Paul Kriwaczek

YIDDISH CIVILISATION

Paul Kriwaczek was born in Vienna in 1937 and, with his parents, narrowly escaped the Nazis in 1939, fleeing first to Switzerland and then to England. He grew up in London and graduated from London Hospital Medical College. After several years spent working and traveling in the Middle East, Central Asia, and Africa, he joined the BBC, where he spent the next quarter of a century as a program producer and filmmaker. Since leaving television in the 1990s, he has devoted himself to writing full-time, catching up on the unfinished business of a life spent exploring places, times, and ideas. He is married and lives in London.

YIDDISH
CIVILISATION

YIDDISH CIVILISATION

The Rise and Fall of a Forgotten Nation

Paul Kriwaczek

VINTAGE BOOKS
A DIVISION OF RANDOM HOUSE, INC.
NEW YORK

FIRST VINTAGE BOOKS EDITION, NOVEMBER 2006

The Library of Congress has cataloged the Knopf edition as follows:
Kriwaczek, Paul.
Yiddish civilisation : the rise and fall of a forgotten
nation / Paul Kriwaczek.—1st American ed.
p.   cm.
Includes bibliographical references and index.
1. Jews—Europe, Central—Civilization.   2. Jews—Europe,
Eastern—Civilization.   3. Ashkenazim—Europe,
Central—History.   4. Ashkenazim—Europe,
Eastern—History.   5. Yiddish language—History.   I. Title.
DS135E8K75 2005
940'.4924—dc22
2005048770

Vintage ISBN-10: 1-4000-3377-2
Vintage ISBN-13: 978-1-4000-3377-5

Author photograph © Noel Chanan
Book design by Soonyoung Kwon

www.vintagebooks.com

Printed in the United States of America
10   9   8   7   6   5   4   3   2   1

In memory of my parents,
Oskar and Alice Kriwaczek,
יצחק בן אפרים ולויה בת מרדכי יהודה ז״ל
who lived out the Jewish story
of expulsion and exile,
and triumphed over them

THE PARLIAMENTARY ASSEMBLY OF THE COUNCIL OF EUROPE
RECOMMENDATION 1291 (1996), SECTION 9, PARAGRAPH VIII:

"The Assembly recommends that the Committee of Ministers . . . commission, for the 50th anniversary of the end of the Second World War, and in order to commemorate the virtual annihilation of the Yiddish Civilisation in Europe, a suitable monument . . ."

ADOPTED BY THE STANDING COMMITTEE, ACTING ON BEHALF
OF THE ASSEMBLY, ON 20 MARCH 1996

"There be of them that have left a name behind them, that their praises might be reported.

And some there be, which have no memorial; who are perished, as though they had never been;

and are become as though they had never been born; and their children after them.

But these were merciful men, whose righteousness hath not been forgotten."

MISHLEI YESHUA BEN SIRA (ECCLESIASTICUS)

Contents

Contents

Contents

Illustrations

Illustrations

The grave of Elimelech ben Eliezer Lipmann Weissblum

Inside the synagogue of the Vilna Gaon (YIVO Institute for Jewish Research)

Second insert

The eighteenth-century synagogue at Przysucha, with its *kuna* or pillory

The synagogue of Zamość, eastern Poland

Isaac Leib Peretz, one of the founders of the Yiddish Renaissance (© Private Collection/Lebrecht)

Shalom Yankev Broido, father of the Yiddish Renaissance (© Private Collection/Lebrecht)

Shalom Rabinovitz, superstar of modern Yiddish literature (© Private Collection/Lebrecht)

Early sail-and-steam ship of the Hamburg-America Packet Shipping Company (akg-images)

Albert Ballin, shipping magnate and friend of Kaiser Wilhelm II (akg-images/ullstein bild)

The Pavilion Theatre in Whitechapel (© Private Collection/Lebrecht)

Page from a Yiddish-English phrasebook (Courtesy of The Jewish Museum, London)

London's Petticoat Lane (© Private Collection/Lebrecht)

New York's Lower East Side (© Private Collection/Lebrecht)

The Jazz Singer, 1927 poster (© Rue des Archives/Lebrecht)

Acknowledgments

I am indebted to Professor John Klier, Head of the Department of Hebrew and Jewish Studies at University College London, and Rabbi David Goldberg, of the St. John's Wood Synagogue, London, for looking over my work for errors and omissions, historical and religious. Any blunders that remain are, of course, all my very own. My thanks are also due to Gosia Cierpisz of Cracow, who guided me expertly around Poland, to Elena Smolina of Moscow, my good friend and helper of nearly fifteen years in Russia and the countries of the former Soviet Bloc, to my former colleague John Twitchin for his helpful comments on my manuscript and my old friend Monte Jacobson for pointing out many slips and inconsistencies. And above all to my wife Jeannette, for her unstinting support and encouragement, even though my long immersion in the Yiddish past must have sorely tried her patience.

Paul Kriwaczek
DECEMBER 2004

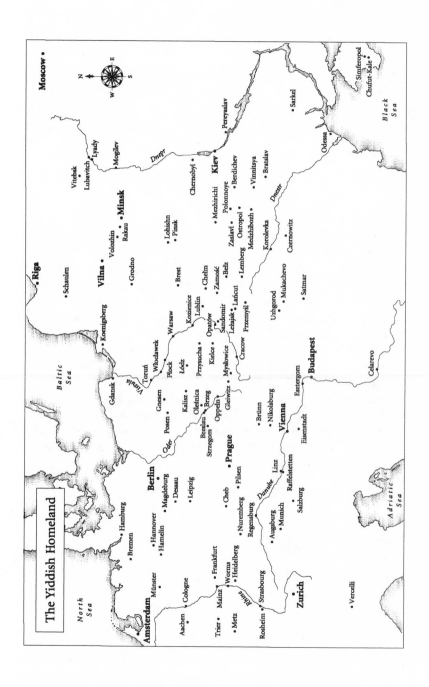

The Yiddish Homeland

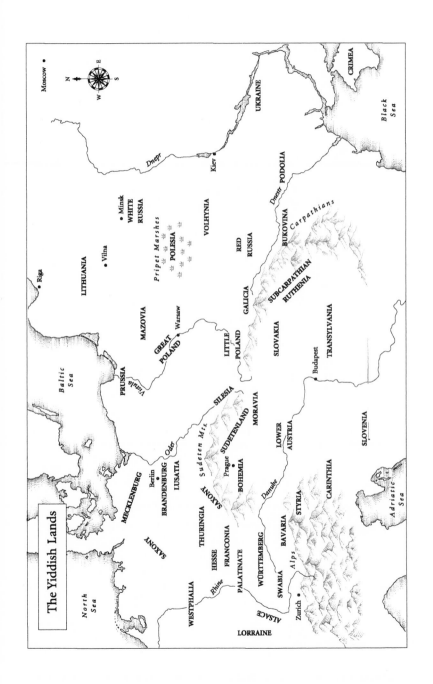

The Yiddish Lands

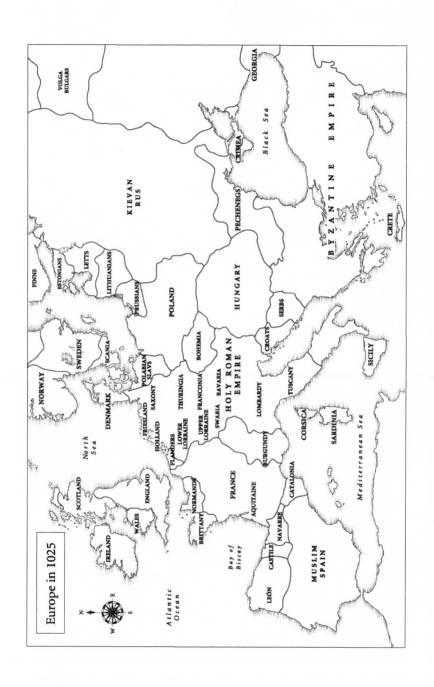

Europe in 1025

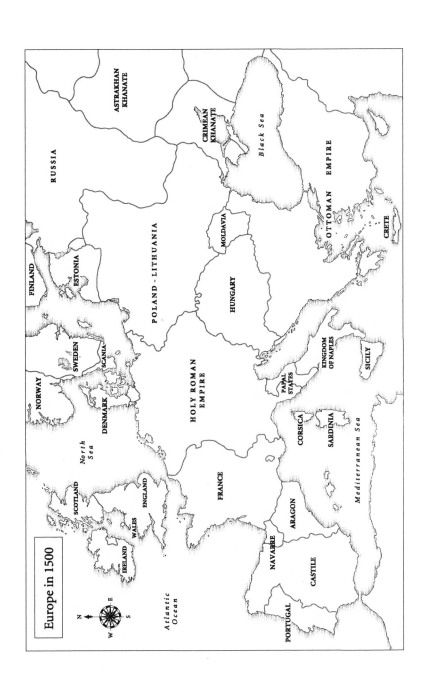

Europe in 1500

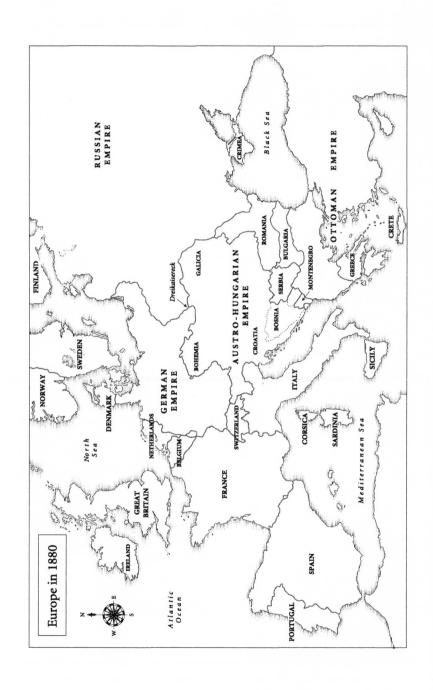

Europe in 1880

YIDDISH
CIVILISATION

Introduction

Easter 1990. The outskirts of a village halfway between Cracow and Kielce in southern Poland. Agnieszka, a young Catholic mother, is sitting under garish strip lighting at the Formica-topped table in her dilapidated kitchen, carefully razoring out Hebrew passages from an Israeli children's book. Next to the growing pile of paper lies a jumble of raw wooden heads, arms, legs and long flat torsos. After painting all but the faces black and the beards grey, she assembles the pieces, sticks on scraps of fake fur, glues a Hebrew text to the hands of each, and stands the resulting foot-high figurines on the shelf behind her, to join a rapidly expanding Chassidic orthodox congregation. The finished dolls, with their fur-trimmed caftans and sable-tail hats, are mounted on springs. If one gently knocks the shelf, they begin to rock backwards and forwards like disturbed, love-deprived children, the authentic movement, called *shockeln* in the Yiddish language, of eastern European orthodox Jews at prayer.

Such a gift at Easter is supposed to bring good fortune and Agnieszka will find plenty of buyers for her handiwork. In the old days, she tells me, children used to run up and touch Chassidic Jews on their way home from the synagogue for luck. Now, I think to myself, the only growing Jewish community in all Poland is made of wood.

Agnieszka can be hardly more than thirty-five years old, born in the mid-1950s at the earliest. I ask her whether she had ever met an orthodox Jew, or even seen one in the flesh. How does she know what they look like? She replies as if it were a thoroughly stupid question, "It is our tradition, part of Polish culture for hundreds of years."

Autumn 2001. On the way to Cracow airport I look out of the taxi at the market square and catch sight of the statue of Poland's national poet Adam Mickiewicz standing high up on his plinth. Though ambivalent in his attitude towards the Yiddish-speaking residents of Poland, in his great epic *Pan Tadeusz* he gave a leading part to Jankiel, a Polish patriot and Jew. "To Israel, our elder brother," Mickiewicz once wrote, "honour, fraternity, and help in striving towards his eternal and temporal goal. Equal rights in all things!" How, I ask the taxi driver, do today's Poles cope with the total disappearance of the community that had such a formative influence on their history?

"You must understand," she explains,

> that the old Poland is gone for ever. After 1945 we had to start from the beginning again. And then again when the Russians left. Today we Poles are a new people. Even our borders are quite different now. Of course we inherited some memories and some traditions from the past but we feel they do not really belong to us.
>
> In the distant future Polish people will recount to each other stories about the time, long, long ago, when Jews lived among us. But they will be like the folk tales other nations tell their children about ogres, giants and fairies.

Spring 2002. Rakau near Minsk in Belarus. The village schoolteacher in a shapeless blue dress lifts the glass top of a display case, pulls out a battered register, blows off the dust and opens it on to the world of 1902. The pages are divided up, one line per name, with the year's marks for each subject in a separate column. Mindel and Slavik did well in arithmetic. Ester's grasp of geography needed improvement. Lyuba, Peschke and Vova received excellent marks for writing. Awrum, Moishe, Yasha and Zima came at the top of the class. Well over half have no figure recorded under the heading Religious Instruction. These are the Jewish children.

I don't need to ask what became of most of them. The schoolteacher had earlier taken me to see the well-intentioned and carefully maintained but indescribably hideous and garish blue-painted memorial erected on the spot where Rakau's synagogue was burned to the ground together with its congregation by Hitler's *Sonderkommando*. So I ask her when Jews first settled here, what brought them and how they lived.

She spreads her hands in genuinely apologetic ignorance. "I don't know. I am really sorry. But you see it is not our Belarusian history."

Then whose history is it, the Jews' thousand-year residence in eastern Europe? The survivors, having moved on and made their homes elsewhere, have mostly shown little interest in recalling the true details of what they take to be no more than a dreadful saga of endless persecution and oppression. Those joining another host society learn the story of their new home, be it France, the UK, Argentina, Australia or the USA. Meanwhile the orthodox pursue their own agenda, keeping in memory only rabbis and sages, those who contributed to the development of their particular religious beliefs. Sephardic Jews, originally from Spain but subsequently displaced to North Africa, Turkey, the Low Countries and seventeenth-century Britain, have their own separate past to look back on. Thus has the life of an entire people faded into a great forgetting. Four hundred years ago a Prague rabbi[1] wrote, "It is as if we were all born yesterday." Little has changed.

This essay is a writer's attempt to make sense of that loss of memory, to try to rescue that Yiddish past from its oblivion, to piece together some of the clues with which historians tease us, and to register how much of the Yiddish story we have forgotten.

We have forgotten how it was the Roman Empire that converted what had been a Middle Eastern and North African people into a European nation; how the division of that empire separated its Jews into western and eastern parental bloodlines; how both sides were nurtured by the Romans' successor states until they mingled again centuries later in central Europe and fused, to give birth to the Yiddish-speaking people—or the Yiddish people, as I shall call them for short. The word Yiddish just means Jewish in the Yiddish tongue and, like English or French, refers equally to the language, the people who speak it, the culture it supports and the civilisation its speakers built.

We have forgotten that Yiddish-speaking Jews were no mere religious or linguistic minority but formed one of Europe's nations, ultimately more populous than many others—eventually to outnumber Bosnians, Croats, Danes, Estonians, Latvians, Slovaks, Slovenians and Swiss, not to mention the Irish, the Scots and the Welsh. What is more, their contribution to central and eastern Europe's economic, social and intellectual development was utterly disproportionate to their numbers. The Yiddish people must be counted among the founder nations of Europe. (Please take note Ireland, Spain, Italy and Poland, who have pressed for "the Christian roots of the continent" to be proclaimed in the constitution of the European Union.)

We have forgotten that the Yiddish language and culture were born, raised and matured in the Slav lands of eastern Europe, in today's Belarus, Poland, Russia and the Ukraine, in originally Slav Austria, Bavaria, Saxony and Brandenburg, as well as in strongly Slavicised Lithuania, Romania and Hungary, from where generations of émigrés travelled west towards the end of the nineteenth century and the first decade of the twentieth to find freedom and improve their material lot.

We have forgotten that it was the association and confrontation with Catholic Slavdom that created the Yiddish way of life. Though in the century before the Holocaust a high proportion of the Yiddish folk inhabited Russian Orthodox countries too, there Yiddish ways were relatively late arrivals, projected into the Ukrainian and Russian domains by accidents of history. In their earlier most formative years, the Yiddish people had grown up among Bavarians and Austrians, Bohemians and Moravians, Poles and Lithuanians, Catholic believers all.

Thus, though neither party may be willing to recognise it, the Yiddish world was a product not just of Jewish but also of Catholic Slav culture; in that sense it was the creation of both Jews and Catholic Slavs together. The inspiration was Jewish; the environment of its growth was Catholic Slav. And just as a rose blooms by reason of its own inherited internal spark of generative fire, but the gardener who tends the bush and nurtures the blossoms has every right to take pride in his or her accomplishment, so Catholic Slavs should justly feel part-ownership, part-responsibility and pride for the achievements of the Yiddish world.

Some hopes! For that would mean confronting the terrible and bitter truth that as the Yiddish speakers were forced at bayonet-point into cattle trucks on their way to Hitler's extermination camps, those who stood by in silence or even cheered were attending the mass murder of their own close kin.

Walking through Cracow's spacious market square, past the imposing fourteenth-century bulk of St. Mary's Church, past the tiny but exquisite

Romanesque church of St. Wojciech, past the great Gothic tower left standing when the original town hall was replaced by the stunning Renaissance Cloth Hall, looking as pretty and pleased with itself as a multicoloured and multi-layered Italian iced pastry, one sees bright new municipal signposts pointing "to the Jewish town." By that phrase the people of Cracow, or the city authorities on their behalf, have recognised in the nearby neighbourhood of Kazimierz more than a town where Jews lived.

Roman Vishniac, a photographer of genius, took upon himself in the late 1930s the perilous and desperate task of recording the outward look of Yiddish life in eastern Europe on the very eve of its final destruction.[2] In Kazimierz one can still pause under the very street sign on the corner of Ulica Izaaka (Isaac Street) that he captured in a shot from 1938. In front of his camera a snowstorm is raging. A woman in a long skirt, brightly coloured shawl and headscarf, and, behind her, an old greybeard in a squashed hat, hurry by, their heads bowed against the weather. Or one can stand in the middle of Ulica Szeroka (Broad Street) on the exact spot where, also in 1938, the great photographer for ever froze the image of three jolly Chassidim conversing animatedly in their long coats, black boots and the kind of wide fur hat called a *shtreimel*—traditionally made up of seven sable tails—on their way to, or from, the synagogue or house of study.

In spite of the Nazi occupation with its anti-Jewish psychopathy and of the Soviet yoke that immediately followed, with its anti-religious political repression, the streets and buildings of Kazimierz are still almost exactly as Vishniac photographed them. Even the many synagogues, after years of desecration, desertion and decay, still stand.

Yet try as hard as one might to invest the bricks and mortar with emotional and spiritual significance, without the Jews inhabiting the houses and walking the streets, one gets no sense of the Yiddish world that had once flourished fruitfully in this environment. Without the rabbis and Talmud students emerging from their religious seminaries, the pedlars and street porters on their way to the market place, the stallholders and shopkeepers touting for customers, the rich fur-clad merchants and their shuffling clerks in wire-rimmed spectacles, without the Chassidim, orthodox Jewish pietists, in their traditional costume and the *cheder* (Hebrew school) pupils in their ragged shorts and torn school caps, without Mrs. Kalitzky stepping out from her doorstep in high-heeled ankle boots to show off to her neighbours the new fox-fur wrap her jeweller husband has bought her, or Josel and Mendel, the pair of bearded old scholars in shiny black caftans and fur hats, old enough to know better, who are blocking the walkway as they angrily and obsessively dispute some fine point of Jewish religious law, without all these the city suburb of Kazimierz has lost the magic it once possessed.

But even stripped of its former inhabitants, the district is a reminder that the vanished Yiddish-speaking people of eastern Europe created more than a Jewish-Polish or Jewish-Lithuanian sub-culture. Kazimierz wasn't just a town inhabited by Jews—it was truly a Jewish town, part of the Yiddish civilisation.

By definition the civilisation that Yiddish-speaking Jews created in eastern Europe formed no part of Christendom. Theirs was a life set apart from the Catholicism that surrounded it, with its own language, its own styles of poetry and prose, its own everyday and ritual costumes, its distinctive decorative motifs, its particular flavour of the Jewish faith, its specific value systems and family traditions, its characteristic social layering. Its artefacts are legion: printed books, Hebrew Bible scrolls, religious requisites, housewares and tablewares, synagogues and cemeteries. Its political organisation was unique: a central legislative council appointed by self-governing communities with the duty to register births, marriages and deaths, levy taxation, the power to commend and shame, to arrest and punish, maintaining close relations with, but quite separate from, the state authorities.

The place where it grew up was the territory of the Western Slavs, the eastern part of which later became the Russian Empire's Pale of Settlement, the area in which Jews were permitted to reside after the eighteenth-century partition and disappearance of Poland and the incorporation of its Jewish-populated areas into the empires of secular Prussia, Catholic Austria and Holy Russia. This was the religious no man's land between Roman West and Orthodox East, sweeping in a wide curve from Riga on the Baltic in the north, to Odessa on the Black Sea in the south. Its time was, roughly, from the eleventh century to the middle of the nineteenth, when the last vestiges of its autonomy were abolished—though the dispossessed remnant survived for almost another century, until the Ribbentrop-Molotov pact delivered one half of Poland's Jews into the arms of Hitler's mass murderers and the other to the hardly less psychopathic if more incompetent depravity of Joseph Stalin's commissars.

The Yiddish civilisation has vanished from its own homeland, its true reality near to forgotten. But it left an indelible mark, and not only on eastern Europe. For towards its end, mass emigration to the USA at the close of the nineteenth century and the opening of the twentieth carried many of its beliefs, values and traditions to the other side of the Atlantic, where they were among the contributors, through film, music, literature and the arts, not to speak of commerce and enterprise, to what we think of as the American way of life—and therefore, in this era of globalisation, to the way of the entire world.

I

Bist a Yid?

Back at the beginning of the 1950s—memory suggests—the world was all in Technicolor and it never rained in summer. Nat King Cole headed the hit parade with "They Try to Tell Us We're Too Young," Tottenham Hotspur was top of the football league and Newcastle United beat Blackpool to the Football Association cup. Butter, meat and sweets were still rationed in Britain and the average weekly wage was around £7, though you could buy a house for under five hundred. Money was tight, particularly pocket money. When the weather was fine, schoolboys like me would save our bus fares for fizzy drinks and walk the couple of miles to school instead.

Our school in north-west London drew its pupils from a wide and diverse area. Every morning, teenage boys—in the rigidly enforced uniform of grey flannel trousers, school blazers and caps (plus satchels and shining morning faces)—could be seen converging on the red-brick Victorian building like wildlife towards a waterhole. We assembled from every part of the suburb: many poorer boys from the working-class terraces leading off the busy, grimy high street, middle-class pupils from upper-bracket apartment blocks with pretentious names like Grosvenor Mansions, and a small number of rich kids from spacious six-bedroomed detached houses with carriage drives, double garages and acres of garden. One young turbaned Sikh was daily delivered to the school gates by chauffeur-driven Bentley. He was the exception; by far the largest religious minority were Jews, for whom Britain's post-war grammar schools offered the irresistible attraction of a free quasi-public-school education.

Back in those days, there was little town-and-gown trouble. True, gangs of adolescent roughnecks did gather in the seedier parts of the district, but we all knew which routes to avoid and which were safe. For some of us, however, there was one peril that was much harder to escape. A section of my route took me through one of the wealthier areas, along streets lined by big houses with wrought-iron gates and plaster-pillared porticoes, past flowery front gardens, tennis courts and recreation grounds—a mock-rural setting which still somehow recalled the real orchards, market gardens and country villas of no more than a generation or two earlier. It was just before entering this quiet would-be pastoral neighbourhood that menace lurked for young Jewish boys like me—a danger that could result in a severe beating.

If we kept our wits about us and our eyes open, we could catch sight of the threat: a group of apparently respectable middle-aged men in dark suits, loitering around the entrance to the alley which led to the local synagogue. If we were quick enough, we could take rapid evasive action. But teenage boys are much given to dreaming, and the long walk to school was the perfect opportunity to let our imaginations wander, leaving our mental autopilots to look after the practical business of working our legs and navigating them towards our destination. All too often a boy would accidentally stray within range of one of the prowlers, who would instantly dash across the road and pounce on his victim. Usually the first a boy would know of his fate was the feel of a hand grasping his shoulder and the dreaded sound of the ominous whisper: *"Pssst! Bist a Yid?"* and he would know that it was all up for him.

The phrase is Yiddish for Are you a Jew? The boy had been captured by one of the synagogue's *minyan-shleppers*, those charged with the duty of dragging (*shlepping*) a quorum of ten ritually adult males (a *minyan*) into the synagogue so that morning service could begin.

I hasten to explain that our reluctance to be caught like this was not prompted by any anti-religious feeling or atheist belief. On the contrary, many of those targeted would have only recently celebrated their religious coming of age, their barmitzvah, and, still enthusiastic, would already have dutifully recited the required morning prayers at home. No, the entirely practical problem was that waiting for the rest of the *minyan* to collect and then taking part in the service threatened to make us late for school, which in those days could still be, and all too often was, a caning offence.

No doubt the *shleppers* spoke in Yiddish so that gentiles wouldn't understand. On us boys, though, it had a different, subtler, perhaps even unintended effect. Had we been asked in English, we'd have been able to argue back, to explain about the penalty for missing morning assembly; about the French homework we had to catch up on before the next lesson; about the early morning rugby football practice, being late for which would earn us a hefty and extremely painful kick up the backside from our games master's sadistic boot. But in Yiddish? You couldn't even begin to talk about such things; they would be quite meaningless. The Yiddish world-view gave no weight at all to school assemblies, French homework or rugby football; it had quite other priorities and totally different values. And the Yiddish language protected this world like a high and unbreachable wall. Once captured and brought inside the language barrier, there was no way for a schoolboy to import his mundane and, to the Yiddish world, irrelevant concerns.

Yiddish excluded not just the gentile world, but other Jews as well. While all Jews share the same religious background and all honour the Torah (the Five Books of Moses), and recognise the Talmud (the compilation of centuries of rabbinical wisdom, like Emerson's "amassed thought and experience of innumerable minds"), their cultures and languages are diverse. The *shlepper*'s words would have meant nothing to the old-established Sephardic community of England, who had first arrived in Cromwell's day, having ultimately come—via a sojourn in the Netherlands—from Moorish Spain. They would have meant no more to *Mizrachi* (Eastern) Jews from Arab lands, nor to those from Iran, Central Asia or India. Linguistically assimilated Jews from Italy and France, however pious, would have been left in ignorance too. Even Bavarians and Austrians would only have understood because—I was going to write "by chance" but of course it isn't—the question sounds the same in Yiddish and Austrian dialect. For though such folk might be Jewish, they were no part of the Yiddish world. The *minyan-shleppers'* words were aimed solely at "our folks," *indzere leyt* as they would have said, Jewish families who had migrated from Poland, Lithuania, Hungary, Romania, Russia and the Ukraine—the Yiddish territories collectively known as *der heym* (the homeland)—and settled in Britain during the previous seventy years.

This was not my first introduction to the rather unsettling idea that different people, though they might inhabit the same place at the same time, could perceive reality in absolutely different ways. As an immigrant child, I was always aware that for a long time after our arrival in England my parents lived in a quite different land from mine. The front door of our apartment marked a boundary between worlds, as sharp as the barbed wire then newly dividing Europe. Inside our flat was pre-war Baden, a small spa town near Vienna. Outside was post-war London. By the time I was ten years old I had absorbed from my parents' conversations an entire imagined landscape, clear as day to me, made up of familiar street names and well-known landmarks. Though I had left Austria before I was two, I felt as if I myself had often walked up Baden's Braitner Street to the plague memorial in the main square, strolled the Kurpark and eaten ice cream by the Undine fountain, climbed the hillside up to Putschaner's Cave, gone on outings to Helena's valley, with its two ruined castles, and visited the family factory at Guntramsdorf—and all without leaving our dismal, rain-stained concrete block of flats in north-west London. The ease with which I still recall the names sixty years later is witness to how thoroughly my parents' memories became my own. (No doubt the same easy familiarity with places never actually seen applies to all immigrant families. The British-born waiters in my local Balti restaurant surely know every house and alley, mosque and madraseh of their ancestral village in Bangladesh.)

The Yiddish world too had its own special topography, dotted with towns like Chelm, Lemberg and Pinsk and Belz, famed in Yiddish legend and song, and peopled by mysterious, but revered, personalities like the *Ba'al Shem Tov*, the Vilna Gaon and the Satmarer Rebbe, and great families like the Landaus, the Brodys and the Rappaports. I had to get to know this world, as did even non-Jewish classmates in our circle, for we had friends whose grandparents—and even parents, though British-born and belonging to the next generation after the mass immigration at the end of the nineteenth century and beginning of the twentieth—still maintained many of the customs and values of their eastern European places of family origin, still prayed in strongly Yiddish-accented Hebrew and still spoke Yiddish at home.

Talk was, however, not conducted exclusively in that language. By now this generation was native English-speaking and would switch with ease between English and Yiddish, depending on the subject. The language chosen could tell the listener much about the speakers' feelings: business and politics would always be argued about in Yiddish—after all, they shared much the same vocabulary: *gonif* (thief), *shvindler* (cheat), *farbrecher* (crook); so would domestic matters like food, clothes, personal feelings and other people's appearance: *sheynere ligt men in drerd* (they bury better-looking people). English seems to have been felt more appropriate for discussing technical issues, like why the *farsholtener* (damned) car wouldn't start that morning, as well as those matters considered to have high status like visits to a doctor or a teacher; I don't remember questions about my school work ever being asked in Yiddish. Surprisingly enough, the same applied to religious affairs. True, our community's rabbi did give regular Yiddish discourses, but in most homes Hebrew religious terms would stand out from their mostly English-language setting: *chazzen* (cantor), *sidder* (prayer book), *kiddish* (a celebratory blessing after the end of Sabbath Service, when small boys would sneak off with slices of honey cake and tiny glasses of whisky, cherry brandy or advokaat). The details of sex were, of course, not to be mentioned in either tongue, while for telling jokes everyone agreed that the language of the gentiles was a very poor substitute.

Consciousness of the distinction between Jew and non-Jew, mostly ignored in English, was always present in Yiddish conversations. The Jewish religion is much given to binary classification: dividing days of the calendar between holy and profane, food between milk and meat, meat between kosher and *treyf* (non-kosher), textiles between wool and linen, Jews between priestly families (Cohens and Levys) and the rest (Israel). So people too were either *Yidn* (Jews) or *goyim* (gentiles), a word borrowed from the plain biblical Hebrew expression for nation, *goy*—plural *goyim*—(gentiles); adjective *goyish* (typically gentile); abstract noun *goyishness* (being drunk in the street and throwing up in the gutter). As with Hindi and Urdu *gora* (white person) or Romany *gajé* (non-Roma), the word *goy* itself has only mild pejorative overtones. To turn it into a real insult, East End Cockney back slang was used. Modelled on the reversal of boy to yob, *goy* became *yog* (pronounced and re-spelled *yock*), a suitable word for the crude louts who would shout obscenities and throw stones at us on our way to Saturday synagogue. But even *yock* could be used with some ironic affection. A close friend's grandmother believed that British Sunday dinner consisted of roast beef and *yockisher* pudding.

It goes without saying that this was a religious world, but in the uncomplicated, unselfconscious manner of a traditional society rather than the stiff piety of committed believers. Religious duties were fulfilled because that was the way things were always done, rather than because they were commanded by God. One attended the synagogue on Sabbaths and holidays because that was where one went at those times. And—how different from the tight-lipped devotions of the churchgoers I knew—having done their duty by turning up, many in the congregation would continue to gossip, tell jokes and discuss business all the way through the long service. So much so that often on Saturday mornings, the conversational hubbub rose so loud that rabbi and beadle were driven to slamming down the lids of their reading desks and calling for silence, so that the cantor's prayers might be audible at least to heaven. Similar feelings surrounded the Jewish dietary code. Unkosher food and the mixing together of milk and meat products were strictly avoided not so much because of Jewish religious law, but because the very idea of eating such foods as pork or shellfish, or veal braised in cream, was as nauseating and repulsive as are maggots or sheep's eyeballs to English taste.

All this was quite a contrast to my own parents' religious attitudes, which were far more cerebral, scriptural and legalistic—my mother having come from a Nikolsburg (now called Mikulov, Moravia) clan with strong rabbinical connections. And that was not the only difference, for each side viewed the other with suspicion and disdain. Those like my family—Jews from Vienna, where they had made up nearly ten per cent of the pre-war population—now saw themselves as a double minority, outnumbered both by gentiles and also by the Yiddish speakers. They suspected the English Yiddish speakers of having profited from the Nazi war and accused them of having done little or nothing to help their co-religionists in their hour of need, seeing them as unreconstructed, ignorant medievalists, their language a barbaric jargon, their religious beliefs hardly distinguishable from vulgar superstition and liable to give the noble aspirations of Judaism a bad name. The Yiddish speakers viewed recent German and Austrian immigrants like us as assimilated apostates, hardly a step away from conversion to Christianity, and blamed the Holocaust on our adoption of modern western ways, denouncing us—in a marvellously antiquated insult—as *apikoyres* (literally: Epicureans).

As a youngster, I had regularly to negotiate these three quite different environments, which seemed to me then almost like parallel universes. Invited to a friend's house for tea, I would leave the continental 1930s at home in the morning, spend my school day in 1950s London, and after lessons enter the Yiddish world of . . . when? It was impossible to put a date on an outlook that appeared both up-to-date and antique, both contemporary and timeless.

It wasn't just that the Yiddish-speakers seemed to live one part of their lives perfectly normally in modern Britain—actively and successfully involved in business or the professions—and the other part in some unfathomable eternal world of their own. But that, unlike German, Austrian, French and Italian, or even Sephardic Jews, they seemed to have no history. Or, to be more exact, no interest in or recollection of people and places outside their own very recent family traditions. Moreover, many didn't know the names of the east European towns from which their families had emigrated, and some had even forgotten what their family names had been before being anglicised to something that the blunt English tongue could more easily negotiate—and, what is more, they didn't seem to care. Twice dislocated, first from the European *heym* to London's East End—where they had originally settled close to their point of arrival in the docks—and in the next generation out to the suburbs, most of the Yiddish families I knew seemed to have abandoned their past altogether.

They presented themselves as if they were a folk society with immemorial roots in Russia, Poland and Lithuania. They had no history, it was implied, because nothing had changed for the Jews since their first settlement of those lands unknowable centuries earlier, since when they had lived, in small towns and villages, as rabbis, artisans, publicans and small traders, making no waves, attracting as little attention as possible to themselves, until the overriding hostility of the religious majority had finally driven them from their settlements a generation ago, to find new homes in the West. So awful had been the memory of what they had left, so painful their struggle to put it for ever behind them, that they had no interest in—indeed strong antipathy to—bringing the old country back to mind.

And yet, at the very same time, the Yiddish speakers did have a powerful sense of ancient history. They were on nodding terms with the kings and queens of biblical days, with the prophets who had walked the Judaean hills before the era of Christ, with the sages who had compiled Jewish law in Babylonia in the first half-dozen centuries of our era. What was missing was the time between then and now: a huge gulf of amnesia separating the ancient Middle East from the modern West.

Perhaps, I thought, the missing millennium was a response to the trauma of the Holocaust. Until Nazi times, the Yiddish speakers of Britain could still have regarded themselves as expatriates and escapees from their eastern European homeland, and many maintained links with their relatives still in the old country—our rabbi, for example, had studied in the seminaries of pre-war Poland—just as South Asian Britons still see themselves as part of the Indian, Pakistani or Bangladeshi diaspora and often return to holiday and even marry in their district of origin. But the annihilation of Continental Jewry had left the Yiddish speakers adrift, like lost and orphaned children, with no links to their past, the grotesque horror of the end of the Yiddish *heym* inducing what psychologists would call a state of denial, pretending that the *heym* had never existed, as if by wiping out the memory of what had been, the pain of its loss could be eased.

Now I have come to believe that in the 1950s a kind of deep shame at Yiddish-speaking Jewry's terrible fate played an important role in British Jews' self-imposed amnesia. Instead, after 1948, they lifted their eyes to a more distant time horizon, and recognised in the new State of Israel the land that two thousand years of daily prayer had assured them was their true ancestral home.

Fifty years have passed since boys like me ran the gauntlet of the *minyan-shleppers*; fifty years in which the London generations that still remembered a kind of authentic Yiddish life have passed into memory. And, in between, a revolution happened: a momentous overturning of previously conformist and deferential, well-behaved British society whose opening salvo was fired off in 1956, when the release of the film *Rock Around the Clock* was accompanied by a sudden and unaccountable outbreak of knife-slashed cinema seats.

The revolution was not just about sex, drugs and rock'n'roll. During the following decade and a half, in addition to Elvis Presley, Bob Dylan and Jimi Hendrix, America experienced civil rights marches and Vietnam protest. In addition to the Beatles and Rolling Stones, Britain saw the failure of her Suez adventure, the end of general literary and stage censorship and a Socialist government committed to the "white heat of technological revolution." The whole western world came to recognise the validity of feminism and the justice of women's rights.

Jews too had a musical and social revolution of a kind—Harnick and Bock's Broadway musical *Fiddler on the Roof*, based on stories by the Yiddish late nineteenth- and early twentieth-century Dickens disciple Sholom Aleichem—but they were also caught up in the drama of Israel's Six Day War. Both were hugely powerful influences. The war made the Jews reassess their identity and fear for the future of their state. But it was the musical that showed them how to imagine the Jewish past.

ROOTS SCHMOOTS!

Back in the 1950s most London Jews dressed like everyone else. Not particularly to make themselves inconspicuous, but because they saw no reason to be different. Some of the orthodox even went bare-headed in the street or wore the then-current fashion in hats. To succeed at their task, the *minyan-shleppers* could only depend on a refined ability to recognise Jewish faces—and not uncommonly made comic mistakes. Today's orthodox take pride in singling themselves out by their apparel, asserting their right to look different. Moreover, many Chassidim, particularly on Sabbaths and holidays, go further and wear what amounts to a historic costume: black caftan fastened with a sash round the middle, knee breeches over white stockings, together with a wheel-shaped brown fur hat—an ensemble apparently attuned to the fashion sense of seventeenth-century Polish noblemen.

The new eagerness to stand out from the crowd isn't simply a consequence of the rise of orthodoxy among part of the Jewish population, paralleling the surge in devotion among Christians and Muslims, but rather a desire to present themselves publicly as Jews. After all, being strictly religious has, in principle, little bearing on attire, which is more a symbol aimed at other people rather than a message to God. Moreover, the eagerness of Jews to distinguish themselves by their dress code does not merely mark them out as different from the non-Jewish majority, the details are equally important in sending out signals to other Jews. For instance a variety of skullcaps, variously called *kippah, kappl, kepl, yarmulka,* and made of different materials—the wearing of which, incidentally, is a matter of custom rather than religious rule—are used as an elaborate code to distinguish Chassidim from the merely orthodox, the orthodox from religious Zionists, and to separate these in turn from secular Zionists. A man who wears a knitted skullcap, a *kippah sruga*, rather than one made of felt or fabric, is declaring his political-religious allegiance as openly as if he carried a banner. And that doesn't even include the *shtreimel, kolpak* and *spodek* fur hats worn on Sabbaths and holidays.

In any case, one might have expected a resurgent Jewish spirituality to be expressed by a return to the clothing of the patriarchs and prophets, or the rabbis of Babylonia, not to the outfits formerly worn in just another part of the world of exile. True, the British climate is hardly suited to Mediterranean dress, but then the ultra-orthodox wear the same uniform in Jerusalem as they do in London.

The renaissance of Polish court style among the Chassidim is, rather, just one aspect of a sudden and surprising rediscovery and reassertion of Jewry's eastern European roots among every section of the community. Far from wishing to erase all recollection of the *heym* as in the past, today's generation is busily trying to revive its memory. Even in Israel, a state founded to allow Jews to return to the Holy Land, many young people are eagerly searching out their connections with the diaspora. "Roots Schmoots,"[1] as novelist Howard Jacobson entitled his account of a trawl through his own ancestral waters.

But as times change, so do fashions and values. What our parents found an embarrassment may be a source of pride to us, what we ourselves deplore our children often praise. Qualities once greatly admired in a nation—power, confidence, ruthlessness, the means and skill to dominate others—are out of favour now. Weakness, formerly despised, is the new strength. Today it sometimes seems as if everybody wants to be part of an ethnic minority that was once (but is no longer) subject to discrimination. Black and Asian lives hold little attraction; the models in Britain are the Irish, the Scots and the Welsh. Jews, it turns out, are as susceptible to the lure of this sentimental and self-deluding vogue as anyone else.

There are fixed and rather romantic ideas about what such a minority should be like. It should, of course, have a minority language; it should have its own folk costume, its own folk traditions, myths, legends and rituals as well as, if possible, its own variety of mysticism; and it should have its own folk music, songs and dances.

In a story well known among aficionados of klezmer, the American-revived dance hall and wedding music of Jewish eastern Europe, Henry Sapoznik, one of the revival's driving forces, who at the time was studying Appalachian-style banjo playing with an old traditional fiddler from Carolina, was asked by his mentor why so many young Jews wanted to learn the old-time music: "Don't your people got none of your own music?"[2]

Sapoznik could have said, "Of course, and we sing it in the synagogue every week." Or he could have said, "Sure; ain't you heard of Mendelssohn, Meyerbeer, Mahler, Offenbach or Schoenberg, or, among more popular songsmiths, Berlin, Gershwin, Kern, Loesser and Bernstein, or any of the other five hundred or so Jewish composers and performers of international repute listed in the *Encyclopaedia Judaica*?" But he didn't. However much shaped by their Jewish background, their music doesn't count. It is simply not ethnic enough.

Sapoznik jettisoned his adopted Hillbilly persona, and his assumed Hillbilly sobriquet Hank, in favour of a new and what he felt was a more personally valid identity. He researched among the dusty collections of 78 rpm recordings long since abandoned to cupboards under the stairs all over the USA, and used them to help resurrect some of the old songs and forgotten dance tunes that were still being recorded in the 1920s and 1930s to remind recent Yiddish immigrants of what they had left behind. Sapoznik was soon joined by others and within a short time klezmer music was once again being heard on the radio and being bought on CD. Fifty years previously, clarinet players like Mezz Mezzrow (Milton Mezirow), Artie Shaw (Arthur Jacob Arshawsky) and Benny Goodman had abandoned klezmer for jazz and swing. Now, in an unexpected reversal of history, young Jewish musicians were returning to the old, previously derided, music. Many Jews who hadn't stepped inside a synagogue since their barmitzvah, and even some marrying outside the faith, now wanted a klezmer band to play at their wedding. Even non-Jews could take part. Klezmer ensembles have sprung up in the most unexpected places, even Japan.

The Yiddish language, too, has experienced a sudden new vitality. While the number of native speakers continues its decline—almost the only groups still using it as a first language are the ultra-orthodox, for whom it serves as a barrier against modernity—young Jews everywhere, many of whom have no connection with the countries where it was still spoken before Hitler's war, want to acquire, if not mastery, then at least a smattering of the old eastern European Jewish vernacular. Formal courses in Yiddish are offered by academic institutions all over the western world, the dreaming spires of Oxford University included. Those not prepared for serious study or who can't get to grips with a foreign grammar and syntax can at least pepper their conversations with Yiddish expressions. Far from being toe-curlingly embarrassing, as when heard on old folks' lips in my youth, the use of Yiddish words now seems to be considered rather hip, even among *goyim*, even in BBC news broadcasts.

It would be wrong to detect in these developments a new interest in or dedication to the Jewish religion. The superficial trappings of ethnicity offer precisely the opposite: a Jewish identity without strings, one which doesn't demand synagogue attendance or knowledge of, and strict adherence to, the 613 commandments, now found over-burdensome by many who apply the standards of the modern western consumer society to ancient religious law. Nor does it require a style of everyday living incompatible with our age's libertarian and egalitarian ideals. That is not to say, of course, that the seriously devout in their dark suits and trilby hats, with the white fringes of their ritual undergarments, *tsitsis*, hanging over their trousers, or the Chassidim decked out in the old Polish-Jewish costume, are not truly pious. But that the adoption of Yiddish ancestry, language, mores and customs by the generality of non-observant Jews—even those whose family origins lie far from authentic Yiddish territory—does serve as a social bridge. It provides a unifying force to marry the disparate sectors of the Jewish world: the ultra-orthodox, the Chassidim, conservative, reform and liberal Jews, agnostics and atheists "of Jewish origin," and even new-age Jewish pagans, believers in astrology, transcendental meditation or with a dilettante fascination for Kabbalah, the medieval mystical Jewish tradition. Now suddenly to be Jewish and to be Yiddish are becoming the same thing. My parents would be perplexed, if not horrified.

NOSTALGIE DE LA BOUE

In the train of the Yiddish revival came the romance of the *shtetl*, the mostly Jewish small market town of Poland and Russia. On every continent, young Jews with a yearning for ethnic roots are busily researching their family backgrounds and seeking out information about the places their great or great-great-grandparents abandoned with relief. Elderly relatives are plagued by insistent questions about where their families had originally emigrated from—all too often the reply is on the lines of "somewhere near Minsk (or Vilna, or Kiev, or Cracow). I don't know the name." A typical story is told by Steven Zipperstein, Professor of Jewish History at Stanford University. As reported in the *Stanford News*,[3]

> when asked by children and grandchildren about their native *shtetl*, his older relatives said Lohishn, their original village, was not in Russia but in Poland. They also said it had been obliterated shortly after his grandfather's exit in 1919 or 1920. "Imagine my surprise," Professor Zipperstein wrote in a conference paper, "when later I glanced at a road map of Belarus and noticed Lohishn, just off a main strip of highway, a small place with little to distinguish it, according to a guidebook I soon consulted, but far from annihilated."

The Internet is beaded with thousands of sites dedicated to researching and preserving the memory of the vanished communities, while Jewish heritage tourists throng the squares of the small towns of Belarus, Lithuania, Poland, Russia and the Ukraine, asking anyone older than sixty if they remember the visitors' great-grandparents. Just as few successful middle-class professionals can resist the temptation to claim impoverished working-class roots, however unlikely, few Jews are prepared to confess that their ancestors were among the overwhelming majority who lived in the great cities of the imperial age and had no *shtetl* connections—and might even have felt insulted by the association with squalid and poverty-stricken rural settlements with their wooden synagogues, tumbledown houses and dirt roads. Yearning for mud, the French call it, *nostalgie de la boue*.

I have in front of me David Grupper and David G. Klein's charming publication *The Paper Shtetl, a Complete Model of an East European Jewish Town*, with cardboard pages for cutting out and assembling. Here, beautifully illustrated in woodcut style, is everything the word *shtetl* brings to mind: the synagogue, with its thatched roof, round-topped windows, the rough plaster rendering on the walls peeling to show the spalled bricks underneath; inside is the Ark, the receptacle for the laboriously hand-calligraphed scrolls of the Torah, above which is written in Hebrew characters the Talmudic injunction: Know Before Whom You Stand; around the back is the entrance to the *cheder*, the children's Hebrew school. Here too is a private house, thatched, wood-framed, planks springing from clapboard walls, with shutters and a farmhouse front door, an axe and a frame saw leaning by its side. Next come a tiny market square with kosher provisions shops, a well, some chickens, a goat and a cow.

Populating the *shtetl* are the expected *dramatis personae*. For the synagogue there is the bearded rabbi at his lectern, sternly scowling, his prayer shawl drawn over his head, pointing accusingly with his finger to a passage in a thick volume. Here is the Torah reader at the raised podium known as the *Bimah*, reciting from a Torah scroll, following the text with the *yad*, a silver pointer in the shape of a hand. A scholar wearing thick spectacles and a deeply gloomy expression sits on a chair with a copy of the Talmud on his lap. Three men draped in prayer shawls sit on a wooden bench, representing the congregation. The one in the centre has his head bowed; maybe he has fallen asleep. Outside in the market place a carter waits with his horse, for some reason the only beardless male in the entire village; is he perhaps the token non-Jew? Another pushes a barrow, and a water carrier stands with two large pails hanging from the enormous wooden yoke over his shoulders.

Elsewhere a klezmer band—fiddle, clarinet and accordion (pictured the wrong way round)—play for a wedding couple who stand under a canopy, the groom smiling to himself in an odiously self-satisfied way, the bride looking doubtfully towards us as if not sure whether she has made the right decision. Even Gimpel the Fool is present—every *shtetl* must have its village idiot, it seems—with a surprised look on his face and what seems to be a fez on his head, one booted leg crossed over the other thigh in a contortion halfway between Cossack dancing and yoga. The blurb on the book's back cover describes how we should imagine the *shtetl* atmosphere:

> In the House of study, men study the sacred texts while children learn to read in a makeshift school called a heder. Outside a wedding is taking place under a canopy with dancers and musicians. Men and women attend to their work in their homes and shops as people in the marketplace kibitz, argue, and play. In the synagogue, a Torah reader chants from a scroll before the Holy Ark. A family at home sits down to enjoy the Sabbath meal.[4]

Never mind that all these activities could never have taken place at the same time. Never mind that the synagogue worshippers are four short of a quorum. Never mind that this *shtetl*'s appearance owes far more to Boris Aronson's Broadway sets for *Fiddler on the Roof* than to any real small east European town. It is no news that revived traditions are more often reinvented out of whole new cloth than truly rediscovered. Just as Scottish folk costume and military bagpipe music, the Tartan Tradition, were largely a creation of Sir Walter Scott and Queen Victoria's British army, and just as the Welsh eisteddfod, with its druidic rites and Gorsedd of bards, was mostly dreamed up in 1770s Primrose Hill, London, by the eccentric scholar Iolo Morgannwg (real name Edward Williams), so in a similar way this image of the eastern European Jewish world owes more to the world of dreams than that of memory, to fond fantasy, rather than prosaic reality.

Jews lived and throve in Poland for centuries—indeed, for about a millennium, if not even longer. But almost all our memories of the Yiddish world are from its final century and our images are of its very last moments. The Yiddish literary renaissance of the late nineteenth century pictured a society in the final throes of decay. The stories of Mendele, of Peretz, of Sholom Aleichem, describe an impoverished, pauperised, tyrannised people, not even a pale reflection of the prosperous and powerful nation that once supplied physicians, diplomats, economic advisers and even music tutors to the royal courts of Europe. Roman Vishniac's photographs were taken at a time when, with the sole exception of Czechoslovakia, every country in eastern Europe was already under authoritarian right-wing, if not openly Fascist, rule, when National Socialism was already on the march and quickly allying itself with every ancient, local anti-Semitic hatred, and when the Yiddish nation already lay in ruins. The artistry of his pictures is in the moving delicacy with which they portray the final gasps of a dying world.

There has to be more to the Yiddish story than a record, however artistic, of its tragic last years. One can no more judge a people's entire history and culture by its appearance at the end than one can value a person's life by the agony of his or her final illness. The glory that was Greece and the grandeur that was Rome are not diminished by the stupidity of the fratricidal wars that fatally undermined Athenian democracy, nor by the stagnation and corruption that attended Rome's final century of decline. Why then remember only the sad closing decades of a backward-looking, impoverished and brutalised Yiddish world?

Yet wherever I asked about the long history of the Yiddish-speaking Jews, in Poland, Lithuania, Belarus or the Ukraine, I was told, as the Rakau schoolteacher had explained to me with a regretful shrug of her shoulders, that after all the Jews' story was not part of their history. They might well have added, like Henry Sapoznik's folk-fiddler, "Don't your people got none of your own history?"

Of course we do. It is outlined in the works of the great figures of nineteenth- and twentieth-century Jewish historiography: of Leopold Yom Tov Lipmann Zunz, Moritz Steinschneider and Heinrich Graetz, of Shimon Dubnow and Salo Wittmayer Baron, of Cecil Roth and Martin Gilbert. Yet it is not surprising that, perhaps apart from Sir Martin Gilbert, these scholars are less than household names, for much of their work reads as irretrievably depressing—a long saga of constant pogroms, oppressive laws invoked by civil authorities, anti-Jewish edicts by the Church, massacres, expulsions, tortures and burnings at the stake. Was Yiddish history truly no more than this?

In a little book by Professor of Medieval History Bernard S. Bachrach, *Jews in Barbarian Europe*, a text assembled for undergraduate students at the University of Minnesota, the author points out that for two thousand years suffering and punishment have been the dominant themes in the writing of Jewish history: what he calls the theology of exile.

. . . those who recorded the deeds of the Jewish people during the Middle Ages and the early modern era emphasised the suffering of the martyrs who died for the faith. They recorded, confounded, and embellished instances of pogroms, forced baptisms, expropriations, and expulsions. These tragic events became the framework of the Jewish view of the history of the Exile and served as evidence to sustain the theological interpretation of the Exile as a period of suffering and as a test for the Jewish people.[5]

And, one might add, those of us who live after Hitler cannot help but see this history as leading inevitably and inexorably towards the *Shoah*, the Holocaust, which brought about the Yiddish-speaking people's horrific final and irrevocable destruction. Such hindsight, Bachrach notes, has led Jewish scholars to misjudge and misread much of the evidence that the past has left us: two thousand years of tradition have made it very hard for learned Jews, he writes, and even professional historians, to escape what Salo Baron memorably called "the lachrymose interpretation" of Jewish history.

Being neither a learned Jew nor a professional historian, I do believe that there is another story to tell. Not an exclusive story, for no story has a monopoly on the truth and many different narratives can be picked out of the same materials. None contain all, but all contain some, of the almost overwhelming, confusing, apparently random profligacy of fact and conjecture, evidence and guesswork. Picking a narrative out of history is like choosing a path through the woods. To decide on any one route between the trees means abandoning all others, to tell one story is to leave all others untold.

The account that I prefer to tell myself avoids harping on the Jews' sufferings and oppressions through the centuries, so comprehensively chronicled elsewhere. Where possible I sidestep the persecutions, skirt the massacres, bypass the Holocaust; others, better qualified than I, have explored these tragic avenues. (My father never spoke of his time in *KZ* Dachau; my mother never dwelt on our imprisonment; my own encounter with Hitler's SS was at too early an age for me to claim personal understanding.) Instead I favour the less frequented but happier and perhaps more important pathways: those that celebrate the success and even occasional splendour of the Yiddish civilisation, its contribution to Europe's economy, society, religion and intellectual progress.

The story of the Yiddish civilisation that I favour rejects a black-and-white clash between gentiles and Jews, between oppression and survival, and embraces a far more nuanced contest conducted within the Yiddish-speaking people themselves: a game of tension and conflict, a tug-of-war-and-peace between East and West, between German speakers and Slav speakers, between intellect and emotion, between orthodoxy and syncretism, between those who identified themselves as "Jews," members of the Jewish people, and those who thought of themselves as "Jewish," nationals of Jewish faith, a tussle in which first one side celebrated victory over the other, then roles were reversed while former winners lost to erstwhile losers, until finally the contending teams were separated by the umpire of history—a long struggle which called up a new interpretation of what it means to be a Jew.

My narrative speaks of that competition as played out in the amphitheatre of central and eastern Europe, hustled and jostled by every crisis and contingency in the surrounding world, fought out before a crowd of Catholic Christian spectators—who would sometimes, like soccer hooligans, run out on to the pitch and attack the players.

It tells of the appearance of a new people, conceived in the Roman Empire, gestated in its successor states, born in central Europe, and raised to maturity in the countries of the East: the Yiddish civilisation, one of Europe's founder nations, whose beliefs and way of life were so attractive to those around that over the centuries uncountable numbers of converts chose them over their own. A civilisation which, as historian Cecil Roth once wrote, "had such a memorable influence on the history of the Western world."

2

The Jews of Rome

The setting is the Forum of Rome, the sanctified old market place outside (*forum* in Latin) the original Italic town, below one of the seven green hills, the Palatine, from which even today the crumbling shells of imperial palaces still project from their foundations like decayed teeth, the ground all around still strewn with collapsed columns, broken busts, and the excavated ruins of several hundred years' worth of temples, courtrooms, assemblies and other Roman religious, administrative and public buildings.

On my last visit to this famous site, walking along the marked visitors' route, I was bemused to hear the unexpected sound of Jewish prayer. I turned to find a group of heavily bearded, black-suited orthodox Jews, trilby hats tipped forward over their skullcaps, white prayer shawls draped over their shoulders, gathered in front of the Arch of Titus, rocking backwards and forwards as they chanted melodious Hebrew psalms, while a group of Japanese tourists, led by a guidette in a tartan skirt with a flag on a stick, stepped single-file in a wide detour around them, studiously and politely looking away from their devotions.

I was struck by the incongruity of the scene: by the contrast between the warm modern Jewish orthodoxy and the cold classical cruelty recorded on the ancient monument; by the realisation that the Judaeans of old would have been utterly mystified by the Jews of our own age with their northern European ways; and by the irony of my co-religionists mourning the very event that gave birth to their own people. For here stands testimony to the genesis of the Yiddish nation, the day the story really begins: the end of ancient Jerusalem and its Temple, the city burned and its citizens crushed by Roman arms in the year 70. Here is inscribed a record of the moment when the Jews dispersed across the Roman Empire, progenitors of the Yiddish people, were suddenly orphaned, cast adrift with no homeland to return to, fated for the next two millennia always to be a minority in someone else's land, the moment at which true diaspora began and, frustratingly, the very point at which collective memory suddenly falls silent.

Yet of that day itself we have good record. It is here on the triumphal Arch of Titus that squats as heavily as a Roman emperor's rule over the remains of the Via Sacra, the Sacred Way, as it runs between the jumbled imperial remains. Where the roadway tunnels the arch, the smoke-stained, weather-eroded Attic marble is sculpted on either side with a snapshot of the triumphal pageant that was awarded by the Roman Senate in June of the year 71 to the Emperor Vespasian and his forty-year-old son Titus on their victorious return from the Middle East, a parade that processed along this very route. The bas-relief is deeper at the centre of the panels than at the edges; the marchers swing out towards the viewer to make certain that its brutal point is taken: Jerusalem, the capital city of the Jews, is no more.

It is not hard to imagine the ear-shattering roar of as many as half a million cheering Romans which greet the head of the procession, the magistrates and senators in their white togas, and, ambling slowly and innocently behind them, the albino oxen that are to be sacrificed outside the temple of Jupiter Maximus at the end of the Way. Then comes a whole fleet of ships mounted on wheels, the ones that carried the victorious army over the seas and, after them, passing by us right now, the spoils of war are being flaunted: the Jerusalem Temple's sacred seven-branched candelabrum,[1] carried by two bearers who have padded their shoulders against its great weight; the two silver trumpets;[2] and the table for the twelve sacred loaves called shewbread.[3]

Flavius Josephus—original name Joseph ben Matthias—the turncoat Roman-Jewish historian who had been military commander of the Galilee and directed the defence of Jotapata but switched sides at the crucial moment, and whose account suggests that he himself was an onlooker, enthused like a schoolgirl: "it is impossible to describe the multitude of the shows as they deserve, and the magnificence of them all . . . for almost all such curiosities as the most happy men ever get piecemeal were here heaped one upon another . . . and all brought together that day to demonstrate the vastness of the dominions of the Romans."[4]

Behind the booty but in front of the victorious emperor and his son the general, today crowned in laurel and dressed in silken robes of imperial purple, as well as the emperor's younger son Domitian, later to become emperor in his turn, prisoners of war are paraded for the public to jeer at, the most important mounted on floats, so elaborate, remembered Josephus, that the onlookers "could not but be afraid that the bearers would not be able to support them firmly enough, such was their magnitude; for many of them were so made that they were on three or even four storeys, one above another."

Some notables, like Jochanan ben Levi of Giscala, one-time commander of rebel Jerusalem, are displayed in wheeled wooden cages, emphasising the tragedy of their fall by wearing their best apparel; Jochanan is to be imprisoned for life. Shimon ben Giora, regarded by the Romans as leader of the rebellious Hebrews, shuffles on foot, hobbled with shackles, a rope about his neck, guarded and whipped on by mounted legionaries, until they come to the space before the magnificent Temple of Jupiter Capitolinus, where Shimon is first tormented and then hanged in sacrifice to the gods, at which "all the people set up a shout of joy." Many of the rest are thrown still living through a hole in the floor into the doorless *Tullianum* (death room) under the grim brick and concrete Carcer, Rome's prison, that broods sullenly nearby.

The savage punishment was for rebellion, not Judaism. Many expatriate Hebrews must have stood among the vast celebratory crowd that cheered and applauded the triumphal procession as it paraded down the Via Sacra. The Jews of Rome had given neither approval nor support to Jerusalem's anti-imperial uprising, having resided in the imperial city for a century and a half or more—some lived there even before the first complete community was transplanted to Italy from Judah in 63 BCE by General Pompey, after capture during the Roman intervention in Hasmonean Israel. By the middle of the first century, Rome already had many synagogues.

These were sumptuous buildings, to judge by the one in Ostia, once Rome's sea port at the mouth of the Tiber, remains of which still stand, the building's earliest phase dating from the time of Claudius, two emperors before Vespasian. Facing south-east, i.e. towards Jerusalem, a splendid *propyleum* or monumental gateway with four slender and graceful columns of white marble leads into a vestibule that in turn gives on to the large prayer hall, fitted out with benches along the walls. Inside, an apse-like brick-built *aron*, or shrine, houses the holy Torah scrolls, apparently replacing an earlier wooden construction that had been donated, according to an inscription, by one Mindus Faustus ("Lucky" Mindus), perhaps to celebrate his good fortune, whatever that may have been. There was also a *triclineum* or dining room with built-in couches for festive meals. Later a kitchen with a beautiful mosaic floor was added, and a large study chamber.

In the surrounding district on the Sabbath, "the lamps on the greasy windows garlanded with violets emit thick smoke, the tail of a tunny fish swims in the red dish, and the white jug overflows with wine," Persius, a first-century Roman Stoic poet, tells his readers. Many city quarters seem unnaturally hushed while "you silently move your lips and turn pale at the Sabbath of the circumcised."[5] (Like several other Roman pagans, Persius apparently believed that Jews fasted on the Sabbath.)

On weekdays, Persius would have met many of the congregation as they went about their business, working, historian Cecil Roth tells us, as actors, blacksmiths, butchers, merchants, musicians, painters, pedlars, poets, singers, tailors and interpreters of dreams: ". . . for a Jew," scoffs the satirist Juvenal, "will tell you dreams of any kind you please for the smallest of coins."[6] Jewish beggars were not uncommon. "As beggars," Roth writes, "they were considered importunate; and, after Christianity established itself, some actually sold holy images on the steps of churches."[7] The Talmud even refers to Jewish gladiators: one of its great sages, Resh Lakish, was first a bandit and then a professional fighter in his youth, who survived "by combining courage with guile." Similarly, the Jewish author Caecilius of Calacte, who wrote in Greek, rose from humble beginnings, having been born a slave, to become famous as a literary critic and historian.

And, of course, there were many traders, the men who rented units in the giant semicircular mall that the Emperor Trajan built off the Via Biberatica (Boozers' Street)[8] in Rome, around which today's private cars and buzzing motor scooters fight with buses, tourist coaches and taxis for domination of the carriageway in a suffocating cloud of exhaust fumes. Had we gone shopping there any day in the first few centuries of our era we would have found many Roman Jews sitting behind their counters under the elegantly brick-arched shop doorways. Among the dozens of goods and commodities that we know they commonly traded, men marketed fowls, clothes, cooking oil, firewood, pots, ironmongery, wine and kosher meat, while their women are documented as wool sellers, jewellers, at least one greengrocer and a fishwife.

Here was no small ethnic or religious minority as in Europe today, but a large and important component of the population. Josephus mentions a lawsuit in which 8,000 Jews from Rome sided with one of the parties.[9] Only male heads of households could take part in the judicial process, so that with their wives and families of three or four children, those 8,000 men could have represented 40,000 to 50,000 people—and those were only those who took part in the case. Given that Rome's ancient population has been estimated at around half a million,[10] this was a community on a par with those of twentieth-century pre-war Prague, Vienna, Warsaw or Budapest (*Yuda-pest*, Jewish Plague, anti-Semites called it), where Jews numbered one in ten or more.

Roman Jews did have their ups and down, of course. The four years, CE 37 to 41, of the half-mad Emperor Caligula were bad—but so they were for everyone. In revolutionary times, when Jewish communities rebelled against their Latin overlords, sometimes committing horrific atrocities against their gentile neighbours as in Cyrenaica and Cyprus, popular Roman sentiment ran against them. Yet generally, until the triumph of Christianity in the fourth century—and to some degree even thereafter—Jews were welcome as followers of a lawful religion and granted special privileges: freedom from military service, the right not to appear in the law courts on the Sabbath, and—usually but not always—exemption from worshipping the emperor as a god. Under the otherwise vicious and bloodthirsty Caracalla (CE 198 to 217), who was rather magnanimous towards the Jews, their position improved still further when they, like all other free inhabitants of the empire, were granted full Roman citizenship.

True, the patricians, aristocrats and literati never approved of Judaism nor of the swelling multitude of Jewish proselytes—including several high-profile converts like the ex-consul Flavius Clemens, a close relation of the emperor, who was executed and his wife banished for "atheism," i.e. not giving allegiance to Rome's gods. Most of the upper class agreed with the philosopher Seneca that Judaism "turned the vanquished into the vanquishers" and concurred with Tacitus, the first-century historian, that this oriental religion seriously threatened Rome by undermining its traditional morality, since the ever-growing number of converts "despise the gods, repudiate the fatherland, and disparage parents, children, and brothers."[11] Other Latin writers derided the Jews' religious gullibility: *credat Iudaeus*

Apella (let Apella the Jew believe it) was—according to the poet Horace—the Latin equivalent of "tell it to the marines," the joke being that, in Latin, *A-pella* means without a foreskin (*pellis*). As for their relentless proselytising, witness another gibe by Horace, referring to his fellow poets: "There are many of us and, like the Jews, we will force you to join our gang."

On the other hand Hebrews straight from Palestine were valued as excellent outdoor slaves, noted for their brawn. Tacitus wrote that their bodies "are healthy and hardy for bearing burdens."[12] Testament to the truth of that claim is the grand project that Vespasian inaugurated to replace the Golden House, his despised predecessor Nero's eccentric, grandiose palace. Known to Romans as the Flavian amphitheatre, after the emperor's family name, Vespasian's remarkable building was constructed by Judaean slaves, captured during the conquest of Jerusalem. Under the name Colosseum (a reference to the colossal statue of Nero that previously stood nearby), the Hebrews' achievement is still today the very symbol of Rome the Eternal City.

Since all roads then led to the centre of the empire and the epitome of its urban life, those who hoped to improve their economic or career prospects would naturally gravitate towards its bright lights, its bread and circuses, much as the boldest and the best in every province of the nineteenth-century Austro-Hungarian dual monarchy made for glamorous Vienna. But Jewish populations on a similar scale were to be found in every city of the empire's vast possessions. Josephus claimed that "there is not a people in the world which does not contain a portion of our kind." The size of the empire's community in Josephus's day has been estimated at some eight million—in a population of maybe thirty million; thus perhaps as many as one in every four.

These were not all immigrant settlers from Judaea. Contemporary sources make it clear that many, perhaps even most, of the subjects of Rome who followed the Torah were not of pure Hebraic origin. Dio Cassius, a Roman historian of the second century, was clear that "all those who observe the Jewish law may be called Jews, from whatever ethnic group they derive."

The expansion of Judaism to include converts from other nations had already begun in the last two centuries before Christ's birth, when the Hasmonean rulers of Israel had vigorously spread the Jewish religion among the surrounding peoples by the sword—and by the *izmel*, the circumcision knife. Ammonites, Moabites, Edomites or Idumaeans, Herod's nation, were progressively incorporated into the Israelite, Jewish, domain. Later conversions, however, were not imposed by force. While today's orthodox rabbis are reluctant to encourage conversion, gentiles throughout the classical world saw Judaism as an attractive and welcoming religion. As the centuries progressed and fewer and fewer intelligent pagans found themselves convinced by the barbaric old gods with their sensual appetites and violent tempers, belief in the prophethood of Moses and reverence for the Torah attracted ever more popular support from the many who, as the historian Suetonius records, "without publicly acknowledging that faith, yet lived as Jews."

In the eastern provinces of the empire, pagan Greeks, known as *sebomenoi*, (God-) Respecters in Greek, called *yereim* in Hebrew, and labelled "proselytes of the gate" by the Talmud, flocked about the synagogues in their thousands—perhaps amounting to millions all told—rejecting, more or less, the old Aryan divinities and keeping to the dietary laws and the Jewish Sabbath. "Some, who have a father who reveres the Sabbath, worship nothing but the clouds, and the divinity of the heavens, and see no difference between eating swine's flesh . . . and that of man,"[13] complained the satirist Juvenal. Circumcision was a deterrent to proper conversion for adult men but, the humorist grumbled, their sons became Jews in the fullest physical sense.

An inscription discovered in Aphrodisias, Anatolia, reveals that about half of the contributors to the city's synagogue were God-fearers and their descendants, rather than ethnic Judaean Jews. And while many *sebomenoi* may have changed their allegiance to the Jewish sect called Christians—which demanded a leap of faith as qualification for entry rather than a painful operation—continued complaint by the Church Fathers suggests that movement in the other direction persisted long after the final break between Church and Synagogue, as marked by Emperor Nerva's exemption of Christians from the Jewish tax, the *fiscus Judaicus*, at the end of the first century.

A BASKET AND A TRUSS OF HAY

To get to know this ancient Jewish community a little better we should venture underground: to the burial catacombs that are recorded as sited next to the ancient routes that once led out of the city on nearly every point of the compass. Part of the magic of modern Rome is that so many of the antique landmarks as well as their names are so perfectly preserved.

Thus we can still walk west along the Via Portuensis, or Ostiensis, that takes us out through the Port Gate in the outer ramparts towards Ostia on the coast—past the ancient sign, amusing to generations of archaeologists, that begs people not to scribble (*scariphare*) graffiti on the walls. We can drive north-east on the Via Nomentana, through the site of the Colline Gate, by the remains of the gigantic and overblown white stucco-rendered bathing establishment built by Diocletian, covering thirty-two acres and so large that it could accommodate 3,000 bathers at the same time, and around the foundations of the great Praetorian barracks that both symbolised and effected the emperor's personal power.

Best of all, perhaps, we can stroll along the Via Appia Antica, the Old Appian Way, Rome's first and best-known intercity thoroughfare, leading south towards Taranto and Brindisi, and called by the poet Horace the Queen of Long Roads (*longarum regina viarum*), that still immortalises, well over two thousand years later, the name of the Censor Appius who began its construction in 312 BCE. Even in the twenty-first century one can follow where the poet Juvenal himself once walked out through the inner, older, Servian city wall, outside which homeless Jewish paupers were encamped: "My friend halted at the dripping archway of the old Porta Capena . . . now the holy fount and grove and shrine are let out to Jews, who possess a basket and a truss of hay for all their furnishings."[14] We would leave behind us the largely Jewish working-class quarter with its narrow teeming streets threading their way between *insulae*, the often jerry-built high-rise tenement buildings of the poor with their distressing tendency to collapse, past the site of the double temple dedicated to the gods of Honour and Virtue, on beside the giant arches and cyclopean walls of Caracalla's magnificent bathhouse and under the Arch of Drusus that once carried its water supply over the road, and on through the Appian Gate, now known as Porta San Sebastiano, that breaches the outer, Aurelian, city wall.

If we were taking this route in classical times we would be relieved, after twenty minutes or so of walking, to find open fields and fresh air at last taking over from the reeking shacks and workshops of the knackers and glue boilers, the tanners, dyers, fish-sauce fermenters and other tradesmen whose stinking works were always banished beyond the city walls. Here, set against the distant romantic backdrop of the Alban Hills, the remains of an extinct volcano, on whose flanks the Roman bourgeoisie built—and still build—their summer retreats, we would have found the road lined by an extraordinary collection, stretching for miles, of tombs, mastabas and mausoleums, constructed of granite, marble and brick rendered in stucco, limewash and paint, a veritable city of the dead, where Romans came at night by torchlight to bury their dear departed.

Just beyond the second milestone, we would have found a fine stone-built portico at the side of the walkway, probably decorated with a *menorah*, the seven-branched candlestick that was the principal Jewish symbol in olden times, behind which a set of steps led down to the Appian catacombs, the underground labyrinth of tunnels, galleries and *cubiculae* (burial chambers), decorated with frescoes of birds, flowers and religious symbols, in which generation upon generation of poorer Roman Jews—those who could not afford a surface tomb—were interred in *loculi*, niches in the wall.

The Jewish catacombs are not now open to the public, and at least one site, that just outside the Ostia Gate, has been lost to landslides. But from inscriptions on the several hundred votive marble plaques that have been recovered, as well as from the dedications that were found scratched into the plastered walls above the funerary niches, we learn more than might be expected about the community that lived here in the first four centuries of our era. We read of at least a dozen synagogues, some known by their location (Synagogue of the Field of Mars congregation, Synagogue of the Subura congregation), others named after a famous personality honoured by the community (Synagogue of the Augustans, Synagogue of the Agrippans), others named for unknowns who may have been their founders (Synagogue of Volumnius, Synagogue of Elaias), yet others named after the place of origin of their worshippers (Synagogue of the Hebrews, Synagogue of the Tripolitanians).

Each synagogue was presided over by a *gerousiarch*, a ruling elder (who may have been a *hiereus*, a member of the Cohen caste), and a governing board of *archons*, supported by *presbyteres*, elders, *grammateis*, scribes, and a *phronistes*, a caretaker. Those described as *pater* (father) or *mater* (mother) *synagogae* were probably generous donors to the congregation. "Veturia Paulla, consigned to her eternal home, who lived 86 years, 6 months. A proselyte of 16 years, [Hebrew name:] Sarah, Mother of the Synagogues of the Field of Mars and of Volumnius. Sleep in peace."

Much of the writing, of names, titles and memorial dedications, is not in Latin but in Greek—sometimes transliterated into Latin characters and sometimes misspelled. Most of the names too, like Eutyches or Evangelos, are Greek rather than Italic. Of 534 names known from the catacombs, 405 are Greek, 123 are Latin and only 5 are Hebrew or Aramaic. Moreover, the distribution of the languages suggests that there may have been separate synagogues for Latin, Greek and Hebrew speakers, as if the congregations were divided on linguistic grounds or between conservative Jews who prayed in Hebrew and others who addressed God in the two vernaculars.

The implication is that the Jews of Rome were divided in their cultural allegiance, that a split between an eastern and a western orientation goes back all the way to classical times. In this respect, they were no different from other Romans. Greek was the lingua franca of the much more populous eastern half of the empire. The educated class of the empire was largely bilingual. Authors needed to write in Greek to reach the widest readership. The first histories by Romans, like the now lost annals of the patrician Fabius Pictor, were written in Greek. Herein lay a source of friction. The Latins had overcome the Greeks by force of arms, but the Greeks had subjugated the Romans by force of intellect. Rome derived a good half of her culture from the conquered nation, and the speech most commonly heard in the city streets was Greek not Latin. How could it be otherwise when so many of the Roman upper and middle classes were reared and educated by Greek slaves and freedmen? The result was eternal ambivalence among Romans towards their eastern cousins. Greek ways were attractive and seductive, but they were also the ways of a defeated and enslaved nation.

The distrust and dislike was reciprocated. The attitude of the Greeks and the Jews to their rich, powerful and over-capable Roman overlords is perhaps a little like the response of some of the world to American power today. Thus the rabbis of the Mishnah: "Rabbi Judah said [of the Romans] 'How becoming are the deeds of these people: they build markets, they build bridges, they build bathhouses.'" The irascible Simeon ben Yochai replied, "Whatever they build they merely do for themselves; they build markets to settle harlots in, bathhouses to delight themselves in, and bridges to take tolls." (For this remark he was condemned to death, was forced to flee and had to hide away in a cave for twelve years.)[15]

This cultural and linguistic tension made the empire fragile, its two wings ever ready to beat to different rhythms. The provinces had already once fallen into Latin and Greek halves, at the time of the civil war that followed Julius Caesar's assassination. It took the ruthlessly applied power of the new emperor, Augustus, to knit them together again. For some three hundred years, the West was strong enough to hold the delicate fabric in one piece, but its eventual unravelling was inevitable.

·   ·   ·

At the opposite end of the Roman Forum's Sacred Way from the Arch of Titus, close to the Arch of Septimius Severus, there stands an apparently perfectly preserved sober red-brick building with a central doorway, three windows on the upper floor and, above them, a pitched and gabled roof. The contrast with the grandiose and histrionic imperial edifices all around is significant, for this was the Curia, the meeting place of the Senate, the supreme governing body of the Roman Republic. Originally ordered into being by Julius Caesar in 52 BCE, burned in Nero's great fire, restored in the time of Titus's brother and successor Domitian, burned and restored again during the third-century rule of Diocletian, the reason it still looks so new is that it was most recently restored from the original materials by that would-be latter-day inheritor of the imperial purple, Benito Mussolini.

It is a tiny building, compared with, say, the Palace of Westminster in London or the Capitol in Washington. True, once there was also a small administrative annexe, a *secretarium*, dedicated in the year 303 but long since gone. Yet from this sparsely furnished hall would have been governed a gigantic empire so vast that its poets could sing of scenes as wildly different as the snowy Northumbrian hills in the province of Britannia, the steaming first cataract of the Nile in Egypt, the storm-battered cliffs of Rabat on the Atlantic coast of Morocco, or far-off Colchis on the eastern Black Sea coast, where Jason and the Argonauts sailed in their quest for the Golden Fleece. As in one of those galumphing dinosaurs that are said to have needed one brain in the head and another in the tail, a single power centre was inadequate to control this huge body politic.

Rome's geographical position posed a problem, sited as it now was on the periphery rather than in the focus of the imperial domains. Of course, history and tradition would always give the Eternal City a special place in Roman hearts, but practical politics demanded a new centre closer to the empire's centre of gravity in the East. It fell to Constantine, the first Christian emperor, to found the New Rome, and give it his name: Constantinopolis, Constantinople, City of Constantine. The emperor had chosen as its site the ancient city of Byzantium—a place sacred to the moon goddess whose crescent symbol would later be adopted by the Ottoman Turks and passed on to all Islam (and whose later emblem, the double-headed eagle, representing a power centre that faced equally west and east, would be adopted by the Holy Roman Empire, the Russian monarchy and others). The official foundation ceremony was held on 11 May in the year 330 of the Christian era.

This change of headquarters could not help but underline the eternal cultural distance between Latin and Greek. The consequences seem inevitable. Within thirty-five years the empire was divided into two—along the same frontier as had separated Mark Antony's realm from that of Augustus in the Roman civil war more than three centuries previously—and two emperors, Valentinian and his brother Valens, were separately enthroned. To quote Edward Gibbon's *Decline and Fall of the Roman Empire*:

> In the castle, or palace, of Mediana, only three miles from Naissus [Niš in Serbia], they executed the solemn and final division of the Roman empire. Valentinian bestowed on his brother the rich præfecture of the East, from the Lower Danube to the confines of Persia; whilst he reserved for his immediate government the warlike præfectures of Illyricum, Italy, and Gaul, from the extremity of Greece to the Caledonian rampart, and from the rampart of Caledonia to the foot of Mount Atlas.

The line of division was almost exactly that which would again separate the continent, this time into capitalist and Communist halves, some fifteen hundred years later.

With the division of the empire, its Jews set out on separate paths. As long as both western and eastern sectors coexisted, intercourse and interchange between the two remained possible. But all too soon the western provinces came under barbarian threat from the Germanic tribes pressing ever harder on their borders and increasingly breaking through. Now the decline of the West accelerated at astonishing speed. Eighty years after the foundation of New Rome, the northern province of Britannia was lost and the unthinkable happened: Rome was sacked by a force of Visigoths led by their chieftain Alaric, the first time in 800 years that the city had been captured by an enemy. Another forty-five years, and Rome was again taken, this time by the Germanic Vandals—and the Jerusalem Temple spoils that had been carefully preserved as trophies in the temple of Jupiter Capitolinus were carted off to Africa, never to be seen again. Twenty-one years later, in 476, the last western emperor, the child Romulus Augustulus, was deposed by the German general Odoacer. After another seventeen years the new kingdom was in turn conquered by Theodoric of the Ostrogoths and Odoacer was assassinated at a banquet, and 163 years after the founding of New Rome in Constantinople, Old Rome was consigned to history.

Here was a complete parting of the ways for the Roman-Jewish world.

From now on the twin, geographically divided, strands of the Jewish experience, the Latin and the Greek, would develop different versions of the Jewish way of life. Two divergent characters would be separately forged under the hammers of two very different histories until, centuries later, both sides would meet up again in central Europe.

3

From the Mediterranean to the Baltic

The ancient Greek city of Miletus lies on the coast of Anatolia by the now silted-up delta through which the River Maeander once meandered into the Mediterranean. On a promontory between the grand City Hall and a *nymphaeum*—a huge water temple also used as an assembly room for weddings (and later as a bordello)—there once stood a magnificent three-storey, fifty-feet-high, white-marble portal that gave access to the southern market place; it now rests in a Berlin museum. Back in the first centuries of our era, had you passed Phineas the barber plying his trade under the notice chiselled into the stone reserving the station for him alone, and walked through one of the gateway's three arched openings, surrounded by twenty-four grand Corinthian pillars, you would have found yourself in a giant *agora*, the largest market place in the Greek world, the size of three soccer pitches or twenty city blocks, boasting warehouses, storerooms and nearly a hundred shops. Here was testimony to the economic success of the most important Hellenistic city of Asia Minor, attracting trade goods and revenue from the colonies she had founded all around the Aegean, the Sea of Marmara and the Black Sea: Abydos, Cyzicus, Sinope, Olbia and Pantikapaion among them.

While the empire of the Italian Latins was based on military conquest of the land, that of the Hellenic Greeks had evolved from mastery of the sea. The Mediterranean coast of Turkey, once called Ionia, Aeolia and Cilicia—today a favourite holiday destination for seekers of sun, sea, sand and sex—is strewn with the bleached marble bones of ruined Greek cities, reminding us that in classical times the Hellenes lived far more widely spread than just in the country we now call Greece, and that the majority inhabited areas that were, geographically speaking, Asian and North African rather than European. For much of its existence the eastern Roman Empire encompassed today's Georgia, Armenia, Turkey, Syria, Lebanon, Jordan, Israel, Egypt, Libya and Tunisia.

This Asian dimension of the eastern provinces of the Roman world brought a very different flavour to the thought, manners, culture and religion of their half of the empire, a tone that came to distinguish it quite radically from the western. The difference seems detectable even in the Miletus gateway's style, with its elegantly fluted tapered columns, its finely decorated entablatures and the graceful coffering of the porch. Latin architecture tends towards the heavy, the stolid and the serious, as if symbolising Rome's ruthless domination of its hinterland and colonies. That of the eastern provinces of the empire is lighter, more airy and delicate, as if expressing a gentler, more subtle and equal relationship between the metropolis and its outposts and neighbours. Latins could afford to govern by brute force. Greeks had to learn to be cleverer and cannier. Before finding themselves included in the rather laissez-faire Roman imperium, Greek outposts in Anatolia like Miletus had to survive long rule by Persian and Seleucid autocrats whose heavy hand could only be circumvented by Greek guile.

This Greek-speaking world was home to millions of the Roman Empire's Jews. The important role that the community played in Miletus's affairs is suggested by the central location of the city's principal synagogue, immediately between the old harbour and the civic centre, as also by the fact that one entire section of the Roman theatre was reserved, according to an inscription, as "the place of the Jews who are also called Fearers of the Supreme God."[1] There must have been other synagogues too, for this particular building seems only to have measured some sixty feet long by thirty-six wide. Compare that with the giant prayer hall, four hundred feet long and sixty feet wide, located on the principal boulevard of nearby Sardis, behind a row of shops (owned by synagogue elders Jacob, Sabbatios, Samuel and Theoktistos), and gloriously decorated with mosaics, marbles and statuary, which could hold a thousand worshippers.

The Jews of the eastern Roman Empire were an important component of the population, as many as one in ten overall. But that is an average, and Jews were more likely to be found in urban rather than rural settings. So here again, in the east of the Roman Empire as in the city of Rome itself, we should think of the towns as having very considerable Judaic populations, some approaching the scale of Vilna or Odessa in the 1920s: more than a third Jewish. Numbers are not everything, of course, but since Judaism was also seen as an acceptable belief, if not to everyone's taste—a situation rarely found until the last century in the European West—we might well conclude that Jewish ideas and idioms, kosher food, chutzpah and mazel-tov were as familiar to gentiles in the east Roman world as they are in today's Britain or the USA

Quid pro quo, it was a very Greek form of Judaism that came to prevail. Prayers were read in Greek, as were parts of the Bible and even the Mishnah, the revered oral tradition of the early sages. Even today, nearly two thousand years later, the only non-Hebrew names by which worshippers can be called to the reading of the Torah in the synagogue, remaining popular even among Yiddish speakers, are Greek: Kalonymos (good name) popularly Hebraised to Kalmen, and Aleksander, Yiddishised to Sender. Indeed, the Hellenic influence on the Jewish people proved so important that the Greek and later Byzantine *Romaniote* rite grew into a separate and distinct tradition of Jewish observance—even surviving into the twentieth century. The last *Gregos* (Greek) synagogue, in Edirne (Adrianople, formerly Hadrianopolis, Hadrian's City), burned down in 1905.

The use of Greek in the holy services hints at the pedigree of those who attended them. Many, perhaps even most, of the Jews of eastern Rome were proselytes, or the descendants of proselytes. Unlike the much more pragmatic Latins, the Greeks had long honoured philosophical speculation and were well prepared to entertain the Jews' novel spiritual and ethical notions. I can put the attraction no more elegantly than Professor Richard Gotheil of Columbia University:

> The purity and simplicity of its theology captivated the high-minded; while the mystery and quaintness of its customs, the welcome Sabbath rest, the privileges enjoyed at the hand of the public authorities, recommended the Jewish faith to those more materialistically inclined . . . In brief, it was a religion essentially supple and elastic under an appearance of rigidity, and one which knew how to be at once authoritative and liberal, idealistic and material-

istic, a philosophy for the strong, a superstition for the weak, and a hope of salvation for all.[2]

Conversion to Judaism continued to be a common phenomenon even well after pagan times, a fact confirmed not only by inscriptions found all over the Greek world, but also by the repeated attempts by Church and palace to prevent it. Decrees forbidding conversion to Judaism, and threatening dire punishment to both convert and converter, were regularly promulgated—on average every fifteen to twenty-five years—for nearly ten centuries after belief in Jesus Christ became the established Greek faith. The authoritative twentieth-century Jewish historian Salo Baron concludes that

> The farther away from Palestine a country was situated, the less pure racially and ethnically its Jewish settlers were. A large section of Syrian Jewry, and probably a still larger section of the Jewries of Asia Minor, the East Mediterranean islands, and the Balkans, must have consisted of former proselytes and their descendants.[3]

Baron doesn't mention the communities established since the first century in the Greek colonies north of the Black Sea, the outposts sited on what would in our times become the Ukrainian and Russian littoral, yet these would prove to be the most important nurseries for the future development of the Yiddish-speaking Jews—the first points of arrival in what would one day be called the Pale of Settlement. As far away as could be from the centre of power, hardly ever more than notionally part of the Roman Empire and mostly completely detached from it by the beginning of the fourth century, these communities were the only ones safe from the ever-increasing imperial pressure on pagans and Christians to stop converting to Judaism and even more on the Jews to stop making proselytes, abandon their religion and admit the superiority of Christian belief.

When Christianity had been declared the state religion of the empire, the situation of Jews and God-fearers had radically changed. Now the two monotheisms were competing for the same pool of potential converts. And while Judaism may have attracted greater sympathy from ordinary people, Christianity, as the faith of the emperors, had the power. The march of history, the transfer of government from Rome to Constantinople, had brought Latinate ways and ideas to the heart of the Greek world. While for the Greeks, religion had previously been largely a matter of personal spiritual choice, saying little or nothing about the believer's other allegiances—they seem to have regarded followers of the Torah simply as Jewish Greeks—to the Latins religion was a matter of politics and patriotism. Jews came to be seen by them as members of a dissident and suspect sect.

The first aim of the newly Christian rulers and their religious mentors was to detach the God-fearers from the synagogue and turn them towards the Church. In the New Testament, the Acts of the Apostles already distinguishes between Hellenes and Israelites, converted Greeks and ethnic Hebrews: "And in those days, when the number of the disciples was multiplied, there arose a murmuring of the Grecians [*Hellenistai*] against the Hebrews [*Hebraioii*] . . ."[4] The rapid growth of Christianity in the East suggests the success of the project to persuade as many as possible of the uncircumcised semi-detached synagogue members to join what had begun as the Jewish Jesus sect but was soon enough to become the separate and antagonistic Christian faith. The next targets for conversion were the real Jews of cities like Constantinople, Adrianople and Alexandria, who numbered several millions. Ever greater legal sanctions were imposed on those who refused to conform to the new politico-religious reality.

In the fourth century the Emperor Constantine, even before his formal deathbed conversion to Christianity, had criticised the "baleful" Jewish religion, and threatened the community, on pain of death, not to dissuade its members from converting to Christianity. His son Constantius forbade intermarriage between members of the sister faiths. The fifth-century code of Theodosius prohibited the building of new synagogues and allowed repairs only if needed to avoid danger to the public. In the sixth century, the Emperor Justinian, builder of the great St. Sophia Cathedral in Constantinople, tried to dictate the form of synagogue services—forbidding the use of the Mishnah in interpreting the Torah, as well as prescribing which translation was to be allowed—and made Judaism altogether illegal in his North African territories.

Matters hardly changed even after much of the Greek peninsula itself, the Hellenes' original homeland, was lost to the barbarians, and the latest of the monotheisms, Islam, had stripped the Egyptian and North African provinces as well as the Middle East from the empire's grasp. In 632, the year of the Prophet Muhammad's death, Emperor Heraclius directed the entire Jewish community to convert. They didn't. In 721 Leo III ordered all

Jews to be baptised. They weren't. In the ninth century Basil I issued another decree of forced conversion. It failed. In the tenth, Romanus I Lecapenus again commanded the conversion of the Jews. In spite of considerable persecutions, it was ignored. Yet the constant attacks on their religion cannot but have suggested to the Jews of the metropolitan Greek world that they would do well to move out towards its periphery, where they might still find the benefits of Greek civilisation and a Jewish community already established, but to which the writ of the Christianising emperors in Constantinople could not stretch. Just such sanctuary was offered by the distant colonies strung like pearls around the shores where the steppes of southern Russia skirt the Black Sea, including the rich and fruitful Crimean peninsula—under non-Christian rule until Catherine the Great annexed it to Russia in 1783.

The Crimean peninsula hangs like a chad from the coast of southern Russia into the Black Sea, almost but not quite closing off the waters that the Greeks called the Maeotian Lake and we know as the Sea of Azov. At 10,000 square miles, it is larger than Wales, mostly covered in age-old grassland, and with a chain of mountains dividing the steppe from the southern coastal towns, where Greek colonists—many of them either full Jews or Greek God-fearers—had already set themselves up to trade with the nomad barbarians during Hellenistic times.

Today there is hardly anything left to see of what was once a flourishing and wealthy society. The winds whistle across the flat miles of scrubby grass, the dreary vista broken only by an occasional nomad burial mound. Here and there a few shattered stones protrude from the dark earth; cobbled roadways and the foundations of walls lie exposed by archaeological excavation. Occasionally, as at the clifftop town where dwellings cling to the rocks like martins' nests—the place later Tatars[5] called *Chufut-Kale* (Jews' fortress)—the roads still show the ruts left by generations of iron-tyred carts, a memoir of the commercial bustle that once enlivened the Crimean coastline. Russian archaeologists have dug beaverishly among the remains of these flourishing overseas colonial city states, providing us with evidence—sometimes to their own chagrin—that Jews served in the army, were organised in communities with synagogues, set up *thiasoi*, private religious societies, and continued in their efforts to turn the heathen towards the one God and His commandments in the Torah. A typical Greek inscription found at Pantikapaion, today's Kerch, where the Sea of Azov runs into the Black Sea, reads: "In the year 377, on the twelfth day of the month of Peritios, I, Chresta . . . declare . . . that my foster-son [i.e. liberated slave] Herakles is free . . . and may travel wherever he wishes . . . he is not however to forsake the fear of heaven and attachment to the synagogue . . . under the supervision of the community of the Jews."[6]

In addition, according to Dr. Uriel Rappaport of Haifa University,[7] Jews exercised appreciable influence on non-Jewish circles, with Jewish symbols and the *tetragrammaton*, the four Hebrew letters indicating the name of God, appearing on otherwise apparently pagan inscriptions.

Greeks and Jews were no strangers to each other, having lived together for centuries. But it was here, in the Crimea and along the surrounding Black Sea shores, that Jews would first come into contact with a quite different kind of nation from those with which they had previously been familiar: nomadic, illiterate, without a recorded history or an intellectually developed religious mythology, peoples the Greeks called barbarous because of their incomprehensible language (sounding to the Greek ear like: baa-baa-raa-ba), but who would turn out, paradoxically, to have the most striking influence on the creation of the Yiddish people.

As an extension of the steppeland, the Crimea had long acted as a sort of reservoir into which successive waves of horse-riding nomads pressed themselves on their way along the great grassy east-west freeway that connects the Tarim basin in eastern Asia to the Danube delta in eastern Europe, then squeezing between the Black Sea's western shore and the swing of the Carpathian mountains into the cul-de-sac of the plain Hungarians call the *puszta*. Scythians, Sarmatians, Goths, Huns, Alans, Avars, Bulgars, Khazars and Magyars all took a bow in the Crimean arena as they passed on their heroic progress, either, like the Bulgars and Magyars, to found European states that have lasted, in one form or another, into the present, or, like the Huns and Avars, to be rewarded with oblivion.

For some six hundred years, from about 400 BCE, the Scythians controlled a great swath of the western steppe, from the borders of Iran to southern Russia and even parts of the north European plain, with their power centred on the Crimean New City, Neapolis, modern Simferopol, and leaving their name to the entire region, Scythia, as well as to the people who lived there. Long into the Middle Ages, Scythian remained the generic term for all eastern European steppe dwellers, nomad or sedentary. In the hinterland to the Black Sea city states, rubbing shoulders with Greek and Jewish colonists with whom they are for ever linked in the passage of St. Paul's Letter to the Colossians: "Where there is neither Greek nor Jew, circumcision nor uncircumcision, Barbarian, Scythian, bond nor free,"[8] the Scythians, though originally horse-riding warrior-nomads, enclosed fields and established farms and grew wheat for shipment over the water to the populous cities of the eastern empire, the start of a trade in Ukrainian grain that would feed much of Europe for nearly two millennia and would in later years become almost a Yiddish monopoly. The Scythian upper class, powerfully attracted to the ways of civilisation, intermarried with their Greek counterparts and intermingled with Jews and God-fearers, a relationship permanently brought to mind by the later application of the name Scythian, Ashkenazi in Hebrew, to all northern European Jews.[9]

The Scythians were only the first of a succession of nationalities who would rule the eastern European grasslands and with whom the Jews would forge relations of surprising intimacy. In the first round of the power game on the steppe, the Scythians were pushed westwards to make way for the Sarmatians, another people speaking an Iranian language and maintaining a nomadic way of life. Here we have the first real evidence of Judaic influence. A letter from tenth-century Constantinople, discovered by the scholar Solomon Schechter in the *geniza*, the attic storeroom, of an old synagogue in Cairo, thus known as the Schechter Letter, refers to the Alans, a Sarmatian tribal group, one wing of which stormed right over Europe, through the Rhineland and across today's Austria, France, Spain and Portugal, where they founded long-lasting settlements like Alençon, while another branch fought their way down to the Caucasus, where they put down permanent roots to become the ancestors of today's Ossetes. "Some of them," notes the Schechter Letter, "observe the laws of the Jews."

The Sarmatians were in their turn displaced by the Goths, a Germanic rather than an Iranian nation. Yet not much changed in the power transfer, for the Goths quickly adopted Sarmatian ways, apparently including the Judaic connection: a tombstone found in Partenit, the main coastal city of the Crimean Goths, is inscribed with the name "Herefridil ha-Kohen," combining a Germanic forename with the title of a hereditary Hebrew priest.

The clues that there may have been Jewish Alans and Jewish Goths are the first signs of a movement of which there is otherwise little record. By the fourth century, Judaism was beginning to expand from its coastal Black Sea enclaves and move into the interior, the wild and undeveloped territories east of central Europe. Now that the uncharted lands were coming under the control of peoples familiar to the Jews and with whom they seem to have felt at ease, there was no reason to go on clinging to the shoreline, and much interest in striking out to bring knowledge, crafts and trade to the primitive interior. Jewish entrepreneurs had discovered a new north-west frontier.

The centrifugal movement was to pick up speed under the impulse of the next great family of tribespeople to thunder up on the eastern horizon under a cloud of dust and a shower of arrows, whose constituent nations began to arrive every few generations from the start of the fifth century and would not stop coming for nearly a thousand years.

These were nations of a completely different background, peoples of Turkic, Tartar or Mongol extraction, born, bred and hardened in the cold, dry, high steppes beyond the Altai mountains of Chinese Turkestan. Over the succeeding millennium one new invader after another would canter on to the eastern European stage, often centring their power in the western-most extension of the Eurasian steppe, the Great Hungarian plain.

At first they must have been greeted by the Judaeo-Greek Black Sea colonists with the same uncomprehending condescension with which, many centuries later, the intrepid Jewish traveller Benjamin of Tudela would look upon the ancestors of Turkmen, Seljuks and Ottomans, the Oghuz Turks of Central Asia, "who worship the wind and live in the wilderness, and who do not eat bread nor drink wine, but live on raw uncooked meat. They have no noses and in lieu thereof they have two small holes, through which they breathe. They eat animals both clean and unclean, and they are very friendly towards Israelites."[10]

The first to arrive from the East in the fourth century were the Huns. Their rule lasted some eighty years. Next, Avars would replace the Huns; after another century Bulgars would replace the Avars. In the seventh century, Khazars would press in on the Bulgars, driving them north along the Volga river and west towards the Danube basin; in the ninth, Magyars would push the Bulgars south and set up their camps in the Hungarian plain, only themselves eventually to fall subject to the Ottoman Turks, who would maintain their occupation of much of the region until after the failure of their siege of Vienna in 1683.

It is clear from the remains that these newcomers were as tolerant as their predecessors of the Jewish religion. The visible consequence was a return from Hellenism and Greek customs to a more authentically Jewish way of life. Tombstones now gave up Greek inscriptions and re-adopted Judaic symbols as a statement of religious identity: the *menorah* (candelabra), the *shofar* (ram's horn), the *lulav* and *esrog* (palm branch and citron fruit, symbols of Succoth, the Feast of Ingathering). Moreover, the Huns appear to have been as susceptible to conversion as other pagan barbarians. The tenth-century Abbot Heriger of the Abbey of Lobbes in today's Belgium—friend of Gerbert, the future Pope Sylvester II, and author of an important mathematics text, a man much honoured in his day for his knowledge and scholarship—wrote that the Huns claimed to be proud of their Jewish origin.[11] This was nonsense, of course; the Huns were no Hebrews. But the reference does suggest that there were Jews among these Turkic invaders when they first appeared and struck terror into the hearts of the West.

And we do know that the ruling class of a very similar Turkic people with a very similar background did indeed become Jews. These were the Khazars, who established a Khaganate north of the Caspian Sea, which was to become for a time so powerful that at least two East Roman emperors, Justinian II and Constantine V, took Khazar princesses for wives. The fourteenth-century Arab cosmographer ad-Dimashqi wrote that, according to an earlier source, "in the days of Harun ar-Rashid," that is, in the eighth century, "the Roman Emperor forced the Jews to emigrate. They came to the Khazar country, where they found an intelligent but untutored race and offered them their religion. The inhabitants found it better than their own and accepted it."[12] The truth of ad-Dimashqi's story is confirmed by the words of the Khazar's ruler himself.

AS STRANGE AS A CIRCUMCISED UNICORN

By the eighth century the Khazars had established a territory at the head of the Caspian Sea with a capital near the mouth of the Volga, and extended their control over an empire which, at its height, stretched all the way from the Ukraine to Central Asia, and took tribute from Sarmatian Alans, Bulgars, Greeks, Goths, Magyars and Slavs, while their raiding parties spread panic even further afield in Europe and Russia. In this they were little different from other eastern conquerors like the Huns before them and the Magyars who followed. It was their response to the power politics of the region that made them unique. For, under sustained military pressure from Christian Byzantines to the west and from Muslim Arabs to the south, as well as having constantly to parry raids by the still pagan Russians to the north, the Khazars chose to keep their distance from all by adopting neither Christianity nor Islam. Instead, the Khazar rulers famously converted themselves and some, or even most, of their people to Judaism.

Far off to the west in southern Spain lay glittering Córdoba, capital of the Umayyad Caliphate which, under 'Abd ur-Rahman III, had grown into the largest and most cultured city in Europe, famed for its mosques and palaces, its silks, brocades and leatherwork prized in both East and West, its scriptoria susurrating with the pen-scratching of the most distinguished assembly of scribes and scholars of the age. The Caliph's director of customs (whom we might now call finance minister), as well as principal diplomat (perhaps foreign minister today), was the Jewish scholar, physician and politician Chasdai Ibn Shaprut (*c*.915–*c*.970), a considerable intellectual, one of the group who translated Dioscorides's classic *De Materia Medica* from Greek into Arabic and thus passed it along the route towards becoming, in its Latin translation, the standard pharmacological text of the next six centuries.

According to his own account, Ibn Shaprut first heard the strange tale of the Turkic Khazars who had converted to Judaism from a party of traders from Central Asia. He thought the idea so unlikely as not to be worth pursuing. However, the story was soon confirmed by a visiting Byzantine diplomatic mission, who also gave their host a much more detailed description of Khazaria. One can only guess at the expression on Chasdai's face as he strolled with the distinguished delegation in his silk robes and his white turban, among the cooling fountains in the shady palace gardens, the air heavy with jasmine blossom and the scent of orange and pomegranate trees, listening to the fantastic saga of a Jewish kingdom held in respect even by the Byzantine emperor himself. As Arthur Koestler put it in his book *The Thirteenth Tribe: The Khazar Empire and Its Heritage*, "A warrior nation of Turkish Jews must have seemed . . . as strange as a circumcised unicorn."[13]

"The name of the ruling king is Joseph," the guests told their host. "Ships come to us from their land, bringing fish, furs and all sorts of merchandise. They are in alliance with us, and honoured by us. We exchange embassies and gifts. They are powerful and have a fortress for their outposts and troops which go out on forays from time to time."

Naturally enough, the Córdoban vizier could hardly wait to make contact as soon as possible. He sat down and wrote King Joseph a letter:

I feel the urge to know the truth, whether there is really a place on this earth where harassed Israel can rule itself, where it is subject to nobody. If I were to know that this is indeed the case, I would not hesitate to forsake all honours, resign my high office, abandon my family, and travel over mountains and plains, over land and water, until I arrived at the place where my Lord, the King rules.[14]

One shouldn't take these protestations too seriously. The use of high-flown poetical language was the order of the day in official correspondence. Indeed the letter seems to have been composed on Chasdai's behalf by Menachem Ibn Saruq, Cordoba's leading Jewish poet and lexicographer. (He was later to fall into disfavour and be replaced by another,[15] the composer of "Dror Yikra," He Shall Proclaim Freedom, the lyric which led to Dana International's downfall in a flurry of feathers at the 1999 Eurovision Song Contest.) Menachem began with a *piyyut*, an elaborate liturgical poem showering praise and honour on the Khazar ruler, in which the first letter of each line spelled out first Chasdai's full name and then his own.

Early on in the text, the Córdoban informs the king of the Khazars about the prosperity of Moorish Spain, where conditions for Jews are so good that "their like has never been known before." Yet the letter ends with an enquiry about the daily awaited return of the Messiah, a subject never far from the pious tenth-century Jewish mind; not, it appears, because of persecution and oppression but because not to have their own country diminished the Jewish people even in their own eyes: "Dishonoured and humiliated by our dispersion, we have to listen in silence to those who say: 'every nation has its own land and you alone possess not even the shadow of a country on this earth.'"

It took Ibn Shaprut a long time to find a way of sending his flowery missive to the khagan of the Khazars. On the first attempt, Chasdai's courier wasn't even allowed to travel beyond Constantinople—the emperor no doubt saw any alliance between Muslim Arabs and Jewish Khazars as spelling twin-pronged danger. However, Chasdai's emissary did meet a learned Khazar Jew, claiming to be a close favourite of his ruler, whom he persuaded to set down a short essay about his country and its relations with its neighbours. A copy of this text, called the Cambridge Document, now rests in Cambridge University.

On his next try, Chasdai sent his letter by a more circuitous route: passing stage by stage, hand to hand, from his own community to the Croatian Jews, in turn to the Hungarian Jews, then on to the Russian Jews, next to the Bulgarian Jews, and finally from the Bulgarian Jews to their contacts among the Khazars. This time, the message does seem to have arrived, for two copies of a response are still preserved, though who can say exactly when it was delivered in Córdoba and whether Chasdai ever got to see it? Perhaps we should not be too sceptical; even during the so-called Dark Ages, people did conduct long-distance correspondence and letters did reach their destinations.

King Joseph's reply, as we have it, gives a full account of the Khazar Empire and its dealings with the surrounding peoples, probably without too much alteration by the scribes who made the copies:

> I live near the mouth of the Volga river and with God's help guard its entrance and prevent the Russians who arrive in ships from entering the Caspian Sea, intending to make their way to the land of the Arabs. In the same way I stop these enemies approaching the Gates of Derbent by land. Because of this, I am at war with them, and were I to let them pass but once, they would destroy the whole land of the Arabs as far as Baghdad.

It was his ancestor Khagan Bulan, Joseph explains, who adopted the Jews' religion after a dream or vision in which God instructed him to set up a tabernacle with an ark, a table for a seven-branched candelabrum, then as now a symbol of the Judaic faith, as well as an altar and sacred vessels and utensils.

> After those days, there arose from the sons of his sons a king named Obadiah. He was an upright and just man. He reorganised the kingdom and established the Jewish religion properly and correctly. He built synagogues and schools, brought in many Israelite sages, and honoured them with silver and gold, and they explained to him the twenty-four books [the Bible], Mishnah, Talmud [the commentaries], and the order of Prayers. He was a man who feared God and loved the law and the commandments.[16]

The correspondence between the Umayyad vizier and King Joseph took place in the mid-tenth century and is the last clear documentary evidence we have of Khazar history. Scattered references in later Muslim, Jewish and Christian sources tell us that attacks from the north increased and that by the year 1000 the Russians had finally achieved their aim of destroying Sarkel, the Khazar city that blocked the Caspian to their shipping. Whether this was the final end of Khazar independence, or whether the Jewish Turks managed to hang on to some of their lands for another hundred years or so, as some historians believe, is a matter of unresolved dispute. Whatever the case may have been, it was only a matter of time before Khazaria vanished completely from the map and from history—though Turks, Arabs and Persians still know the Caspian as the Khazar Sea.

SENNAN AND ZIPPAN

There has been much debate about what proportion of ordinary Khazars, as opposed to their rulers, took up the religion of the Hebrews. Their empire held many different peoples, with many different beliefs, within its borders. Turks, Iranians, Slavs, Germans and Celts, Jews, Christians, Muslims and traditional, Tengri, shamanists were all represented among the population. Such tolerance ensured that immigrants professing the Jewish religion would have continued to flow into Khazaria from more unfriendly parts of the Byzantine world as enthusiastically as did Yiddish speakers flock to America from intolerant Russia at the end of the nineteenth century. A tenth-century letter in Hebrew from the Khazar Jews of Kiev is signed with eleven names, of which seven are Hebrew and four Turkic. One of the Hebrews is a Levy, but two of the Turkic names are suffixed Cohen.

It was not just the Crimean Jews who were affected by the millennial east-to-west flow of successive nomad conquerors, of Huns, Avars, Bulgars, Khazars and Magyars. This great extended population movement that began in the fourth century and ended in the tenth changed the ethnic composition of all Eurasia, sweeping along with it many of the other peoples the Turks encountered in their path, like a series of giant tidal waves that picked up communities, bore them along for great distances and finally, when the waters at last receded, dumped them, like deposits of precious minerals, in new surroundings, among unfamiliar peoples, far away from their original locations.

The Hun and Avar surges towards the west and into the Balkans spread Slav-speaking farmers from their original homes east of the River Vistula as far west as Hamburg and the River Elbe and as far south as the Greek Peloponnese. The hordes retreated, the pioneers stayed. This was a massive population movement with far-reaching historical consequences. Central Europe, including today's Austria, the Czech and Slovak republics, even much of Germany, became overwhelmingly Slav-populated; the

South Slav nations—Croats, Serbs and Slovenes—were born. To the horror of Byzantium, the whole of Greece became ethnically more Slav and Turk than Greek. Now Slavic dialects could be heard all the way from the Saale river near Leipzig (itself a Slav name) to beyond Moscow, from the Gulf of Finland to the Gulf of Corinth, from the mountain slopes of the Tyrol, the forested bowl of Bohemia and the grassy plain of Hungary, to the chilly uplands of Russia and the baking steppes of the Ukraine. Folklore still remembers three Slav brothers, Lech, Czech and Rus, fathers of the Polish, Czech and Russian nations respectively, who set off travelling together, looking for new lands to settle, and then parted company east, west and north, each to find and found his own new homeland.

And with them and among them, floated up from the Crimea and the Black Sea steppe, borne along into the body of Europe by the very same series of waves of advance, almost but not quite invisible, were settlers professing the Jewish faith. In the tenth century Ibn Shaprut would send his letter to the khagan of the Khazars via established communities in Croatia, Bulgaria, Hungary and Russia. The intermixed Hebrew, Gothic, Greek and Turkic synagogue communities, augmented by new converts from among the other peoples that surrounded them, had long given up the Greek language for Turkic. Now they adopted the Slavic language, what they called the *loshen kna'an*, the Cana'anite tongue—parallel to the Latin *Sclavus*, which meant both slave and Slav, since to the Hebrews the original slave nation had been the Cana'anites. A letter recommending its bearer to the community in Salonika on the Mediterranean explains that he, like other Slavic Jews, knew neither Hebrew nor Arabic nor Greek, "since the people of his country speak only *kna'an*."[17]

Such were the bare foundations on which the Yiddish world was to be built. From this time onwards we find hints and indications, tiny traces, of Jewish life in eastern Europe and the Balkans. Ninth- or tenth-century mixed pagan-Jewish graves in Čelarevo, Serbia, contain bricks with Jewish motifs—*menorahs*, rams' horns—and even one with a Hebrew text that rings out down the ages: *Jehudah, oy!* A ninth-century Latin text from Salzburg[18] notes Jewish merchants in Austria and refers to *medicum iudaicum vel slavianiscum* (a Jewish or Slav physician). A legend, popular if unbelievable, has it that the very first king of Poland was a Jew. The Dalimil text, the oldest Czech rhyming historical chronicle, written in the 1200s, tells of how in the tenth century Czech Jews joined their Slav brethren to defend their homeland against German attack. The *Austrian Chronicle*, compiled in Vienna in the thirteenth century, claims that the first rulers of Austria were a series of twenty-two Jewish princes bearing Turkic names, such as Sennan, who ruled for forty-five years and is buried by the Stubentor in Vienna, or Zippan, who ruled for forty-three years and is buried at Tülln. Others bore names like Lapton, Ma'alon, Raptan, Rabon, Effra and Sameck.[19] Taken with the needed grain of salt, what these tales suggest is a folk memory of early overlords, some of whom professed Judaism, at the time of Avar domination or Magyar assault.

Even when the eastern Europeans became Christian and began to found states, the Jewish influence continued. In a ninth-century exchange between Boris, Czar of the Bulgars, and the pope, the new Bulgarian Christians sought guidance on such matters as the proper regulations for offering the first fruits; the law concerning *tefillin* (phylacteries);[20] which day is the day of rest, Saturday or Sunday; which animals and poultry may be eaten; whether it is wrong to eat the flesh of an animal that has not been ritually slaughtered; should burial rituals be performed for suicides; how many days must a husband abstain from sexual intercourse with his wife after she has given birth; should a fast be observed during a drought; should women cover their heads in houses of prayer.[21] These questions show how widely Jewish beliefs and attitudes were still held even among the newly minted Christians. Bulgarian lords called their sons by Hebrew names like David, Moses, Aaron and Samuel. And the conversions continued. In his reply to the Bulgarians' enquiry, Pope Nicolas I complained of the way Jews were attracting proselytes and even persuading non-Jewish pagans to avoid work on the Sabbath.

Similar conditions applied all over the eastern half of the European continent. In the Ukraine, a Jewish quarter is thought to have existed in Kiev from the eighth or ninth century—a Jewish Gate still stood in the twelfth.[22] In his definitive history of Poland, *God's Playground*, the historian Norman Davies finds little reason to doubt that "Jews had lived in Poland from the earliest times, and that Judaism . . . had actually antedated Christianity."[23]

These were not, strictly speaking, "Jews," if by that name one means people who self-consciously belong to a distinct national community, with their own separate history, identifiable as different from all others around them, with an awareness of having lost their homeland and with the expectation that a Messiah would one day lead them back there. Were that the case, there is surely little doubt that the existence of Jewish communities in eastern Europe would have been noted and recorded by observers and travellers, particularly by other Jews. It was not.

By mischievous chance, the very first known description of Poland, written soon after 966, was by a Jew, Ibrahim Ibn Ya'qub, from Tortoba in Muslim Spain, who in that year accompanied a diplomatic mission to Bohemia, and probably also to Cracow, on behalf of his master, the caliph of Córdoba.

> The lands of the Slavs stretch from the Syrian Sea to the Ocean in the north . . . They comprise numerous tribes, each different from the other . . . At present, there are four kings: the king of the Bulgars; Bojeslav, King of Faraga [Prague], Boiema [Bohemia] and Karako [Cracow]; Meshko, King of the North; and Nakon on the border of the West . . .
>
> As far as the realm of Meshko is concerned, this is the most extensive of their lands. It produces an abundance of food, meat, honey, and fish. The taxes collected by the King from commercial goods are used for the support of his retainers. He keeps three thousand armed men divided into detachments . . . and provides them with everything they need, clothing, horses, and weapons . . .
>
> In general, the Slavs are violent, and inclined to aggression. If not for the disharmony amongst them, caused by the multiplication of factions and by their fragmentation into clans, no people could match their strength. They inhabit the richest limits of the lands suitable for settlement, and most plentiful in means of support. They are specially energetic in agriculture . . . Their trade on land and sea reaches to the Ruthenians and to Constantinople.[24]

In the fragments of his account cited in the work of a later Arab geographer,[25] Ibn Ya'qub records seeing Jewish travelling merchants in a number of Austrian and German towns. It is not known what was in the rest of his travelogue, since it was of little interest to his Arab countrymen. But progressing as he did in a delegation of high status and dignity, he might not have noticed his co-religionists who, though professing love of Israel's God and veneration of Torah, did not yet distinguish themselves as a separate community. Much as in today's multicultural world—where British Jews, Christians and Muslims, or Jewish, Christian and Muslim Americans share most of their habits and values, and only the most orthodox and self-consciously separatist identify themselves as different from others when walking the streets—before the twelfth century the eastern lands surely knew many who were of Jewish religious faith, but who did not yet identify themselves as of the Jewish people.

Scholars and historians have argued long and loud about the percentage of ethnic Hebrews in this mixed population scattered over the Slav world. It has seemed very important to some writers that the Jews of eastern Europe should be shown to be of pure Hebraic descent. Apart from the sour taste of racism inherent in such concerns, an echo of the Nuremberg laws, they miss an important point. As equally do attempts by other scholars to prove that European Jews are almost without exception the progeny of proselytes. There is no gene for Jewishness. After several generations, ethnic Hebrews, descendants of Middle Eastern, Roman and Greek converts, German, Slav and Turkic proselytes would have been so intermingled that even modern DNA analysis would be quite unable to separate the different strands in their genetic inheritance.[26]

In any case, distinguishing between ethnic Hebrews and the descendants of proselytes is profoundly un-Jewish. An established principle in the tradition has it that all converts, wherever from, adopt the ancient Hebrew lineage as their own. No matter what their origins, Turkic, Greek, Slav, German, even African or Chinese, all Jews can rightfully claim Abraham, Isaac and Jacob as their progenitors. This judgement was put on record for all time in the twelfth century by the greatest theologian, philosopher and physician of his day, Moshe ben Maimon, Maimonides, who was asked by a convert whether he might properly, as required in prayer, refer to his "father Abraham." Maimonides replied,

> It was our father Abraham who taught the whole people, educated them, and let them know true faith and divine unity . . . therefore, everyone who converts, to the end of all generations, and everyone who worships the name of God only according to what is written in the Torah, is a pupil of Abraham. All are members of his family . . .
>
> Abraham is the father of the righteous ones of his descendants who follow his ways, and a father to his pupils and to each and every proselyte . . . There is no distinction between them and us in any respect whatever.
>
> And do not treat your ancestry lightly; if you are related to Abraham, Isaac and Jacob, you are related to Him who created the world.

4

The Remaking of Western Europe

Had you travelled through western Roman territory in the fifth century, during the early years of the new tangle of squabbling nationalities, the Germanic states that took the place of the ordered Latin imperium, you would have found most cities and towns deserted, their buildings collapsing to rubble, trees piercing the roofs, foxes and crows colonising the ruins, the surrounding fields overgrown and returned to shrubby wilderness, the irrigation canals blocked, the aqueducts fallen, the forests spreading as if trying to restore the pre-human landscape. The great, straight, Roman roads are now grown head-high with grass and weeds, for who is there to tread them? The milestones are fallen, for who is there to read them? Of the former inhabitants, most of those who could do have fled; of those who could not, more than a third have died: of atrocity, famine and disease.

Between the beginning of the fifth century and the end the sixth, a mere two hundred years, the time of the barbarian remaking of western Europe, the population crashed. From an estimated forty million citizens in the year 400, it halved to not much over twenty million, the greatest population slump known to western history,[1] such was the catastrophic effect of the collapse of Rome's empire, the ruin of its productive and economic systems, the disintegration of its communications networks.

Those who still remembered their ancestral rural origins returned to the countryside, where the Roman great estates, the *latifundia*, forgot cash-crop production for a market that no longer existed and reverted to self-sufficient subsistence farming, reducing their horizons and shrinking their bounds to become small, self-contained communities, protected from internal crime and external attack by local warlords, who often gave little more than nominal allegiance to a distant royal court, and were fed, clothed and otherwise supported by the estate's own produce. Cash money almost ceased to circulate.

A few towns survived: Rome itself, Genoa, Lucca, Pisa and Mediolanum (Milan) among others in Italy, Augustonemetum (Clermont), Narbo Martius (Narbonne), Aurelianum (Orléans), Massilia (Marseilles) and Lutetia (Paris) in Gaul, throwing up around themselves primitive defensive walls of stone cannibalised from now unwanted governors' basilicas or temples to forgotten gods. Town dwellers abandoned masonry buildings, haunted by the ghosts of the past, where the under-floor heating no longer functioned and the water supply no longer operated, instead setting down cosy thatched wooden shacks in the forum, animal pens in the circus, pigsties in the public baths.

Among the Jews, those who were able, particularly the Greek speakers, trekked to the coast and took ship for the East, as like as not on Jewish-captained vessels, no doubt hoping for a safer voyage than the one survived in the fourth century by Synesius—then a pagan writer but later a Christian bishop—who described in a letter to a friend[2] how he feared that all was lost when the captain stopped commanding the vessel in the middle of a storm to say prayers for the onset of the Sabbath. The Jewish population of the lands of the former western empire diminished in even greater proportion than that of the gentiles. Military attack, economic collapse, disease and starvation hit the Hebraic middle and working classes disproportionately hard. The teeming Jewish quarters of the cities of Italy emptied. Many must have fled with their families to the self-sufficient country estates, giving up their freedom, their religion and their Jewish identity to avoid starving to death.

Those who did stay put had to find a new way of life for themselves. There was no longer any call for actors, painters, poets and singers; the new Germanic rulers had their own blacksmiths and didn't need tailors; keeping shop no longer provided a living where markets and malls were deserted and nobody came to buy. On the other hand, a new opportunity did knock, one not much previously exercised by Jews: the long-distance wholesale commodity trade. The fall of Rome turned the religious minority of workers and shopkeepers into a business community.

To those for whom Judaism is synonymous with business it comes as a surprise to discover that this was far from a traditional pursuit. In the Bible, merchants or traders are always Cana'anites rather than Israelites; in the first century Josephus had written that Hebrews "do not indulge in commerce either by sea or otherwise"; later rabbis disparaged commercial activity on the grounds that "the more trading the less Torah."

But now, after the fifth century, there was a new situation. Roman trade had been largely under official control, but with the coming of the barbarians, the imperial economic bureaucrats had vanished back to their great hereditary farming estates and cultivated their own gardens, in the process establishing themselves as the new, local, nobility. Jewish smallholders, on the other hand, whose produce was insufficient to pay taxes to the king, whose faith prevented them from dedicating tithes to the local bishop and whose traditions were hostile to providing manpower for war—the three obligations placed on landowners in the new dispensation—faced the difficult prospect of either abandoning their property and retiring to the towns or fleeing overseas, otherwise finding themselves for ever tied to their patch as unfree serfs or villeins in a feudal system that became ever more rigid by the century and which, moreover, insisted on conformity to the Christian religion. It wasn't much of a choice and unsurprisingly most elected to leave the land.

The new kingdoms of Italy, Gaul and Spain, however, desperately needed experienced businessmen. The rough new lords of the West knew little about finance and less of economics, while the arcane art of bookkeeping, which had already been mastered by the Hebrews in Babylonian days (there are clay tablets to prove it from Marashu and Sons' banking and trading house of Nippur, Babylonia, in the fifth century BCE), and without which no commercial concern can successfully operate, must have seemed to beer-quaffing German warriors like so much magic. To them, the Jews of their kingdoms represented the highly valued last remaining survivors of Roman commercial practice. As a result, the 1906 *Jewish Encyclopedia* explains,

> as soon as the Teutonic nations had settled down after the great migrations of the fifth century, Jews are found mentioned together with Syrians as merchants at Narbonne and Marseilles. The

Frankish kings bought goods from them, and they occur as traders at Naples, Palermo, and Genoa. They even chartered ships: Gregory of Tours mentions a Jew who owned a vessel sailing between Nice and Marseilles. It is recorded of Charles the Great that, after watching a ship nearing Narbonne, he decided that it was not a Jewish, but a Norman, vessel.

This international trade led inexorably to what would, over the following centuries, become the stereotypical Jewish specialities: banking, money-lending and exchange.

There are two kinds of money. There is money of account—the units with which bookkeepers calculate and in which account books are kept, which may really exist, like US dollars, or may not, like British guineas. And there is money of exchange—real coins swapped in the market place. Until recently, the two hardly ever coincided. The financial reform of Charlemagne gave us the ninth-century equivalent of the euro, standard pounds, shillings and pence—"librae," £, livres or pounds, supposedly the value of a pound of silver, worth 12 "solidi," ſ, s, sous, or shillings, and 240 "denarii," d, deniers or pennies—a system faithfully preserved in conservationist Britain until decimalisation some twelve hundred years later. But Charlemagne never had librae actually minted—not surprisingly since each coin would have weighed a pound. Indeed, pounds never existed in Britain even as paper money until the nineteenth century. As for dollars, in the USA elderly and conservative folk were still keeping their financial records in pounds sterling as late as the 1830s, half a century after independence.[3]

Goods, on the other hand, can only be bought with whatever kind of cash is to hand. Until the modern age, merchants in international markets needed not just to make lightning conversions between the many fractional exchange rates (in 1247, one Valencian sou was worth 1 sou 6 deniers of Barcelona, 1s. 4d. of Montpellier, 1s. 3d. of Tours; it was worth 4 English silver pennies, and 48 of them were worth 1 silver mark;[4] in 1265 the livre de Tern was worth 1.4 of the Tours livre, in 1409 it was worth 1.5, and from 1531 till its disappearance, it was worth twice the livre Tournois)[5] but also needed to maintain a large store of real coinage with which to trade.

Here, however, lies a serious problem. As all who keep their savings hidden under their mattresses know to their cost, cash money slowly loses its value in inflationary times, which means most periods of history. Capital can be used to buy a fixed asset that keeps its value, like land, but then money can't be released quickly when urgently needed. The alternative, so commonplace to us that we give it little thought, but a step fraught with future dangers for merchants during the Dark Ages, was to invest it in loans, charging interest to make up for loss of value over time. Today we call it banking. However, all pre-capitalist religions and most cultures, Judaism included, referred to it pejoratively as usury and regarded it as evil, even though monetary investment was as desperately needed by the new kingdoms of the European Dark Ages as it is by poor countries in today's developing world. Germanic rulers intent on economic growth constantly needed capital, which it seems only the Jewish merchants were able to provide. For many centuries there was no other source of finance for churchmen wanting to build cathedrals, nobles caught in financial embarrassment, merchants obliged first to buy what they would then sell, even peasants needing seed for the next growing season.

In her book *English Society in the Early Middle Ages*, Lady Doris Stenton records the loans made to a compulsive twelfth-century litigant, Richard of Anstey, to enable him to pursue a legal case in the King's court.

"When," he says, "I sent my brother over sea for the king's writ I borrowed 40 shillings from Vives the Jew of Cambridge, paying in interest 4 pence a pound a week, and I kept the money 14 months and paid 37 shillings and 4 pence in interest." The following Easter Vives lent him 60 shillings at the same rate. He kept it 6 months and paid 24 shillings in interest. When he went abroad himself to get the king's writ he borrowed £4 10s. from Comitissa of Cambridge at the same rate, kept it 9 months and paid in interest £2 14s. When he was pleading at Canterbury at Whitsun he borrowed £2 at the same rate from Deulecresse the Jew, kept it 2 months and paid in interest 5 shillings and 4 pence. When he went abroad he borrowed £3 from Jacob the Jew of Newport at the same rate, kept it 13 months and paid £2 12s. interest. When he sent his clerks to Rome, Hakelot the Jew lent him £10 at 3 pence a pound a week. He kept it 7 months and paid £3 0s. 10d. interest. After Michaelmas Hakelot lent him another £3 at the same rate. He kept it 3 months and paid 9 shillings interest . . .[6]

The interest rates seem exorbitant by today's standards, excusable only by the extreme scarcity of capital and the very real danger of the borrower defaulting. As with insurance premiums, the greater the risk the more expensive the loan. Yet wherever the Jews were expelled, as they would be from England in 1290, and from the kingdom of France in 1395, ordinary people were quick to bemoan their loss, complaining that the gentile—usually Italian—bankers who replaced them had raised the rates even more. High returns were a consequence of the desperately insecure financial environment rather than Jewish greed.

Thus, it was not, as Karl Marx would have it, the Jews' worship of gold, but the collapse of the Roman economic system in western Europe that eventually turned much of the remaining Jewish farming, petit-bourgeois, artisan and labouring classes into businessmen and money dealers—a change of occupation over which they had little choice, though a trade that would serve them ill in coming centuries. That was striking change enough. But the new European order managed a transformation even more profound, and one whose importance for the Yiddish civilisation cannot be overstated. For it turned Roman citizens of Jewish faith into a separate nationality: the Jews.

The Germanic Lombards (Long-Beards) and the two wings of the Gothic nation, Visigoths (western) and Ostrogoths (eastern), who set up their kingdoms in what today are Spain and Italy, had already converted to Christianity before their arrival in the West. But it was the Arian version of Christianity that they favoured. Arianism taught that God the Son is not equivalent to God the Father but subordinate to Him, an idea closer to the Jewish conception of the Messiah than the full divinity of Jesus as preached by the Catholic Church. Indeed, Arians were often accused by Catholics of Judaising, perverting Christianity in a Jewish direction. In addition, Arianism promoted a much more tolerant attitude to religious belief than Roman orthodoxy. An Arian bishop reproved the staunchly Catholic Bishop Gregory of Tours thus: "Blaspheme not a doctrine which is not thine. We on our part, although we do not believe what ye believe, nevertheless do not curse it. For we do not consider it a crime to think either thus or so,"[7] an attitude summed up in King Theodoric the Great's definitive statement: *"Religionem imperare non possumus, quia nemo cogitur ut credat inuitus."*[8] (We cannot command religion, for no man can be compelled to believe anything against his will.)

As long as the new rulers maintained their dissident faith, Jews were seen as fully equal to Goths, Romans, Syrians, Greeks and any of the other subcultures within their borders. A nineteenth-century German scholar reported that at times the Goths' Jewish subjects even exercised some kind of jurisdiction over Catholics, and found that marriages between Arians and Jews were not uncommon.[9]

However, all that changed once the Gothic ruling class in Spain, and the Frankish adventurers who had taken control of Gaul, had been coaxed into the Catholic fold in the course of the sixth century, and after Italy was retaken for the eastern Roman Empire by General Belisarius—with Jews fighting valiantly on the side of the Goths, particularly at Neapolis (Naples), where they manned the walls and, almost alone, undertook the defence of the city. Since the time of the otherwise awful Emperor Caracalla, members of all faith communities and none had been equal citizens of the empire. Now Christianity—of the right flavour—came to be a prerequisite for membership of the nation. All who could not and would not accept Christian belief were from now on to be considered outsiders, alien residents in lands to which they had no birthright and in which they all too often had few rights of any kind. Never mind that many Torah-observing families had been settled in western European territory for centuries, certainly for far longer than the recently arrived invaders; that they had been literate and civilised townspeople at a time when the Germanic nobles were still living in squalid huts in the northern forests and eating gruel. Never mind that many, perhaps even most, could claim impeccable Latin or Greek pedigrees. Those who refused to conform to the religious demands of the new western European kingdoms were no longer to be considered nationals of a different faith. They were not held to be nationals at all. Henceforth Jewish residents were to be "Jews," a separate and alien race.

Nobody knows exactly what forms of Judaism had been practised by the citizens of the western Roman Empire. Most scholars believe that they were very varied, with different communities praying in different languages, celebrating the festivals with greatly different degrees of fastidiousness and obeying the laws of the Torah with widely different levels of scrupulousness—if they even knew what they were. Probably many of those who called themselves Jewish were, like today, little more so than in name, if a seventh-century inscription from Narbonne in the south of France is representative. It bears the symbol of a Jewish candelabrum, but mistakenly with only five branches, and is written entirely in Latin except for the three Hebrew words, *Shalom al Yisroel* (Peace upon Israel), which are spelled wrongly.[10] France's, Spain's and Italy's Judaic population was completely cut off from the great international centres of Judaic thought during the first Christian millennium. The Holy Land and the flourishing rabbinic academies of Babylonia lay out of reach within the borders of Rome's powerful enemy, the Iranian Empire of the Parthians and later the Sassanians.

Yet now the novel form of internal exile imposed by the newly Christian monarchs resulted in a renaissance of Judaism, a dramatic and positive reworking of the Jewish self-image and a rekindling of enthusiasm for Jewish orthodoxy. One can almost hear the response: "Very well, if we are not to be accepted as full subjects of Visigothic Spain, of France of the Franks, or of Byzantine Italy, then let us reconnect with our roots and make ourselves once again a separate nation of priests, as commanded in our Bible."

Yet how could this be achieved? The answer came with an event that was unnoticed and unsung in the annals of the Germanic kingdoms. A new prophet, the Prophet Muhammad, appeared in a small desert town in far-off Arabia and began to write a new volume in the history of the world. Soon enough the conquest of the Iberian peninsula by Muslim Moors would lead to the birth of the other great branch of the European Jewish family, the Sephardim, and thus take us outside our present story. But it also made possible the Yiddish civilisation, for it was the Muslim Empire that reconnected the Jews of western Europe to their ancestral and religious roots.

CHARLES'S ELEPHANT

At roughly the same time as King Reccared of the Visigoth kingdom in Spain was converting to Catholicism and beginning to insist on the religious conformity of his subjects, the Prophet Muhammad was starting his own spiritual revolution in Arabia. Six years after his death, Muslim armies took Mesopotamia from the Persians. Two more years and the Holy Land fell from Roman into Arab hands. Another two and Egypt had been wrested from the Byzantine Empire. Slowly Islam crept westwards across the Mediterranean coast of Africa until towards the end of the seventh century all the Byzantine forces had withdrawn. Tunisia, Algeria and Morocco were now incorporated into the Muslim world as the province of Ifriqiyah.

The Visigothic kings trembled as they saw the forces of Islam massing a mere eight miles off the coast of Spain across the Pillars of Hercules. In their anxiety, they looked around for potential traitors to the Christian cause and fixed their eyes on the Jews, whom they—rightly—suspected of favouring the Muslim cause over theirs. Drastic action seemed to be called for. Now it was no longer enough to denounce Judaism, order the Jews to accept baptism and pledge themselves loyal to the Christian faith, or else face corporal punishment, have their belongings seized and go into exile. What more could be done? In the year 694 King Edica made a disastrous decision. He confiscated the remaining Jews' possessions, declared them all to be slaves and gave them to Christian masters who had to ensure, by whatever means they saw fit, that their human property no longer practised the Jewish religion in any form. Their children were taken away from them to be brought up as Catholics. Those Jews who could, fled; the rest had to submit. It was a servitude even severer than that in Egypt under pharaoh nearly 2,000 years previously. Fortunately it was to last a much shorter time, though long enough for those who had to suffer it: seventeen years.

This time God did not send the enslaved Hebrews a princely Moses to deliver them, but a man who was himself a former slave: the Berber general Tariq Ibn Ziyad, his intervention sought by one of the parties to a dispute between contenders for the Visigoth throne. Tariq crossed the narrow strait in the year 711 with a force some 7,000 strong packed into small boats and landed at Gibraltar (Arabic: *Jebel Tariq*, Mount Tariq). Over two years of fighting he won almost the entire Spanish peninsula for Islam.

Those many Jews who had pretended to accept Christianity to save themselves and their families from slavery now came out to welcome the Muslim forces and flock to their standard. Arab sources tell us that the invaders called the Jews of every city together and set them to garrison the towns they had conquered. Córdoba, Granada, Toledo and Seville came under Jewish control. Later Arab geographers cited Lucena, Granada and Tarragona as wholly Jewish cities.

Now, for the first time since Roman imperial days, European Jewry was once again linked to its Holy Land, and to the Mesopotamian heart of Jewish tradition and scholarship, in a single universal empire. Islam's Jewish subjects could travel unhindered between East and West, from Babylon through Palestine, Egypt and North Africa to Spain, without crossing an imperial border. The rabbis of Babylonia could correspond at will with Jewish centres like Barcelona. Teachers and prayer books were sent to the Spanish community from the Middle East. Rabbinic academies were established, like that in Lucena, which became so prestigious that by the beginning of the ninth century its rulings were regarded as authoritative.

Rediscovering their Jewish identity and reconnecting to the mainstream of Jewish intellectual culture sent the Sephardic Jews off on their own historic journey, by the end of which they had made a central contribution to one of the giants of European civilisation, Muslim Spain, and so to the development of the modern world.

From now on until the nineteenth century, though sharing origin, religion and history with their cousins over the Muslim-Christian border, the Sephardim would be regarded, by both gentiles and Jews, as a separate and superior Jewish race, naturally noble and elevated in every respect above their co-religionists. Yet their contacts with the communities in neighbouring Christian-ruled countries changed the destiny of the religious minority there too.

In October 801 a storm-battered ship—probably two-masted with triangular lateen sails, for such were the common carriers of the Mediterranean trade—tied up at the dockside in Porto Venere on the Ligurian coast of Italy. Down the gangplank stepped two creatures, each of which must have seemed in its own way as exotic as the other to the buzzing crowd of onlookers that would have gathered from far and wide to stare. The first was the Jew Isaac, the second the elephant Abu'l'Abbas (Father of the Stern Countenance).

The elephant was a flattering, perhaps also a little condescending, gift from Harun ar-Raschid, fabled Caliph of Baghdad, the greatest ruler of the period, to his admirer Carolus Magnus, Charlemagne, King Charles the Great of the Franks—as if saying "Look on my beast, ye mighty, and despair." Actually, Harun had merely inherited the elephant from his predecessor who had himself received it from an Indian rajah. The Jew Isaac, who was the sole survivor of an embassy that Charles had sent east three years previously, now set off along the old Roman road, the Via Cassia, that led by way of Genoa to Turin and then up over the Alps. He was, in effect, trailblazing the route that over the following centuries would lead many of Italy's Jews to new homes in Germany and beyond—at roughly the same time as those from the Black Sea coast were arriving in central Europe from the East. Like many who would follow in his footsteps he was unable to continue his 600-mile journey north to the imperial capital at Aachen as the Great St. Bernard Pass was already blocked by snow, so he waited for the spring thaw at the little town of Vercelli. (Actually, this was not the first time an elephant had been seen in those parts: the Raudian Fields nearby were the site of Hannibal's elephant-assisted victory over the Roman General Scipio after the Carthaginian general's historic crossing of the Alps a thousand years before.) Isaac and Abu'l'Abbas finally arrived at Charlemagne's court the following summer, where the elephant survived for another ten years, until he expired on Lüneburg Heath during a military expedition against Danish rebels on the North Sea coast.

Not mentioned, however, in the *Annales Regni Francorum* (*Annals of the Kings of the Franks*), from which this account is taken, was a gift to the Jews of France that ultimately had far greater significance. For Jewish tradition records that on his return Isaac brought with him a learned Jew by the name of Machir, the Babylonian scholar credited with founding the important rabbinical academy of Narbonne. A twelfth-century author, Abraham Ibn Daud of Córdoba, claimed in addition that Charlemagne invited Machir to found a dynasty of Jewish kings in that city. Others say that when the town was taken by Pepin the Short in the year 759, Jews helped to drive out the Muslims and, as a gesture of appreciation, were granted the right to be governed by Jewish kings.[11] Records do indeed show that for long afterwards male members of the Machir family bore the title *Nasi* (prince), and lived in a building known as the Cortada Regis Judaeorum (Court of the Jewish King).[12] Me'ir of Narbonne, the community's representative at the emperor's court in the thirteenth century, wrote that this was in reward for an episode when "at the siege of Narbonne, King Charles, having had his horse killed under him, would himself have been killed but for a Jew who dismounted and gave the king his horse at the cost of his own life." (First a pachyderm and now an equine; Jews seem to have been regular animal suppliers to the Carolingian household.) The divergent stories suggest that, though its true origins were lost in the past, a princely Jewish dynasty really did once rule in the greatest city of the western Mediterranean.

The tale of Charles's elephant also affords us a revealing glimpse of the place of the Jew in Frankish society. The emperor viewed Isaac as a go-between, a mediator neither Christian nor Muslim, between the civilisation of Islam and his own world. After all, next door in Islamic Iberia, did not the Jews live with mutual honour and respect among those who followed the Prophet? Seen as halfway in faith between St. Paul and Muhammad, only a Jew would be able to interpret Charles to Harun and Harun to Charles.

However burdensome to the Jews this problematic identity must have been over the next centuries, through the eyes of the common Christian folk they appeared to hold an enviable position. Some Jews were suppliers to the royal court and others were administrators of Catholic religious institutions. They engaged in agriculture and vine-growing—even the wine for Mass was bought from Jews. Beneficial charters were granted them by the rulers. There were numerous converts to Judaism, particularly among the upper classes, of whom perhaps the best-known was Bodo, a former deacon to Louis the Pious. But the common people were sympathetic to the Hebrew faith too, to judge by a letter of protest sent in the 820s by Agobard, Bishop of Lyons, to the emperor, in which he complains:

> the Christians celebrate the Sabbath with the Jews, desecrate Sunday, and transgress the regular fasts. Because the Jews boast of being of the race of the Patriarchs, the nation of the righteous, the children of the Prophets, the ignorant think that they are the only people of God and that the Jewish religion is better than their own.[13]

A later prelate advised a countess of Flanders against letting Jews have private conversations with "women or other simple folk" who might too easily be persuaded to convert.[14]

Indeed, after the Germanic Lombards had driven the Byzantines out of most of Italy and the Franks were constructing what would become the Holy Roman Empire in France and Germany, the Jews, though still seen as a foreign community, had been awarded an honourable place in society. Even after joining the Catholic confession, Lombard rulers had treated the Jewish minority on a par with their Christian subjects, and the popes, who had become de facto rulers of Rome, Naples, Palermo, Ravenna and their hinterlands, had protected them, more or less, from the excesses of the Catholic bishops and lower clergy. Pope Gregory the Great (590–604) had insisted on the balanced principle that would apply for centuries afterwards: "Just as the Jews in their communities may not be allowed liberties beyond the measure allotted them by law, so must they, on the other hand, suffer no violation of their rights."

Now that the Muslims had settled down in their new-won land, there was much interchange of both goods and ideas between the communities of Spain, France and Italy, restoring a religious identity to many who had long forgotten what being Jewish actually meant and bringing traditional Jewish scholarship to places where it had previously been unknown. Yet in spite of their connections with the Islamic world, in spite of their rediscovery of a Jewish identity, the Jews of the Christian kingdoms were well assimilated to their environment. Where today English is the lingua franca that is spoken and understood in most places, so Jews, like others, spoke Vulgar Latin, the popular language of western Christendom, that was starting out on its much-branching path towards Catalan, French, Italian, Provençal, Romansch, Spanish, or any of the other members of the modern Romance language family.

For "to pray" they said *orare*, the Latin verb; for "to bless" they used *benedicere*; "to read" was *legere*; "to doze" was *dormitare*. Some of the men were called Senior; a popular woman's name was Gentile.[15] Like Charlemagne's "£ s d," these words and names, with many others, would hang on into the present, taken along wherever their users went, their latinate polysyllables rounded and smoothed by generations of lazy tongues, their conjugations Germanised, until *orare* became Yiddish *oren*, *benedicere* became *bentshn*, *legere* became *leyenen*, *dormitare* became *dremeln*, Senior became Shneur and Gentile became Yentl.

Since the Jews had been rejected as true nationals of the kingdoms where they had, in most cases, lived for generations, they were not tied by bonds of sentiment to any particular European soil and, like most emigrants even in our own time, felt free to move to wherever liberty and opportunity beckoned.

For several centuries, on any day of the summer travelling season except for Sabbaths and religious holidays, one might have observed Jewish family groups and larger expeditions, accompanied by covered mule-drawn wagons bearing all their worldly possessions, trekking north across the Alps, mostly taking the same route as King Charles's elephant over the St. Bernard Pass—or else further east over the St. Gotthard and Brenner Passes—crossing from Italy into the Rhône valley, then travelling north into Germany and following the Rhine basin, eventually arriving in the entrepôt towns that gathered agricultural produce from the interior of the continent and traded it on to the Scandinavian sailing masters of the North and Baltic Seas. There the Jews would slowly abandon Latin speech and take up the German of the day, though retaining a few familiar Latin phrases, and adding a sprinkling of their newly relearned Hebrew vocabulary as a badge of their newly re-adopted Hebraic national identity.

Previously the Franco-German borderland, the so-called Rhineland, had been a frontier zone separating Romanised Gauls from barbarian Germans, and many towns like Cologne and Trier had already known Jewish settlement in earlier days. Now as part of the Frankish, later to be Holy

Roman, Empire, they were ripe for further development and economic expansion. As markets expanded, so did a need for ever more people who understood business. Rulers were keen to encourage Jewish pioneering and by the end of the millennium substantial communities of Jewish merchants had been attracted—or commanded—to Cologne, Frankfurt, Mainz, Speyer, Trier, Worms and even Regensburg in Bavaria.

Typical was the experience of the family called Kalonymos. A branch of the family, recognisable from their name as descendants of Greek speakers, had long been resident in Tuscany under the rule of the Lombards. Starting from Lucca, the old trading city from where roads radiate towards Parma, Florence, Rome and Pisa, their progress represents the history of western European Jewry in miniature, including the new-found link to the source of tradition in Mesopotamia and the move north into Germany. In the words of Eleazar ben Judah ben Kalonymos of Worms,

> Abu Aaron . . . came from Babylonia because of a misadventure, and was forced to wander from place to place, until he came to the country of Lombardy, to a city named Lucca, where he found Master Moses . . . and transmitted to him all his secrets. Master Moses, son of Kalonymos, son of Master Judah . . . was the first to leave Lombardy, he and his sons . . . together with other important persons. King Charles brought them with him from the country of Lombardy, and settled them in Mainz, and there they multiplied and flourished greatly . . .[16]

The Charles in question was probably Charles the Bald (823–77), Charlemagne's grandson.

To make resettlement as attractive as possible the Jews of Worms were granted freedom to travel wherever they wished and to engage in commerce without paying customs duties. They could trade, act as money changers, hire Christians to work for them and own property. In 1084 Rüdiger, the Catholic Bishop of Speyer, gave Jews the village of Altspeyer, which he incorporated into the municipality and allowed its new inhabitants to fortify, "to increase the honour of the town a thousandfold." Note that the Jews were kept out of Speyer itself not out of anti-Jewish prejudice, but "lest they should be too easily disturbed by the insolence of the citizens."[17]

Why were Jews in particular so sought after? Were there no others practised in commerce who could bring trade and prosperity to the region?

Apparently not. The religious minority, the facts insist, was the only group that had preserved some memory at least of Roman business techniques. Moreover, the social organisation that we call the feudal system gave everyone a fixed place in society and allowed few other commoners the freedom to travel at will. Right up until the nineteenth century in the Russian Empire, it was still mainly Jews and gypsies who could travel from place to place without special permission, as tinkers, tailors, pedlars and musicians. And while Jews, like Christians, were forbidden by their faith to grant loans at interest to their own kind, both sides closed their eyes to moneylending across the religious divide.

Tradition was not their only stock-in-trade, but innovation too, learned from exchanges with the Islamic world. The location Lucca gives us a clue, for somewhat later that was one of the cities in which the Spanish-born scholar Abraham Ibn Ezra, memorialised in Robert Browning's poem "Rabbi ben Ezra" ("Grow old along with me! The best is yet to be . . .") and one of the two medieval rabbis honoured by having a lunar crater named after them,[18] stayed for a time to study and write during his wanderings through Italy. It was Ibn Ezra who, while visiting Verona in 1146, wrote in his *Sefer ha-Mispar* (*Book of Number*) the earliest explanation in Europe of the new decimal system in arithmetic, using place notation and the figure zero, though not employing the Hindu-Arabic numeral signs themselves, but taking the first nine letters of the Hebrew alphabet for the digits 1 to 9 and a small circle for zero, which he called *galgal* (Hebrew for wheel)—our number system inherited his *galgal* rather than the Islamic dot. Long before then, contact with their brethren in Spain and the Middle East had almost certainly introduced Christendom's Jewish merchants to these newfangled calculation aids. Now for the very first time it was possible for those who were in on the secret of the new numbers to do arithmetic on paper, without having to perform the maniacal "gesticulations of dancers" as Martianus Capella, an influential fifth-century author from Carthage, had scathingly described the then-current system of finger calculation, or else needing to go off and find an abacus, counting board or other mechanical device.

Displaying numbers in decimals—the hundreds, tens and units that we learn as infants in school—does not only make arithmetic easier. Even more important, it offers the possibility of writing numbers in columns, with all the hundreds, tens and units lined up under each other. This can't be done with Latin numerals. For example the number 48, when written as XLVIII, would occupy six places, while 51, written as LI, would take only two. Their sum, 99, XCIX, takes four:

XLVIII
<u>LI</u>
XCIX

whereas of course,

48
<u>51</u>
99

This was a revolutionary development. Putting down figures in columns opened up an entire new world of arithmetical and therefore financial possibilities. The new number symbols could easily be added, summed, subtracted, abstracted, multiplied, divided. Once the idea of columnar format had taken hold, handling long series of figures became easy, and bookkeeping in the modern sense was for the very first time possible and only a small intellectual step away.

Proper accounting methods became available to the Jewish merchants of the Frankish Empire centuries before their help was permitted to Christian traders. The Church expressly opposed the use of Arabic numerals, as heathen devices, well into the fifteenth century. A 1299 ordinance of the Florentine bankers' guild prohibited members from recording accounts in "what is known as the style or script of the abacus" and required them to "write openly and at length, using letters."[19] As late as 1510 the Freiburg Municipality still refused to accept accounting documents as legal proofs of debt, unless they were prepared using Roman numerals or had their sums written out in words.[20] Jewish businessmen, at least those among them who could quickly grasp new ideas, had for the moment a great advantage over their competitors. It would be some time before their gentile rivals would catch up.

NEW BORDERS, NEW ALLEGIANCES

But catch up they did—in the end. New borders were drawn, new allegiances sworn, new languages born out of old. The economy of the German Empire grew and naturally, as locals learned the arts of business ever more successfully, the special Jewish role lost its importance—indeed, it became an affront. Where, in the beginning, the ruling class had treated

Jewish traders as honoured guests and felt themselves lucky to have attracted such clever specialists who promised economic development to their petty domains, now local Christian artisans and merchants became increasingly jealous of Jewish expertise. From the tenth century onwards, they began to join together in guilds, trade associations that specifically excluded Jewish membership and fought vigorously against Jewish competition. As German society progressed and the new monarchs sought to ape their illustrious supposed predecessors, the Roman emperors, renewed attention was paid to the compilation of Roman law that had been made in the year 534 for the eastern Emperor Justinian, hammer of Goths, heretics, pagans and Jews alike, with its several injunctions limiting Jewish freedom of operation and worship: "Jews must never enjoy the fruits of office," was the principle, "but only suffer its pains and penalties."

All was not well politically with the German world either. A power struggle between Church and state could not be resolved. Pope and emperor battled each other for primacy, the dispute leading to a scandalous crisis when in 1076 Pope Gregory VII excommunicated the Emperor Henry IV, and in response Henry set up an anti-pope of his own choosing. Ordinary people saw little to admire in either camp, turning for spiritual support to the lower clergy—who were far from learned—or to the monasteries, who had their own agenda of industrial expansion. The centralised Roman Church was in danger of abandonment by its flock.

Reacting to these social and political strains, Church leaders had little option but to reform their institution and stretch out a hand of kinship to the common people. In this flat-earth world, where sun and moon were lanterns placed by God in the sky solely for human convenience, the character of the Ruler of Heaven had long been determined by experiencing how rulers of the earth behaved. In an age of arbitrary autocracy, priests had threatened their congregations with a God the Father possessing the same irascible, intolerant temperament as kings and emperors. Now, in a reaction to this harsh vision, the Church began to spread a different idea, one not derived from obvious human models, of a God who cherished his human worshippers and "so loved the world, that he gave his only begotten Son, that whosoever believeth in him should not perish, but have everlasting life."

Away with the representation of pope and bishops as great and wealthy lords of the world, an image that had in the past gained the priesthood the admiration and adoration of the multitudes. Away with pomp and circumstance. Riches were now out, poverty and asceticism were in.

Jesus began to be portrayed as a poor man rather than as King of Heaven, a simple preacher as well as Son of God—a very human Christ who had sacrificed himself for humanity and had himself suffered as so many in the medieval population were suffering. The saints were shown as simple and fallible human beings just like their worshippers. Ordinary people were encouraged to take a hand in their own salvation instead of relying entirely on the over-rewarded work of religious professionals.

The rebranding of the Church largely succeeded. From the eleventh century the common, plain, folk became spiritual enthusiasts as never before and took to the streets in processions and displays of holy fervour. Religious passion expressed itself all along the great pilgrimage routes to the shrines of saints and martyrs: to the shrine of Our Lady of Walsingham in England, to St. Winifred's Well in Holywell, Wales, to the shrine of St. James in Santiago de Compostela in Spain, to the grave of St. Rupert in Salzburg, Austria, to the tomb of the Apostles in Rome, to the relics of the Three Kings in Cologne. "When April has pierced the drought of March to the root with its sweet showers . . . then do people long to go on pilgrimage,"[21] as Chaucer would write.

Religious devotions centred around meditations on the agony of Jesus, often before the sign of the cross and with relics of the passion. There was an obsession with the details of the crucifixion. And the more that people concentrated on Christ's death, the more they were directed by the Gospels to blame the Jews. And the more they blamed the Jews of old, the more likely it was that their anger would boil over and that the Jews of the present would be physically attacked. The ruling class of state and Church did what it could to restrain popular anti-Jewish violence, though the support of the hated nobility and higher priesthood won the Jews no less unpopularity among the mob. The first reports of persecution of Jews in Germany date from the early eleventh century. They were expelled from Mainz in 1012 after a priest had converted to Judaism. (They were, however, soon asked to return; the city couldn't do without them.)

This ecclesiastical revolution, which some have called the New Piety, however popular among the masses, was not able to reform the habits of the class of wayward warlords who now ruled over western Europe. Theirs was still a culture of honour and its violent defence; incessant private warfare was the order of the day and human life and security counted for little. When the average person expected to live to an age of no more than perhaps forty years—and that only if they were lucky, for in those times famine and plague were a constant and very present danger—to die gloriously in combat may have seemed preferable to expiring miserably in a sickbed. But the Church refused to accept that rampaging armies constantly criss-crossing the continent were an unavoidable evil. From the tenth century onwards it tried hard to bring an end to the eternal fighting and to limit violence against people and property by instituting a so-called Peace of God. Synods in France in the 990s forbade, under pain of excommunication, every act of private warfare or violence against ecclesiastical buildings, clerics, pilgrims, merchants (including Jews), women, peasants, cattle and agricultural equipment. At the Council of Bourges in 1038, the archbishop demanded that every Christian of fifteen years or older take an oath to observe and enforce the peace.

The Peace of God didn't work, nor did the Truce of God that followed it. The solution would have to be radical. If the warlords could not or would not stop fighting, then at least their aggression should be directed away from each other and away from the smiling fields and shady woods of Europe, towards where it might do some good. Let them instead go and attack the Muslims of the Middle East who had overrun Christian Armenia, Syria, Palestine and the Holy City of Jerusalem, and were now on the threatening march towards the Second Rome, Constantinople.

At a synod at Clermont in France's Auvergne region, on 27 November 1095, Pope Urban II seated himself upon a papal throne set up where the hillside slopes down from the Romanesque yellow sandstone basilica of Notre-Dame to the old market quarter known as the Vieux Port. Behind and above him stood an old sanctuary where, a century and a half later, work would begin on the grand blackstone cathedral that would not be completed until 1902. Before and below him sat a huge audience, hundreds of bishops, priests, nobles, tradesmen and peasants, who had gathered from far and wide to hear him send out a ringing appeal to all of Christendom to come to the aid of the Byzantines in their struggle with the Turks: "I, or rather the Lord, beseeches you, as Christ's heralds, to publish this everywhere and to persuade all people of whatever rank, foot-soldiers and knights, poor and rich, to carry aid promptly to those Christians, and to destroy that vile race from the lands of our friends."[22]

The crowd responded with the passionate roar *"Dios lo volt"* (God wills it), and Urban declared a Papal Indulgence, an immediate remission of all sins, for anyone who participated in the expedition to recover the Holy Land from the infidels. The knights brandished their weapons, a cardinal sank to his knees and, beating himself on the breast, recited the prayer of confession, while Bishop Adhémar of Le Puy handed out cloth crosses for the Lord's new holy warriors to sew on to their surclothes. Thus began the First Crusade.

It may not have been the pope's intention, but he had succeeded in unleashing a wave of vulgar, ruthless brutality that carved a bloody wound across Europe on its way to the Middle East. The Jewish communities in France shuddered. They understood only too well that in their traditional position as mediators and go-betweens, halfway between Christ and Allah, the crusaders could hardly fail to see them as infidels also, closer to hand and less able to defend themselves than the distant Muslim Turks with their great armies. A Jewish chronicler known to scholars as the Mainz Anonymous wrote shortly after: "Each said to his fellow, 'Lo, we are going to a distant land to fight its kings. We have put our lives in our hands to kill and subdue all the kingdoms that do not believe in Him who was hanged. But it was the Jews who killed and hanged Him!'" (Incidentally, the use of "the hanged one," *Tola* or *Talui*, is the expression medieval Jews always chose for Jesus, to avoid the religiously charged words Christ, Cross and Crucified.) "When the communities of France heard of this, they were seized with fear and trembling . . . writing letters and sending messengers to all the Rhineland communities, that they should fast, sit in abstinence, and beg for mercy from Him who dwells on high, that He save the French Jews from the Christians' hands."[23]

But when the letters arrived in the Rhineland, the Jewish communities were rather more sanguine in their estimate of the danger to themselves. Their lives were peaceful and undisturbed; they thought themselves immune from the virus of violent unrest that was racing across Europe. "All our communities have declared fasts—we have done what is ours to do. May the Omnipresent save us and you from all troubles and tribulations. We fear for you greatly, but need not fear so much for ourselves, as we have not even heard any rumours."[24]

Their lack of concern was a tragic error. Wherever the crusaders came across them, Jews were to be among their first targets. Though the road to the East did not pass directly through the Rhineland, 15,000 holy warriors led by a murderous thug by the name of Baron Emicho of Leiningen made it the target of a purposeful detour in the spring of 1096, travelling north through Speyer, Worms and Mainz, some diverting further west to Trier and Metz, and coming together again for a grand gory reunion in Cologne, slaughtering Jews wherever they could be found. Solomon bar Samson, writing some fifty years later, recalled the awful scenes. In Speyer:

It was the eighth of Iyyar [third of May]. The Crusaders and burghers rose first against the holy ones, the pious men of Speyer, planning to capture them all together in the synagogue. But they were forewarned. They rose early on the morning of the Sabbath, prayed quickly, and left the synagogue. When the Crusaders saw that their plan to catch them all together had failed, they rose against Jews everywhere, killing eleven. That was but the start of the massacre.

In Worms:

> they said: ". . . let not a single one escape—even the young and the suckling in its crib!" They came and smote those remaining in their homes—fine bachelors, fine and pleasant maidens, and the elderly—all stretched out their necks to be slaughtered; even freedmen and maids were killed among them, to honour the name of God.

In Mainz:

> Young and old put on their armour and girded on their weapons. At their head was Rabbi Kalonymos ben Meshullam, the chief of the community. Yet because of the many troubles and the fasts which they had observed they had no strength to stand up against the enemy . . .

(It is worth recording that Emicho's thugs were eventually crushed by the Hungarians, and that the bloodstained baron slunk home, where he died some twenty years later. His family line, unlike that of his victim Rabbi Kalonymos ben Meshullam, became extinct in the thirteenth century. For long after, a Christian legend had it that the baron's tortured spirit forever haunted Mainz, begging people to pray for his damned soul's release from the agonies of hell.)

We can never know how many were killed, or—what may seem even worse—rather than save their lives by accepting baptism chose to kill themselves and their families in a horrific perversion of the technique of ritual slaughter that they called *Kiddush Hashem*, sanctification of the (Holy) Name. Eleazar ben Judah ben Kalonymos of Worms wrote, "God's fury hit all the holy communities in the year 1096. And then we were all lost, all perished, except the very few who were left from our kinsmen." Albert of Aachen, a Christian chronicler, describes how the crusaders rose "in a spirit of cruelty against the Jewish people scattered throughout these cities and slaughtered them without mercy." Yet Professor Bernard Bachrach contends that "a careful examination of a great variety of sources in Latin and Greek as well as in Hebrew makes it clear that the accounts of the suffering endured by various Jewish communities are so overwhelmingly exaggerated in the Jewish Chronicles as to give them little value as historical sources."[25]

It used to be claimed that it was these attacks—as well as those which later followed the outbreak of the plague called the Black Death in the fourteenth century, popularly blamed on Jews for poisoning the wells—that drove the Jews eastwards from the Franco-German borderlands, across the width of Germany and into Poland, in headlong flight from the bloodstained self-appointed avengers of Christ. Yet in all the records of the period, both Jewish and gentile, there is no mention of mass emigration. True, on hearing that the crusaders were approaching, many communities fled, but to nearby towns and castles, where the nobles and bishops mostly did their best, with varying success, to protect them. Jews would temporarily hand over their property and movable goods for safekeeping to trusted neighbours and friends, and return to their homes when the peril had passed. The Emperor Henry IV, in the teeth of ecclesiastical opposition, allowed the Jews of Bamberg, who had escaped slaughter by accepting baptism, to return openly to their true faith. Professor Simon Schwartzfuchs of Bar Ilan University,[26] emphasises that "the communities destroyed in the Rhine valley were quickly re-established: Worms, Speyer, Mainz, Cologne, and Trèves [Trier] rapidly regained their former importance." And further: "There is nothing to suggest that during this period the Jews in Western Europe lost their sense of security in the localities where they were living: no great exodus took place in 1096 or in 1146."

Yet something devastating had indeed happened. To begin with, it was not just in Germany that the crusaders wrought havoc among the communities. Those already resident in the eastern territories were hammered by the soldiers of Christ too. Bishop Cosmas, Dean of Prague Cathedral and the earliest Bohemian chronicler, wrote that the persecutions of the First Crusade caused Jews to move from Bohemia to Poland in 1098—from one Slavic territory, in other words, to another.

Even more significantly, the First Crusade gave a signal that could not be dismissed, marking in blood and fire the final end of an era. Jewish life in Germany had been comfortable. Jews had held an honourable place in society, aliens maybe, yet a respected minority, valued for the prosperity they seemed able to conjure out of thin air wherever they settled. But for years the mood had been changing. Jews had begun to feel the contempt of the petty nobles, the envy of the burghers, the revulsion of the churchmen, the hatred of the masses. The mob had come to believe that attacking Jews was acceptable whenever there was social or religious unrest. The ejection of the community from Mainz in 1012 was the first expulsion of many; from now on Jews would all too often be driven out of their home towns. Trials of Jews on preposterous trumped-up charges, their guilt long prejudged, sent all too many to the stake or the gallows.

Can one really believe that persecution on such a grand scale failed to direct the eyes of at least some individuals towards safer havens? Surely not. Yet that is far from the whole story. The centuries that bracketed the year 1000 saw developments which would set in place the shape of all Europe for the next thousand years, and not just of its Jews. For another great movement of people, another *Völkerwanderung*, was beginning. German speakers—many, though not all, led by churchmen or monks—started steadily moving eastwards, into the lands of the Slavic and Baltic peoples, in the great movement that came to be called the *Drang nach Osten*, the Eastward Impulse.

DRANG NACH OSTEN

Historians have long debated the reasons for the German drive into the Slav world. It was underpopulated, to be sure, offering new unclaimed lands for farming and new unsatisfied demands for trading. But such a large population movement can hardly be explained by the mere pull of opportunity unless there was also a major push from behind. The best explanation so far ventured is that the move was a consequence of continued population growth. After the upheaval and turmoil, the attacks and invasions, the cultural collapse and religious confusion that followed the ending of the western Roman Empire, tenth-century Christian Europe began to feel more stable and secure than it had for many hundreds of years. At long last the corner was turned, the future looked brighter. In consequence, women gained the confidence to start bearing their children earlier. Families increased in size.

It was under pressure from this growing population, and a resulting scarcity of local resources, that around the beginning of the second Christian millennium German landowners, townspeople, clergy and peasants began first to infiltrate, and then to take over outright, the Slav-populated lands of Brandenburg, Bavaria, Austria and parts of Bohemia and Polish Silesia. Many of the first expeditions were led by militant monks whose motives were both conversion of the heathen as well as finding new outlets for their pent-up energies. "There were numerous holy colonies which they sent out from their midst like swarms of bees endowed with reason, and they dispersed them . . . amongst the barbarous nations,"[27] recounts the English chronicler William of Newburgh. "Our manor of Alchuseren was originally forest that had been cleared by the men called Wends [Slavs]. It was made into a manor by our provost Gottfried,"[28] explains a twelfth-century German annalist. The monks' progress can be followed by observing the sudden appearance of new varieties of crops across the eastern regions. Like a particular strain of apple, the Reinette Guise, whose complex itinerary across the continent was minutely detailed in a seventeenth-century account: first travelling from Morimond Abbey in Burgundy to the daughter house of Altencamp in the Rhineland, and thence from abbey to abbey across Thuringia, Saxony and Silesia right into Poland.[29]

Some colonists arrived at the invitation of local lords keen to develop their lands for agriculture and commerce:

> He need only go to the bailiff, who takes him behind on his horse and brings him to the land. And, so soon as the stranger is on the land, in that place where it pleases him and he springs from the horse, and is willing to do tillage, there shall the bailiff measure him fifteen *morgen* in width and breadth [about a hundred acres], and grant him this in fee, and offer him fellowship on the manor.[30]

Organised expeditions were led by so-called locators, *zasadźca*, who, in return for a fee or a plot of land, prepared the pitch, squared the locals, arranged the transport. Henryk the Bearded, Prince of Silesia, launched a campaign in 1205 to attract 10,000 families to settle 400 new villages on his territory.

Among these pioneers, naturally, travelled the formerly Latin-speaking, bnow German-speaking Jews. As Dr. H. G. Wanklyn wrote in an often cited essay that she read to the Royal Geographical Society in January 1940, when Hitler's maniacal programme had, for the first time, drawn the attention of serious academic geographers to the story of the Yiddish civilisation:

> More persistent and more important than sudden outbursts of persecution was the positive attraction of trade in these regions. Just as in the early period the Jewish colonists had followed the Greeks and shared with them the profits of the Black Sea trade, so in the north the Jews with the Germans saw the commercial possibilities of eastern Europe. They took part unconsciously in the medieval period of the German *Drang nach Osten*.

It was not just the commercial possibilities that attracted Jewish emigrants into the Slav lands, any more than it was mere business opportunities that prompted Horace Greely's famous 1850 admonition in the *New York Tribune*, brilliantly expressing the dream of the pioneer: "Go west, young man, go west and grow up with the country." The motivations and aspirations of those who gave up their predictable, if constrained, lives in the cities of the Rhineland to brave the perils and insecurities of the Wild East were surely as multiple and complex as those that attracted citizens of Chicago or Kansas City or St. Louis to follow the Oregon, Santa Fe, Chisholm, Smoky-Hill or Goodnight-Lovin' Trails and seek a new life in the wilderness. Some were looking for land to farm, others for space to pursue their skill or craft, yet others for markets to trade in. Two hundred years before Horace Greely, the itinerant Polish preacher Jedidiah ben Israel Gottlieb had proclaimed, "The land is wide open, let them be mighty in it, settle and trade in it, then they will not be sluggards, lazy workers, children relying on their father's inheritance."[31]

Nineteenth-century American frontiersmen prepared themselves to face the wilderness and hostile natives. Medieval Jews forearmed themselves against malicious phantoms.

> When you build houses in the forest, new inhabitants may be stricken with plague if the site is haunted by spirits . . . Take the Ten Commandments and a Torah Scroll and stretch out a cord the length of the site, and bring the Torah Scroll to the cord . . . at the end say: "Before God, before the Torah, and before Israel its guardians, may no demon nor she-demon come to this place from today and for ever."[32]

Self-defence from human enemies in the medieval Wild East was a heavy-metal affair. Breastplates and coifs, iron skullcaps, were must-haves for trailblazers in an age when, as economic historian David Hackett Fischer of Brandeis University explains in *The Great Wave*,[33] his fascinating account of price and money movements through the ages, body armour was more a necessity than a luxury. Records show that, like today's washing machines and refrigerators, the growing demand and therefore the boosted production of these "consumer durables," which were "mainly designed to make a more durable consumer," consistently pushed down their price relative to other commodities.

Pioneers were more at risk from their own kind than from the natives, just as in the Wild West fights mostly broke out among the settlers, between bandits and bankers, cattlemen and clodbusters, cuckolded husbands and wandering Lotharios. A typical event, which tells us something of the flavour of life in the new territories even as late as the fifteenth century—and which would have been settled with gunshots had it taken place in Tombstone or Dodge City—was drawn to rabbinical attention by "the holy company of Lvov." A drunken argument in Pereyaslav, a town on the eastern bank of the Dnieper river that would one day host the birth of Yiddish author Sholom Aleichem, ended with one Jew being set upon by a gang of others. He was knocked to the ground, and Nachman, one of the mob, shouted: "Simchah, hit him! Beat him to death!" So Simchah struck him about the head as he lay there until he expired. The excuse given was that the victim was a totally ignorant man, "he couldn't recognise a single Hebrew letter and had never in his life put on *tefillin* [phylacteries]. The murderer was drunk at the time and the victim had started the quarrel; they were all in a large company of Jews."[34]

Indeed, in the Wild East there would be relatively few attacks from an indigenous population trying to defend its lands from expropriation. Quite the reverse. The pioneer Jews would discover to their astonishment that scattered all over this old new world, living in towns and villages, forest clearings and open country, were people with a thoroughly mixed Hebrew, Slav, Greek, even Turkic, ethnic background who claimed to be Jewish, yet had few recognisable synagogues or religious schools, couldn't recognise a single Hebrew letter and didn't even know what *tefillin* were. These were men who called themselves by Slavic names like Lewko, Jeleń and Pychacz, and women who answered to Czarnula, Krasa or Witosława. They spoke Slavic dialects with a component of ancestral Turkic and Greek vocabulary; their religion was a half-forgotten memory of Byzantine, *Romaniote*, Judaism—if it was remembered at all. They were generally as poor as the peasantry and labouring class. As unlearned too: "In most localities of Poland, Russia, and Hungary," writes a correspondent at the turn of the thirteenth century in wonderment, "there are no students of Torah. Because of their poverty, the communities hire any competent man they can to serve as their reader, judge, and schoolteacher."[35] Even as late as the 1500s, scholars would still bemoan the lack of mastery of Hebrew, the sacred language, among the Jews of the East:

> young people . . . have learned nothing and understand nothing of grammar. They make masculine into feminine, and vice versa, second person into third person and vice versa, singular into plural and vice versa. That all stems from the fact that the young do not become accustomed to grammatical categories in their youth . . .[36]

And, just as the Germans, particularly those organised into militant missionary organisations—like the Teutonic Order and the Knights of the Sword, who would carve out Christian states along the Baltic coast—saw it as their sacred duty to spread faith in Jesus among the heathen, so the Jewish pioneers too began their own millennial mission to reclaim for the Torah and Talmud those easterners who professed to be followers of the Jewish religion. To turn them back, as they saw it, into proper Jews.

Both wings of the Roman Empire's Jewish diaspora, the two halves, western and eastern, Latin and Greek, of the nascent Yiddish people had finally come together again after many centuries of separation. One might almost say that each had long been waiting for the other.

Ulica Szeroka (Broad Street), Kazimierz, Cracow, 1938. Three jolly Chassidim captured by Roman Vishniac as they converse animatedly in their long coats, black boots and the kind of wide fur hat called a *shtreimel*—traditionally made up of seven sable-tails—on their way to, or from, the synagogue or house of study

Top: Entrance façade to the southern *agora* of Miletus on the Mediterranean coast of Anatolia. The largest marketplace in the Greek world, it was the size of twenty city blocks. Nearby stood the main synagogue and the theatre, where a large section was reserved as "the place of the Jews who are also called Fearers of the Supreme God." *Above left:* Roman Ostia's first-century synagogue, excavated 1961–62. The apse-like brick-built *aron* shrine for the holy Torah scrolls, replaced an earlier wooden construction, donated—according to an inscription—by Mindus Faustus ("Lucky" Mindus). *Above right:* "Portico of the Jewish Synagogue of Ratisbon. Destroyed on the 21st of February in the year 1519." Engraving by the local landscape painter Albrect Altdorfer, one of the Outer City Council delegated to inform the Jews that they had two hours to empty the synagogue and five days to leave the city

Minnesinger Suesskind von Trimberg (c. 1200–50), on the right, wearing a blue cloak with an ermine collar, presented as a dignified, honourable and respected Jewish member of the Bishop's court, his Jew's hat, like the Bishop's crosier, coloured in with gold leaf

Above: Prague's Altneuschul, Europe's oldest synagogue still in regular use. The entrance lobby dates from the 1220s, the double nave from the 1280s and the brick comb-edged gable from the fifteenth century. Behind it stands the more recent Jewish Town Hall. The hands of its lower Hebrew-lettered clock turn in reverse. *Inset:* The banner, combining a Star of David with a Jewish hat, was awarded to the Jews of Prague in 1648 for their help in resisting a Swedish invasion, and is still proudly displayed in the Altneuschul synagogue. This is the first known use of the Star of David to symbolise Judaism. From here, the custom spread to the wider Jewish world.

Left: The synagogue in Strzegom, southern Poland—once a bustling little town of inns, baths, brothels, dance halls, trading bureaux, and storage depots—was built on land donated to the Jews in 1370 by local Duke Boleslaw the Small. It was reconsecrated as a church in 1454 when the Jews were expelled during anti-Hussite agitation.

Above: The tomb of Rabbi Judah Loew Ben Bezalel (c. 1525–1609), the Maharal, in the Old Jewish Cemetery of Prague. He was reputed to have moulded a Golem out of clay, bringing it to life by placing a piece of paper bearing the name of God into its mouth, and withdrawing it every Friday evening to prevent his creature from violating the Sabbath. *Right:* "Here is buried our teacher, the righteous David Gans, author of *The Shoot of David.*" Gans (1541–1613), a rabbi and educator, published the work of the intellectual few in a form accessible to the many: "I did not write this book for great scholars who are filled like pomegranates with the Torah, but for householders, and humble and young students, of my own standing."

Above: The seventeenth-century Old Synagogue of Kazimierz, now a suburb of Cracow, stands by the Old Town Wall on a site originally chosen by King Casimir the Great for his University. After expulsion from Cracow itself in 1568, the Kazimierz Jews sought, and were granted, the *Privilegia de non tolerandis Christianis*, a ban on gentile residence. *Below:* The remains of a seventeenth-century Prague palace built for Jacob Bassevi von Treuenburg (1570–1634), the first Yiddish-speaking Jew to be ennobled. In return for certain privileges, such "Court Jews" rendered financial, commercial and diplomatic services to the crowned heads of Europe.

The Counterfeit Messiah of the

Above left: The grave of Elimelech ben Eliezer Lipmann Weissblum (1717–87), author of *No'am Elimelech*, the definitive formulation of the role of the Chassidic *Tsaddik*, or holy man. The scraps of paper poked through the grill are prayers to his spirit. *Above right:* Sabbatai Zvi (1625–75) of Smyrna, the highly learned but severely disturbed individual who led what has been called "the largest and most momentous messianic movement in Jewish history subsequent to the destruction of the Temple."

Inside the synagogue of Elijah ben Solomon Zalman (1720–97), known as the Vilna Gaon, the founder of modern Jewish orthodoxy and staunch opponent of both the Chassidic movement and rabbinical casuistry

5

At the Crossroads

A young Christian scholar, Anselm of Parengar, head down against the wind on a gloomy wet autumn afternoon, some time early in the fifteenth century, navigates the empty, narrow cobbled streets of the Jewish quarter, *Judaeorum habitacula*, in Bavaria's normally bustling city of Regensburg, once also known as Ratisbon. It is the Sabbath, with most people closely closeted inside. About the only sound, from all directions, is that of indoor voices murmuring prayers, perhaps punctuated, from a nearby courtyard, by chickens clucking around muddy wisps of straw lying by an upended cart that looks, in the old engraving of Ratisbon in front of me now, as if it has been waiting years for a new wheel. Anselm turns into a lane between timber-framed houses, already ancient of days—we first read of Regensburg's Jewish district in 1008—where plaster grey with age peels from the walls and cracked shutters over the windows droop from their hinges, longing desperately for a fresh coat of paint. He steps over the open drain that runs down the middle of the alleyway and makes for the crumbling pile at the very end of the passage, to which he has been invited for a festive meal.

The house was a dark-grey, moss-covered, hideous pile of stones, provided with closely-barred windows of various sizes, irregularly placed. It seemed scarcely habitable. A passage, more than 80 feet in length, feebly lighted on the Sabbath, led to a dark, partly-decayed, winding staircase, from which one had to grope one's way in the gloom along the walls to reach the structure in the rear.[1]

In a paragraph whose modern translation owes something to Charles Dickens's descriptions of nineteenth-century London, the fifteenth-century chronicler introduces his account of a visit to the house of Samuel Belassar, the wealthiest Jew in the most important free city of the German East. Ratisbon, "Plain Fort" in Celtic, was where the Romans sited their Castra Regina (Fort Regen, German Regensburg), sitting on "the knee of the Danube" at the crossroads of Europe. Two millennia later the Praetorian Gate through the Roman wall still survives, next to the base of one of the defensive towers now built into the side of a thirteenth-century bishop's palace.

Anselm's route to Belassar's house would have taken him right across the sector of Regensburg that the Jews had built in the centre of town, hardly more than a bowshot from the quaysides and warehouses that provided their income, and no more than a stone's throw from the Wahlenstrasse, the street of the Welsch or foreigners, in those days known as "Inter Latinos," where—unlike its near namesake, the Byzantine-Latino district of Los Angeles—the wealthiest traders of all lived. A part of one merchant's fortified residence, now called the Golden Tower, still stands here to remind us of the striking wealth and power of Regensburg's mercantile upper class. Of their insecurity too: most of the patricians' houses here were built as strong as castles with walls six feet thick.

Yet of Regensburg's Jewish quarter itself no vestige remains today. For centuries the rulers of Regensburg had withstood demands by churchmen and jealous burghers to expel the Jews from the city. During the civil war that broke out in the 1290s between rival claimants for the German crown, when a beefy nobleman named Rindfleisch believed himself called by God to lead attacks on Jews all across eastern Germany and Austria, a contemporary report said that "the citizens of Ratisbon desired to honour their city by forbidding the persecution of the Jews or the slaying of them without legal sentence."[2] In 1348, during the anti-Jewish agitation that followed the Black Death, the city magistrates declared that they would protect "their" Jews. They couldn't hold out for ever. In 1519, during the city's last-ditch attempt to avoid bankruptcy in the turmoil of the Reformation, urged on by the rabble-rousing preacher Balthazar Hubmaier after the death of erratic Emperor Maximilian, a mob finally succeeded in expelling the Jews to Stadtamhof on the other side of the Danube bridge, expropriating their money and goods, and tearing down their entire quarter. All that remained was the rabbi's house, a large hip-roofed and gabled three-storey building—looking in contemporary drawings as if constructed from children's wooden blocks—which survived until 1838. (Hubmaier was himself burned at the stake in Vienna for heresy in 1528.)

Built with some 5,000 gravestones from the old Jewish cemetery,[3] the Neupfarrkirche, the New Parish Church, rose in place of the old synagogue. All we know of the original Jewish place of worship comes from two prints. One is of the lobby, with a sober-looking bearded man entering, carrying a large leather-bound book, wearing a prayer shawl and the kind of medieval stuffed hat called a chaperon, the other is of the empty, lofty, vaulted prayer hall, with tiny high windows and the podium from which prayers were led, squeezed uncomfortably between the central columns. The pictures were hurriedly produced by the local landscape painter Albrecht Altdorfer, as if conscience-stricken for having been one of the Outer City Council delegated to inform the Jews that they had two hours to empty the synagogue and five days to leave the city. But though demolished half a millennium ago, the Old Synagogue of Regensburg still keeps a place in history: Altdorfer's etchings—according to the website of New York's Metropolitan Museum of Art, which owns one of them—constitute "the first portrayal of an actual architectural monument in European printmaking."[4] Today the parish church, with twin towers strapped on either side of the nave like Gothic rocket boosters, stands cast adrift in the centre of an open shop-lined square, rows of cars parked where Regensburg's Jewish community once walked to Sabbath prayers and Master Anselm of Parengar came a-visiting.

The Jewish quarter aside, the landlocked Bavarian port is one of the best-preserved early medieval towns in all central Europe. Having escaped damage during the Nazi war, the Romanesque and Gothic architecture of its churches and fortified patricians' castles seem to promise the modern visitor a true glimpse of past times.

Regensburg's workaday atmosphere is very different now from what it was in Anselm's time. As you walk through the prosperous streets of the old quarter of town, not a ruinous or moss-covered construction in sight, between pinnacled towers, carefully restored and painted, and filigreed Gothic façades pierced with pointed-arch stone window frames, you can easily forget that this is still one of Bavaria's commercially most important towns, hosting Germany's second-largest inland harbour, miles of docks and quays handling huge annual tonnages of iron, steel and oil as well as the many other miscellaneous goods that travel the Danube river between the Balkans and western Europe's extensive inland waterway system. Port Regensburg is a mute memorial to the success of medieval Yiddish enterprise.

A Jewish trading community had prospered in Regensburg since at least the 980s when records show that a landowner called Samuel, resident here, sold property to the monastery of St. Emmeram, and long before an eleventh-century charter, renewed a hundred years later by the Emperor Frederick Barbarossa, conceded: "to our Ratisbon Jews" and confirmed with imperial authority "their good customs, which their ancestors secured through the grace and favour of our predecessors until our time." The charter spelled out the Jews' important role in promoting trade with the East, specifying that "they be allowed to sell gold, silver, and any other kinds of metals and merchandise of any sort, and also to buy them, according to their ancient custom."

It is clear that the presence of Jews was believed an absolute necessity for any ruler concerned with the economic development of his fiefdom. Indeed, until the end of the eleventh century the Latin word *mercator,* merchant, was more or less synonymous here with Jew. In the year 905 King Louis the Child's *Inquiry into the Tolls of Raffelstettin*, the major riverside market not far downstream, where "Bavarians and Slavs of that country [Austria]" came to exchange "serfs, horses, oxen, or garments," states, "Merchants, that is Jews—as well as other merchants, wherever they come from, from that country or from others—shall pay the just thelony [toll], both for their servants and their goods, as was always the case in the time of previous kings." Over the first centuries of the second Christian millennium some of these merchants became very wealthy. Anselm the chronicler, in spite of his distaste for the ruinous outside appearance of the Jew's house, positively gushed over its impressive interior:

A well-protected door opened, and one entered into an apartment cheerfully decorated with flowers, with costly and splendid furniture, richly and splendidly appointed. Here, the walls panelled and decorated with polished wood, with many-coloured waving and winding hangings and artistic carved work, was the owner's domestic temple, in which the Sabbath festival was celebrated with alternate religious exercises and luxurious regalements. A costly carpet, rich in colour and design, covered the brightly-scrubbed floor. A flame-red cloth of finest wool overlay the round table, which rested on gilt legs, and above it hung, fastened to a shining metal chain, the seven-armed lamp, bright as when fresh from the casting, and streaming with radiance from seven points. The festal board, adorned with heavy silver goblets, the work of a master-hand, was surrounded by high-backed, gilt-decorated chairs, and cushions of shorn velvet. In a niche a massive silver urn, with a golden tap, invited you to the ceremonial hand-washing, and the finest linen interwoven with costly silk, dried the purified hands. A superbly inlaid oak table, girt with garlands of flowers, was laden with the festive viands and the glittering wine-jug; a couch of oriental design, with swelling side-cushions, and a silver cupboard filled with jewels, golden chains and bangles, gilt and silver vessels, rare and precious antiques, formed the rich frame which worthily embraced this picture of splendour and magnificence.[5]

It is no surprise that Belassar's house should have such sumptuous interior arrangements. By the fifteenth century Regensburg had long been the principal trading city of the entire region. Much of its history, both political and commercial, is summed up at the single point where its ancient bridge, completed in 1146 as the first in stone over this stretch of the Danube and still the oldest in use in Germany, steps almost gingerly with thirteen delicate arches across the water, like a game of ducks-and-drakes frozen into solid masonry. Here was the meeting point from which the armies of the Second and Third Crusades had set out on their blood-stained eastward progress in the twelfth century. The wide-arched gate-house, surmounted by a rectangular tower and topped by an open lantern, carries sculptures of King Philip of Swabia and his wife, who awarded the city its first charter in 1207, and of Emperor Frederick II, who granted Regensburg the status of a free imperial city in 1345. On either side of the roadway, representing Regensburg's commercial success, stand what must be among the most elegant storage facilities anywhere in the world: the town's two great salt silos whose red, steeply pitched roofs are pierced by numerous sloping dormers looking like narrowed eyes suspiciously watching over the river traffic—the one to the left of the bridge, the Amberger Salzstadl, dating from just after Anselm's time.

Downstream, the Donau-strudel—not a pastry but a series of rapids that mark the gateway to the East, the swirling confluence of the Danube with the River Regen—once rocked sailing barges stacked to the gaff-fork with sacks of grain or sunk to the gunwales under loads of iron, copper, salt, hides, salted meat and live cattle. On the river bank, long strings of wagons would arrive with a commotion, or set out hopefully, to waves, cheers and good-luck prayers. Some take the path of least resistance, loading their goods on to the boats that ply the smiling Danube, sailing downstream towards Raffelstetten, Linz and Vienna in today's Austria, and then on to Esztergom (aka Gran) and old Buda (aka Ofen) in Hungary, where they would connect with mule trails across the Tatra Mountains towards Mukachevo (Munkacz) and Uzhgorod in Carpathian Ruthenia and ultimately out on to the Ukrainian steppe, or even navigating all the way downriver to the Black Sea, from where commercial shipping lanes lead to Asia Minor, India and the entire Orient. Others set off by land to brave the difficult northerly route through the Bavarian forest following the River Regen towards Pilsen and then Prague in semi-Germanised Bohemia, and after that the long, slow climb and swifter descent over a high pass through the Sudeten Mountains towards Polish Breslau (now Wrocław). Yet others again, leaving all security behind, turn north through the gap in the mountain chain known as the Moravian Gate—aiming for Cracow and other burgeoning townships in the wilder territories of the Slavs and Baltic peoples.

Major international traders like Samuel Belassar ran their own fleets of wagons manned by Jewish carters, and river craft commanded by Jewish watermen, who faced not only the dangers of storm, flood, piracy and warfare, but also the severe rulings of the Jewish authorities to whom they were increasingly answerable, and who accepted no excuse for disobeying God's laws. The eleventh-century Rabbi Kalonymos ben Shabbetai of Esztergom in Hungary, for example, famously found against two Jewish merchants from Ratisbon, who were on the road with goods from Russia when the wheel of their wagon broke late on a Friday afternoon, only an hour or so before the onset of the Sabbath. They fixed it as quickly as they could, but were unable to reach town before sunset and found the congregation already leaving the synagogue after the service. In spite of their protests, Rabbi Kalonymos imposed a heavy fine on them for Sabbath breaking.

Even as late as Anselm's day, some five hundred years ago, Regensburg would have still felt very much like a frontier town. Medieval Ratisbon represented the last major eastern outpost of the Holy Roman Empire, to which Bavaria, including part of modern Austria, had belonged since the tenth century. Further afield and only half tamed, semi-detached Bohemia and Moravia owed merely theoretical, rather than actual, allegiance to the emperor. Beyond them, the wild places where Poles, Lithuanians and the Baltic peoples lived were as unpredictable and unstable as their religion— it would take centuries for country people to give up their pagan beliefs. Though Poland had been, at least officially, part of Christendom since the year 966, Lithuania would not be completely won over to faith in Jesus until nearly five hundred years after that, and since Christianity and nation building went hand in hand, eastern Europe would have to wait centuries for full political consolidation.

IN EVERY CASTLE A KING

In the early Middle Ages names like Bavaria, Austria, Bohemia, Moravia, Poland, Lithuania meant little or nothing. The different segments of the west Slav nation—Sorbian, Polabian, Bohemian, Slovakian, Polish—had not yet become distinct, their forms of speech no more separate languages than those of modern working-class London, Cardiff, Newcastle and Glasgow. As Norman Davies puts it in *God's Playground*:[6] "In the first half of the eleventh century, there was a real chance that a united West Slavonic state might have been permanently established under Czech or Polish leadership."

Moreover in this first half of the second Christian millennium, national borders were not as they are today. The territories they designated were ill-defined.

> In times when land was in superabundant supply and people alone had a political value, there was no point whatsoever in defining the territory of a state or of staking out its boundaries with a tape measure. Rulers were less concerned to claim land as a whole than to dominate the people who could work and develop the scattered oases of settlement and industry.[7]

Populations were sparse, towns and cities were small, surrounded, here in the East, not by a vista of smiling fields and lush pastures as the romantic imagination and the Brueghels' paintings might suggest, but by terrifying forest, wilderness and heath, where dangerous outlaws, ferocious wild beasts and evil spirits lurked—perhaps even *volkelakes*, werewolves, as Jews believed—ready to attack any traveller with the temerity to enter their domain.

The political power centres in this undeveloped landscape were widely dispersed. A ruler's ability to command loyalty stretched little further than the few days' ride from his fortress on which he could send an armed band to assert his authority. When, in 1180, the Holy Roman Emperor Frederick I Barbarossa awarded the dukedom of Bavaria to the Count Palatine Otto of Wittelsbach—founding a dynasty which would survive until the end of the First World War—the duke's power was in reality limited to his private estates around the small towns of Kelheim and Straubing.[8] Even as late as the sixteenth century the great Rabbi Moses Isserles of up-to-date, fashionable Cracow, the city that had trained the astronomer Copernicus, wrote: "Every city has its special tax and its special governor; and even the King does not rule over them, but only their own lord of the manor," a situation summed up in the sarcastic adage "In every castle a king."

Further afield—and, given the scarcity of towns and cities, that meant most places—power and authority were much more diffuse and its sources uncertain. Here warlords and robber barons held sway, gambling to extract maximum freedom of action without losing a more powerful lord's protection in case of serious attack by more distant foreign enemies. In the quarrelsome and murderous Middle Ages, when noble males were bred, like prize horses, for combat and war, such invasions came often.

These were the lands through which Turkic invaders had cut a bloody track in past centuries and through which Genghis Khan's grandson Batu would lead his horde in the 1240s, laying waste everything in his path, including the cities of Breslau, Sandomir and Cracow, where to this day the tune of the hourly trumpet call, the *Henal*, from the top of St. Mary's Church in the Great Market Square, is cut short in memory of a trumpeter struck dead in mid-alarm-call by a Tartar arrow to the throat. Further west in 1241, Batu's bowmen killed the duke of Silesia at the battle of Legnica, famous in military history as the first conflict in which rockets were deployed, and then smashed a Hungarian force on the banks of the Sajó river, leaving three-quarters of Hungary a desert. Contemporaries perceived the hand of God at work when Batu, poised to take over the whole of central—perhaps even western—Europe, unexpectedly withdrew back to Central Asia, anxious to take part in the battle for the succession when his overlord, the Great Khan Ögödei, died.

But this was of little relief for eastern Europe, which was left subject instead to another hundred years or so of deadly power struggle between local princelings, ambitious military commanders and bands of mercenaries—some of infantry brigade strength—who left broad swaths of devastation in their wake, until at last most of the Polish territories were taken in hand and reunited under the firm rule of Casimir III (1310–70), known as "The Great," who was said to have "found a Poland of wood and left a Poland of stone," whose concern for social justice led to his contemporary reputation as "King of the Serfs and the Jews," and who was indeed so well disposed to his Jewish subjects that the story of his love for his Jewish mistress Eszterka of Opoczno, by whom he had two daughters, became a staple of both Jewish and Polish folklore.

In the north, continuous raids on his Christian principality by the still pagan tribes along the Baltic coast led another duke, Conrad of Mazovia, to forget every lesson of history and invite the help of a German crusading order, the grandly titled *Haus der Ritter des Hospitals Sankt Marien der Deutschen zu Jerusalem* (House of the Knights of the Hospital of St. Mary of the Germans at Jerusalem), understandably better known as the Teutonic Knights, offering them a base on the naïve assumption that after subduing and converting the pagan coastlands they would meekly go home again. Instead, as one might have predicted, the Teutonic Knights absorbed another order, the Knights of the Sword, conquered what are now the coastal provinces of Poland, Lithuania, Latvia and Estonia, outdid the Turks and Mongols in exterminating most of the native population—a ghastly massacre at Gdansk in November 1308 would be long recounted by Polish storytellers—and, with the backing of the pope, set up a state of their own that native dynasties would take centuries to reclaim.

In all the turmoil, large areas of what we now call Poland, Belarus, Lithuania and the Ukraine were devastated, fields were left untilled, cities and towns ruined, their economic development halted or even reversed—walls crumbled and grass grew in the streets. Desperate rulers called for new immigrants to come and help restore their broken fortunes, offering whatever inducements they thought might attract new waves of settlement.

One of the most powerful incentives was the offer of what would today be called extraterritoriality: incomers were granted self-government and legal autonomy. In the case of the Christian German communities, this meant the so-called Magdeburg Law, the political and commercial urban constitution first developed during the thirteenth century in Magdeburg in central Germany, a charter which was, in the course of the next hundred years or so, adopted by many important centres of German immigration like Lublin, Sandomierz, Lemberg, Vilna, Brest and Grodno. It was to prevent these new German burgher communities from harassing or excluding Jews that Bolesław the Pious, Prince of Cracow, issued his famous General Charter of Jewish Liberties, the Statute of Kalisz, in 1264. He based the text on a similar document previously granted to the Jews of Bohemia by King Otakar, guaranteeing their freedom to travel round the country, to engage in trade, to be exempt from slavery or serfdom, and to follow their own religion, worship in their own synagogues, be buried according to their own customs, and—most important—to be governed under their own, Jewish, law. Bolesław's bond was the basis for all subsequent grants of Jewish independence in eastern Europe up to the end of the eighteenth century, the legal foundation of a separate, self-governing Yiddish world.

The attraction to Jews living elsewhere on the continent is self-evident. This pioneer territory was now, in Chasdai Ibn Shaprut's words, "a place on earth where harassed Israel could rule itself."

For one should not imagine that even in distant western Europe these events taking place far away at the eastern extremity of their continent were happening—as Neville Chamberlain would for ever damn himself by claiming—"in a far-away country between people of whom they knew nothing." In actual fact, even back then Europe was a much smaller world, and eastern Europe much closer to the West, than one might think. Mieszko, Poland's first Christian ruler, was grandfather to Canute, the eleventh-century King of Denmark and England who famously demonstrated his humanity to his courtiers by failing to turn back the ocean tide. After Canute's conquest of England, the sons of the previous Anglo-Saxon King, Edmund Ironside, took refuge in Hungary. John of Luxembourg, King of Bohemia, known as Blind King John, died fighting the English on the battlefield of Crécy, northern France, in 1346—and may, or may not, have bequeathed his emblem, three ostrich feathers, and his motto, "*Ich Dien*," to the Prince of Wales. And, in spite of their name, the Teutonic Knights were no more all-German than is the *Légion Étrangère* all French. A spell of fighting along the Baltic was regarded as useful practical battle experience for a European aristocrat of any nationality willing to disguise his bloodlust under a cloak of Christian piety. The Knight in Chaucer's *Canterbury Tales*, for example,

a worthy man,
That from the time that he first began
To riden out, he lovèd chivalry
Truth and honour, freedom and courtesy.
Full worthy was he in his Lorde's war,
And thereto had he ridden, no man farre [farther],
As well in Christendom as in Heatheness,
. . .
Full often time he had the board begun
Above alle nations in Prusse [Prussia].
In Lettowe [Lithuania] had he reysed [travelled],
   and in Russe [Russia] . . .

Chaucer's protector Henry Bolingbroke, who became Shakespeare's Henry IV parts I and II by usurping the English crown in 1399, took an active part as a young man in the Teutonic Knights' assault on Vilnius in Lithuania. And it was not only the upper class who took an interest in what was going on far away in the East. Even ordinary townsfolk were touched by the Slav world, whose clothing designs were seen as particularly trendy. A style of exaggeratedly pointed winkle-picker shoes, known as Crackowes (from Cracow) or Poulaines (Polish), were the height of western European fashion from the fourteenth century onwards for more than three hundred years—in spite of repeated attempts to ban them on grounds of health and safety.

Let us then think of Regensburg in this period, and even Vienna, as being—rather like nineteenth-century St. Louis, Missouri—gateways, but not in this case to the Wild West, rather to the Untamed East. Or perhaps—since those on the far side of the Pale, however rude, rustic and barbarous, were nonetheless, unlike native Americans, of a related European race—more like Comrie, Crieff and Perth in eighteenth- and nineteenth-century Scotland: roaring towns on the edge of the rough and lawless highlands, through which the cattlemen annually drove their herds southwards to lowland English markets—and ran drunken riot while they were about it. Indeed, the parallels are even closer, for livestock on the hoof was for many centuries one of the most important commodities of eastern European trade. Cattle were fattened on the Ukrainian steppes and driven along the rich pastureland north of the Carpathian Mountains, through Lesser Poland and Silesia, to Germany and even as far as France.

For many centuries Jewish cattle dealers would be a familiar sight at the great international fairs, like that in Brzeg (Brieg) on the River Oder. By the 1600s, herds of thousands of head of cattle were regularly driven west from Poland and Lithuania by Yiddish-speaking cowboys to supply the armies of central Europe, in a prequel to the great cattle trails of the nineteenth-century American West. A similar expansion of role saw the horses of most of the cavalries, too, supplied by Jewish horse-traders. An old Westphalian folk song runs:

> Jew Itzig bought a cow
> And a calf as well;
> Itzig Jew didn't notice,
> The calf was *moberes*.[9]

Extraordinary to find that last word—Yiddish for pregnant, from a Hebrew root—in an old German folk song.

And just as the rambunctious Scottish frontier territory was the seedbed from which there sprang the Gaelic-permeated version of the English language that came to be called Lallands (Lowland) and which the poet Robert Burns chose as a medium for high art, so was this boisterous continental borderland the area where German and Slav collaborated to develop the particular and peculiar Bavarian and Austrian varieties of German language, and where these distinctive dialects were adopted and further adapted by the Jews into *Juden-Teutch*, Judaeo-German, now known as Yiddish.

Today's scholars are convinced that it was in frontier towns like Regensburg that there first came into being the mixed Jewish-Germanic-Slavic language and culture that underlies the Yiddish civilisation. Indeed, Oxford and Vilnius Professor of Yiddish Dovid Katz, and others too, have proposed that it was actually in Regensburg itself, or places very like it and very near it, that the Yiddish language first developed from a variety of south-east German city dialects[10]—rather as in certain districts of south London an identifiably African-Caribbean style of English has developed, the adoption of which by native English youth to boost their street credibility is the subject of much mockery. Perhaps, in the early years, Regensburg's non-Jewish students and apprentices also affected a Yiddish accent and manner in a similar spirit of fashion-conscious rebellion. Certainly in later centuries, local varieties of German owed something to Yiddish, as did *Gaunerwelsch*, the argot of the Viennese underworld. More likely, though, it would be those with upper-class pretensions since, far from constituting an underclass, the Jews were a prosperous and enviable community.

From here in twelfth- and thirteenth-century Bavaria the Yiddish language and its culture would spread east, first through Austria, Bohemia and Moravia, then to Poland and Lithuania, and finally out into distant White Russia and furthest Ukraine, becoming ever less German and more Slav in the process. Regensburg thus marks both the place of origin of the Yiddish world and its later western edge.

A BLESSING UPON MIESZKO, KING OF POLAND

Historian Cecil Roth wrote in his book *The Dark Ages*:

> The record of the earliest settlement of the Jews in Eastern Europe is involved in obscurity . . . We know that Jews travelled there for purposes of trade, we have vague statements that Jews resided there, we are told legends regarding the activity of the Jewish settlement there. It is out of these ludicrously sparse elements that we have to reconstruct the prehistory of what was to become the most numerous and most vital section of the Jewish people . . .[11]

Occasionally, as if in the darkened amphitheatre of a vast *son et lumière* display, a spotlight suddenly flicks on, narrowly illuminating a single point, and just as suddenly snaps off again, before the eye has time enough to register exactly what it has seen, or the mind to work out its meaning.

The note by Cosmas of Prague, that Jews were driven from Bohemia into Poland by the crusaders of 1098, suggests that the move from Germany into the nearer Slav lands, i.e. Bohemia and Moravia, must have been well under way before the eleventh century. On the other side the reference in the *Sefer ha-Dinim* (*Book of Laws*) by Judah ha-Kohen, probably written before 1028, that Jewish merchants on their way to Russia displayed their wares to the Jewish residents of Cracow, confirms that Slavo-Turkic Jews had long since arrived from the opposite direction.

Some time later, a lost decree—referred to by a later chronicler—was issued by Mieszko III (1126–1202), bynamed "The Old" and otherwise best-known for his brutal and despotic rule, imposing a severe fine on anyone who seriously assaulted a Jew. The measure smacks of a hasty response to an event of some kind, an outrage, perhaps a riot, in twelfth-century Poland, as well as the concern that the ruler felt to protect a valuable human resource, since he recorded no such concern for the welfare of other inhabitants of his lands. Whatever prompted Mieszko to issue his pronouncement, it confirms a Jewish presence not mentioned in any other source of the period.

In the thirteenth century, more nudges, winks and hints. Jews are mentioned as living in the Polish township of Płock in 1237. And though Bolesław's Document of Privilege is dated 1264, the actual presence of Jews in Kalisz is only first mentioned in 1283. In 1304 a Jewish Street is noted in Cracow. By 1350, according to the historian Salo Baron, there are brief references to at least sixteen organised Jewish communities in seventy-five Polish cities, though precisely how they arrived there, and where from, can be no more than guesswork.[12]

Judging from what is recorded about other travellers in the early Middle Ages, one can assume that parties would have journeyed in covered carts, drawn probably by mules rather than horses, and more than capacious enough to hold all the meagre household possessions owned by families living the simple life of the early Middle Ages. (Two standard cabin trunks—one for my father, one for my mother and me—contained what my parents were grudgingly permitted to take on our flight from Austria in 1939.) Later illustrations—there are none from contemporary times—show the vanguard leading the way, seated like Indian rajahs, two up, in wickerwork howdahs strapped on to mule-back, a servant walking along behind, goading the mount forward along the rutted and stony path with prods from a sharp stick.

Such were the dangers of the open road that a twelfth-century religious text[13] allowed Jewish men the normally unthinkable: to dress and disguise themselves as Christian priests, for robbers were believed less likely to attack members of the Church. Women, uniquely, were permitted to carry swords and to dress as men, complete with false beards woven from human hair, a breaking of the law of nature that was otherwise regarded by the rabbis as an abomination punishable by excommunication or worse.[14] At night, if they were between settlements, they would have slept in their carts on straw palliasses, often with an iron object, a knife or even a sword, placed under it for protection, not against human assailants, but in defence against demons, as recommended in the Talmud.[15] Masters and servants would have taken turns on watch, having drawn up the wagons end-on around the cooking fire for warmth and protection. On the

Sabbath and on holidays, the expedition would stay encamped in one place; keeping the Sabbath holy by stopping work and travel was one commandment to which all who called themselves Jewish, however otherwise unobservant, were likely to pay lip service at least.

Supplying themselves with kosher food was no big issue, given the usual medieval diet. Grains and pulses and vegetables, the main staples, with perhaps a little milk, a crumb of cheese or a few eggs, could be bought from farmers anywhere along the way—by barter rather than coins, for which peasants had neither need nor use. Ordinary folk in the Middle Ages ate very little meat—even the best-off did so mostly on Sabbaths and holidays. For a celebration along the way—a wedding, a childbirth or circumcision—animals would be bought on the hoof and killed according to the prescribed religious procedure by the head of the household—until the thirteenth century when valid ritual slaughter was restricted to qualified professionals.[16] In villages and towns, Jewish travellers would most likely be housed and fed (sometimes for a small fee but often none) in the homes of local co-religionists, where they could be assured of a meal and a clean bed. Unlike Christian pioneers, Jewish migrants must often have been able to find congenial temporary berths outside the major cities, in the villages and hamlets where others of their religion, either earlier immigrants or Jewish Slavs, made their homes.

The pioneers were not just blindly pushing on into the complete unknown. They were actually following well-trodden commercial pathways. Trade routes across the Slav world were well established by the year 1000. One trail led from Magdeburg in Germany via Posen and Kalisz, and another from Regensburg via Prague and Brünn in Bohemia, and Cracow in Poland. They joined at Przemyśl in Red Russia, led on to Lvov, and subsequently divided again, one branch striking out north-east to Kiev and the other south-east towards Vinnitsya and the Ukrainian steppe. For centuries these roads had carried the long-distance Jewish traders called *Radanites* (from a Persian word meaning to exchange), described in the ninth century by the caliph of Baghdad's postmaster, Ibn Khordadbeh:

> These merchants speak Arabic, Persian, the languages of the Roman Empire, of the Franks, the Spanish, and the Slavs. They go from west to east and from east to west, sometimes by land, sometimes by sea. From the west they carry eunuchs, female and male slaves, silken cloth, various kinds of furs, and swords . . . On

the return . . . they carry musk, aloes, camphor, cinnamon, and other goods from eastern lands . . .'[7]

Their descendants, Jewish slavers called *holekhei Rusyah* (travellers in Russia), also plied their trade—so unsavoury to us but taken for granted by Church and synagogue—right across the Slav lands; some set up residence in Poland for extended periods. Stories would have filtered back to civilisation, speaking of the freedom and opportunity to be found in the underdeveloped Slav world, a chance to capitalise on craft skills unknown to the peasantry of the wild places, not to speak of the potential for setting up wholesale and distributive networks between the cities, towns and their rural hinterland.

Transport of bulk commodities across the countryside was very difficult in the early medieval period. The ruling class, as the new arrivals would soon discover, could often amass considerable surplus produce but had no means of conveying it to market or trading it for other goods. In times when harvests were very variable, ever subject to the vagaries of the weather, surplus and scarcity were close neighbours. In *The Great Wave*, Fischer quotes an example from Normandy: during the year 1180 the price of wheat fell to 1 livre at Norrancourt where the market was glutted, while only a few miles away at Mortain, where there was a shortage, the price was 10 livres, and even rose to 16 livres on the nearby Cotentin peninsula, where local people went hungry. If this was true even of the advanced western kingdoms, with paved roads going back to Roman times, how much more would it apply to the untracked eastern wilderness with its huge swaths of underdeveloped territory desperately in need of investment, a fact as obvious to the noble rulers of the backwoods as to incomers looking to make a living.

To sum up: from the eleventh century onwards, underdeveloped eastern Europe must have looked to potential migrants as inviting a *Goldene Medine*, a golden land, as the USA seemed to Yiddish-speaking eastern Europeans in the 1880s: a territory wide open to all, to which Jews were as welcome as any others, where the risks may have been great, but so were the potential rewards. By the fifteenth century, German-speaking and Slavic-speaking Jews were united in a flourishing, wealthy Yiddish-speaking civilisation, extending right across eastern Europe, such that Samuel Belassar, its representative in Regensburg, could make of his home enough of a "picture of splendour and magnificence" greatly to impress any visiting Christian scholar.

That much is, necessarily, mostly inference. The true details of the rejoining of the two wings of Europe's Hebrews are obscured in historical shadow. What one yearns for is physical evidence. Suddenly, as if in answer, confirmation is brought up out of the ground—significant confirmation, for it could not better represent the important role the newly arrived western Jews would play in the founding of the states in the East.

In Great Poland, as well as near the resort town of Włocławek where the Vistula river north-west of Warsaw crosses the Polish Lakeland and where, according to an old account, "the gardens attract visitors with swings and barrel-organ music,"[18] archaeologists dig up the first solid proof of a Jewish presence: twelfth- and early thirteenth-century coins issued during the reigns of Mieszko III (The Old), Casimir II (The Just), Bolesław (The Curly) and Leszek (The White). These silver bracteates, undamaged by their long sojourn underground, though so thin that the design is stamped only from one side but appears on both, are inscribed with Hebrew characters. Some bear the name of the minters, others spell out a Jewish blessing on the ruler, for example: *Brochoh Mishko Krol Polski* (a blessing [upon] Mieszko, Polish King).

What can we deduce from these artefacts that sit so stubbornly dumb on velvet cushions in their museum cases? Before we imagine some Jewish coiner in skullcap and prayer shawl labouring over the money press, we should pause to remind ourselves that these coins are very simple to produce—when the raw materials are available. A silver blank of the appropriate size is placed on a round metal base, a die with the reversed design is rested on top and struck with strong hammer blows. The engraved metal stamps that left the unexpected Hebrew letters could have been commissioned from craftsmen as far away as Cairo in Egypt or Córdoba in Spain. Yet some coins bear the names of the mint masters, and at least some of these worthies, like Joseph of Kalisz, are local residents and not from foreign parts.

They must have been men of great wealth, presumably Jewish bankers from the West, owning enough liquid capital to underwrite an issue of coinage. The minting must have been sanctioned by the king, as evidenced by the inscribed blessings showered on Mieszko and other lords. Indeed, it seems that Mieszko gave a lifetime grant to the Jews to produce coinage under his name.

Why inscribe the coins with Hebrew lettering? The legends would have been meaningless to all but those who could read the Jewish liturgical language. Even literacy in Polish, using the Latin alphabet, was a preserve of the Christian clergy. Most if not all the nobles, like the peasants they owned, had no use for reading and writing, and all alphabets, whether Hebrew or Roman, probably looked equally foreign and inscrutable to the illiterate. But how would educated German burghers have responded to keeping the money of their deadly competitors in their cashboxes? How would Catholic priests have reacted to being forced to conduct Church business through the medium of a coinage marked with the sign of the hated ancestor religion? In fact, this may not have been so unusual. In the west of Europe some money bore the mark, not of Judaism, but of Islam. As late as 1266, after seven Crusades against the Muslim world, Pope Clement IV still had to rebuke the bishop of Maguelonne in southern France for allowing the minting of coins bearing the Muslim declaration of faith in Arabic: "There is no God but Allah and Muhammad is the Prophet of Allah." Coins that preached Islam were, the pope protested, "displeasing to God and unprofessional in a bishop."[19]

David Fischer's *The Great Wave* suggests an explanation for the Hebrew coins of early Poland. The eleventh century, we read, began a time of severe money famine. The growth in population and prosperity created the demand for a much greater circulating medium of exchange—in other words, many more coins—which proved ever harder to satisfy. Paper money, a symbol of wealth rather than its substance, though known in the far Orient from the ninth century, was not yet in European use; the value of a coin was in its precious-metal content. When that became scarce, money substitutes were put into use all over Europe: high-value assets, *mobilia*, movable goods such as silver vessels, jewellery, furs, fine textiles and even books. "By the year 1100, the hunger for specie was so great," Fischer writes,

> that the canons of Pistoia's St. Zeno Cathedral melted down their great crucifix and used it for money. German princes sold their imperial seals. English nobles exchanged their silver sword mounts, and French bishops converted their golden chalices into cash. The theologian Fulbert of Chartres justified these practices with the casuistry that it was better to sell sacred vessels to Christians than to pawn them into the hands of Jews.

The money famine was, however, only the beginning. From the eleventh century onwards there began a three-century-long period of price inflation, to which rulers responded in the classic way, by attempting to increase the money supply. In the absence of paper money, they could not simply print more, as modern governments can. Since their problem was the result of a shortage of precious metal, their only recourse was to adulterate the coinage, melting down the pure silver and incorporating copper and other base ingredients into the mix. Of course, once discovered, this adulteration reduced the coins' value and such devaluation simply increased the rate of inflation. Merchants began to refuse coin from any sources other than those that could be trusted, carrying their silver to mints with a reputation for honesty, even if that meant moving to another country. England was one place whose Royal Mint's reputation stood high. "Moneyed men carried their silver across the channel, and had it struck as English Sterling. In 1305, John de Everdon, England's Warden of the Exchange, reported that the 'merchants were daily bringing silver there in great quantities,' so much so that the mint was running six weeks behind."[20] (The result was to increase the money supply so greatly that, as the monetarist economists of the 1980s would have predicted, prices immediately went up. In a single year eggs, for example, rose from 4 pence per hundred to 6, an annual rise of fifty per cent.)

Why did the English mint have such a high international reputation? The Elizabethan antiquary William Camden wrote,

> In the time of . . . King Richard the First [1157–99], monie coined in the east parts of Germanie began to be of especiall request in England for the puritie thereof, and was called Easterling monie, as all inhabitants of those parts were called Easterlings, and shortly after some of that countrie, skillful in mint matters and allaies, were sent for into this realme to bring the coine to perfection; which since that time was called of them Sterling, for Easterling.

By this account the name sterling for English money is a reference to eastern European minters—surely meaning Jews—brought over in the twelfth century to improve the quality of the coinage. Perhaps the "monie coined in the east parts of Germanie" referred to the very same silver bracteates dug up in Włocławek. Camden's etymology of the word sterling has since been questioned, but his anecdote indicates the high repute in which Jewish mint masters were once held—and that the fact was still remembered centuries later in Jew-free England.

If Jewish mint masters in Poland were considered more trustworthy than other strikers of coin, and their money more reliable, the Hebrew lettering, even if it could not be read by its users, may well have represented a kind of visible guarantee of the coinage's value.

In that case these mysterious coins stand as an appropriate symbol for the crucial and indispensable economic service the Jews performed as they moved out into the Slav lands, to build the foundations of eastern Europe's financial development, and therefore the economic underpinnings of a whole new world. It would be going too far to say that the entire commercial infrastructure of the medieval Bohemian, Polish and Lithuanian states was built by Yiddish enterprise, since local lordlings as well as other foreigners like Germans, Italians and Scots also took a hand—but not much too far. To quote Rabbi Dr. Isidore Loeb, a respected Jewish historian of the nineteenth century, "The Jews rendered particular service to Europe by teaching it commerce; by creating, in the teeth of the Church, that instrument of credit and exchange without which the existence of a state is impossible."[21]

And in helping to lay the economic foundations of the new eastern European states, the Jews built into them, right from the beginning, a place for their own civilisation, their own new Yiddish world.

6

The New Yiddish World

Civilisations are defined by, among other qualities, language, literature and religion, but perhaps most of all by their overall character. So how should we then think of the new Yiddish world that the pioneers created in twelfth-century eastern Europe?

The Yiddish civilisation was first and foremost a medieval creation, and our attempts to envisage the true reality of the distant past usually fail because in our fantasies, to quote one distinguished museum director, there are "no slave lines, no starving beggars, no mad and deformed in the streets, no corpses hanging on gibbets, no excrement in the gutters. The children aren't scabby and they don't smell."[1]

Such sights, sounds and smells would have assaulted the eyes, ears and nose of anyone who ventured into a medieval city's warren of streets, alleys, courts and yards, and wandered among the tall, narrow-fronted Gothic houses, backed by church spires and pinnacles, all straining up towards the sky like a drowning man's upstretched fingers, representing in wood and stone a universal heartfelt longing to rise above a corrupted earth and reach towards salvation. If many medieval folk despaired of their worldly condition—as they did—how much more would a modern visitor stand aghast at the reality of eleventh-, twelfth- or thirteenth-century city life.

A time traveller seeking the reality of the Middle Ages would be assaulted by the constant, clangorous, extravagant contrast. A contrast between ready laughter and easy tears; the most abject and miserable poverty beside the most excessive displays of wealth; fat, richly adorned burghers in their sumptuous furs and elaborately embroidered silks passing starving beggars wrapped in rotting rags; joyful and colourful aristocratic processions making stately progress in one direction, accompanied by trumpet and drum, onlookers cheering and saluting, while plodding inexorably in the other, lugubrious parades escorting cartloads of convicts on their way to horrible execution, the gallows, the stake, the disembowelling table, pursued by jostling, jeering crowds.

Violence was constant. To the rabbis of the eastern outposts, armoured warriors setting off to war on their caparisoned chargers were both an everyday sight and models to be emulated: "We should take a lesson from the knights who ride off into battle to show their bravery at their lord's command," wrote Judah the Pious.

> They would rather be maimed or die than flinch from the sword. This is because of shame; for it is considered a disgrace if they flee. Yet if they fall in battle, they will receive no reward from their lord. Therefore, how much more must we bravely endure suffering and pain to the point of giving our lives at the command of our King, the Lord of the universe, blessed be His Name.[2]

And when no real conflict offered, men were encouraged to entertain themselves with mock fighting, though one Moravian rabbi disapproved of pointless "jousting tournaments, where men take pleasure in racing towards each other on horseback while holding lances."[3]

In this distant land and long-gone age with its shockingly different mentality, it is hardly possible for us to place ourselves in the shoes of our medieval forebears, who would surely seem to us ridiculously childlike in their innocence, ignorance, irrationality, fatalism, credulity and savage cruelty. Terror and dread were a dominant feature of life during medieval times: dread of the weakness of the body, of sickness and the perils of childbirth; dread of the unpredictability of nature: of drought, crop failure and famine. And a particular dread of the excesses of the proud and the strong: of injustice, torture, execution, and constant, constant warfare. The ruling class was among those most to be feared. "The court is a sea," wrote Charles de Rochefort in the fifteenth century, whence come

Waves of pride, storms of envy . . .
Anger stirs up quarrels and outrages,
Which often sink the ships of state,
Treason there shows his face.
Swim somewhere else for your fun.[4]

And as if that were not already quite enough, there was also the obsession with the end of the world, with the very real fear of hell, of sorcerers,
of devils. And for the Jews, to the list of universal terrors must be added
the ever-present possibility of anti-Jewish rioting, like the unprovoked and
unmotivated pogrom that exploded among the common crowd after the
coronation of Richard I of England, the Lionheart, in September 1189.

> While the king was seated at table, the chief men of the Jews came
> to offer presents to him, but as they had been forbidden the day
> before to come to the king's court on the day of the coronation, the
> common people, with scornful eye and insatiable heart, rushed
> upon the Jews and stripped them, and then scourging them, cast
> them forth out of the king's hall . . .
>
> The citizens of London, on hearing of this, attacked the Jews
> in the city and burned their houses; but by the kindness of their
> Christian friends, some few made their escape. On the day after
> the coronation, the king sent his servants, and caused those
> offenders to be arrested who had set fire to the city; not for the
> sake of the Jews, but on account of the houses and property of the
> Christians which they had burnt and plundered, and he ordered
> some of them to be hanged.[5]

To keep the record straight, it must be emphasised that, despite the
ever-present risk of attack and irrational outbursts of aggression against
them, early medieval Jews were not especially singled out for particularly
barbaric treatment. There were plenty of other targets too. If it were not
the Jews, it might just as well have been foreigners, lepers, heretics or anyone else who attracted the evil eye of the mob, like the sad and strange old
women burned alive as witches in their thousands to popular applause.
Thirty-five London-resident Flemish merchants and weavers were, for no
particular reason, savagely hacked to pieces by the insurgents of the Peasants' Revolt in 1381—by then there were no Jews left in England for popular fury to vent itself on.

Yet perhaps the Jews had one advantage over their neighbours. Their religion taught them that history was an ongoing message from God, and they did not see themselves as the constant targets of unpredictable bolts of fate as Christians did. "Oh Goddess Fortune . . ." wrote one monk, the thirteenth-century composer of "O Fortuna," one of the medieval lyrics found in a manuscript from a Benedictine monastery in Bavaria, not a hundred miles from Regensburg, and set to music by Carl Orff in his *Carmina Burana,*

> Like the moon always changing,
> Ever waxing and waning,
> Hateful life first oppresses
> Then soothes as fancy takes it.
> Poverty and power,
> It melts them like ice.[6]

If it is hard for us to come to terms with the physical conditions of earlier centuries, it is even more difficult to empathise with what people thought of their lot and their place in the world. We who live such different lives in such a different era would find it hard to accept that, for all but the few, the idea of an individual person's significance was not yet recognised. Men and women saw themselves, and were seen by others, as members of their class or estate, each of which had its specified rules, costume, occupations and position in life. It was impious, even blasphemous—not to speak of dangerous for the stability of the social and world order—to break conventions which were an expression of God's will and His prescribed pattern for the universe. In much the same way as for today's religious Jews mixing milk and meat in food[7] or linen and wool in a garment[8] is to muddy a distinction that God wants kept sharp and clear, so the many separate treads on medieval society's power ladder must be openly distinguished and publicly acknowledged by adopting a particular form of dress and manner of self-presentation.

Out on the streets, where the drama of medieval life was mostly played, nobles and lords were fêted by dazzling displays of arms and heraldry; lepers and others disfigured by disease went in procession, announcing their presence with wooden rattles; as in many Third World cities even now, disabled beggars made open and theatrical display of their deformities. Uniforms were de rigueur, and not only among the military classes: servants and retainers wore the livery, colours, badges and blazons of their masters; clergy distinguished themselves in their clothes from laymen. Lovers proudly displayed the "favours" bestowed on them by their ladies; those who had been on pilgrimage wore emblems as a sign of their holy travels—like the scallop shell, the badge of St. James, adopted by visitors to the shrine of Santiago de Compostela in Spain.

How a group presented itself in public tells us much about where its members saw their place in the medieval world. European Jews of the early Middle Ages generally wore the same clothes as did everyone else of their gender and station in life. Representations of Jews in earlier gentile sources distinguish them neither by costume nor by facial appearance.[9] The one unique item that they seem to have favoured was a "Jewish Hat" that appears in many images of the period, looking like a handbell placed on top of the head, or a short, wide-mouthed, inverted ice-cream cone, sometimes with a knob on the end. Commentators have at times interpreted the curious shape of this headgear as designed to humiliate the Jews by making them look ridiculous. But that is to apply modern taste inappropriately to medieval fancy. In earlier years, before the Church made the Jewish Hat mandatory in the West and the Breslau church council of 1266 ordered its adoption by all Jews in the Polish bishopric of Gnesen—instructions that led to its speedy abandonment—this headgear was freely chosen and worn as a small proud sign of their different faith, just as many Jews now wear skullcaps in public. It appears on a fourteenth-century Jewish seal from Koblenz, which bears the sign of a lion rampant crowned with a Jewish Hat.[10] The banner awarded to the Jews of Prague in 1648 for their help in resisting a Swedish invasion, and proudly displayed in the ancient Alt-neuschul Synagogue, combines a Star of David with a Jewish Hat (though some describe it as Swedish).

The origin of the Jewish Hat is a mystery. As far as I know, not a single example has survived. We don't know how it was constructed, nor what precisely it was made of. (The only other people associated with this kind of headgear were the long-gone Scythians, whom the Greek historian Herodotus had described as the "pointed-hat Scythians" more than a thousand years before. How odd that two nations who shared similar headgear should also be linked by name: Scythian-Ashkenazi.)

The lack of outward distinction between Jews and Christians reflected the considerable intercourse between the communities—in every sense of the word. The Fourth Lateran Council, sitting in 1215, which among much else was trying to meld the disparate European peoples into a single Christian nation that could effectively challenge the Muslims who had taken the

Holy Land, was greatly concerned about the absence of visible signs of a person's religious, and therefore social and political, affiliation:

> The confusion has reached such proportions that a difference can no longer be perceived. Hence it happens at times that, through error, Christians have relations with Jewish and Saracen women and Jews and Saracens with Christian women. Therefore . . . we decree that such of both sexes in every Christian province shall at all times be distinguished in the eyes of the public from other peoples by the character of their dress.

In some places the response was the enforced wearing of the Jews' Hat, in others the colour of their costume was prescribed: pale-green in Barcelona, yellow in Augsburg. As late as the eighteenth century, Jews in Habsburg Prague still had to wear yellow collars over their coats, and the memory was strong even at the end of the nineteenth—"O'er the Moldau bridge trotted the throng of yellow-caftaned Jews," wrote New York poet Emma Lazarus (author of "Give me your tired, your poor, your huddled masses yearning to breathe free") in her 1889 poem "Raschi in Prague." Elsewhere even odder rules were enforced: Salzburg in 1418 ordered all Jewish women to attach bells to their dresses so that they could be heard coming; and to emphasise an even finer distinction, Jewish visitors to Nuremberg had to wear a special hood to distinguish them from the locally resident Jews. These impositions should, however, be taken in context. Almost all classes in society had their costume prescribed by law. Polish ordinances of the sixteenth century decreed that the following must be distinguishable by their dress alone: peasants, burghers and city dwellers, merchants and craftsmen, members of the Council and patricians, nobles, doctors, counts and lords, orderlies, soldiers, cattle guards, scribes, clerics, servants, secretaries, cashiers, bailiffs, attendants, officials, common and faithless women, messengers—and Jews.[11]

The most frequent and obvious marker, adopted in much of western Europe, was a badge. Badges were a familiar feature of medieval society: aristocrats wore the badges of their lineage; retainers wore the badges of their lords; guild members wore the badges of their associations; those who had been on pilgrimage wore the badge of the saint or martyr whose shrine they had visited, like Santiago de Compostela's scallop shell, or the crown badge one could buy at Edward the Confessor's tomb in Westminster

Abbey. Lovers exchanged badges, often in the form of sprays of tin flowers, and wore them as tokens to denote the constancy of their affection. There were even badges making political or social points, much like today's lapel buttons or ribbons: an English badge of the early fifteenth century depicts an ape urinating on to a pestle and mortar, symbol of the physician, and seeming to mean "I piss on doctors," apparently made to be worn by those who bore a grudge against the medical profession.[12]

Thus that there should be a Jewish badge, in the shape of a coloured patch, a wheel (*rota*), a target (*scopus*) or an image of the two round-topped Tablets of the Law (*tabulae*), was in itself no great novelty. That it was legally enforced, exposing Jews to immediate recognition and therefore danger, as the world became ever less friendly towards them, was oppressive. Even the law allowed that, when travelling, they could take it off.

However, it would take a long time for the prescription of a Jewish badge to reach the eastern margins of western Europe and points beyond—England in 1253, the Papal States in 1257, France in 1269, Ofen (Hungary) in 1279, but Augsburg not until 1434, all Germany only after 1530 and Austria after 1551—and by then the focus of the Yiddish world had long moved east and firmly established itself in the Slavic world, where the idea of making Jews wear badges was resisted in the highest circles. King Sigismund I of Poland decreed in 1534 that Jews must not be compelled to wear any distinguishing sign on their clothes. In spite of resolutions to the contrary by other interested parties, the king's decision was final. His son Sigismund Augustus, who united his country with Lithuania, declared, "The Jews pay taxes and are therefore entitled to the same rights as everyone else."

When Jews of Europe's East wore a special form of dress, it was by their own volition. The earliest record of a recognisable Jew in Poland,[13] on a twelfth-century miniature, shows him wearing typical Byzantine clothing: a tunic and a man's cloak, a *paludamentum*, sign of his eastern, Greek, ancestry—though he almost certainly spoke Slavic. I take him to represent the typical target of the major missionary effort that was now being undertaken by the formerly Latin-speaking, now German-speaking, western Jews, moving eastwards to join their long-separated formerly Greek- and Turkic-speaking brethren, and marking their progress by establishing among their co-religionists the language that would come to characterise them: Judaeo-German, *Juden-Teutch* or Yiddish.

THE LANGUAGE

The culture of the Jews is not very visual. Scripture commands us to revere the word and abjure the image. So it seems quite natural that the sign with which the Jews of central and eastern Europe chose to distinguish themselves from others was not their clothing but their language. More than a sign, of course, for out of the masonry of language both walls and civilisations are built.

The Jewish dialect of German, the fusion with Hebrew and Slavic that would in time become Yiddish, spread rapidly among the eastern Jews because the speech of the incoming westerners offered clear advantages. German was the language of international commerce and culture across most of central, northern and eastern Europe. The German-speaking Jews were of a higher class; they were better educated and better connected; they were richer and more powerful, part of an international network with access to royalty and the nobility; and their version of the ancestral religion laid claim to being more authentic than the half-forgotten Byzantine Judaism of the Slavs. To learn the language and become part of the Yiddish-speaking community was to better one's prospects. To bring up one's children bilingually in the international, as well as the local, language was, as it is today with English in India and even Israel, to give them access to modernity and prosperity.

To the incoming western missionaries, concerned to forge a single unified Jewish people with a single uniform faith out of the fragmented and disparate communities of Bohemia, Moravia, Poland and Lithuania, their language would serve as glue to hold the new nation together. In the surprisingly short period of a couple of centuries, a distinct, unified, identifiable and separate Yiddish-speaking people appeared, though the name Yiddish would gain common currency only in the nineteenth century. The adoption of Jewish-German, *Yiddish-taytch*, as the language of a populous, eventually powerful and prestigious, Jewish civilisation in the East eventually spread its use right across Europe, to be adopted as the tongue of Jews from France to Russia, from Scandinavia to Italy, the self-chosen identity tag of European Jewry.

According to the often-quoted saying by Max Weinreich, the greatest of modern Yiddish scholars, "a language is a dialect with an army and a navy,"[14] i.e. when it is used by a group with political power. So the near-universal tongue of European Jewry shouldn't count as a language at all.

But that is to take far too narrow a view. Yiddish as we know it today is undoubtedly a language, though a rather unusual one. It may have derived from a mix of south-eastern dialects of German, but it quickly left its antecedents behind. "Their *Teutchen* [Germanising] is very *un-Teutch* [un-German]," wrote Christoph Helwig, a sixteenth-century scholar and translator. "You will easily hear the contrast between *Juden-Teutch* [Jewish German] and *Waren-Teutch* [true German]," Johann Wagenseil pointed out in 1699.

Its modern grammar and sound system derive partly from German, partly from Slavic and partly from neither, the consequence of the natural evolution of language along idiosyncratic and unpredictable lines. Apart from the two main source languages, its vocabulary also contains words from Hebrew, Aramaic, Latin, Turkic, French, Greek and more—a record, albeit hard to decipher, of all the peoples among whom Jews have lived. Particularly characteristic is its use of diminutive suffixes derived from both German and Slavic but developed further than in either. For instance "town" is *shtot*, "little town" is *shtetl*, and "dear little town" is *shtetele*. Or take the Hebrew name Avrohom, Abraham. Among Yiddish speakers it can appear as Avrom, Avreml, Avremele, Avremche, Avremenu, Avreminke, Avremchik, and yet more.

The speech of religious minorities usually includes many specialist words that are unfamiliar to the majority. Listen to the way Muslim immigrants to Britain and the USA speak English, and you will hear many expressions ultimately taken from Arabic, Persian, Urdu and Bengali to express concepts for which no English words are available—or suitable. So you might expect a language like Yiddish, which began simply as Jewish-German, to differ from its source language mainly in its religious vocabulary. Equally, eavesdrop on the way Asian immigrants speak the languages of their former home countries and you will hear many local English words, borrowed to name objects and concepts unfamiliar in the places they came from. So one might expect Yiddish to be basically German, with Slavic words imported to describe phenomena familiar in a Slav but not a German environment, and with Hebrew words and phrases applied to those special items and ideas derived from a Jewish way of life.

Today's Yiddish is not like that at all. It is a real fusion of the Germanic, the Slavic and the Hebraic, with words like the pronoun *mir* (we), reflecting both German *wir* and Slavonic *my*, such expressions as *khotch* (although), taken from Polish *choć*, in spite of German having the perfectly adequate *obwohl*; *shmate* (rag) from Polish *szmata*, a piece of cloth, rather than German *Lappen* or *Fetzen*; and *efsher* (perhaps), and *tachlis* (goal or purpose) from the Hebrew, where a German would say *vielleicht* and *Ziel*. True, a few of the Slavic imports are words for things which only exist in the Slav world, while Hebrew is applied to some items which have no gentile equivalent, like the prayer shawl, the *tales*, or the phylacteries, the *tefillin*.

According to the linguistics scholar Paul Wexler,[15] some or much of the Hebrew vocabulary in Yiddish is of relatively late adoption, the result of a conscious injection of Hebrew words to replace older usages from German or Slavic. Yet in many cases where one would anticipate a Hebrew expression to refer to a Jewish matter, we have instead a loan word from the non-Jewish world: usually Latin or German in the west of the Yiddish range, and Slavic or Turkic in the east. Consider the verb to pray. In the western part of the *heym*, the Yiddish for praying is *oren* from the Latin *orare*, to pray, while in the east the word is *davenen*, which is ultimately Turkic in origin. Saying grace at meals is known as *bentshn*, from *benedicare*, Latin for to bless. Or take the word for the head-covering Jewish men don while praying. In the West this is called a *kappel* or *kepl*, from the German for little cap, while in the East it is known as a *yarmulka*, the probable derivation of which is through Polish from Turkish.

Even less expected is what linguists call Lexical Bifurcation, where an item, idea or action has two labels: one Hebrew and one not. Unusually, several instances label a Jewish idea with a non-Hebrew word, while the non-Jewish bears a Hebrew expression. While *oren* or *davenen*, of non-Hebrew origin, are used for Jewish prayer, the standard Yiddish for praying by Christians is *tfile tun* (Hebrew: *tefilah*, "prayer"). And sometimes the Germanic-derived word is for standard use, while the Hebrew-derived is used as an earthy, slangy alternative. The Yiddish for ordinary eggs is Germanic *eiyer*, but where German speakers use the same word to refer vulgarly to testicles, Yiddish speakers keep the German reference, but translate the actual word, turning to the Hebrew for "eggs," *beytsim*, instead.

Yiddish is traditionally written, like other Jewish languages, right to left, in the Aramaic characters used for scripture, Torah and Talmud, and known as Square Hebrew, though the sound value of some of the letters has been changed to adapt them to their new use. The Jews of central Europe had no access to any other form of writing. Though archaeologists assure us that writing began in ancient times as a tool for accountants and tax gatherers, literacy was introduced to barbarian northern Europe by the

Church, and both reading as well as writing were accessible only to those with a Christian education. Reading Latin characters—or, in the East, Cyrillic, the symbols devised in the ninth century for the Slavic language of Moravia by Saints Cyril and Methodius—was thus a religious Christian act. Jews had either to use the alphabet with which they were already familiar from their own sacred texts, or forgo literacy altogether. To this day Latin characters are still known to some Yiddish speakers as *galkhes*, from Hebrew *galeakh* (shaven), referring to the Catholic priesthood.

Of course it goes without saying that there were always some or even many who broke the rules and secretly took lessons from a friendly cleric, or eavesdropped through an open window on the local nobleman's children learning to read from their Psalter, though had it become publicly known, such near-apostasy would have attracted heavy censure from the community leaders. It is said that even in the early twentieth century some immigrants to the USA from the most pious and sheltered quarters of the *heym* were shocked to find that their children were expected to learn to read and write English in Latin characters. Only after the Holocaust, particularly in the United States, has Yiddish come to be most commonly written—as in this book—in the formerly rejected alphabet of its religious enemies. For seven centuries Yiddish literature was inscribed exclusively in the Hebrew characters of Judaism's own proud tradition.

THE LITERATURE

If the first requirement of a civilisation is the possession of its own language, the second must be the pursuit of a literary tradition. Books are, in historian Barbara Tuchman's words, the carriers of civilisation.

Yet the earliest suggestion of a Jewish literature in the German of its day is actually set down in Latin characters. This is the legacy of the poet Suesskind von Trimberg (*c*.1200–50), several of whose short works are included in the early fourteenth-century Manesse Manuscript, probably written in Switzerland and now kept in the University of Heidelberg. There is a picture of the poet too, under the heading *Süskint der Jude von Trimperg* (Suesskind the Jew of Trimberg)—an illustration which used to be interpreted as showing the poet himself, clearly depicted in a Jewish Hat, reciting his verses before an audience of an ecclesiastic, a monk and a layman. More recent scholarly analysis[16] suggests a different interpretation: that the picture shows a legal dispute argued before a bishop of Cologne seated on his ceremonial chair and holding a crosier. The plaintiff is shown in the middle of the image, pointing his finger accusingly at the Jew.

So far, so ordinary: a Christian takes a Jew to court for some supposed affront. However, it is the treatment of his subject by the manuscript's illuminator which is particularly interesting. The figure of Suesskind is presented as the most important character in the scene, slightly separated from the others, depicted as a handsome bearded man in a fine blue cloak with an ermine collar, quite as sumptuously dressed as the bishop himself, and his Jew's Hat coloured in with gold leaf, just like the bishop's crosier. Here is pictured no grovelling, guilty Jesus-denier, but a dignified, honourable and respected Jewish member of a bishop's court, the equal of his master.

The picture is in striking contrast to Suesskind's own description of himself in one of the poems, where he complains that the nobility are not giving him his due:

> Forsooth I shall leave your gates
> With my art of song.
> The lords give me no gifts;
> I will flee from their court
> And I will grow a long beard
> Of grey hair.
> From now on I will live
> Like an old Jew.
> My coat will be long,
> My forehead deep beneath a hat,
> My step will be humble,
> And I will rarely sing courtly songs
> For the Lords deny me their generosity.[17]

Scholarship is divided on the question of whether Suesskind was really a Jew, or whether he adopted a Jewish persona as an ironic comment on the commercialisation of art, the fickleness of the public and the isolation of a poet fallen out of fashion.[18] Certainly, presenting himself as a humble Jew was consistent with the fashionable self-pity of the courtly bards known as Minnesingers—from *Minne*, an old-fashioned word for love—who, like the French Trouvères and Provençal Troubadours, usually sang of their desperate, never-to-be-requited passions for unreachable noble ladies. Whether Suesskind was indeed Jewish or not—and as well as the illustrated scene, the illuminated first letter of his first poem, a "W," is entwined with a strange human-headed bird wearing a Jew's Hat—there seems to be nothing in the language that differs from the German written by non-Jews in the early thirteenth century.

For the first clearly Jewish variety of the German language, except for the occasional marginal gloss in manuscripts of the Hebrew Bible, we need to move on fifty years or so to a cheeky little rhyme written into a prayer book from Worms and dated to the year 1272:

Gut tak im betage	A good day be vouchsafed to him
Shewer dis machazor	who carries this *machzor* to the Synagogue.
in beth hakneseth trage!	

Here we already find some of the typical characteristics of the later Yiddish language: a slightly Slavicised flavour to the construction (which echoes Hebrew *she*, Slav *že* and German *wer* in the relative pronoun "who") and the use of two Hebrew expressions for specifically Jewish religious items: *Machzor*, a prayer book for festivals, and *Beth haKnesseth* (House of Assembly), a rather formal Hebrew phrase for synagogue—today's Yiddish speaker would be more likely to say *shul* (literally: school) but of course that wouldn't scan.

And a rollicking scansion seems to have been much to Yiddish taste in this early period, to judge by the examples that remain to us of early Yiddish literature. The thirteenth-century tale "Our Father Abraham" (*Avrahom Ovinu*), for example, a retelling of the story of the Patriarch, bowls along in a ballad metre as catchy as any. Abraham makes ready to leave the door of his father's house.

Er vaßte si wil ebene	He got up unhurriedly
er machte sich hin vür	he went out.
Er korte siene verßen	He turned his heels . . .
zu sieneß fater tür	towards his father's door

He has been told to take his father's idols to market in a sack.

Er warf den ßak zume rüken	He threw the sack on his back
er machte sich zu den velden	he made for the fields
Er began di apgote	He began to curse the idols severly.
se'ere schelden.	

Avrohom Ovinu is but one of many early Yiddish renderings of familiar Bible stories. In the same document—the Cambridge Manuscript, found in a synagogue attic in Cairo—we find the story of Joseph the Righteous and of Moses. These are not simply translations into the vernacular but true retellings, full of wit and even a certain degree of *lèse-majesté*, the tone of their language far from the plodding pedestrianism of Christian equivalents of the time, like the *Ormulum*, a Middle English paraphrase of the Christian Gospels in 20,000 lines of clumsy verse. Theirs is the lively Yiddish of daily conversation, of the street, the counting house, the taproom and even the cowshed.

Over the next centuries a large corpus of works was composed in Jewish German, many using the jaunty metrical structure of popular poetry of their time. There were well-known biblical tales like *The Binding of Isaac*, of *Esther in the Persian Court*, of the narratives in the Book of Kings[19] and of Samuel,[20] this last, the *Shmuel Buch*, composed by a woman, the brilliant and learned Litte of Ratisbon, in the metre of the *Nibelungenlied*. The genre culminated in the *Tseynareyna* (Hebrew: *Z'enah u R'enah*) by Rabbi Jacob ben Isaac Ashkenazi of Janow, a sixteenth-century Yiddish version of parts of the Bible, composed in a lively, popular style, generously larded with proverbs, anecdotes, legends, commentaries and homilies culled and translated from the preceding thousand years of Hebrew literature. There have been more than two hundred editions of the *Tseynareyna* and it remains in print to this day; an astonishing publishing phenomenon.

The book was originally called *Taytch Chumesh* (*German Pentateuch*), but the first printer, noting that the work was particularly popular among women—who mostly did not study Hebrew and to whom therefore the sacred texts were inaccessible in their original tongue—used the words of an appropriate line from the Song of Solomon on the title page: "Go forth and behold [*Z'enah u R'enah*], O ye daughters of Zion . . ."[21] Yet a readership restricted to women was not the author's original intention. "This work is designed to enable men and women . . . to understand the word of God in simple language," states the introduction.

Prayer books too were written in Yiddish, and much new devotional poetry and prose, including the so-called *tchines* (Hebrew: *techinnoth*, devotions), which were considered women's prayers and most of which were attributed, perhaps falsely, to women composers. Written in simple, often tear-jerking and sentimental style, they frequently ended with a rhymed couplet, like a Shakespearean curtain line. A typical prayer to accompany *challah*, the separation and burning of a portion of dough when preparing the Sabbath bread—in memory of the sacrifice made by the priests while the Temple still stood—concludes with this:

Vi ikh tu mayn mitsve fun khale mit gants hartsn,
(As I fulfil my commandment of *challah* with all my heart)
zo zol Got, borukh hu, mikh hitn far payn un shmartsn.
(So may God, blessed be He, protect me from anguish and pain.)[22]

One could stock a respectable library shelf with the known products of the early Yiddish religious writers—and we have probably lost nine-tenths if not more of the works that were written.

It would be a mistake, however, to think that medieval Yiddish literature was wholly religious, or that the Jews were completely cut off from contemporary developments in the literary arts of other Europeans. Quite the contrary. It is clear that Jews were well aware of what their Christian neighbours were reading and wanted their versions too. Indeed, wrote the late Professor Chone Shmeruk of the Hebrew University of Jerusalem,[23] much of the material on Jewish themes was "born out of the conscious need and intent to produce a suitable offset, and possible substitute, for the alien 'fictitious' adventure stories which had found their way to the mass Jewish public." (Evidence of cultural exchange in the opposite direction, from the Yiddish civilisation to the surrounding Christian society, is found in works such as Jans von Wien's *World Chronicle*, written in the thirteenth century, which is said to show clear signs of having incorporated Jewish narrative materials.)[24]

Epics like *Dukus Horant*, a version of the German *Hildebrand Saga*, a cousin of the more famous *Song of the Nibelungs*, appeared in Yiddish versions. In fact, in this particular case, the Yiddish transcription pre-dates the oldest known copy written in German by more than a hundred years (grind your teeth, Richard Wagner). Jews also avidly read *Melech Artus*, stories about the court of King Arthur (*Artus Hof*), and even a set of yarns based around Till Eulenspiegel, the German peasant prankster made internationally famous by Richard Strauss's tone poem. The aesthetic pinnacle of this development was probably the *Bove Buch*, an early sixteenth-century poetic adaptation of the then well-known Italian chivalric romance, *Buovo d'Antona*.[25] The Yiddish version by Elieh ben Asher haLevi, pen-name Elijah Levita or Elieh Bachur, prolific author, grammarian and one of the foremost Yiddish intellects of the sixteenth century, used the same metre as the original, called ottava rima (the metre of

Byron's *Don Juan*). However, not having read the Italian romance, I can't say whether the distinctly misogynist tone was carried over from the Italian or introduced by its adapter.

> Thus, dear Sirs, you shall see
> What bad luck comes from evil women,
> See what King Solomon's books write,
> How he sought a good woman,
> But in all his days never found a single one.[26]

This work, too, rewritten in Yiddish prose, survived into the twentieth century, the title Yiddishised to *Bubbe Mayseh* (Grandma's Yarn), which became the standard Yiddish idiom for any tall tale. The Yiddish civilisation was always receptive to inspiration from outside.

And this was the case even in matters of faith.

THE RELIGION

The *Book of the Pious*, a Hebrew text that was the basis of much Yiddish religious observance, not only gives us frequent examples of non-Jews whose actions should be emulated, but also tells us that "Jews generally adopt the behaviour of the gentiles among whom they live. For example, if in a certain locality the gentiles are heedful to refrain from adultery, the Jews who live there will be equally scrupulous in that regard." Presumably elsewhere they were not so particular.

The New Piety too, the softer, gentler vision of God promoted by the Church leaders from the eleventh century, however baleful had been its crusading consequences, found a ready response among the Jews. It came in the form of the *Chasidei Ashkenaz* (the Pious Ones of Germany), antedating by more than five hundred years the Chassidim of our own day. If any one group can be credited with the effort to return the lost Jewish sheep of the Slav world to Torah and Talmud, it was these earlier Pious Ones.

The mantle of leadership in this religious movement was largely worn by members of the family called Kalonymos, whom we met earlier after their move north from Italy into Germany, and whose pedigree, as given by Eleazar ben Judah ben Kalonymos of Worms, claimed a link with the ancestral Hebrew world of Mesopotamia ("Abu Aaron . . . came from Babylonia . . . and transmitted . . . all his secrets"). This long-established clan with their hotline to authentic tradition, even bearing heraldic arms, a lion rampant ("Judah" is a lion's whelp),[27] arrived during the thirteenth century from eastern Germany to find, scattered all over the Slav world, the ethnically mixed Hebraic, Slavic, Hellenic, Turkic community which, it seems, observed a kind of nominal Judaism that had drifted far from its origins. It had forgotten not only the sacred languages, Hebrew and its semi-sacred cousin Aramaic, but much else besides—particularly the many instructions, commandments and rules which prescribe how to live as a Jew.

The *Chasidei Ashkenaz* saw it as their duty, not only to lead pious lives themselves, but also to bring the light of true Judaism to those who had lost contact with their faith and broken their links with tradition. Here was the opportunity to re-establish their faith across the new world opening up to them in the way they themselves now interpreted it: gentle, loving and tolerant, honest and sincere, rather than doctrinaire: "Deceive no one intentionally, not even the non-Jew; quarrel with none, no matter what his belief."[28] And with a conviction, unusual among rabbis, that good intentions are more meritorious than strict observance: "This is the essence of piety: to be lenient in all things rather than adhere to the strict letter of the law."

The quotations are from the book that might be called the key to their creed, the *Sefer Chasidim*, the *Book of the Pious*, a compilation in Hebrew of writings by successive Kalonymos rabbis of the twelfth and thirteenth centuries, notably Samuel ben Kalonymos the Pious, and his son, Judah ben Samuel the Pious, intended as a compendium to correct their lapsed brethren and lay out before them what it meant to be a proper Jew.

> This book is called the *Book of the Pious*. It is a delightful and pleasing work, written for the benefit of God-fearing people.
>
> There are pious men who sincerely love their Creator and want to do His will, but . . . they lack understanding. They do not know what to do, what to avoid and . . . how to do the Creator's will.
>
> . . .
>
> This is the reason that *Sefer Chasidim* was written: so that all who fear God and those returning to their Creator with sincerity may see, know, and understand what they should do and what they should avoid.[29]

In its earliest edition, a manuscript found in Parma, the *Book of the Pious* is an oddly arranged work, disorganised and rather jumbled, showing clear signs of having been assembled from several shorter texts, each being itself a collection of separate passages. Avraham Finkel, its most recent translator, explains, "its teachings and case histories are arranged arbitrarily and follow no discernible pattern. Often a number of unrelated topics are discussed in the same paragraph." The result is not so much a code of ethics and religious observance, or even an exposition of philosophical or mystical ideas—though it contains all of these—but "a tapestry that reflects Jewish life in all its multifaceted variety."

But even if the *Book of the Pious* is far from a complete portrait of medieval Yiddish life on Europe's eastern marches, it does give us some brief and touching glimpses of the reality prevailing in the Slav world, as well as of the difficulties faced by the missionaries now setting out to bring back strayed brothers and sisters to the orthodox Jewish fold.

They were confronted with many whose Jewishness was hardly more than notional, who knew nothing of the Torah, the Five Books of Moses, and its laws, yet whose communities were nonetheless thriving. Orthodox religious teaching had always stressed the importance of adhering to God's word, and held that transgressions were punished by divine retribution in this world too, not only in the next. To the Chassidim, the congregations' success was confirmation that good intentions were more significant than legalistic pedantry: "If, where Jews are ignorant of Torah, they enjoy peace and prosperity, you can be sure that there is no Torah scholar among them to reprove them—or if there is, he does not admonish them. Thus their transgressions are done unintentionally and an inadvertent sin is not like an intentional one." And—an almost Christian thought, this—love conquers all, even sin: "Or maybe they are benevolent and charitable and harbour love and affection for each other." Those who called themselves Jewish frequently had no knowledge of the sacred language: "If God-fearing people who do not understand Hebrew ask how they should pray, tell them to learn to recite the prayers in the language they do understand."

Leaders of synagogue services were not overfamiliar with the contents of the prayer book. They are admonished to rehearse often: "A *chazzen* (cantor) should practise frequently so that the prayers come out fluently." Some who had set themselves up as rabbis here in the East, away from the supervision of their peers, were far from well-qualified: "If you know that some of the rabbis are not God-fearing men, you should direct your enquiries only to the righteous ones." On the other hand some aspects of human nature never change, in spite of the great gulf in mentality between medieval times and ours, not to speak of the centuries' radical transformation of attitudes, beliefs and aspirations: "There are . . . emotions that cause a person to waste time that could be devoted to Torah study: . . . the enjoyment of children, the yearning for women, socialising with friends, amusement and empty chatter." For here, out in the eastern wilderness, a man was a man's man, like any nineteenth-century American cowboy: "There are two things that are on a man's mind day and night: women and money. For these he gives up his life."

Reading between the lines, it is obvious that the Jewish communities shared many beliefs with their gentile compatriots that the strictly orthodox would have written off as pagan superstition and tried to suppress. Yet here too, the Chassidim promoted tolerance and accommodation. As far as folk beliefs were concerned their counsel was to hedge one's bets: "Though one should not believe in superstitions, it is better to be heedful of them." Indeed, one of the passages in the *Sefer Chasidim* warns the reader: "Do not be sceptical and say 'these are not lessons of piety; this smacks of superstition' . . . This book is called *Book of the Pious* and it is exactly what the name implies."

The example and teachings of the *Chasidei Ashkenaz* are not just historical curiosities. They would retain great influence over all the following centuries, in spite of the many transformations, both social and political, that Jewish life in eastern Europe would experience, not to mention the turmoil it would have to survive. In later times the Yiddish-speaking Jews of Poland-Lithuania would still point out with pride that "we are of the lineage of the *Chasidei Ashkenaz*."[30]

Even when the teachings of the *Book of the Pious* were veiled in mystery, they were followed to the letter for centuries. Thus it tells us that "a man should not marry a woman if her name is the same as that of his mother." It does not explain why. More than six hundred years later, the carpenter Mordechai Gebirtig of Cracow (1877–1942), perhaps the greatest of all modern Yiddish bards, wrote a catchy song in which a girl called Soré complains about the succession of unacceptable suitors brought to her by a matchmaker. Finally a young man appears who wins her approval.

> The matchmaker brings me a bridegroom,
> An exception from all the others.
> He name is Vladek. But there's a problem—
> Vladek's mother is also called Soré,

Exactly like me, his bride—
So she won't have me as a daughter-in-law.[31]

It should come as little surprise that the missionary efforts to bring lost Jews back to the Torah should spill over into the Christian and pagan world, and that Judaism should attract proselytes from among the Slavs. Jewish-owned slaves, while they were still legally allowed,[32] had good reason to convert, for they might thereby gain their freedom. But there were also many who found that the spiritual wealth of the Jews, as well as their worldly success, offered greater rewards than their own Christian lifestyle. The *Sefer Chasidim* confirms that this was a far from uncommon occurrence. The authors emphasise that converts should be fully accepted: "The Torah urges us to love converts and cautions us not to wrong them, either monetarily or through words. God loves them more, and they are more precious to Him than Israel." Their origins must never be held against them: "When talking with a convert, a Jew should not mention the convert's former religion, nor speak contemptuously of it." Even mixed marriages should not necessarily be frowned on: "The offspring of a Jew who marries a wife not of the Jewish race, but who is a woman of good heart, modesty and charity, must be preferred to the children of a Jewess by birth who is, however, destitute of the same qualities."

One might imagine that converts to the Jewish religion came only from the dwindling pool of pagans, many of whom continued to resist the Church for several centuries after the official acceptance of the Christian faith by their rulers. However, the many edicts that condemned fraternising between Jews and Christians, that tried to ban the employment of Christian servants by Jews, that forbade Christians from attending Jewish celebrations and religious services, that barred Jews from participating in Christian festivals and weddings, or that—as in the 1267 Synod of Breslau—ordered Jews and Christians to stop living among each other, indicate not only that such promiscuous mixing was commonplace, but that Judaism was actually attracting converts from among the Christian community too:

Since the Polish country still is a young plant in the body of Christendom, the Christian people might the more easily be infected by the superstitions and the depraved mores of the Jews living with them. In order that the Christian faith be more easily and quickly implanted in the heart of the faithful in these regions, we strictly prescribe that the Jews . . . of [the Bishopric of] Gniezno should not indiscriminately dwell among the Christians . . .[33]

Attempts to separate Christians from Jews were largely impossible since the Jewish quarter was sited close to the centre of nearly every medieval Slav town, the Jews having been among the settlements' first founders. However, the antagonism of the Christian prelates combined with that of the German burghers—who were in strenuous competition with the Jews and co-opted every possible ally to fight their rivals' economic power and success—would in later years all too often lead to the Jews' expulsion from any town where either bishop or *Bürgermeister* was able to impose his will.

Yet in spite of such vehement opposition, the attraction of Judaism to the Slavs would continue down the centuries—as shown by regular complaints of Church leaders against Judaising: the tendency to incorporate Jewish values and customs into Christian belief. Some Judaisers were accused of abandoning the Trinity and downgrading Jesus to the status of prophet rather than Son of God. Others apparently celebrated the Sabbath on Saturday, ate only kosher food and even circumcised their male children. Many, protested the Church, eventually became fully Jewish. Catholic and Eastern Orthodox clerics promulgated regular decrees to turn Christians away from this heretical path, but in spite of burning at the stake all whom they caught straying across the forbidden borderline, failed to block it.

A Russian chronicle relates that in 1471, Prince Michael Alexandrovich of Kiev came to Novgorod with several Jewish merchants in his retinue. The Jew Zechariah, "Skhariya Zhidovin," apparently "corrupted to Judaism" two clergymen, Alexis and Denis. In 1479 Grand Prince Ivan Vasilevich (Ivan III) of Moscow visited Novgorod and invited Alexis and Denis to officiate in the church of Moscow. There they influenced many members of the grand prince's court, among them his daughter-in-law Helena.[34]

Judaism went on attracting converts in later centuries too. In Vilna, before the Second World War, the grave of Count Walentyn Polocki, known among Jews as Avrohom ha-Ger, Abraham the Proselyte, who was reputedly denounced by a Jewish tailor and burned at the stake in 1749 on the second day of the festival of Pentecost, Shevuoth, regularly drew crowds of pilgrims on the anniversary of his execution. Sects of Judaisers and Sabbath observers continued to appear in Russia right up to modern times, a notable example being the pacifist Molokans (milk drinkers) founded around the year 1800 by Simeon Uklein, a Bible scholar who introduced much Jewish lore to his sect, and whose disciple Sundukov called for greater association with the Jews. Cruelly repressed by the czars, they emigrated to the Americas en masse. Even in the twentieth century, the religious freedoms introduced after the Constitutional Revolution of 1905 allowed numerous Russian "Sabbatarians of the Jewish faith" to emerge from the shadows and gain legal recognition as semi-Jews. In 1997 an expedition funded by the Amsterdam Jewish Museum found Russian Sabbatarians still living a Jewish life in Azerbaijan.[35] Even in Germany, hard to believe though it may be, official records show that in the decade just before the First World War, some seventy or so citizens per year officially registered their withdrawal from the Christian Churches in order to embrace Judaism.

This steady flow of incomers, which in every generation brought hundreds if not thousands of non-Jews into the Yiddish-speaking communities, not only swelled Jewish numbers in the *heym* but also made the Yiddish-speaking world receptive to many originally foreign ideas, beliefs and customs. Slowly but surely the religion of the eastern European Jews came to adopt a unique Yiddish accent, different from Judaism elsewhere.

Some of the newly adopted ways were merely trivial, like lighting a candle on the anniversary of a parent's death, *yortseyt* in Yiddish, from the German for "time of year," which was first a Catholic German custom. Other new practices were more far-reaching. The tradition, original to the Yiddish-speaking world, that Jewish men must don hats to pray, and that the most pious should keep their heads covered at all times, suggests oriental influence. The habit certainly perplexed the rabbis. A distinguished sixteenth-century Polish authority[36] claimed to know no reason why Jews pray with covered heads, and was particularly irritated that many were unwilling to go bare-headed at any time, "imagining that such is Jewish law, and not merely an instance of superlative scrupulosity."[37]

But one change went even further, transforming the very spirit of Judaism itself, by reversing the relative importance of the two fundamental sources for all Jewish observance. This was something entirely new.

THE SCHOLARLY TRADITION

Debate is at the heart of Judaism. Jews are not only inheritors of a particular divine revelation, but are also a community united around an agreed programme of constantly evolving religious interpretation. Adherence to Judaism is, in this sense, not only a religious but also a political affiliation. To be defined as a Jew, a person must give allegiance not only to the Written Law—the Five Books of Moses, the Prophets and the other Writings which make up the Hebrew Bible—but, more important, to the so-called Oral Law, the authoritative interpretation of Scripture. Those who reject this, like the Karaites of Lithuania and the Crimea, however faithful to the Bible, are not to be counted among the Jews.

The framework of Jewish law was revealed to Moses—so the orthodox believe—some twelve hundred years before the birth of Christ. The keepers of the tradition, the priestly legal experts of the Jerusalem Temple, were killed or dispersed when their city was burned and its defenders crushed by Roman arms in the year 70. Ever since then the full mental resources of generation upon generation of sages have had to be sharply applied to keep the Word of God from being forgotten or its meaning lost. For the task of reading His intentions from the ancient Hebrew text is not easy. The language is so distant that its words and phrases are commonly unclear and confusing, often mysterious, and sometimes downright incomprehensible—"even that which is plain in the Torah is obscure, how much more so that which is already obscure," wrote poet and philosopher Judah Halevy in the twelfth century.

The interpretation of the Torah, the Oral Law, was expounded over centuries in the Talmud (that which is to be taught, or learned), which thus serves as a sort of Jewish constitution. This encyclopaedic work, written in Hebrew and Aramaic, which is really two books: the Mishnah (repetition) and the Gemara (completion), is a collection of law and lore, of precepts, rulings and reminiscences about the days of the Temple, of explanations and interpretations of Holy Scripture, of moral tales and uplifting anecdotes, and of voluminous commentary on all these, that define in sum what is demanded of a person who wishes to call him- or herself a member of the Jewish people. Thus the Talmud is no ordinary law code. It is, in fact, a kind of religious equivalent to the British *Hansard*, or the American *Congressional Record*, an exhaustively detailed account of several hundred years' worth of discussion in the rabbinical academies of Judaea and Babylonia during the first half of the first Christian millennium.

In its standard presentation, as originally devised by the Christian printer Daniel Bomberg for his Venice press—"The feet of his fathers did not stand at the foot of Sinai but . . . he was one of those who spend their money freely in the service of God"[38]—the debate continues on the page.

The text is laid out with a passage from the Mishnah in the centre, the related section of the Gemara above it, commentary by the eleventh-century French Rabbi Solomon ben Isaac, Rashi, on the fold-side, super-commentaries to Rashi's words on the outside, and all around a series of marginal notes and glosses, cross-references and pointers to other works. This richness of connections gives the printed Talmud almost the quality of hypertext, the closest to a page of the World Wide Web that could be devised before the advent of modern technology.

Those centuries of discussion and debate, first in the religious academies of Javneh and Tiberias in the Holy Land as well as Nehardea, Sura, Pumbedita and other Babylonian towns, then later in the seminaries of North Africa, Spain, Italy and France, had developed the technique of biblical exegesis to a fine art. (Which continues to this day, keeping religious practice in step with social change. Otherwise how could a bronze-age text give instruction to a world of aeroplanes, telephones and computer-controlled washing machines?) From the thirteenth century onwards, as the *Chasidei Ashkenaz* were achieving their aim of returning strayed Slav brethren to the fold, the rabbis of Germany and Austria began to pass the scholarly tradition eastwards into Bohemia and the rest of Yiddish territory. New Yiddish-speaking exegetes took up the mantle with alacrity, and by the fifteenth century all the major cities of Poland and Lithuania, Bohemia and Hungary had dedicated to the study of the Talmud one or more religious seminaries, yeshivahs (where one sits), some purpose-built, others making use of pre-existing buildings, some sumptuous and even grandiose in style, others little more than earth-floored wooden shacks.

Soon every Jewish quarter resounded with the chanting of Talmud students and voices strongly raised against each other in religious disputation, for yeshivah study is an oral activity in which different points of view are encouraged to contend aloud. The use of musical tropes to bring out the contending threads of an argument is a basic yeshivah technique. The Talmud itself pours scorn on anyone "who reads without melody and studies without a tune."[39]

The seminaries were open to all who had the mental capacity to benefit from them. The traditional passion for learning among Jews, in an era when religious education was the only form of instruction and nobody went to school to learn arithmetic or geography, led to every family's desire to send at least one son, and preferably all, to a yeshivah. It was the highest aspiration that any Jewish male with intellectual ability could pursue, an ambition assiduously cultivated among participants in the Yiddish civilisation.

The consequences are with us to this day. The traditional teaching methods of the yeshivah are the source of the Jews' reputation for always answering one question with another. It was the dialectical melodic cadences of Talmud study[40] that gave rise to the characteristic up-and-down intonation of the Yiddish language, which is heard in other vernaculars too, even in Israeli Hebrew, where "sing-song" is the description most often applied to Jewish ways of speech.

By the fifteenth or sixteenth century, the proliferation of yeshivahs in the Yiddish-speaking lands had made them the focus of Jewish religious wisdom. No longer were the greatest and most important authorities to be found in Spain or Italy or France. Indeed, soon the new eastern European centres of learning felt confident enough to challenge the old. We read that already in 1234, "Rabbi Jacob Savra of Cracow that sits in Poland, a great scholar and fluent in the entire Talmud, put forward his own opinion against that of the greatest contemporary scholars of Germany and Bohemia."[41] Later Yiddish-speaking scholars like Yom Tov Lipmann Muelhausen, appointed *Judex Judaeorum* (Judge of the Jews) of Prague in 1407, Moses Mintz, rabbi of Posen from 1474, Solomon Luria (1510–74) of Ostrog, Brisk and Lublin and Moses Isserles (*c*.1520–74) of Cracow, rapidly gained international reputations with their writings and pronouncements. In fact, the last-named even had the temerity to take on the definitive summary of Jewish practice, the *Shulkhan Aruch* (the Prepared Table) of Spanish-born Joseph Caro, for which the Polish sage provided a gloss, which he rather audaciously called *ha-Mappah* (the Tablecloth), covering up the sturdy functionality of his older contemporary's work with a decorative overlay that responded to the different spirit, conditions and therefore traditions of eastern Europe.

In the new centres of learning a subtle yet profound change came over the pursuit of religious knowledge. By long tradition students pored over both Torah and Talmud in equal measure. Maimonides taught that "a person should divide his time in learning: a third for Bible, a third for the Mishnah, and a third for Gemara." So did Rabbi Caro. But the yeshivahs of Poland and Lithuania, so different in time, space and mentality from the Judaea of antiquity, now raised the importance of Talmud study well above that of the Torah, quoting the dictum: "Study of the Torah is an accomplishment, yet not an accomplishment; but the study of Oral Law, there is no greater accomplishment than this."[42] Perhaps the rabbis feared that access to the primary source would lead to each man deciding on its meaning for himself and thereby falling into heresy. Or perhaps it was the very different intellectual atmosphere of the European East that led to the change of emphasis. For whatever reason, there was a consensus that "True future salvation . . . can only come through the merit of Talmud study, for Talmud study leads to saintliness and purity . . . while study of Torah does not even produce righteousness . . . Even a little Talmud study creates more fear of Heaven than much Torah study."[43] In the end, Talmud became so much the exclusive subject of study in the yeshivahs of Poland that a Frankfurt scholar wrote in the seventeenth century of rabbis "who have never seen Scripture before in their lives."[44]

There would be a penalty to pay. Without firm grounding in the Hebrew Bible, the rabbis' creative interpretation of the Talmud was set free to soar to ever greater imaginative heights. Flights of fancy replaced pedestrian scholarship as ever more difficult challenges were invented to extricate ever more arcane meanings from the recalcitrant ancient sources, until the entire enterprise, however worthy and well-intentioned, reached well beyond what ordinary folk could comprehend. Elaborate casuistry became the order of the day.

At its most extreme, as introduced into Poland by Jacob Pollack (born between 1460 and 1470), Rabbi of Cracow and founder of its first Talmudic academy, this became a sort of wild and wonderful metaphysical calculus called *pilpul* (pepper), in which unconnected phrases were connected, expressions minutely dissected, words read in reverse, the numerical value of the characters computed and interpreted, and all on the understanding that since divine inspiration had been concealed in the original text, there were no limits to the mental contortions which should be deployed in decoding its hidden meanings. Sophistry and scholarly wordplay would tease out the truth of God's word.

Polish *pilpul* appealed particularly to the eastern rabbis. In vain did the anonymous fifteenth-century treatise from Germany, *The Ways of the Righteous*,[45] or great rabbis like Jehudah Loew of Prague and Jair Chayyim Bacharach of Worms protest against these methods; in vain did Isaiah Halevi Horowitz of Prague describe practitioners of *pilpul* as: "a sect of madmen who say that hairsplitting [*hilluk*] sharpens the wits—those who say this deserve censure." They were merely reflecting the flat-footed, legalistic, Germanic, western outlook, so much despised in the eastern *heym.* In the Slavic Yiddish tradition, a predilection for the esoteric and the unintelligible easily overcame the authority of the prosaic and the mundane.

Rabbis who excelled in the art of *pilpul* publicly vied with each other for glory and social status, not to mention lucrative appointments and political influence—for when government authorities sought out representatives from among the Jews and when communities selected those it wished to represent them, who could be a more obvious choice than the most celebrated rabbi of the locality?

It is a very brief journey from peer-selected spokesman to co-opted member of the ruling establishment. Power soon accrued, of course, to the most agile mentally and the most devious intellectually—not often a prescription for good governance.

Eventually there had to be a reaction. And when it came it would be shattering, splitting the Jews of the Yiddish world into a number of mutually antagonistic fragments, which remain apart to this day. But that was not to happen for half a millennium yet. For most of those centuries the rabbis had unchallenged control of the wheel, as they did their best to steer the Yiddish civilisation round one the most difficult obstacle courses of history: eastern Europe's political consolidation.

7

Political Consolidation

The crisis of the fourteenth century began with the collapse of the Italian banking system, continued with disastrous weather right across the continent, leading to floods, crop failure and famine from the Pyrenees to the Carpathians. Edward II of England could hardly get enough bread to feed his court. In Breslau—like London, Paris and Utrecht—citizens lay dying of hunger in the streets. A Hundred Years' War began between England and France. Scots fought the English under the banners of William Wallace, Robert the Bruce and his son David. Flemish burghers and weavers hacked an armed French garrison to pieces in the grisly event known as the Matins of Brugge and defeated the French cavalry in the Battle of the Golden Spurs—700 pairs were collected from dead French knights. Swiss peasants with pikes skewered the flower of Austrian chivalry on the shores of Lake Ägeri. Breadless Edward II was assassinated, a red-hot iron driven up his anus. Mid-century came the Black Death, the pandemic of plague that slashed Europe's population with shocking speed by perhaps a third. For nearly all of what historian Barbara Tuchman called the "calamitous fourteenth century,"[1] western and central Europe experienced starvation, disease, warfare gotten out of hand, riots, peasant uprisings, flagellant processions and disturbing episodes of dancing mania. "There spread along the Rhine . . . a strange plague . . . in which persons of both sexes, in great crowds . . . continuously danced and sang, inside and outside the churches, until they were so exhausted that they fell to the ground."[2] Jews, lepers, foreigners, priests and whatever lords rioters could get their hands on were massacred; survivors were driven out of town. Economic analyst David Fischer writes that "the people of Europe suffered through the darkest moment in their history . . . This was more than the collapse of the medieval economy. It was the death of medieval civilisation."[3]

Yet as the west of Europe convulsed, the east throve. The small population spread over a huge productive area slowed the spread of disease—the Black Death hardly penetrated Poland at all—and drew the claws of famine. The primitive economy, far less fragile than that of the much more developed western states, flourished, as hunger in the West offered new opportunities to grain producers in the East. The Polish population grew, more than doubling in the course of a hundred years—though, at about twenty people per square mile at the end of the fourteenth century, this was still a little less than in parts of the Congo today.

Hand in hand with growing prosperity came political consolidation. Bohemia, from the end of the twelfth century a kingdom within the Holy Roman Empire, had by the end of the fourteenth brought Moravia and Silesia as well as the Slav-speaking parts of eastern Germany within its jurisdiction. After Casimir the Great had united most of the Polish lands, Poland and Lithuania were joined together under the personal rule of Lithuanian Grand Duke Jogaila (Polish: Jagieło) in 1385, when he converted to Christianity and married the Polish Crown Princess Jadwiga. (Full political union under an elective monarchy would come in 1569.)

By the year 1400 Poland-Lithuania was the largest state in Europe, covering more than half a million square miles, populated by Poles, Lithuanians, Armenians, Germans, Tartars and Jews, following the Christian Orthodox, Armenian, Catholic, Jewish and Muslim faiths. In the course of the following century the German Knights on the coast were brought to heel and the twinned nation extended itself from the Baltic to the Black Sea.

Bearing in mind the meaninglessness of national borders in the premodern period, we should not think of these states as in any way monolithic. As ever, great lords had little lords upon their backs to bite 'em, and little lords had lesser lords. Ownership of the land changed from generation to generation with bewildering arbitrariness. The peasant and townsman had no dealings with the one who sat on a golden throne in a distant capital city, but must sway to the desires and follow the orders of the war-lord whose band of swords- and spearmen held the nearest fortress.

Nevertheless, the official borders of Bohemia and Poland-Lithuania now in the fifteenth century contained almost the whole of the Yiddish homeland, the *heym*, directly connecting the communities of the West with those of the East, from Germany to the Ukraine. In the western lands expulsions, restrictions and physical attacks had turned the Jews' eyes—and feet—eastwards. Though in France and Germany there remained sub-stantial, if insecure, Jewish populations, the eastern lands—largely free, mostly tolerant and principally under the suzerainty of rulers eager to encourage innovation and enterprise—had become the centre of European Jewry. There, the Jewish population, well-established, returned to ortho-doxy by the *Chasidei Ashkenaz*, united by the Yiddish language and a long way down the process of alloying the German with the Slavic-Greek tradi-tions, acted like a magnet to attract a great surge of further immigration from all points of the compass. Newcomers streamed in from an increas-ingly Jew-hostile Germany to the west and from the Tartar Khanates in the south-east, tolerant but backward, economically depressed and frag-menting under the blows of a new Mongol onslaught by followers of Tamerlaine the Great. After 1492 they would be joined by Sephardic com-munities expelled by Ferdinand and Isabella, Catholic monarchs of a de-Judaised Spain. Bohemian, Polish and Lithuanian nobles, anxious not to miss out on the Jewish contribution to the prosperity of their domains, competed with each other to make the conditions of life appealing to Jews. Against the furious opposition of German burghers and Catholic bishops, the lords of the Silesian borderlands gave land to Jews to establish syna-gogues in towns like Jawor (German: Jauer), Olesnica (Oels) and Strze-gom (Striegau).

The little Silesian market town of Strzegom (pronounced, roughly, Shtshegom) lies on the main medieval road coming over the mountains from Prague in Bohemia. In the fourteenth century this was a bustling place of business, of inns, baths, brothels, dance halls, trading bureaux and storage depots, the mule trains' last major overnight halt, about thirty miles to go, before arrival in Breslau, where the ancient north-south Amber Route between the Baltic and Adriatic Seas crossed the east-west Salt Route from Cracow to Regensburg. Here in Strzegom travelling mer-chants would have made their final preparations to put themselves and their goods in best order before tackling the last leg of the journey to the regional capital down the road.

Today this is a rather sleepy minor provincial centre—known only, if at all, for its closeness to Hitler's gross Gross-Rosen concentration camp—and hard to imagine as an important way station on a major thoroughfare. Only a single relic testifies mutely to what the town had once been. Next to a crossroads, in front of a railway viaduct and surrounded by tired, fly-spotted shop vitrines, clapboard roadside kiosks and peeling nineteenth-century apartment buildings, stands isolated a chunky red-brick construction, sole local survivor of six hundred years of turbulent history. A long time ago this was Strzegom's synagogue.

Medieval Silesia, mostly populated by Slavs but with a large and growing German minority, was an area over which both Bohemian and Polish royal houses had long disputed for control, until the province fell under the permanent control of Prague in 1335. But the real rulers were the proliferating number of local dukes. In 1370 one of these, Bolko (Bolesław) II, known as "The Small," whose territory and writ ran—in theory—all the way from his palace in Schweidnitz (Świdnica) as far as the suburbs of Berlin, gave a plot of land in Strzegom to the Jews, to establish a place to pray.

They were not alone. Silesia—at just under 8,000 square miles a little smaller than Wales—had even back then significant communities in Beuthen, Breslau, Bunzlau, Glogau, Goldberg, Grollkau, Haynau, Hirschberg, Kosel, Löwenburg, Münsterburg, Namslau, Neumarkt, Nimptsch, Ohlau, Oppeln, Potschkau, Preisketscham, Ratibor, Reichenbach, Schweidnitz, Strehlen, Trebnitz, Troppau and more.[4] (I will spare you the Polish equivalents.) Breslau, the province's main city, had at least three synagogues under the charge of a rabbi addressed by the authorities as *Episcopus Judaeorum*, Supervisor of the Jews. In 1351, the position was held by a Rabbi Yitzchak. A synagogue building still stands in Oleśnica, while just up the road from Strzegom, at Jawor, the Duchess Augusta went one better than Duke Bolko when in 1420 she transferred a Catholic church to the Jews for conversion to their own use—less, I imagine, as a pro-Semitic gesture, than as a blow in the struggle then beginning between Catholicism and a rising tide of Christian nonconformism.

Unfortunately Bolko the Small's good intentions were undone in 1454 by this same religious conflict, when the Jews were expelled from Strzegom as collateral damage of papal envoy Saint (*sic*) John of Capistrano's bloody and brutal campaign to suppress heresy, which brought destruction on the heads of all non-Catholics. The synagogue was reconsecrated for Christian use and dedicated to St. Barbara, protector against storm, lightning and fire—an appropriate choice for a brick building in a town otherwise constructed mainly of wood and much given to rioting and arson.

The fact that the synagogue is not built of stone confirms that granite quarrying had yet to begin in the nearby hills, though that is a major local industry today—the Berlin Reichstag was built of Strzegom granite—and is a resource elsewhere associated with Yiddish enterprise, as at Olkusz near Cracow, where in 1658 the Jew Marek Nekel was granted the first concession. It looks nothing like the usual form of a synagogue, or even much like a church, notwithstanding the small cross now perched atop the summit at the front. What it most resembles is a miniature castle with a rectangular keep, a rounded apse at the rear end, thick walls pierced by arrow slits and a large arched window above the sturdy iron-bound door at the top of the entrance steps, straddled by two rather phallic hexagonal conical-roofed towers—one of them extended, in the course of conversion to a church, as if with an erection. In the same period the French peasantry were converting their stone churches into castles, and turning the bells from summoning worshippers to prayer, from marking birth, marriage and death, to sounding a warning if marauders approached their village.[5] In the western Slav lands, the very word for church, *kostel* in Czech and *kościół* in Polish, derive from the Latin *castellum*, a little fortress. The Strzegom synagogue too must have been built to double as a refuge for the community in troubled times.

It would have meant a tight squeeze for the entire community to shelter behind the synagogue's thick brick walls. This is a fairly small building, capable of holding a congregation of at most a hundred or so—men only, at this time in history. The community, though influential enough to be given building land, cannot have been all that numerous, in contrast to other towns, like Cheb (Eger) further west in Bohemia, where even in the fourteenth century Jews made up a quarter of the townspeople. Its location points us towards the heart of the Jewish quarter, not far from the river bank and just round the corner from the market square.

Had you walked the narrow cobbled medieval streets within earshot of the commercial hubbub early in the fifteenth century, you would have passed rickety wooden tenements closely packed together as if for mutual support, black-and-white timber-built merchants' trading halls and warehouses, the *mikveh* or bathhouse—essential in an age when ordinary homes had no sanitary arrangements—and the hospital. You would have caught a whiff of the beery tang from the Jewish inn funded by the community, where travellers might lodge for free—brewing had long been an established tradition in this part of the Slav world—and smelled the rich aromas wafting from the communal cookhouse in which families left their Sabbath meal to simmer over Friday night—the dish of meat, beans and grains called *cholent*, ultimately from the Latin *calentem* (kept warm), about the only dish totally unique to Yiddish cuisine, though according to cookery writer Claudia Roden, it perhaps developed from the Mediterranean *cassoulet*.[6] The community must also have owned a plot for Jewish burial, though this would have lain outside the town walls.

Competing with the cries of street traders and market stallholders, the warning curses of porters and carters, the work songs of labourers, you would undoubtedly also have heard the children chanting their lessons in the private *cheder*, or the communally-funded *Talmud-Torah*, the only schools in the whole town, attended by every Jewish boy above the age of three or four, where they learned to read and write Hebrew, and were inducted into the study of Holy Scripture.

The significance of these schools can hardly be overestimated. In an age when almost everyone else was illiterate, in places where even aristocrats had difficulty in signing their own names, obligatory universal schooling for Jewish boys raised the Yiddish speakers' cultural level far above that of their gentile contemporaries. Even more so when, in later centuries, the syllabus was extended to include literacy in Yiddish. In the sixteenth century the communal ordinances of Cracow stipulated that each school appoint a *shrayber* (scribe) to teach all children "to write the sounds of the language that we speak." Other subjects too, like arithmetic, geography, and a grounding in the national language of their neighbours, crept into the curriculum. In Yiddish-speaking society, unlike the Christian feudal world, any boy with intelligence, ability and the necessary *sits-fleysh* (patient perseverance), no matter how humble or degraded his origins, could aspire to rise to intellectual eminence and rabbinical respectability.

And you could hardly have missed the sounds of musical jollity emanating from the *Tantshoys* or *Shpilhoys*, the dance hall,[7] where celebrations and receptions were held. Sabbath afternoon dances were a popular activity among young people in spite of the insistent Jewish prohibition on mixed dancing, derived from the line in the Bible that runs: "though hand join in hand, the wicked shall not be unpunished"[8] and the many jokes on the subject (Why does Judaism forbid premarital sex? Because it might lead to mixed dancing). Regular informal gatherings were held outside; the *Tantshoys* building itself was reserved mainly for special occasions like circumcisions, barmitzvahs and marriages. But wedding festivities lasted a week or more. "The seven days' wedding feast," says Israel Abrahams in *Jewish Life in the Middle Ages*,[9] "was marked by incessant musical performances, which not even the Sabbath day itself interrupted . . . Christian musicians were employed for that purpose and Christian guests were entertained." So even with a Jewish community of only a hundred or so, the *Tantshoys* would rarely have been left dark and empty for long, but would have resounded regularly with the strains of *der Mayen Tants* (the May dance), *der Umgeyender Tants* (a Circle dance), *der Shpring Tants* (a jumping dance), *der Fish Tants* (the Fish dance), *der Totentants* (Dead Man's dance), *Doktor Foysts Tants* (Doctor Faustus's dance) and *der Alter Kakers Tants* (the Old Farts' dance). Solomon Luria, known as the Maharshal,[10] one of the great rabbinical authorities of Poland, strongly disapproved: "I condemn the youth who frequent dance halls even if the music is furnished by Gentile musicians. Moreover, those who participate in these revelries are doomed to mental and physical degeneration. For at such boisterous gatherings they imbibe freely and indulge in sexual indecencies."[11]

What did the music played for these dances sound like? Probably not much like the klezmer music we know today, which has much more recent roots and links with the music of the Balkans and the Greek islands. One might imagine that, since Jewish musicians also played for Christian clients, and Christian musicians played for the Jews on Sabbaths and holidays, the tunes and rhythms heard in the *Tantshoys* were much the same as those to which surrounding gentiles made merry. Yet we have evidence that the playing of Jewish bands was even then spiced with the exotic flavour of strange scales and unfamiliar rhythms.

We even have a piece of music—of sorts. The sixteenth-century Nuremberg-based composer Hans Neusiedler wrote down a dance tune that he heard played by a Jewish band at a royal wedding. Yet so weird is the tune that the composition—he called it *Judentanz* (Jews' dance)—has been taken for parody rather than accurate transcription. In the following century the Christian musicians' guild of Prague complained that Jewish instrumentalists "keep neither time nor beat, and mockingly deprive noble and sweet music of its dignity."[12] Obvious professional rivalry aside, the implication is that the music of the Yiddish Jews was unlike that of their gentile neighbours. Perhaps Jewish musicians, members of the working lower orders after all, remained close to their eastern Slavic and Turkic musical roots, and resisted the western German Baroque style, which was then the coming fashion among the middle and upper classes.

Many of Silesia's Jews were poor immigrants from further east. Well into the 1400s medieval Strzegom's streets and alleyways would have still echoed with the West Slavonic language that was only just beginning to separate into Czech and Polish flavours. But you would also have caught a word or two of the Judaeo-German that would one day be called Yiddish, though mostly from the mouths of the wealthier and better educated. As in today's England, language was a marker of social class.

For it is far too simple to speak baldly of a Jewish community. There were as many striking differences among Jews as there were among the surrounding gentiles—in the Jews' case between ethnic backgrounds: German and Slavic-Greek-Turkic; between social classes: diplomats, bankers, physicians and dealers in bulk commodities on the one hand, and petty traders, pedlars, artisans, musicians, labourers and servants on the other; between levels of wealth or the lack of it; between employment or lack of that too. Though there may not have been quite the contrast to be found in Christian society between the noble and the pauper, there were always glaring disparities.

LANDOWNERS, MERCHANTS, ARTISANS, SERVANTS

Some Jews, early pioneers, had long been farmers—not bound peasants but free yeomen, since they were not attached to their land by bonds of servitude. "The Jews are not tied to any particular place as gentiles are; for they are regarded as impoverished freemen who have not been sold into slavery," wrote Me'ir of Rothenburg in the thirteenth century. Nevertheless in the 1220s Jewish tillers of the soil on the estates of Count Henryk I near Bytom in Silesia had to pay a tithe of their produce to the bishop of Breslau, just like their Christian neighbours. Some among them even owned entire landed properties together with the tenants. In the year 1200 the Silesian village of Sokolników had already belonged to the Jews Joseph and Khaskel.[13] The Bohemian villages of Tynice and Sokohrice to the west of Strzegom were in the early Middle Ages known to be owned and managed by Jews, as was the town of Mały Tiniec near Cracow to the east.

But by the year 1400 or so most of the Jewish population would avoid any too permanent attachment to a particular patch of earth. Expulsions from so many places in west and central Europe had been a hard lesson in the unwisdom of tying up assets as immovable property, which became a near total loss if—or rather when—the owner was forced to leave at sword point. After the Jews were driven out of France in 1306, fifty large and fine formerly Jewish stone-built houses in the city centre of Narbonne were acquired by a French landlord as a job lot from the royal receiver for less than 80 livres each (perhaps £15 sterling). After the Spanish expulsion of 1492, Andres Bernaldez, chaplain to the archbishop of Seville, wrote that anyone could have a Jewish vineyard for the price of a piece of cloth.[14]

Caution was wise in Silesia. It was not only the Strzegom community that was to be expelled in the course of the religious upheavals of the fifteenth century. Jews from almost every town in this disputed borderland between Bohemia and Poland found themselves refugees, heading east along the trails towards the Polish interior, when all distinctions between Jews—landowners, merchants, artisans, domestic servants and the unemployed—were levelled by their common fate.

Jewish inequality was, in any case, always rather different in kind from that prevailing among the gentiles. Instead, it resembled a kind of inverted version of the surrounding feudal system. Among Christian Slavs the movement of wealth was upwards, from the worse-off to the better-off, from the base of the social pyramid towards its summit. Riches were sweated from the soil by the multitude of peasants and passed upwards to swell the coffers of the noble few. Among the Jews, the movement of money was in the opposite direction, flowing from the prosperous, middle-class, Yiddish-speaking merchant minority, growing wealthy from the export trade—the entrepreneurs of Cracow, Lemberg and Lublin, men like Izaak Brodawka of Brest, Eleazar Abramovitch of Tykocin and Aron Izraelovitch of Grodno—down to the mass of the Jewish Slavic working class who serviced their social superiors' religious and existential needs: the kosher butcher, the matzo baker, the Sabbath candlestick maker, the vintner, the dyer, the weaver, the tailor, the musician and the man who drove the mule cart. (The important twentieth-century Polish anthropologist and ethnographer Jan Czekanowski detected traces of this ethnic class distinction, between a Slavic-Turkic-origin working class and a German-origin business class, in pre-Second World War studies of the Jewish population of Lvov.)[15] Thus where the Christian nobility depended on, exploited and was sustained by its peasants and serfs, the Jewish proletariat depended on, exploited and was maintained by its own bourgeoisie.

On these foundations an entire economic world was constructed. The meeting of West and East that had begun in cities like Regensburg and had continued with the migration of the German speakers across the Slav world imbued the new mixed community with the vigour of the hybrid. Despite the many setbacks, despite executions, expulsions and exclusions—or perhaps because of them, in a stubborn refusal to be bowed—a wave of energy, optimism and unquenchable entrepreneurial spirit lifted the communities and sowed them liberally across the Slav world to grow with the country, as the skills they had honed in servicing Jewish religious needs were directed outwards to provide for the surrounding peoples, expanding their markets to include a gentile clientele and stimulating economic growth in new industries and novel applications.

Such Jewish success was greatly resented by the Church, which was in competition with Judaism for the souls of the people, and by the Christian townsmen who vied with the Jews for worldly profit. Wherever they could, the two combined forces to drive out their rivals. Yet experience had already shown that expelling the Jews resulted in little commercial improvement. Quite the contrary, in fact. Instead of expanding markets delivering increasing profit to German monopolists, trade dwindled and everyone became poorer. Jewish bankers, it had turned out to everyone's surprise, were less rapacious than local moneylenders, Genoese, Venetian and Lombard bankers, and even the clergy. St. Bernard of Clairvaux (*c.*1090–1153), founder of the Cistercian monastic order, had long since excoriated "those Christian moneylenders, if they can be called Christian, who, where there are no Jews, act, I grieve to say, in a manner worse than any Jew."[16] In 1290, the very year of the expulsion of the Jews from England, a jury in Norwich had found that "John the Chaplain is an excessive usurer" and the abbot of Bristol was accused of taking from a poor man "more than a hundred per cent of usury, which even civil law forbids to all men."[17]

As a result, wherever the Jews were expelled from the cities, towns, duchies and principalities of central Europe, on the instructions of rulers pressurised by the Church, egged on by the Jews' competitors or driven by personal animosity, the outcasts were almost invariably invited to return within a few years; their contribution was simply too valuable to be lost. After the Black Death massacres in 1349 Augsburg's Jews were expelled and excluded and then, in the very next year, the emperor granted the request of the bishop, no less, to readmit them. When the 300 Jewish families were again driven out in 1439 on the insistence of the burghers, the town council had to pay Albert II of Austria 900 gulden in compensation.

(The expelled Jews were, however, encouraged to enter the city during the day for business and also granted the right of asylum in times of war.) They were excluded from the Bavarian city of Aschaffenburg in 1349, readmitted in 1359 and granted protection by the archbishop of Mainz in 1384. Jews were expelled from Speyer in 1405, readmitted in 1421, banished again in 1430 and begged to return in 1434.

Given the fragmented jurisdiction between dukes, counts and lords, those driven out did not usually have to travel far to set up new homes. In Regensburg it was to the far side of the river. In other cities—in those days conurbations were hardly ever more than a mile across and mostly rather less—it was to the suburbs or the neighbouring baronage. When Cracow, for example, expelled its Jewish community at the end of the fifteenth century, they moved to Kazimierz, which is about the length of a football pitch from the site of Cracow's walls. Only occasionally were Jews thrown out of entire provinces or countries. They were expelled from the whole of Lithuania in 1495, apparently at the whim of its Grand Duke Alexander, and resettled themselves just over the border with Poland. When Alexander became king of Poland in 1503, he mysteriously changed his mind and asked them to return, ordering that their houses, lands, synagogues and cemeteries be restored to them, and their old debts repaid. A new charter of privileges invited them to live throughout Lithuania as before, and commanded the vice-regent to ensure that they were restored to the enjoyment of their former property and helped to collect all outstanding monies.

The crucial role of the Jews was made explicit in Poland-Lithuania with the emergence of a fivefold division of society, the so-called "estates" of the realm, separate and exclusive collectives each with its own legally enforced and jealously guarded rights and duties: the nobles, the clergy, the burghers, the Jews and the peasants (though these last had few rights, only duties). Norman Davies explains in *God's Playground* that:

> membership of an estate was principally determined by a person's birth, and movement between one estate and another was strewn with obstacles. The process whereby the clergy and the nobility reinforced their privileges in the country as a whole was matched by the actions of the Guilds in the cities. It was as difficult for a burgher to become a nobleman, as it was for a Jew to aspire to the rights of a burgher . . . or for a peasant to engage in the activities that occupied Jews.[18]

In the eyes of the rulers, the Jews' estate, like the other social groups, needed representation, if for no nobler purpose than the efficient and effective extraction of taxes. It was not appropriate for the local lord or prince of the Church to speak for the Jews within his domain or diocese. The Jewish communities must be answerable for themselves.

Other estates had their own forms of representation. The nobles had their *Sejm*, their parliament, the clergy were represented by the princes of the Church, the burghers by the municipalities, only the peasants remained mute. The question for the king was—to paraphrase Henry Kissinger's well-known barb about Europe—"When I need to talk to the Jews, whom do I call?"

An obvious answer was to light upon the only known authority figures within the communities—the rabbis. Thinking, mistakenly, that these were in some sense like priests of the Church, whose hierarchy exercised power in lands owned by the Church, rabbinical specialists in the interpretation of religious law were now elevated to positions of secular power over their co-religionists: *Episcopi Judaeorum*, Supervisors of the Jews. Since the Jewish estate governed itself under its own religious law, there must have seemed as good a reason to put rabbis in charge of their society as there is for modern nations to turn to lawyers for their presidents or prime ministers. However, legal experts are acceptable as politicians where there exist checks and balances to their power, and where the legal code has democratic legitimacy. This was no more the case in medieval Jewish Poland than it is in modern Islamic Iran.

The total authority that rabbis would come to exercise over the everyday lives of their congregations, with none of the restrictions to their power that even Christian lords had to recognise, would in later years come to be strongly resented. They had the right to excommunicate, to expel, to imprison, to order physical punishment and even to execute. Appealing to the gentile authorities against the rabbis' rulings risked appalling sanctions. As late as 1674 the Jewish Council of Konice in Moravia ordered, "It is the duty of every Jew to shatter the slanderers and those who burden the princes with their lies and to cut off their hands and their feet," though this was, one hopes, intended as a metaphor. In Poland rabbis were not permitted to issue sentences of death though, according to Moses Isserles,[19] Rabbi Solomon Luria sanctioned the lynching of informers—by which was meant those who allowed Jewish affairs to come to the attention of the civil power. Local tradition in Posen remembers the last execution of an informer at the end of the eighteenth century.[20]

King Casimir tried appointing two chief rabbis, one for the Polish, the other for the Lithuanian half of his domains. This proved unsatisfactory, however, as the Jews refused to accept leaders imposed on them from above by gentile authority. Each community insisted on retaining the management committee, the Kahal, in Yiddish *Kehile*—pronounced "*ke-hi-leh*" and short for *Kehillah Kedoshah*, Holy Community—that had administered its affairs since its original establishment centuries before. In small towns like Strzegom the *Kehile* had but a single chief functionary, usually known as the *parnas* (Hebrew for Leader). Travel the trunk road to Cracow, however, or any other great city and you would have found an entire bureaucracy of chiefs (*roshim*), aldermen (*parnasim*), trustees (*ne'e-manim*), tax assessors (*shamma'im*), tax collectors (*gabba'ei ha-mas*), diplomats (*shtadlanim*), members of the board of morality (*berurei averah*), as well as supervisors (*gabba'im*) of the synagogue, cemetery, school and a host of others. This being the Middle Ages, these were by no means democratic institutions, as the *Encyclopaedia Judaica* makes plain: "There was a patrician tendency to limit election rights . . . to make the ruling circle a closed and self-perpetuating one. Membership of this ruling class depended on riches, learning, and patrician descent, in most cases a combination of all three."

The Kahals vied with each other furiously, particularly over shares of the tax burden, fought strongly against any artisan and craft association unauthorised by themselves, and indeed guarded the locality jealously against outsiders who might offer competition to those already established. The Ban on Settlement (*kherem ha-yishuv*) was rigorously imposed and most Jewish communities became closed to newcomers. Even refugees were sometimes denied asylum.

Communities were governed according to Jewish law, but its precise interpretation was a matter of local custom and preference and could thus vary in its prescriptions and demands from place to place. Long-drawn-out legal disputes between Kahals regularly arose, quarrels that not infrequently boiled over into violence and threatened to break up the Yiddish-speaking world. The leaders soon realised that some form of national congress was sorely needed, where representatives from all communities could meet together to iron out their differences, cement agreements and ensure the consistency of Jewish rulings right across the territory. But how and where?

All over the *heym* regular fairs were held, as at Lemberg and Lublin, where Yiddish speakers from every quarter gathered to trade, do business, exchange news—and to meet prospective marriage partners: "To the fairs held at Lemberg and Lublin come young students and their teachers in shoals. He who has a son or daughter to marry journeys to the fair and there makes a match, for everyone finds his like and his suit. At every fair hundreds of matches are made, sometimes thousands."[21] What more suitable location could there be for community leaders to hold regular meetings and match their principles of governance?

By the early 1500s, a month-long convocation of *Kehile* elders and rabbis at Lublin's Candlemass Fair in February had become a regular yearly fixture, perhaps evolved from the "pie-powder" (i.e. dusty-footed) courts that traditionally dispensed summary justice among merchants and visitors at markets. Later, a second annual meeting at the fair in Yaroslav just before the autumn High Holidays was added to the calendar—though the venue was for a time moved some ten miles out of town when Yaroslav proved to be, according to one surviving proclamation, "a pernicious and dangerous place," though the text gives no details of what had gone amiss.

In time these fairground meetings developed into sessions of what was called the Council of the Lands (Hebrew: *Va'ad Aratzoth*, Yiddish: *Vaad Aratsoys*), most often of the Four Lands (Great Poland with its capital at Posen, Little Poland centred on Cracow, Red Ruthenia around Lemberg, and Volhynia, now north-west Ukraine), sometimes of Five (the four plus Lithuania), but sometimes of only Three (Poland, Lithuania and Red Ruthenia). One representative from each *Kehile* attended, plus six of the leading rabbis of the day. Around 730 communities were eventually represented, with an elected president at their head. Lithuania broke away in 1623 to set up its own council, the *Vaad Medinas Litoh*.

Here were the supreme legislative and administrative bodies of the Yiddish civilisation. Like national parliaments everywhere, they concerned themselves with defining the law, regulating taxation and maintaining relations with the ruling monarch. They arbitrated on boundary disputes, regulated the rabbinical courts, prescribed the curriculums of schools and seminaries, acted as censor of published books—the Council of the Three Lands authorised the printing of the Talmud for use in all schools in 1559—and adjudicated on disputes over property and leases. The Councils also delivered edicts on social matters. In 1607, for example, the Council of the Four Lands proclaimed that Jews must not drink at inns where Christians congregate, on penalty of being struck off the list of reputable members of the community, that Jewish costumes should show modesty and moderation and differ in cut from those of Christians, and that the chastity of women living among Christians in villages must be safeguarded. The *Vaads* acted as the highest Jewish legal Court of Appeal, sent their agents to attend the Polish parliament, the *Sejm*—particularly the so-called Coronation *Sejm*, held upon the enthronement of a new monarch, when charters of Jewish liberties had to be reconfirmed—and made direct appeals where necessary to the king himself. In sum, as a contemporary annalist observed,

> The representatives of the four lands resembled the Sanhedrin in the session chamber in the Temple of Jerusalem. They had jurisdiction over all the Jews of the kingdom of Poland, with power to issue injunctions and binding decisions and to impose penalties at their discretion. Every difficult case was submitted to them for trial.[22]

Legal judgements were written in Hebrew, while proclamations were composed in Yiddish, to be read out in all synagogues. Both were recorded in a record book, the *pinkes* (from the Greek *pinax*, a wax writing tablet). This, for example, from 1671:

> The Council of the Four Lands reports that a violent quarrel having arisen which almost ruined the whole district [of Chelm] and—which God forbid—might have harmed the remnant of Israel and involved the loss of thousands, the Council of the Four Lands has taken upon itself the task of punishing those who initiated the quarrel or subsequently participated in it, whose names, out of respect for their positions, are withheld . . .
>
> The Council of the Four Lands hereby fully authorises the leaders of the communities and districts to prosecute any persons so intriguing and offending, and to punish them with the ban, with fines, or with imprisonment . . . Such persons should never be nominated to any office in any community or district.[23]

Poles referred to the Council of the Lands as the Jewish Congress, *Congressus Judaicus.* It was formally recognised by King Sigismund in 1533 when he characterised one of its decisions in a private case as a decision of the "Supreme Court for the Jews," thereby implicitly recognising the Yiddish Jews not just as a separate estate but as a semi-independent nationality. Even Jews outside Poland, like some communities in Germany, gave partial recognition to its authority.

Of course, like the Kahals themselves, of whose representatives it was composed, the Council of the Lands was a far from democratic institution. The same self-appointed oligarchy who ran the communities ruled the roost in the *Vaad* too. To be sure they were elected, but only by the great and the good—in total no more than about one per cent of Polish-Lithuanian Jews were eligible to vote. Whenever disputes arose between ordinary community members and their leaders, the allegiance of the Council was never in doubt. Having nothing but contempt for what it characterised as "the rabble in the streets and markets, who make light of the opinions of their betters," it issued ever harsher ordinances against those guilty of what it condemned as sedition and scorn. It was, the *Vaad* decreed, the duty of every community leader to deter these offenders with the severest penalties, "reaching even to the gates of death."[24]

AT THE JEWISH INN

Thus in spite of the ups and downs of history, and in the teeth of energetic opposition from both religious and commercial rivals, an autonomous Yiddish-speaking civilisation had crystallised within the interstices of Christian Slav society like veins of precious metal branching out through mother rock. In the early 1400s the congregation of Strzegom's fortified synagogue could look out from their little town towards a Slav world generously planted with communities much like theirs, stretching all the way from Prague in the south-west to Cracow, Przemyśl and Kiev in the south-east, to Grodno and Vilna in the north-east. The promise of Jewish opportunity in the new territories had been amply fulfilled, the people had become fruitful and multiplied mightily. In many places, particularly in important towns like Prague, Cracow, Grodno and Kiev, the Yiddish-speaking community now made up a significant proportion of the citizenry, with land, houses, synagogues and cemeteries.

By the year 1400 Vilna's Jewish quarter occupied a full fifth of the urban area. In Płock, north-west of Warsaw, customs lists mention some thirty local Jewish merchants, including importers of textiles, of metal utensils, of perfumes and spices, and exporters of grain, cattle, hides and timber, dealing as far afield as Breslau, Leipzig and even Nuremberg. Among artisans and craftsmen there are recorded weavers, glaziers, bakers, butchers, shoemakers, furriers, tailors, and even a blacksmith who made swords. A little later, revenue lists refer to Jews who paid taxes on fields around the town, and Jews who owned flocks of sheep and herds of cattle. In 1561 Joseph the Physician was the Płock community's *parnas*.

Thus any Strzegomers who ventured out of town along the old, well-trodden road towards Breslau, seat of the Bohemian governor of the province, crossed the River Oder at the great livestock market at Oppeln, travelled on past the massed breweries of Gleiwitz to reach the Polish capital of Cracow, would find ample confirmation of the growth and prosperity of their fellow communities.

One can imagine them stopping for the night at an inn like the huge village tavern preserved in the remarkable open-air ethnographic museum at Sanok in south-east Poland: an enormous construction, all of wood—shingles on the roof, sidings of long planks cladding a giant timber frame the size of an aircraft hangar. In the centre: the taproom; to one side: the innkeeper's lodgings; to the other: some six or eight guest rooms; at the back: a huge drive-in hall where loaded carts and carriages could be kept secure overnight behind heavily barred doors and under armed guard; the upper storey under the high-peaked roof—accessible only by a ladder leading to a loading window in the gable end surmounted by a winch—given over to storage of fuel, animal fodder and other bulk supplies.

An inn like this would almost invariably have been a Jewish enterprise. The overland routes between central and eastern Europe had become better trodden in the centuries since the turn of the first millennium. Most Jewish voyagers were now no longer migrants but diplomats, merchants, scholars and businessmen on their regular rounds between courts and fairs, travelling without cooking equipment and other domestic possessions. In response to their needs, many of the sparsely distributed inns along the trails had installed a lockable "Jewish cupboard" somewhere on the premises, in which religiously observant traders would keep their own supplies, as well as ritually clean cooking utensils, stored safely against their next arrival. In those feudal times most people had neither cause nor permission to leave their homes, and in any case to go on a journey was to take a risk that might well prove fatal, an activity definitely not to be undertaken lightly by those who had no pressing need to move about. But for some occupations it was a necessary gamble, and Jewish wayfarers proceeding from place to place, village to village, city to city, must have made up a high percentage of those likely to knock late at night on a wayside hostel's door. It did not take much to recognise that here was an opportunity for networks of Jewish inns to be established by enterprising souls who would not, of course, restrict themselves to a solely Jewish clientele.

Winemaking had been an important Jewish occupation from earliest times, as kosher wine is needed for religious services and domestic ceremonies. The greatest of eleventh-century Talmudic scholars, Rabbi Solomon ben Isaac, Rashi of Troyes in France, had made his living as a wine producer and merchant, having learned the trade from his religious teacher who, as he wrote, used to sell "from his barrel to the gentile."[25]

An understanding of the techniques of fermentation led Jews, in northern grapeless climes, to beer brewing. In the thirteenth century, Rabbi Meir of Rothenburg was even asked whether the *Kiddush*, the blessing made over wine that refers to "the fruit of the vine," could be pronounced over beer instead. He rather stuffily told his questioner not to be so daft:

> There is no wine in Westphalia, but in all other principalities there is abundant wine; and there is wine in your city throughout the year. It seems to me that you personally drink mostly wine; and if at the end of the year there is some dearth of wine you will find it in your neighbourhood . . . Certainly you know that it is proper to recite *Kiddush* over wine.[26]

Close relations with the Arab world in Spain had early on introduced western Jews to the secrets of distillation. The result when they moved east into the Slav world was vodka. Though patriotic nineteenth-century Russian writers attribute the introduction of vodka—"that pernicious drink"—to the Genoese, it is far more likely that the archetypal Slav tipple was actually first introduced into these parts by Jews coming from the West.

The professions of innkeeping, brewing and distilling, natural bedfellows, combined to create the Jewish tavern, an institution that quickly became familiar all over the Yiddish *heym*, starting a long tradition that began early and continued to thrive, one way or another, until the Nazi extermination. In later years vodka manufacture became a virtual Jewish monopoly and village inns were leased almost exclusively to Jewish publicans. Campaigners attacked the Jews long and loud for encouraging the poor Slav peasantry to drunkenness, perhaps not entirely without justice; an old Yiddish nursery rhyme teaches: *Shicker iz a goy, trinken muss er*— The gentile is a soak, he has to drink. (Yet now that the Jewish tavern keepers are all gone, is there any sign that Poles and Russians imbibe any less copiously? Not in my experience.)

Even today, kosher spirits are market leaders in twenty-first-century eastern Europe and Yiddish surnames confirm the story: Brenner (distiller), Bronfen (brandy), and thus Bronfman (brandy-man) and Bronfenbrenner (brandy distiller) are common from Queens, New York, to Queensland, Australia. The Seagram Company of the United States, according to the *Encyclopaedia Britannica* the largest producer and marketer of distilled spirits in the world, was founded by Samuel, one of the Bronfman family, in 1928.

Had you looked around the dark and smoky bar room of a Jewish inn, smelling of beer, kosher cooking, unwashed bodies and clothes, on any of the trade routes that closely criss-crossed the German-Bohemian-Polish-Lithuanian lands throughout the central centuries of the second Christian millennium, your eyes would have fallen across an assortment of types representing all Yiddish society, comprising a whole gamut of businessmen, craftsmen, emissaries, labourers, physicians and religious functionaries with their clerks, servants and hangers-on, men whose activities called on them to journey between the villages and urban centres of their world. Many of these would have been plying trades with their origins in the needs of the Jewish community. Just as the need for kosher wine for religious use gave rise to the Jewish interest in alcohol production, so the need for guaranteed kosher clothing—without the forbidden mixture of different fibres—led to the practice of tailoring; the need for bread over which to say blessings, to milling and baking, while the universality of wedding and other celebrations cued the demand for Jewish musicians and entertainers. Other specialists, like glaziers, were continuing a long Jewish tradition without obvious religious motive—glassmaking had originally come from the East and may well have been first brought to central Europe by Greek and Khazar Jews before the turn of the millennium. Later Polish rulers encouraged Yiddish-speaking glassmakers to set up factories in Oppeln, Breslau, Kruszwica and Miedzyrzecz.

Many of these trades were by their nature peripatetic, the craft workers travelling from village to village and living a style of life that would continue wherever the feudal system, with its ban on leaving the land, hung on to near the present day. Before the First World War, tailoring the clothes of country people in Russia's Baltic provinces was still undertaken by travelling craftsmen, Jews and gypsies in the main, who were obliged to combine the needlework trade with playing the violin for village fêtes—in those parts long a traditional combination.

Sitting in the Jewish inn, you would have quickly observed that nobody became rich from making clothes or baking bread. The mass-production methods that would arrive with mechanisation and would make a millionaire of Bavarian Löb (Levi) Strauss, the fashion industry that would make Calvin Klein from the Bronx an international star, were still far in the future. Other religious needs did, however, lead Jews to occupations which might promise a fortune. The demand for animals that conformed to the complicated rules of ritual purity led to stockbreeding and cattle raising, from which many grew extremely wealthy. Salt is required to render meat kosher, ritually fit to eat (unless it be roasted over an open flame). So it is not surprising that from an early date European Jews were involved in its mining and preparation. In the tenth century Ibrahim Ibn Ya'qub had already mentioned Jews operating a salt mine in Halle in Germany. In the fourteenth century the Polish salt mines at Bochnia and Wieliczka near Cracow were under Jewish management. In 1452 King Casimir Jagiełło entrusted to the Jew Natko the salt mines of Drohobych, on account of his "industry and wisdom, so that thanks to his ability and industry we shall bring in more income to our treasury."

Indeed, mining of all kinds was a particular Jewish speciality, from the twelfth century when Jews were involved in tin extraction in Cornwall in England, through the sixteenth when Queen Elizabeth's principal secretary, Francis Walsingham, invited Joachim Gaunse to come to England from Prague and reorganise the "makeing of Copper, vitriall, and Coppris, and smeltinge of Copper and leade ures"[27] first in Keswick in Cumberland and then in Neath, South Wales, right up to the eighteenth century when the coalfields of Katowice in Silesia were opened up by Yiddish-speaking mining engineers from nearby Bytom.

Walking over to the bar to collect a drink, you might have spotted in a corner, surrounded by acolytes, one of those major international figures, later to be called "court Jews," whose business acumen, financial probity, tactical sense and political sensitivity made them valuable assets to the local rulers, on whose behalf they acted as agents, brokers, financial advisers and tax farmers—and who were often personally exempted from the rulers' anti-Jewish decrees. During her visit to Hamburg in 1667, Queen Christina of Sweden—a land from which Jews, "revilers of Christ and His communion," were completely excluded until the eighteenth century—she and her entourage happily stayed for several weeks in the sumptuous home of her Jewish bankers, Abraham and Isaac Teixera.[28] Such exemptions became the tradition in central and eastern Europe. In 1496 the Holy Roman Emperor Maximilian I expelled the Jews from the Austrian provinces of Carinthia and Styria, and forbade them to live in Vienna—except for his personal financier Herschl of Zistersdorf, with whom he said he "had to have patience." In the mid-1500s his grandson Ferdinand I banned all Jews from Lower Austria, Silesia, Prague and Vienna—except for Abraham Levi, known as Abramo dall'Arpa, Abraham of the Harp, whom he invited from Mantua to give music lessons to his children. When Karl Lueger, founder in 1893 of the anti-Semitic Christian Social Party of Austria, was taken to task by a colleague for including Jews among his personal friends, he famously replied, "*I* decide who is a Jew,"[29] a quote repeated by Hermann Goering when taunted that his co-founder of the *Luftwaffe*, Erhardt Milch, was the son of a Jewish pharmacist. (He arranged for Milch to be declared an honorary Aryan.)

If the tavern in which you were staying was in Poland and the time was the fourteenth century, you might have found yourself in the company of the Jew Jordan of Cracow, or one of his sons, Lewko and Cana'an, the wealthiest Jews of Poland at the time, perhaps even the wealthiest Poles *tout court*, in money terms as opposed to landholdings. A century later, you might have been lucky enough to meet the financiers Jakub Slomkowicz of Łuck, Szania of Belz, Samson of Zydaczow, Josko of Hrubieszow or Natko of Lemberg—perhaps even, if it was the year 1425, Volczko, lease-holder of the Lvov customs, who might proudly tell you of King Ladislaus II Jagiełło's recent grant of a large and empty tract of land: "As we have great confidence in the wisdom, carefulness, and foresight of our Lvov customs-holder, the Jew Volczko . . . after the above-mentioned Jew Volczko has turned the above-mentioned wilderness into a human settlement in the village, it shall remain in his hands till his death."

Another century on and in Bohemia, or in Germany, if you yourself were sufficiently distinguished, you might have found yourself being introduced to Joseph ben Gershon, popularly known as Josel or Yosselmann of Rosheim in Alsace (who lived from *circa* 1478 to 1554) and heard from the horse's mouth some of the stories of his extraordinary adventures, about which he left a brief Hebrew account.[30] His diary gives us a series of snapshots of the troubles visited on the Yiddish-speaking Jews of the Holy Roman Empire in the late fifteenth century that had Josel constantly tramping the roads of central Europe in attempts, mostly successful, to rescue as many of his co-religionists as he could from calamity.

He might have recounted to you how he first came to prominence in 1507, when the expelled Jews of Obernai in Alsace asked him to persuade the authorities to allow them back and how his rapid success had led to his appointment in 1510 as *Parnas u-Manhig* (Leader and Guide) of the Alsatian Jews—though he would probably not have mentioned that when he later wrote to the Imperial Diet in Speyer under the grandiose German title of *Gemeiner Judischheit Regierer im Deutschen Lande* (Ruler of All Jewry in Germany), he was quickly slapped down and fined two marks with costs, for only the emperor might call himself ruler of the Jews. Whereafter he took to signing himself more acceptably as *Befehlshaber der ganzen Judenschaft* (Commander of all Jewry), a designation under which he was addressed by the emperor himself.

He might have reminisced about the terrible time when in 1514 he himself was arrested at Mittelbergheim and imprisoned on a charge of ritual murder. "We were shut up in the dungeons of Oberenheim. After seven weeks, our innocence was accepted. May God never withdraw his love." After that, as was the general custom in those dangerous days, he made sure to wear his burial tunic under his outer clothes when on the road, so that he might at least be properly interred should the worst come to pass.

He would surely have described how well he got on with the Emperor Maximilian and his successors Charles V and Ferdinand, how he raced around Europe after them, travelling to Coblenz, to Nuremberg, to Hagenau, to Günzburg, to Brabant, to Ratisbon, to Schwabach, to Anspach in Silesia, mostly on horseback but sometimes on shanks's pony—"my horse being lamed, I had to leave on foot in search of Ferdinand, whom I finally found in Prague"—and almost always managing to persuade his ruler to undo whatever edict of expulsion, execution or other outrage was being threatened against his community. "I presented myself before him and, with God's help, found a favourable reception" is the typical outcome of most of his anecdotes.

He might have sadly reminisced about how at Ratisbon in 1532, he tried to persuade the proselyte and pseudo-Messiah Solomon Molcho to give up his dangerous notion of recruiting a Jewish army to aid the emperor in fighting the Turks.

> As soon as I got wind of his project, I wrote to him to try to dissuade him, as I feared the worst. I left Ratisbon so that the Emperor couldn't accuse me of being party to his ideas. As soon as

he arrived, Molcho was clapped in irons and taken to Boulogne, where he mounted the pyre and sanctified the Holy Name [i.e. was martyred]. Many there were whom he rescued from sin. May his soul rest in Eden.

Josel's one failure sat heavily on his heart: he could not save his own home town:

> The same year, an edict of expulsion was made against the Jews of Rosheim and those of the provostship of Kaisersberg. I got the Emperor to annul the order of expulsion from the Provostship of Kaisersberg, but could get no result concerning our brothers of Rosheim. We obtained delay after delay, but the matter is still in suspension. Let us place our faith in God, that he save us from our enemies.

Jews were still living in Rosheim when Josel died there in 1554; there is no trace of his grave.

But he is not forgotten. For he was a witness to, and even a participant in, the coming upheaval that would shake all European Christendom to its very roots: the challenge to the Catholic Church.

8

The Reformation

If you walk north through the centre of Oxford along the old road that is now called St. Aldate's—an ancient north–south route that crossed the Thames where in Anglo-Saxon times it marked the border between the kingdoms of Wessex and Mercia at a ford for oxen (an Ox Ford) over which Folly Bridge now springs across the much-punted waters of the Isis—you approach the eleventh-century Carfax Tower, seventy-two feet high, marking the busy four-way crossing (in the original Latin *Quadrifurcus*, hence Carfax) with what are now called Queen Street and High Street. Once these were named Great Bailey and La Boucherie, for their line marks the site of the old town wall, and the field just outside it where the slaughterers plied their trade. St. Aldate's itself was once known as Fish Street, and even before that the Great Jewry, for around here spread what had become, by the thirteenth century, one of England's most prosperous and distinguished Jewish settlements.

Splendid stone-built houses lined the final furlong of the road, on land purchased from the Priory of St. Frideswide, with a synagogue on the eastern side directly opposite the place where the steeple of St. Aldate's church rises today, and on the spot where, in the sixteenth century, Cardinal Wolsey would found Christchurch College.

The story of Oxford's university and Oxford's Jewish community were strongly linked, for several of the halls around which the university was founded—Moysey's Hall and Lombard's Hall—had been owned by Oxford Jews and it was the Jew Jacob who sold two houses to Walter of Merton on the site of which he built Oxford's first residential college. When, after a century of increasingly pitiless expropriation, the Jews of England had lost all economic value to the crown and had therefore become more trouble than they were worth, so that their entire population was expelled from the kingdom by King Edward I on All Saints' Day 1290, the imposing stone properties along Great Jewry, including the synagogue, fell into the hands of Balliol College.

Several important rabbinical authors had flourished in Oxford during the preceding century. Rabbi Yom Tov and his son Moses, the latter known to the English as "Magister Mosseus," wrote several works that are quoted as authoritative by their contemporaries and immediate successors, and Moses penned the standard medieval work on biblical Hebrew punctuation and accentuation.[1] Another Jewish savant, Berechiah, known in English as Benedict the Punctuator,[2] wrote a number of ethical works while resident in Oxford, and translated into Hebrew several important books of the day, such as a popular twelfth-century account of the natural sciences by Adelard of Bath,[3] and—best-known—a collection of fables culled from the Arabic and from Aesop, called in English the Fox Fables,[4] that ran to eighteen editions. "These fables are well known to all mankind and are in books by people of all languages," wrote Berechiah in his introduction, "but my faith differs from theirs."

In his *Social and Religious History of the Jews*, Salo Baron suggests that after the expulsion, the important intellectual heritage left by such a well-organised and conspicuous community could hardly vanish overnight. Particularly as there would have remained living in Oxford and its surrounding villages the families of Jews converted to Christianity "by the exemplary carriage and gift of preaching" of the Dominican priory planted in the midst of the Jewry in 1221, a few doors away from the synagogue. (Proselytes in the reverse direction, like the deacon of the church in 1222 whose desperate love for a Jewish woman led him to convert, were handed over to the secular power and burned.) There might well have remained a strong residue of Judaic influence on the ways of thinking of Oxford's scholars even seventy years after the exodus, when a young graduate, a Yorkshireman by the name of John Wycliffe, was appointed Master of Balliol College in 1360.

. . .

Perched on the outermost western boundary of the European continent, dipping its toes into the Atlantic Ocean, about as far as it could be from the Yiddish *heym* in central and eastern Europe, England had nonetheless long played a leading part in the destiny of European Jewry. Before becoming the first state to expel her entire Jewish population, she had earlier hatched the most dangerous and longest-lasting canard, the blackest lie, to haunt Europe's Jews all the way into the twentieth century: the Blood Libel.

This wicked falsehood, that Jews need the blood of Christian children for their rituals, was invented in Norwich in 1144 when the body of a young boy, William (later St. William), was discovered in Thorpe wood near the town. The murder was immediately blamed on a Jewish conspiracy. A Jewish convert to Christianity, Theobald of Cambridge, was said to have revealed that every year a secret cabal of Jews cast lots to decide where the annual sacrifice of a Christian child at Passover should take place. In the preceding year the vote had been taken at Narbonne and the finger of fate had fallen on Norwich. They "bought a Christian child before Easter and tortured him with all the tortures wherewith our Lord was tortured, and on Long Friday hanged him on a rood in hatred of our Lord."[5] Similar charges were brought at Gloucester in 1168, at Bury St. Edmunds in 1181, and at Winchester in 1192, whereafter the myth quickly spread to the continent of Europe to become the most enduring anti-Semitic calumny in history—and the most generally believed.[6] One only has to be aware of the overwhelming, blind outrage so easily whipped up even today in our own times against child molesters and killers, to understand what forever facing that false charge has meant to Europe's Jews.

After 1290, however, with all Jews gone, the commons looked around for other scapegoats. They now directed their anger and blame towards an unexpected target.

The calamitous fourteenth century—leaving aside the plagues, the famines, the manias and massacres—also brought low the English Catholic Church. The hierarchy was believed corrupt, the clergy ignorant, the monks greedy and the sale of indulgences—originally intended as a temporal, this-worldly penalty to accompany true spiritual penitence and remorse—was becoming a scandalous racket. In the Catholic capital Rome, a power struggle among the patrician families and a dispute with the king of France led first to the kidnapping of one pope, then to the hostile takeover by France of the entire Vatican enterprise, with a Frenchman made pope and the headquarters relocated from St. Peter's in Rome to a small town in Provence, until then known mainly for a twelfth-century bridge miraculously erected by a certain St. Benezet the shepherd—*on y danse.*

The Avignon papacy—morosely mourned by Italians as the pope's Babylonian Captivity (it lasted some seventy years, as had Israel's biblical exile) and triumphantly trumpeted by the French as the New Gallic Rome (*Roma Nova Gallica*)—was welcomed enthusiastically by the Jewish community that lived along the Rue des Marchands and around what is today the busy Place Jerusalem in the town they called City of Vines (*Ir ha-Gefanim*). Jews serviced the Avignon papal court with foodstuffs, bed and table linen, horses, perfumes, parchment, coral and pearls for rosary beads, as well as with tailors and bookbinders. In contrast, the power shift was particularly threatening to the English, since the head of the Universal Church was now a Frenchman, one of the traditional enemy race across the Channel.

The situation called for strong protest and John Wycliffe, the Morning Star of the Reformation, was ready for the call. Born between 1325 and 1330, awarded a doctorate of theology in his forties, Master of Balliol College—owner of the former synagogue in Oxford, a town still resonating with the echoes of a vibrant Jewish tradition not long abandoned—this Catholic priest and foremost English theologian of the day vigorously attacked the failings of the Church. Not only opposed to indulgences, to the consecration of sinners as priests, to the worship of saints, images and relics, to the doctrine of transubstantiation—the claim that the bread and wine of the Eucharist literally and miraculously become the flesh and blood of Christ—Wycliffe went so far as to reject altogether the automatic legitimacy of the church hierarchy with the pope at its head: "It is blasphemy to call anyone head of the church, save Christ alone." For him the sole religious truth was to be found in the Bible which, as in Judaism, should be accessible to all. "Those Heretics who pretend that the laity need not know God's law but that the knowledge which priests have had imparted to them by word of mouth is sufficient, do not deserve to be listened to."[7] To make it possible for the laity to approach God's law directly, he had the Bible translated into English, "for it is maad, that alle pupils schulden knowe it."[8]

At any other medieval time Wycliffe would surely have ended his life at the stake—no less than five papal edicts were issued against him—but one of his patrons was John of Gaunt, into whose dying mouth Shakespeare would put the most patriotic speech in our language before the age of Winston Churchill: "This royal throne of kings, this sceptred isle, this earth of majesty, this seat of Mars . . ." He and the other proud English nobles were damned if they would heed the commands of a despised French pope, so in spite of losing his Oxford job, being excommunicated and arraigned before the courts on a number of occasions, Wycliffe managed to survive into his fifties and die in bed.

The followers that he left behind, however, of whom there were a great many, were mostly less fortunate. Less than twenty-five years after their leader's death in 1384, reading the Bible in English was outlawed and actually owning one was made a capital offence. In 1415, thirty years on, the pope decreed that Wycliffe's bones should be dug up, burned, and the ashes scattered in the River Swift in Leicestershire.

It is tempting to believe that Wycliffe's opposition to idolatry, his insistence that the Bible and not the Church was the ultimate religious authority and on the common people's right, not to say duty, to read that Bible for themselves, was a Judaic idea—after all, Judaism knows no priesthood and the whole thrust of Jewish education from the very beginning of the diaspora was to equip every man to be able to read and understand the Hebrew Scriptures. Those who attacked Wycliffe and his followers certainly accused them of Judaising. However, overwhelmingly more important was another of the Yorkshire clergyman's beliefs, which had nothing to do with Jewish influence, yet when spread abroad would utterly change the Jewish situation. "It is supposed," he wrote, "and with much probability, that the Roman pontiff is the great Antichrist."

The pope as Antichrist? After all the claims made by Rome throughout the centuries that the greatest opponents of Jesus were the Jews? Wycliffe's stand shifted the fault line between the saved and the damned from where it had been drawn for a thousand years, between Christians and Jews, and redrew it within Christendom itself, dividing Catholics from those whom the 1529 Diet of Speyer would label Protestants. Almost overnight the Jews were turned from active participants in the historic melodrama of faith to bystanders.

Had any Jews remained in England in the fourteenth century they would surely have been amazed. As they would have been further perplexed to see two rival popes spring up in 1378, one in Rome the other in Avignon, and perhaps even driven to laughter when a third pope, intended by the Council of Pisa to replace the two rivals and heal the schism, simply added himself to their number. But they would probably have concluded that England was so far from the mainstream of thinking in Europe that whatever happened on that damp and distant island, however promising, could hardly have much effect on the future of the large, increasingly Yiddish-speaking Jewish communities of central and eastern Europe.

But England was not so very distant from the European continent. In 1382 the fifteen-year-old King Richard II married the pious teenager Ann, daughter of the Holy Roman Emperor and sister of the king of Bohemia—she was the one responsible for first importing the fashion for pointed Crackowe shoes to England. She quickly came to appreciate Wycliffe's work, apparently using his Bible translation to teach herself the English language. After her early death at the age of only twenty-seven, the lord chancellor spoke glowingly at her funeral (with a predictable sideswipe at the Church): "Although she was a stranger, yet she constantly studied the four gospels in English. And in the study of these, and in the reading of Godly books, she was more diligent than the prelates—though their office and business require it of them." The enthusiastic queen had her attendants send copies of Wycliffe's writings back home to Prague, and the intellectual links between England and central Europe were yet further strengthened when a Prague religious scholar[9] left money in his will for Bohemian students to travel to Oxford for advanced instruction.

HUSSITES

Once Wycliffe's ideas reached Prague, they found a particularly friendly hearing among a people where ill feeling between German speakers and Czech speakers had long festered and whose relationship with the Catholic Church was as ambivalent as it was among the English. At the end of the fourteenth century, in the University of Prague, Czech masters clashed with German masters over Church reform. Arguments of high philosophy were also involved. In the country, peasants resented the Church for its enormous landholdings and for the heavy tax burden it laid on them. Within the Church itself, poor priests were embittered by the enormous wealth and deep corruption of the higher clergy. The Great Schism with first two, then three rival popes brought Roman Catholicism into general disrepute. The dissenters, however, were not well organised and had no fully thought-out programme or theological position.

Wycliffe's writings from Oxford proved to be the seed around which could crystallise an increasingly anti-Catholic, Slav-nationalist, popular movement, led by Jan Hus, Dean of the Prague University Faculty of Philosophy and a popular preacher in the Czech tongue at the Bethlehem Chapel near the old town centre.

A twentieth-century replica of this chapel stands on the original site, not far from Prague's Old Town Square, the white-painted rendering pierced by a single row of dark pointed-arch windows, revealing that what had been originally sanctioned by Rome as a small building where Mass might be held in the Czech language, was actually a great barn, able to house a congregation of some 3,000 under its twin steeply pitched gables. Modern Czech tour guides assure the visitor that this is the very spot where the Reformation actually began. If Wycliffe was the Morning Star—which always precedes the dawn—of the Reformation, Hus's movement was the first actual ray of sunrise.

The lessons that Hus preached in his chapel in the first decade of the fifteenth century already emphasised many of the features that would come to characterise the rise of Protestantism: a conviction that the Antichrist would appear out of the ranks of the Catholic Church rather than from among the Jews; a passionate belief in the supremacy of scripture over the all-too-human papacy—indeed, a refusal to accept any features of Christianity, like saints, icons, relics and papal supremacy, not accounted for in the written word of God—a concentration on the Old rather than the New Testament—it constitutes, after all, two thirds of the Christian Bible—and a resulting keen interest in the Hebrew language and in important Jewish commentary writers like Rabbi Solomon ben Isaac, Rashi—they called him "Magister Shelomo." Hus himself probably learned his Hebrew from Jewish neighbours, while he and his followers had contact with the principal Prague rabbi, mystic and poet of the day, Avigdor Kara. Hus and his disciples may well have been influenced by Kara's views, for the rebellious Bohemians took up a poem he had penned on the unity of God, beginning: *"Ekhod yakhid u-meyukhad"* ("One, Single and Unique," an elegant Hebrew play on words, as all three are variations on the same root, meaning oneness), which they recited in Czech, while Jews apparently sang it, both in the original Hebrew and in Yiddish translation, to the tune of a Christian hymn.[10]

It is for good reason that the reformers' enemies charged them with Judaising. The Yiddish-speaking community of Bohemia must also have perceived a turning back towards Christianity's Hebraic, Jewish roots, for many of its leading lights expressed sympathy for Hus's movement, while a Hebrew text[11] of 1449 would retrospectively, and wildly, claim in a hot flush of wishful thinking that: ". . . there arose a priest named Hus . . . He attracted the city's inhabitants and taught them true faith in the unity of God. They destroyed churches, burned images, and punished the priests. Most inhabitants of that province followed them, and they decided to give up their Christian faith."

In reality Hus felt that he was a truer Christian than his opponents. He revered the Sacrament of Communion; in fact, one of his most important demands was that lay worshippers should receive Communion "in both kinds"—i.e. the wine as well as the bread—instead of only the bread, which had become the Catholic tradition. As for the Jews, Hus, like other Church reformers both before and after, however much they may have glorified ancient Hebrew society back in the land of Israel, was not particularly well disposed towards those in his own country who continued stubbornly to persist in refusing to recognise Jesus as the Messiah, or to accept the redeeming truth of the Trinity. However, even the most strongly anti-Jewish among the reformers strongly disapproved of forced conversion and taught that Jews should be tolerated, not just to show off Christian mercy and generosity, but more because they had once been the recipients of divine revelation. They quoted the words of an earlier Bohemian nonconformist preacher, Matthew of Janow: "When at the end of days the Jews will be converted, they will lead such exemplary lives that the Holy Church will be amazed and will follow their example."

Bohemia's Yiddish community was divided in its attitudes towards the growing dissent within the Christians' ranks. Most initially supported the Catholics and opposed reform. Community leaders recalled that the pope and the curia had, after all and in the main, been a restraining influence on the anti-Jewish excesses of the lower clergy, city burghers and the fickle common crowd. Conservative rabbis disapproved in principle of tearing down traditional structures, seeing novelty as a threat to the inviolability of their own inheritance. Business people feared the loss of lucrative contacts with the higher Roman clergy who had—in spite of theological differences—been strong supporters of Jewish enterprise. Other ordinary Yiddish-speaking folk, their survival instincts well attuned to the crosscurrents of ethnic discord in central Europe, feared that the massive support of the Bohemian peasantry for Hus and his anti-German reformers boded ill for other non-Slav communities too. Those with a good memory for history feared—with good reason—that any instability in the non-Jewish world usually ended by putting their own people in danger.

Ultimately they were given no choice but to support the movement.

For Hus was unluckier than Wycliffe. Lured with a promise of safe conduct to appear before the Council of Constance, he was almost immediately arrested, tried for heresy and, after defending himself valiantly at three public hearings, condemned, urged to recant and in 1415, after refusing to do so, publicly burned—naked and wearing a pointed dunce's hat labelled Arch-Heretic—in a field on the edge of Constance town. As a torch was applied to the faggots, the secretary to the council read out the following significant malediction: "O curse'd Judas, because thou hast abandoned the pathways of peace, and hast counselled with the Jews, we take away from thee the cup of redemption."

Bohemian nobles came together and published a formal protest. Artisans and peasants among Hus's flock seethed with fury and a barely suppressed thirst for revenge. The authorities responded in the usual way: by arresting troublemakers. Bohemia's Jews looked on anxiously.

After four years of bargaining, arm-twisting and stand-off, the king of Bohemia dismissed the heretic's sympathisers from the Prague Municipal Council. On 30 July 1419 a mob of Hus's followers, now calling themselves Hussites, stormed the town hall on Charles Square in the New City quarter, ten minutes' walk from the Bethlehem Chapel, claiming that stones had been thrown at a Hussite procession. A delegation broke into the council chamber to demand the release of several imprisoned brethren. In response to the Catholic councillors' refusal, the insurgents bundled up seven of them and flung them to their deaths from a third-storey window—an event known as the "First Defenestration of Prague." On hearing the news, the king apparently burst a blood vessel and died. Rioting broke out in the city. The Bohemian nobility, mostly sympathetic to the Hussites' cause, took de facto control of the state, which was now effectively in open revolt against its overlord the Holy Roman Emperor. The pope called for a Catholic crusade "for the destruction of the Wycliffites, Hussites and all other heretics in Bohemia," and Prague's Yiddish speakers found themselves helping their fellow citizens dig a defensive moat round Vyšehrad castle hill.

The Hussite Wars that raged across Bohemia, Moravia and Silesia, with murderous forays into Germany, Austria and Poland, lasted more than thirty years. In spite of five attempts, the Catholic forces were quite unable to defeat the religious rebels—led first by one general of genius, Žižka (The One-Eyed), then after his death by another, Prokop Holý (Procopius the Great)—and eventually recognised that they had no option but to try to negotiate a settlement. Talks were begun in 1431. (The Hussite delegation included the Englishman Peter Payne, a man seemingly in love with the sound of his own voice, whose address lasted three days.) However, the resulting agreement split the Hussites into two parties: the moderates, who only sought reform of the Church and were willing to accept compromise with Rome, and the radicals, who demanded total religious and social revolution, and rejected any deal with the pope out of hand.

The extremists' principal headquarters, a hilltop fifty miles south of Prague on the River Lužnica, they renamed Tabor, after the mountain in Palestine where, according to tradition, Jesus had foretold his second coming. Salo Baron tells us that they dragooned the local Jews—men, women and children—to work at building the fortifications. But the radicals, who became known as Taborites, were, as revolutionaries often are, deeply divided among themselves. Some tried to emulate the simple life led by Jesus's apostles. Jewish observers noted with enthusiasm that some *Bnei Hushim* (children of Hus) based their social arrangements on their reading of the Old Testament, even observing the Sabbath on Saturdays, obeying the Jewish dietary laws and practising ritual slaughter.

More worrying to the Yiddish merchant class was that most tried to establish communities run on principles of primitive Communism: "Mine and Thine do not exist at Tabor, but all possession is communal, so all people must always hold everything in common, and nobody must possess anything of his own. Whoever holds private property commits a mortal sin."[12]

A later rabbi would write that "all of Bohemia was filled with robbery, so that the people of the land became weary and stopped cultivating the soil."[13] Žižka, the moderate Hussite general leading the fight against the Catholic crusaders, had often to take his one good eye off the enemy to deal with the more dangerous heretical communities, which he did with utmost ruthlessness.

In 1434, while peace talks between the Catholics and moderate Hussites were taking place in Basel, they joined forces to suppress the revolutionaries for good and all, and succeeded in utterly crushing the radicals' army at the battle of Lipany. Many individual fighters escaped, however, and the struggle continued for nearly twenty more years, until Tabor itself was captured in 1452 and all the ringleaders burned at the stake. Bohemia now settled down to an—albeit slightly troubled—accommodation between Catholics and moderate Hussites, broken only by a few outbreaks of violence. In 1483 a Catholic mayor would be thrown into the street from a window in the Old Town Hall, the Second Defenestration of Prague, while in the same year a massacre of Hussites planned for St. Bartholomew's Eve would only be averted by a timely forewarning.

Those radicals who escaped slaughter at Lipany and immolation at Tabor gave up their revolutionary aims and millenarian expectations, restricting themselves from then on to a purely spiritual, peaceful programme. The Bohemian and Moravian brethren, as they became known, nevertheless continued to be bitterly persecuted, an experience which brought them ever closer in sympathy to the Jews. Much later, after the Thirty Years' War, when all varieties of Christianity other than Catholicism were strictly forbidden in the Habsburg realm on pain of execution, many communities chose outright conversion to Judaism rather than Catholicism or exile. Several well-known Czech Jewish families trace their descent to these converted brethren, among them those of the writers Max Brod and Franz Kafka. The name Kriwaczek also suggests the same origin. According to an official Czech report, "after the Holocaust, many synagogue buildings in Czechoslovakia became prayer rooms of the Bohemian Brethren, where they also took over the care of the Jewish cemeteries. They had a special prayer for these occasions."[14]

War is kind to no community that stands in its way. The Yiddish people suffered along with all others as the Hussite and Catholic armies fought their way across central Europe, particularly since the Catholic side was mostly made up of mercenaries who subsisted on pillage and despoliation of the lands they passed through. Though attacks were not specifically directed at Jews, their quarters were sacked along with those of all other citizens when towns were taken by the Catholics or retaken by Hussites, even in Prague.

Yet the victory of the moderates over the enthusiasts and their agreement with the Catholic Church ushered in a period of relative stability that allowed the Yiddish speakers to take stock of their gains and losses through the Hussite wars. True, in some places outside Bohemia proper Catholic actions in response to the heresy—"all bad Christians and Jews," it was claimed, "had escaped to the Hussites"—resulted in the murder and exclusion of many cities' and provinces' Yiddish-speaking communities. The rabble rousing of John Capistrano, sent by the pope in the 1450s to return the Hussites to the Catholic fold, was largely responsible for the subsequent expulsion and destruction of the Yiddish-speaking communities of Austria, Bavaria and Silesia.

In Bohemia, however, the triumph of Hussite tolerance over Catholic bigotry brought practical rewards to the Jews. Thousands of peasants and townspeople had died in the fighting, untended fields in many areas were running to scrub, and the cities were impoverished by the desertion of so many of the artisan and shopkeeper classes to join the revolutionaries' ranks. The Bohemian nobility, Hussite sympathisers nearly all and animated by the new spirit of religious tolerance, were keen to attract Jews to help re-establish the economies of their impoverished fiefdoms. Areas abandoned by the millenarian fantasists were now made available for Jewish settlement. In Prague, though there were mob attacks and attempts at expulsion here too, the Yiddish community seems to have shrugged them off. A 1546 list of Jewish residents—doubtless incomplete—detailed nearly a thousand Jewish households in a city where no Jews at all were supposed to have been living after being charged with arson and temporarily expelled, by order of the emperor, in 1542. The Hussite wars, while bloody enough and temporarily destructive, ultimately improved the lives of all the people of Bohemia and Moravia, Yiddish speakers included.

By contrast, during this very same period, another reformist movement was developing to the west which, when exacerbated by the economic roller-coaster of the times, would have much profounder consequences. Perhaps because the Hussites were mostly Slavs and the new reformers were mostly German speakers, the outcome of the later movement would be very different: vastly more destructive for all, yet paradoxically at the same time bringing great, if temporary, benefit to the Yiddish civilisation.

LUTHER

How might the Yiddish-speaking Jews have first become aware of the momentous change being incubated in Germany in the sixteenth century? Even devout students of Talmud, closely cloistered in their seminaries against intrusion by the Christian world's affairs, or simple artisans, traders and shopkeepers, more concerned with earning a livelihood than keeping up with the politics of religion, would almost certainly have heard tavern talk about the protracted dispute between the great Christian humanist Johannes Reuchlin (1455–1522), scholar of the Hebrew language, publisher of the first Hebrew grammar book by a non-Jew, staunch defender of the Talmud, who insisted that Jews were *concives* (fellow citizens) of the Holy Roman Empire ("both sects are citizens of the Holy Roman Empire, we Christians by virtue of the Emperor's choice by electors, the Jews through their submission and their public profession"), against the Jewish apostate to Catholicism Johannes Pfefferkorn, butcher, convicted thief, protégé of the Dominican Order and indefatigable issuer of scurrilous pamphlets and tracts attacking Jews and the Jewish religion—for the last and most outrageous of which the publisher, though not the author, was arrested and imprisoned.

Yiddish speakers passed among each other the amazing report that in 1523 a Catholic Augustinian monk and consecrated priest, a self-avowed follower of Reuchlin, had written a book with the title: *Dass Jesus Christus ein geborener Jude sei* (*That Jesus Christ was born a Jew*), expressing such opinions as: "Our fools, the popes, bishops, sophists, and monks, these coarse donkey-brains, dealt with the Jews in such a manner that any Christian would have preferred to be a Jew. Indeed, had I been a Jew and had I seen such idiots and dunderheads expound Christianity, I should rather have become a pig than a Christian"; or: "If I were a good Jew, the Pope could never persuade me to accept his idolatry. I would rather ten times be racked and flayed"; and finally and most welcome:

> I would advise and beg everybody to deal kindly with the Jews and to instruct them in the Scripture; in such a case we could expect them to come over to us. If, however, we use brute force and slander them, saying that they need the blood of Christians to get rid of their stench, and other nonsense of that kind, and treat them like dogs, what good can we expect of them? Finally, how can we expect them to improve if we prohibit them to work among us and to have social intercourse with us, and so force them into usury? If we wish to make them better we must deal with them not according to the law of the Pope, but according to the law of Christian charity. We must receive them kindly and allow them to compete with us in earning a livelihood, so that they may have an opportunity to witness Christian life and doctrine.

And if that did not persuade the Jews to convert, well then: "If some remain obstinate, what of it? Not every one of us is a good Christian."

Jews would soon have learned the name of this unlikely supporter, Martin Luther, though they would not have heard tell of how in 1517 he nailed his ninety-five theses to the door of the Castle Church in Wittenberg, as that pretty tale was not circulated until after the reformer's death. It appears that some Jews made it their business to distribute Luther's book as widely as they could, to judge by his later bitter complaint that they had misused and taken advantage of his work.

Luther's early opposition to the Catholic treatment of the Jews was, of course, only a very small part of his much greater challenge to the Church. Nor was he the only churchman to question the principles by which the Catholic enterprise claimed a monopoly over western Christianity. The Jews, unversed in the details of Christian observance, uninterested in the minutiae of Christian religious politics, must have been surprised and disturbed by the rebellion now bubbling up all over northern Europe. The Hussite revolt had been understood as a Slav reaction to German religious and social hegemony over Bohemia; and though protracted and bloody, the dispute had been settled, by and large to the benefit of all, by a compromise within the borders of the Slav kingdom. This new revolution, however, was upsetting the status quo right across the continent: in England, France, the Low Countries, Scandinavia, Germany, Poland and Lithuania. Even the Knights of the Teutonic Order, once dedicated warriors for the pope and committed missionaries for Rome, now hanging on grimly to their last territories around the Gulf of Riga, woke up one morning in 1525 to find that their Grand Master Albrecht von Hohenzollern had converted to Lutheranism, turned their lands into a secular state under Polish suzerainty and appointed himself its duke.

By the time accounts of what was going on in Europe reached the Holy Land, where several important Spanish rabbis like the mystic Abraham ben Eliezer haLevi had fetched up after their expulsion in 1492, they had been greatly embellished and Luther's reputation had been transformed into that of a "secret Jew" whose purpose was to infiltrate Christianity from the inside and prepare the followers of Jesus for their return to the Torah. HaLevi recalled a prophesy by a certain Rabbi Joseph that "a man will arise who will be great, valiant, and mighty. He will pursue justice and loathe butchery. He will marshal vast armies, originate a religion, and destroy the houses of worship and clergy. In his day Jerusalem shall be rebuilt."[16] Who else could this have meant other than Martin Luther?

Yet whatever flights of fantasy Jews living far from Germany, and from reality, may have had, the Yiddish people closer at hand were quickly brought back down to earth. They may have seen themselves as uninvolved bystanders in the momentous changes that were sweeping across northern Europe but, as Francis Bacon wrote at much the same time, "in this theatre of life it is reserved only for God and angels to be lookers on." Jews would soon enough discover that, as an identifiable European nation, many on both sides saw them as fully implicated.

The Lutheran revolution in the 1500s was not a replay of the Hussite rebellion. Hus had burned but Luther won a great moral victory when arraigned before the emperor at the 1521 Diet of Worms, where he made his famous declaration that he would recant only if convinced of his error either by Scripture or by evident reason. Otherwise, he protested, he could not go against his conscience, which was bound by the word of God. "Here I stand," he is said to have declared, "I can do no other." The meeting broke up in a shouting match and Luther, disguised and renamed Junker Georg, was spirited away by his patron Frederick the Wise, Elector of Saxony, to a hilltop castle called the Wartburg. There, out of the pope's reach, the excommunicated reformer dedicated himself to developing a new, non-Catholic, church service, to beginning his seminal, ground-breaking German translation of the Bible and to go on working the strings of his revolution safely out of sight in the wings.

Economically these were again difficult times. Inflation had been steadily rising for a century, imposing severe hardships on the peasantry. In an atmosphere of ever greater impoverishment, popularly blamed on the Church's sinfulness, the social unrest triggered by the heady new teachings of the religious reformers broke out of control. The result was almost inevitable. A contemporary chronicler recorded:

> Anno 1525, soon after the new year, there occurred a great and unheard of insurrection of the common man throughout the Allgäu, Swabia, Bavaria, Austria, Salzburg, Styria, Württemberg, Franconia, Saxony, Thuringia, Alsace, and many other places. Calling upon the Gospel as their justification, the common folk rose against their lords in protest against the injustices, taxes, burdens, and the general oppression under which they were forced to live.[17]

This is the moment when *Shtadlan* (diplomat) Josel of Rosheim, confidant of the emperor and self-styled Commander of German Jewry, enters the story. Rushing across Europe from city to city in his everlasting efforts to protect his co-religionists from exile, prison and the stake, and having got wind of the intentions of the peasants to ravage Alsace, he first alerted the city council of Strasbourg to their danger, then found himself not far from his own home town of Rosheim trying to reason with the leaders of the insurrection. "1522. The peasants were in revolt in Germany," he wrote in his diary.

> In Alsace they were bent on massacring us. The massacre had already begun before I could meet the rebel leaders at the Convent of Altdorf. I succeeded in persuading them to abandon their plan, and they sent letters to that effect to all the provinces of the country. But they failed to keep their promises. We were saved when the Duke of Lorraine defeated them and decimated their troops.[18]

There is more to this account than first strikes the eye. It seems that by "us" and "we" Josel was in this case referring to the whole urban population, not just the Jews, for otherwise he would have ascribed their rescue, as he does elsewhere, to God rather than to the duke of Lorraine. And if one wonders how he managed to persuade the leaders of the insurgents to "abandon their plan," it helps to know that one of the main peasant leaders was a man called Ittel Jörg, who in quieter days had been provost of Rosheim and whom Josel must therefore have known well. A modern mural in the Rosheim tourist bureau shows both men together, Josel wrapped in a black cloak and hat, and Jörg dressed up like Henry VIII for a Holbein portrait. As for the decimation of the rebels, reliable reports tell of 20,000 peasant fighters left dead on one battlefield and 6,000 more on another, perhaps one in ten of the population. Ittel Jörg was captured and hanged in Strasbourg. Josel's town of Rosheim escaped attack.

Luther turned violently against those who thought themselves his protégés, publishing a typically crude and brutal pamphlet, "Against the Thievish and Murderous Hordes of Peasants,"[19] in which he advocated: "Let everyone who can, smite, slay and stab, secretly or openly, remembering that nothing can be more poisonous, hurtful, or devilish than a rebel. It is just as when you must kill a mad dog; if you do not strike him, he will strike you, and a whole land with you."

The Peasant War was a sideshow, however, to the main conflict between Lutherans and the Catholic emperor. At the Diet of Augsburg in 1530, the Emperor Charles, "the Last Medieval Emperor of Germany," made a frantic attempt to preserve the unity of Christendom in the face of the Turkish threat from the East. For in 1529 Suleiman the Magnificent had besieged Vienna and—it was rumoured—had sworn by the beard of the Prophet not to rest till the muezzin's call to prayer was heard from the tower of St. Stephen's Cathedral. (Several months previously, Josel had managed to reassure the emperor that, contrary to popular talk, the Jews were not acting as Turkish spies.) The Protestants, however, insisted on prioritising the religious dispute and on presenting their Augsburg Confession—still today the foundation document of Lutheranism. It was a momentous meeting. The emperor took the side of the Catholics and dismissed the Protestants' claims—not surprisingly as he had been anointed as Emperor Charles V by the pope only two months before, the last Holy Roman Emperor to be so confirmed.

Any decision on the future religious disposition of Europe naturally had to take account of the Jews. Included in the programme was to be a formal public debate, a *disputatio*, between Joseph ben Gershon of Rosheim in the Jewish corner and in the other, a certain Antonius Margarita, originally Margolis, a Jewish apostate to Catholicism who, like too many converts, had justified his betrayal by publishing a vicious libel of his former people. His was entitled "The Whole Jewish Faith"[20] and it was a best-seller. As Josel and Anton squared up to each other, the future status of the Yiddish population of the empire hung in the balance, for a win by the apostate would have made Jewish life there impossible.

But Josel of Rosheim was endowed, Salo Baron suggests in his *Social History*, with "a quiet, tactful, and yet magnetic personality." Fully versed in contemporary religious and political issues, he was able to find the right tone for nearly every occasion. At Augsburg, as the two opponents stood and debated in front of the emperor himself, with the other Christian divines all listening attentively, Josel's calm, patient logic scored such a victory over Margarita's furious arguments, that in the end it was the apostate who was first imprisoned and then expelled from Augsburg. In a last-ditch accusation, the Catholic side tried to pin on the Jews the guilt of leading Luther and his followers into their errors. Josel convincingly brushed away the accusation as hardly worthy of answer.

The Augsburg Diet ended without agreement. The Protestant representatives withdrew, while their leaders began to assemble a joint army and sought alliances abroad among the emperor's enemies. War was brewing. The emperor was losing control of more and more of his dominions. The Jews faced a difficult choice. In theory the beliefs of Germany's Protestants were far closer, in some cases very close indeed, to Jewish principles. On the other hand, pope and emperor were in practice the traditional supporters of the Jewish cause against the petty interests of townsmen and working clergy. City councils had always needed to petition the emperor for the privilege of excluding Jews, *non tolerandis judaeis*. Now, however, chaos threatened. Every princeling, every local lord, perhaps even every city mayor, would henceforth be free to decide on a Jewish policy for himself. It was not hard to guess what that policy might be—it was unlikely to be favourable to the Yiddish-speaking inhabitants.

Josel, perhaps from personal conservatism or out of political acumen, chose to back the emperor and pope. Having persuaded the pope's representative to give him a copy of a charter issued to the Jews by Emperor Frederick Barbarossa 350 years previously, he put it before the emperor, who responded by declaring it a binding precedent for himself and all the German states. Josel's choice turned out to be astute, for Luther's mood was changing, and with it the whole political atmosphere.

The reformer's violent shift of attitude towards Jews has embarrassed many modern Lutherans, who can trace both the very highest in German culture, as well as the most frightful, back to the influence of their greatest ever religious leader. Luther was disappointed to find that his earlier generous treatment of the Jews did not result in the expected tidal wave of conversions. He claimed to be outraged to hear reports that, on the contrary, in Bohemia and Poland, Jews were taking advantage of the upheaval to make new proselytes for their own faith. He complained that "in Moravia they have circumcised many Christians and call them by the new name of Sabbatarians. This is what happens in those regions from which preachers of the gospel are expelled; there people are compelled to tolerate the Jews." He was personally affronted when a Jew he had converted to Lutheranism relapsed and returned to Torah and Talmud, saying that the next time he baptised a Jew he would take him to the River Elbe, hang a stone round his neck and drop him in with the words, "I baptise you in the name of Abraham." He encouraged his new patron, John Frederick I, Elector of Saxony, to expel all Jews from his territory.

Josel tried his best to have the expulsion rescinded, approaching his good friend the reformer Wolfgang Koepfel, known as Capito, whose sermons in Strasbourg the Yiddish diplomat often attended "because of his great scholarship"—claiming, a little unconvincingly, that he always left immediately when matters of faith were discussed. He asked for a letter to Luther, seeking help in arranging an audience with the elector. This Capito wrote, naïvely expressing the hope that "in accordance with our office, in which we hold God as a model of supreme mercy, you will decide to plead their cause before the prince." Luther responded to the High Representative of the Yiddish Jews with a polite letter of refusal:

> My dear Josel,
>
> I would have gladly interceded for you, both orally and in writing, before my gracious lord, just as my writings have greatly served the whole of Jewry. But because your people so shamefully misuse this service of mine and undertake things that we Christians simply shall not bear from you, they themselves have robbed me of all the influence I might otherwise have been able to exercise before the princes and lords on your behalf . . .
>
> For the sake of the crucified Jew, whom no one will take from me, I gladly wanted to do my best for you Jews, except that you abused my favour and hardened your hearts.

Josel tried six more times to see Luther, but with no success. Even worse, from the Yiddish point of view, was to come later. In his increasing bitterness and ill health towards the end of his life, Luther delivered himself of two poisonous diatribes: "On the Jews and Their Lies,"[21] and "On the Ineffable Name,"[22] containing such invective as "There is no people under the sun more avid for revenge or more bloodthirsty, believing itself to be God's people merely in order to murder and strangle the heathens," or "they are thieves and brigands who do not eat any food, do not wear on their bodies a single thread which they have not stolen from us and taken away by the most voracious of usuries." His last sermon, "An Admonition Against the Jews,"[23] delivered three days before he died in 1546, was hideously predictive of Nazi policy, prefiguring passages in Goebbels's infamous propaganda film *The Eternal Jew*.[24] Luther proposed to dispatch all the Yiddish speakers back to the Middle East. "Who prevents the Jews from returning to Judaea? Nobody. We shall provide them with all the supplies for the journey, only in order to get rid of that disgusting vermin. They are for us a heavy burden, the calamity of our being; they are a plague in our midst."

Such crudity even offended his partners in the reform movement. One protested at Luther's "lewd and houndish eloquence" and deplored his crude and vulgar tone, "which is appropriate for no one, still less for an old theologian." Josel of Rosheim lamented "such a boorish and inhuman book containing curses and vilification hurled at us hapless Jews, such as by the will of God can truly never be found in our beliefs." He approached the Strasbourg city councillors and asked them for permission to publish a refutation. This they refused, but in the light of the *shtadlan*'s persuasive submission, they themselves forbade the distribution of Luther's pamphlets within their area of jurisdiction. Even ordinary readers seem to have been uncomfortable with the violence of the language. Salo Baron points out that the two anti-Jewish tracts sold far fewer copies than Luther's other works.

Sadly, the effect of these poisonous publications proved long-lasting. Luther was not only a religious but also a literary genius, and his writings, particularly his hymns and translations from the Bible, were as formative for the German language as were Shakespeare's poetry and King James's Bible for English. Just as his German prose and verse would inspire the sublime works of Goethe, Schiller and Heine, so would his attacks provide powerful ammunition for Jew baiters from his own time right up to the twentieth century.[25]

To be scrupulously just, we should note that while advocating that the Jews' synagogues be burned, their houses torn down, their books taken from them and their rabbis prohibited from teaching, Luther was no racist anti-Semite: "If the Jews wish to be converted . . . and accept Christ . . . we shall treat them as our brothers." Neither was the coarse and violent style unique to him. This manner of argument, known as *Grobian* (ruffianly), was then all the rage in German polemical literature. (The German language strikes me as particularly well suited to the expression of crude brutality, often achieved by applying to people words normally reserved for animals. Thus when humans eat, they "*essen*"; animals "*fressen*." Using "*essen*" of a beast implies a ludicrous daintiness; using "*fressen*" of a person suggests unrestrained, unmannered, uncivilised vulgarity.) Nor did Luther restrict his abusive rants to Jews alone. In other publications he referred to the pope as "Roman Duke Antichrist, servant of error, apostle of Satan, man of sin and son of depravity." The elector of Brandenburg was a "liar, mad bloodhound, devilish papist, murderer, traitor, desperate miscreant, assassin of souls, arch-knave, dirty pig and devil's child, nay the devil himself." The inquisitor Hoogstraaten was "a mad bloodthirsty murderer, a blind and hardened donkey, who should be set to scratch for dung-beetles in the manure heaps of the papists." It is hardly surprising that other reformers looked askance at the excesses of his language. "Nothing has been more painful to me than to be compelled to pour such things into decent ears," wrote Sir Thomas More about Luther's pamphlet attacking Henry VIII, calling it an "unclean book."

NOW A MIRACLE HAPPENED

Luther was the most prominent partisan for reform of Catholicism, but he was far from alone. There were many other pious preachers against Roman doctrine too: John Knox the Scot, Thomas More in England, the French exile John Calvin in Geneva, Huldrych Zwingli in Zurich, the Spaniard Miguel Servet (Michael Servetus), Sebastian Castillio in France, as well as many less well known but still important activists in Germany itself. While opposing Judaism on religious principle, they expressed no hostility towards Jewish people themselves. Indeed, Andreas Osiander, Protestant theologian and Professor of Hebrew at Koenigsberg, wrote to the prolific Yiddish author Elijah Levita, composer of the *Bove Buch*, such a passionate denunciation of Luther's last works that he became terrified of the consequences when the letter was made public. He also wrote a detailed demolition, in twenty arguments, of the lie of the blood libel. And on one celebrated occasion the author of the Augsburg Confession, a friend and supporter of Luther known as Philipp Melanchthon (Greek for his real name Schwarzerd), had actually used the Catholic Church's cruel treatment of one group of Jews to illustrate the papal institution's general corruption and tolerance of injustice.

The event was a meeting intended to bridge differences between the Catholic and Protestant princes. After Luther's rebuff to Josel, his refusal to intercede with the elector of Saxony, the Commander of Germany's Yiddish speakers had no choice but to pursue John Frederick "The Magnanimous" directly. In 1539 after a fruitless foray into Thuringia in eastern Germany, Josel caught up with him at a council of electors held in Frankfurt. Here was an opportunity to sway the rulers of both Saxony and Brandenburg into repealing their ban on Jews living in or even entering their territories. In his diary Josel recalls "standing up in the presence of numerous gentile scholars, and arguing, with proofs from our holy Torah, against the words of Luther, Butzer and his faction. I was given a favourable hearing."

Philipp Melanchthon was present, representing his friend and mentor Luther. In the sermon that he preached to the assembly attacking the sinfulness of the Catholic Church, he gave as his example of papal injustice a celebrated trial that had taken place in Berlin twenty-nine years previously. A tinker by the name of Paul Fromm had been arrested for stealing a gold monstrance from a village church, still by chance containing two hosts, the wafer-thin discs of bread that, in Catholic teaching, become the body of

Christ during the Mass. Under torture Fromm claimed to have sold one of these to a Jew, Shelomo of Spandau, who was thereupon also tortured until he confessed to ritually desecrating it and selling pieces to several other Jews. The whole district had then exploded in popular anti-Jewish uproar. A swift trial in Berlin sentenced Fromm to death by torture with red-hot irons, and thirty-six Jews to the stake; two who agreed to baptism suffered a supposedly more merciful beheading.

Mayor Hans Brackow, who had presided over the trial, read out the sentence to the crowd from a high podium specially erected against the red-brick walls and tall Gothic windows of St. Mary's Church in the New Market—significantly the scene is the subject of the very first recorded artist's view of Berlin. The condemned were executed on a giant pyre just outside the city wall. All Jews in Brandenburg had then been expelled. "Now a miracle happened," Josel continues. "We learned at that moment [from Melanchthon's address] that the thirty-eight Jews who had been executed at Berlin in 1510 had been innocent. The monstrance thief had admitted his crime, but the Bishop, wicked man that he was, had forbidden his confessor to reveal the truth to their master Duke Joachim." The thief had in fact confessed to having been pressed by the bishop to invent the story of Jewish involvement. "On hearing this, the dukes renounced their aim of expelling us. All of them, including Duke Joachim, kept their promise. Only the Elector of Saxony betrayed us and did us great harm. He was punished for it." (The punishment was his arrest, imprisonment and condemnation to death after being defeated by imperial troops in a misjudged invasion of Bohemia. Though he was not executed but eventually released, he lost the title elector.)

Melanchthon's attack on Catholic morality, using this Jewish cause célèbre as an example, is as noteworthy as it is surprising. It demonstrates how far the attitudes of Luther's partners differed from those of their leader and mentor, who would never have used the stubborn and blasphemous Jews as an example of miscarriage of justice.

But though Martin Luther was the inspirer and figurehead of the German Reformation, as well as its greatest, most outspoken personality, Philipp Melanchthon was the scribe and the practical thinker. And it was the latter's generally more conciliatory and practical stance towards the Yiddish-speaking people, rather than the former's fervency, which represented the mainstream of Protestant thinking across Europe.

Several reformist-minded countries like England, the Netherlands, France and Switzerland in any case no longer supported Jewish communities at all and were unconcerned with the religious minority's relationship with the body politic. Indeed, one French pastor, later famous, who attended the Frankfurt colloquy in a private capacity, may well never actually have met a professing Jew before being exiled from Geneva to Strasbourg the previous year and coming face to face with Josel of Rosheim in Frankfurt.

His name was John Calvin and he was destined to have an even greater influence on world history than Martin Luther. In his *Social and Religious History of the Jews*, Salo Baron argued that during the 1539 assembly Calvin met and verbally jousted with Josel, who reported that he had been vocally assaulted by one of the divines present at the conference "in a violent, angry and menacing" way. This, Baron says, sounds very like Calvin, who himself admitted to losing his temper too easily, for example writing to a colleague: "Here I have sinned greatly, for I could not keep moderation." (Calvin's usual foul moods may have been the result of ill health; he suffered greatly from many ailments including excruciatingly painful kidney stones that made his every movement agony.) Josel, ever the diplomat, no doubt remembering that "a soft answer turneth away wrath,"[26] responded, perhaps with a slightly superior smile, "You, a learned man, wish to threaten us poor people? Well, God our Lord has preserved us from the days of Abraham. He in His grace will doubtless preserve us from you also."

This brief exchange can be matched up with a document later penned by Calvin himself called "An Answer to Some Jew's Questions and Objections,"[27] delivered in dialogue (*disputatio*) form, in which the Christian protagonist argues using evidence mainly from the Old Testament, and the Jewish antagonist largely from the New. Salo Baron is persuaded that "it summarises a real discussion which Calvin at some time had with a Jew" and that this Jew was probably Josel.

The playlet seems to be Calvin's attempt to respond to the Jew's questions with answers that he had been unable to come up with at the time, the tract representing a sort of theological *esprit de l'escalier*, finding a smart response too late after the event. The subjects were all the usually disputed issues but, strangely enough, even having had the opportunity to consider his replies at leisure, Calvin produces arguments that, unlike the Jew's, seem rather lame. Thus Josel—if it was indeed he—contended that "if it be true, as it is written, that, in the hour of his death, Jesus begged his Father and said, 'Father, forgive them; for they know not what they do', and if

Father and Son are identical and both have the same will," then how could Christians justify the treatment meted out to the Jews, supposedly in the name of God?

To which Calvin could only bluster that the Jews' oppression was fully justified by their obstinacy and their perseverance in error, and by the cumulative sins of their ancestors, as fully detailed in the Bible. This sounds very much like the kind of "violent, angry and menacing" response of which Josel complained and is in truth an unsatisfactory answer. But Calvin's mind may well have been on other things—namely on finding a wife to look after him. Melanchthon apparently chided him for his pensiveness during the conference and for drifting away on dreams of getting married.[28]

That is not to say that John Calvin was at heart in any way a man of gentle disposition. He was not. In the first four years of the theocratic totalitarian tyranny he founded in Geneva, he had fifty-eight heretics consigned to the stake and seventy-six exiled; in one single year he had forty-three women burned as witches; during a three-month outbreak of plague he executed thirty-four unfortunates for "sowing the pest." In 1553 he unforgivably sent to the pyre the brilliant Michael Servetus—scientist, philosopher and theologian, first discoverer of the circulation of the blood—though it is said that Calvin would have preferred a less brutal form of execution.

Yet movements begun by religious reformers, like those started by political philosophers, indeed by thinkers in general, are usually overtaken by developments that their founders had not and could not have foreseen. Just as Moses would be perplexed by modern Judaism and Jesus would be astonished by the Vatican, the future of Lutheran and Calvinist Protestantism would probably have surprised both founding fathers. Luther's teachings became ever more associated with narrow German nationalism. As Alfred Rosenberg, the Nazi theorist, trumpeted, "It was Luther, we must understand, who began to Germanise Christianity," adding, "National Socialism must complete the process."

Calvin's contribution, on the other hand, set in train an international religious movement that was far wider-reaching in its impact, spreading rapidly east and west. It was his work rather than Luther's that led to the reshaping of Christendom, to the founding of the Reformed Churches not only of France, Germany, Scotland, the Netherlands and Hungary but also the Church of England, which follows a sort of Calvinised Catholicism. William Pitt, the British politician who made his country an imperial power, explained it like this: "We have a Calvinistic creed, a Popish liturgy, and an Arminian clergy."[29] (Arminius was a Dutch theologian who opposed Calvin's ideas on predestination.) Moreover Calvin's views were extended further by those English Puritans who broke away from Anglicanism and eventually brought Calvinism to North America. Today both the Church of England and the Episcopal Church of the USA, as well as nonconformist and dissenting churches like the Methodists, Baptists, Presbyterians and even Unitarians, could all justly name Calvin among their founding fathers.

The Geneva reformer's promotion of Old Testament law, particularly the Ten Commandments, his loathing of images, his acceptance of financial trading, perhaps even his belief in predestination—which absolves the sinner of total responsibility for the sin—turned Christianity in a new direction. The consequences have been incalculable. Scholars with persuasive arguments have ascribed much of what we prize about our modern world to Calvin's legacy: the separation of Church and state, the Enlightenment, liberal humanism, religious tolerance, capitalism. We owe the existence of the State of Israel and today's wealthy and influential Atlantic diaspora at least in part to the man who wrote, "If we compare the Jews with other nations, surely their impiety, ingratitude and rebelliousness exceeds the crimes of all other peoples." The *Encyclopaedia Judaica* compares Calvin with the biblical soothsayer Balaam, who was called upon by the king of Moab to curse Israel, but who blessed her instead. "The Geneva reformer, too, set out to curse the Jews, but in the end turned out to have blessed them."

Nowhere was this truer than in Poland-Lithuania, where Calvinism bore a political meaning: resistance both to the great families and powerful bishops of Catholicism as well as to the Lutheran preferences of the German burghers. Calvinism ensured that, east of the Oder, Catholics were for a time no more than a dominant minority. Thus Poland-Lithuania was, as Norman Davies writes in *God's Playground*, "a 'land without bonfires.' There were no campaigns of forced conversion; no religious wars; no *autos-da-fé*; no St. Bartholomew's Eve; no Thomas or Oliver Cromwell." A Polish Benedictine wrote, "Beautiful harmony is born from contrary things, as on a lute strung with different strings."

As for the Jews, it is even said—not least by nineteenth-century Polish historian Sergei Bershadski[30]—that in 1587, during the interregnum between the death of King Stefan Bathory and the election of Swedish Prince Sigismund to the Polish crown, because the constitution of the

Polish-Lithuanian commonwealth did not allow for the throne to remain vacant, a wealthy and worthy merchant, Saul Judisch, spokesman for the Yiddish-speaking community of Brest and son of a famous rabbi in Italy,[31] was nominated "king for one night" and was known ever after as Saul Wahl (German for election). Even if untrue, the tale demonstrates how the country's ecumenical, multi-faith spirit made the Jews believe such an event to be entirely possible.

In this generous atmosphere, Poland's Jewish community would become the scholarly beacon of the Yiddish world, the site of an intellectual renaissance among European Jewry, a demonstration that the Yiddish civilisation could contribute not only to European economics, but also to European thought.

9

The Yiddish Renaissance

While the Protestant Reformation was beginning to build up its irresistible head of steam back in the 1530s, the European economy was again careering towards hell in a handcart. Economic historians have argued convincingly that this was not by chance, that the two were closely connected, that if you chart the uprisings, wars, civil disturbances and expulsions of the sixteenth and seventeenth centuries, all usually attributed to religious enthusiasm, you will find that the peaks and troughs coincide with a graph of the value of money and the prices of commodities like food and fuel. Not that the religious divisions played no part, but that those with little or nothing to lose were more likely to risk their all in a dangerous cause.

Across Europe what we today would call stagflation took hold. The contrast between rich and poor became ever more grotesque. Landowners grew fat, while peasants starved. Rising prices persuaded lords to convert their tenants' rents to labour obligations, opening up new lands to the plough and forcing their peasants to work on them unpaid.

Even in Poland with its dense forests, its rich and fertile cornfields, records from the beginning of the sixteenth century show a slow but unstoppable rise in the prices of firewood, Toruń rye and Cracow oats.[1] But it was much worse in the West. In some places the price of grain rose by

nearly a thousand per cent. Hunger sent destitute country people streaming into cities everywhere. In 1534 the city secretary of Strasbourg asked,

> What drives the poor here in such numbers? Answer: the great
> need and dearness of things. And where does this dearness come
> from? From God. Why did he send it to us? Because of our disbe-
> lief and sins, our ingratitude and selfishness, from which develops
> great cruelty and unbrotherly hardship for our neighbours.

In 1538 a German chronicler complained, "There are so many people
everywhere no one can move."

In the train of overcrowding and hunger came disease. Outbreaks of
pestilence decimated the cities. Six attacks of the mysterious *sudor anglicus*,
the English Sweating Sickness, spread all the way across the continent
through Germany, Austria, Bohemia and Poland into Russia, killing hundreds of thousands. In England as much as twenty per cent of the population perished in epidemics during the mid-century reign of Queen
"Bloody" Mary.

The social strains could not be contained. Mobs rioted; violent crime
rose tenfold. In a religious age, social protest and antisocial aggression were
channelled through the funnel of faith. Religious sectarians attacked each
other's buildings and fought running battles in the streets. When the price
of grain in the Low Countries suddenly surged even higher, the Iconoclas-
tic Disorders of the Low Countries broke out, new Calvinist converts
trashing the interiors of Catholic churches and attacking the priests. In
cities where epidemics raged, witches burned, a score at a time, in a holocaust of misogyny. At the height of the disorders Pope Gregory XIII took
it into his head to reform the old out-of-step Julian calendar, inherited
from pagan Rome; the citizens of Paris, Frankfurt and elsewhere rose in
fury against the theft of eleven days from their lifespan.

Minorities and outsiders were expelled or fled. The entire Catholic
population was driven out of Münster at the point of the sword in 1535 during the brief takeover by John of Leyden, the mad millenarian who ended
up in the iron cage still today suspended above the clock on the spire of St.
Lambert's Church. Some fifty thousand Protestant refugees took flight
from the Netherlands in 1557; a similar number trekked the roads out of
France after the St. Bartholomew's Day Massacre of 1572. And, of course,
the Jews: expelled from cities and entire principalities across the whole
empire.

Germany's loss was the Slav world's gain. Yiddish refugees arrived in Bohemia and Poland with few assets, but with their knowledge, experience and skills intact, their frustrated energies ready to be put to the service of the flourishing Jewish centres of Prague and Cracow, re-enriching the energetic but disorganised Slav-Yiddish communities with a strong Germanic influence—the Teutonic virtues of rationality, self-discipline and hard work. New arrivals swelled the communities to ever larger size. New Yiddish enterprises transformed the towns. In 1618 a Christian chronicler noted,

> In Lvov, in Lublin, in Poznań, and particularly in Cracow, not to mention Vilna, Mohilev, Slutzk, Brest-Litovsk, Lutsk, and elsewhere, the Jews have in almost every brick house five, ten, fifteen, or sixteen shops. These shops are full of merchandise and all kinds of wares.
>
> . . .
>
> They trade in spices and all kinds of grain, in honey and sugar, in milk products and other foodstuffs. There is scarcely any kind of goods, from the most expensive to the cheapest, in which the Jews do not trade.[2]

Soon, from among the prosperous business class, leading personalities emerged: brilliant engineers like Joachim Gaunse, invited to far-off England as a mining consultant; like the fabulously wealthy Bohemian philanthropist Mordechai Meisl, who paid for Prague's Jewish quarter to be paved; and like the stunningly successful international trader Jacob Bassevi von Treuenburg, probably the first Yiddish-speaking Jew to be ennobled, his coat of arms consisting of a blue lion with eight red stars.

But no civilisation can survive by commerce alone; it must also cultivate the life of the mind. Here too the populous and materially successful Yiddish communities of Bohemia and Poland-Lithuania were not found wanting, as they nurtured the movement to give the Yiddish civilisation its proper place in a modern, rationalist and scientifically advanced Europe.

Not, however, without opposition.

The Saturday of 18 March 1559, the Great Sabbath that preceded the Passover festival, was a red-letter day in the annual calendar of Poznań (German Posen), which had once been Poland's capital and which, with its duty-free trade privileges, had by the mid-sixteenth century grown to be one of the country's most prosperous centres. The Jewish population of the great city crowded into the Old Synagogue, to hear Rabbi Aaron Land, the community's highly respected spiritual leader, deliver his most important sermon of the year.

This was an old and important community, one of those for whose benefit Prince Bolesław the Pious had promulgated his famous Statute of Jewish Privilege in 1264. In the sixteenth century the 3,000 or so Jewish households formed nearly one-half of the entire population.[3] They owned 137 houses in the area of Jews' Street (*Judengaße*), Shoemakers' Street (*Schumacherstraße*) and Wreckers' Street (*Wrackerstraße*), of which 80 were built in stone, no doubt the dwellings of the merchant upper class, while into the shingle-roofed wooden tenements were crammed in multiple occupancy the families of the workers that are recorded among the sixteenth-century Posen Yiddish working class: the bakers, barbers, braiders, butchers, button makers, cap makers, cooks, furriers, glaziers, gold embroiderers, gold refiners, goldsmiths, horn workers, jewellers, musicians, porters, seal engravers, silk dyers, tanners and tailors.[4]

Like congregations today, they probably sat gossiping with each other on the synagogue's crowded wooden benches, watching as successive members of the great and the good were "called up" to recite a blessing as another section of Torah was chanted by the reader, and eagerly waiting for the rabbi to mount the central podium and deliver his address. They would have expected to hear the usual homilies—as recorded in the sermons of the period—attacking selfishness and greed, the haughtiness of the rich and their hypocritical self-righteousness, all of which would have gone down very well among a congregation largely composed of working people. In return, they would have to put up with being harangued about their failure to observe the commandments as strictly as they should. For, according to a leading Polish Talmudist of the day, "in this generation only a very few are scrupulous about the observance of the Sabbath laws."[5] It was, surely, ever thus.

However, what they received from Rabbi Land was something entirely different and quite unanticipated: a savage attack on reading books about science, philosophy and, in fact, anything other than the Talmud and commentaries upon it. According to a campaigning pamphlet issued by a certain Abraham Horowitz some time afterwards, "The Great Ass . . . said in his impudence that no Jew should study anything but the Talmud alone, and that all other books are 'books of Homer' [a phrase used by the early sages for pagan or heretical works]." No books? Not even the Hebrew

Bible? Indeed not. "No Jew," he had apparently thundered, "should study the Twenty-four Books very much or closely."[6]

The great majority of the congregation must have been rather bemused by this attack, since vanishingly few of them would have been readers of anything at all, let alone "books of Homer." In any case, the sermon on the Great Sabbath is traditionally dedicated to explaining and emphasising the laws governing the Passover festival and the moral lessons to be drawn from them, rather than what should or should not be in a student's private library. As the pamphlet protested: "You need not have informed them of any of these things, which for them are as a sealed book. Rather you should merely have rebuked them for their common transgressions, such as fraudulent dealings, oaths taken in vain, slander and gossip, and many similar things, not for things of which they know nothing."[7]

Unlucky Rabbi Aaron Land, the Great Ass, was not really the target of the attack. Rather out of his depth, he had dutifully weighed in, out of a spirit of family solidarity, to support his son-in-law, Rabbi Joseph Ashkenazi, dismissed in the same text as the Great Fool, who had been conducting a running verbal fight with the pamphlet's author in seminaries across the width of Yiddish Europe. They had argued their case in front of yeshivah students at Posen, probably elsewhere in Poland too, and certainly at the yeshivah of Prague, where the budding rabbis of that famous establishment had concluded—vainly as it turned out—that the egregious opponent of philosophy should henceforth be forbidden from publicly airing his opinions, on pain of excommunication. Now he had drawn his father-in-law into the dispute.

The results were inconclusive. Eventually Ashkenazi retired hurt, removed himself to Italy and then to Egypt, where he felt more in tune with conservative local opinion. His attacker, Abraham Horowitz, writer of the pamphlet, mellowed with age, turned from philosophy towards mysticism and left behind an ethical testament[8] that is still read by the pious today.

Rabbi Land's public protest was not so much, as it may at first appear, evidence for the Yiddish-speaking rabbis' incorrigibly reactionary views. Like most attempts at prohibition, what his outburst actually demonstrates is the reverse: that enough people were reading "books of Homer" to disturb traditionalists. Which is not surprising, given the date. A dispute over the place of science and philosophy in the Yiddish world-view was an inevitable consequence of the arrival of the Renaissance among the Jews of central and eastern Europe.

When, in the fifth century, the western Roman Empire collapsed under barbarian assault, its intellectual, philosophical, scientific and technical traditions were not erased, merely frozen. A place mark was inserted between the pages of history and the book temporarily closed. Now, after a millennium of barbarian rule, the feeling had spread, first in Italy and then across the continent, that it was time to open the book once again and continue writing the story from where its previous authors had left off. But to traditional Jewish scholars, however sorely their people had suffered under a thousand years of barbarian ignorance and cruel idiocy, the re-emergence of the classical world was a most unwelcome development.

Enshrined at the centre of the Jewish faith is a deep distrust of what it calls Greek Wisdom,[9] the product of the only culture ever to have offered a serious challenge to Jewish principles, at times perilously successful, particularly during the centuries that bracketed the birth of Christ. Now Renaissance rationalism, based on the Greek philosopher Aristotle's analysis of the physical world, and Renaissance humanism, based on the Greek philosopher Protagoras's proposition that "man is the measure of all things," threatened once again to confront the followers of a divinely revealed plan, to whom the world existed miraculously from moment to moment only by heaven's decree, and to whom the measure of all things could only be God.

Even more disturbing than physics and humanism was the introduction of printing with movable type, the archetypal Renaissance invention. As the chronicler David Gans wrote:

> No other invention, no other discovery can be compared to it since God created man upon the earth. It is not only the metaphysical sciences and the seven secular sciences which have profited from this invention, but all the applied sciences—metalworking, architecture, wood-engraving, and lithography—have also benefited. Each day reveals some new aspect, and innumerable books are published which benefit all professions whatever they may be.[10]

Jews took to the art of printing early. At the very same time as Gutenberg, in 1444, a Jewish dyer of Avignon, Davin of Caderousse, was experimenting with the "art and science of writing" using Hebrew letters "well cut in iron."[11] The first printed Hebrew books appeared in Italy from the 1470s, only some fifteen years after Gutenberg's famous Bible. Soon

Hebrew presses were set up in distant eastern Europe—in Prague (1512), Oels (1530), Cracow (1534) and Lublin (1550). This had a devastating effect on the Yiddish intellectual tradition, which had until then been an entirely oral affair that had passed its wisdom down the generations by word of mouth.

The old ways were unable to compete with the flood of printed books that surged through the Yiddish arena. Historians believe that the litany of philosophers attacked by Rabbi Ashkenazi in Posen's Old Synagogue on that March morning was in fact a roll-call of works that had been printed shortly before and which were now reaching the Polish seminaries. As Horowitz's pamphlet listed them:

Maimonides, Nachmanides, Don Isaac Abravanel, Rabbi Isaac Arama, Rabbi Shem-Tov, Rabbi Abraham Ibn Ezra, Rabbi Bahya the Elder, the second Rabbi Bahya, Gersonides, Rabbi David Kimchi, Rabbi Joseph Albo, Rabbi Isaac Israeli the second, Rabbi Solomon ben Adret, the Sage Rabbi Jonah who composed a commentary on Alfasi, and Rabbi Saadia Gaon.

It must have seemed to Rabbi Ashkenazi that the traditions of centuries were in danger of being overthrown by an uncontrolled and uncontrollable profusion of books. Once again the question of whether the study of science and philosophy was compatible with religious belief became an inescapable public issue for a God-orientated community.

It did not happen overnight. Since the late 1400s Yiddish-speaking scholars in eastern Europe had been quietly occupying themselves with the study of rationalist philosophy and its offshoot which we today call science. A scribe by the name of Yerukham Fishl was hard at work in Poland, dividing his time between copying out manuscripts by such philosophical greats as Aristotle, Averroës and Al Gazali in Hebrew translation, plus other original Jewish works, and tramping the roads of eastern Europe to sell them to the learning hungry. He and those like him did well. In 1517 the Polish chronicler Maciej Miechowicz noted that Lithuanian Jews studied sciences and arts, astronomy and medicine from Hebrew books,[12] an observation later confirmed by a visiting papal legate.

The author most commonly studied by the Yiddish-speaking scholars was the great Maimonides, Moses ben Maimon (1135–1204), a contemporary of the Arab thinker Averroës (Ibn Rushd), and the Norman martyr

Thomas à Becket, a product not of the Yiddish but of the Judaeo-Arabic world, and of an earlier time of rebirth, the abortive twelfth-century renaissance.

His story, and the violent discord that it generated, should have given his sixteenth-century Polish followers pause for thought.

Turn the calendar back from the sixteenth century to the twelfth. Ben Maimon is the most widely influential of all the Jewish philosophers—even among Christians and Muslims.

A lifelong exile from his Spanish birthplace Córdoba, after it was taken over by an intolerant fundamentalist Berber dynasty, he travelled first to Fez in Morocco and finally settled in Cairo, where he made himself a thorn in the flesh of the religious authorities of his time. He attacked the head of the Babylonian rabbinic academy and his son-in-law, "a very foolish man . . . miserable and an ignoramus in every respect," and sought to replace study of the Talmud, which needs years of intense work, with his own, concise, systematic and above all accessible law code, the *Mishneh Torah*. Maimonides favoured Greek logic and analysis over rabbinical casuistry, explained as allegories passages in the Torah and Talmud that would not stand up to rational scrutiny, opposed astrology in favour of astronomy, and made an attempt, brilliant if not wholly successful, to reconcile the teachings of Aristotle with those of the Hebrew sages. Apart from that, he wrote treatises on astronomy and on medicine.

Maimonides split the Jewish community of his own day into warring factions, who conducted a savage battle of words, flinging cruel insults and vicious accusations against each other. Had not Judah Halevy, the greatest Hebrew poet of the previous generation, declared, "Let not Greek wisdom tempt you, for it bears flowers only and no fruit."[13]

This was not just a dispute between faith and rational thought, but also a conflict between separation and integration, and a class struggle between the workers and the intellectual upper stratum of Judaeo-Arabic society. In a letter to the rabbis of northern France the leading Talmudist of the period, Moses ben Nachman, Nachmanides, expressed strong criticism of those like Maimonides who earned their living by serving the ruling class:

> They have defiled themselves with the food of gentiles and the wine of their feasts. They have mixed with them and become used to their deeds. . . . Courtiers have been permitted to study Greek

wisdom, to become acquainted with medicine, to learn mathematics and geometry, other knowledge and tricks, that they may make a living in royal courts and palaces.

This dispute, known to historians as the Maimonidean controversy, simmered on for more than a century after the philosopher was laid to rest in his tomb at Tiberias on the shore of Lake Galilee. Supporters and opponents continued to pour out a deluge of letters, commentaries, sermons and pamphlets. Anti: "They have filled their belly with the foolishness of the Greeks . . . They do not enter profoundly into the ways of our Torah; the ways of alien children suffice for them." Pro: "Know ye . . . that God differentiated men from animals and beasts through the reason, wisdom, and understanding which He granted them." Anti: "As he does not quote proofs from the sayings of the Talmudic sages for his decisions, who is going to follow his opinion?" Pro: "Reason was implanted in each and every one of the seed of Israel before his knowledge of Torah."[14]

Eventually verbal conflict boiled over into shocking violence, when some opponents of philosophy, letting their passions get the better of them, vandalised Maimonides's grave and, even worse, when Rabbi Solomon of Montpellier ran "crying and begging" to the Franciscans and Dominicans: "Behold, there are among us heretics and infidels, for they were seduced by Moses ben Maimon of Egypt. You who clean your community of heresy, clean ours too."[15] The Dominicans didn't have to be asked twice and in 1233 happily burned the great man's books at Montpellier. Nine years later, having acquired a taste for book-burning, they tipped twenty-four wagonloads, containing 12,000 copies, of the Talmud, on to a great pyre near Notre-Dame on the Île de la Cité of Paris.

This outrage quickly sobered up those drunk on their own self-righteousness and brought both warring sides up short. The controversy abated for several generations. Only to flare into life again when in 1305 a synod of rabbis met at Barcelona and excommunicated anyone "who, being under the age of twenty-five, shall study the works of the Greeks on natural science or metaphysics, whether in the original or in translation," saying, "How can any man dare to judge between human wisdom based on analogy, proof and thought, and the wisdom of God, between whom and us there is no relation nor similarity?" A counterblast, defending philosophy, was issued by the chief rabbi of Provence, who denied that studying philosophy led to heresy and claimed that an understanding of mathematics and astronomy was needed to comprehend many passages in the Talmud. In any case, he wrote, the ban was unenforceable, for "each individual will search out what suits him according to his natural inclination." His supporter, the prolific poet and essayist Rabbi Jedaiah Bedersi, pleaded, in an ironically titled "Letter of Apology,"

> Relinquish your excommunication, for the heart of this people will not turn away from philosophy and its books as long as there is breath in their frame and soul in their bodies . . . Even if they had heard it from the mouth of Joshua . . . they would never have accepted it, for they intend to do battle for the honour of their great teacher [Maimonides] and his works. For the holiness of his teaching they will sacrifice fortune, family, and soul as long as there is a breath in their bodies.[16]

Thus ended the last major bout of the slanging match. The troubles of the calamitous fourteenth century, the overall economic collapse, accompanied by plagues, insurrections, expulsions, massacres and burnings at the stake, dunked the flames of cerebral intellectual conflict into the cold waters of sober everyday reality. For more than two centuries Jewish thinkers, despairing of Christendom's crude and ignorant uncivility, put away philosophical investigation and clove to ancient certainties for comfort.

But the Reformation of Christianity had made everyone, Catholic, Protestant and Jew, think again. Now, in the sixteenth century, a new Jewish renaissance was breathing life on to the still smouldering ashes of the old. Rabbis began once more to take an interest in matters outside their narrow remit: scholars like Jonah Landsofer from Moravia, who appended notes on a number of Euclid's geometrical propositions to his collection of responsa,[17] and Yom Tov Lipmann Heller of Prague and Cracow (1579–1654), keen student of philosophy, linguistics, mathematics, astronomy and the natural sciences, and author of *Tosafot Yom Tov* (Yom Tov's "additions," commentaries on the Mishnah), as far as I know the only Hebrew religious work to be named, complete with Yiddish pronunciation *Tausves-Jontof*, in a canonical German text, Heinrich Heine's poem "The Disputation":

> *Gilt nichts mehr der Tausves-Jontof,*
> *Was soll gelten? Zeter! Zeter!*

which is itself quoted in Karl Marx's *Das Kapital*, in a discussion of bills of exchange, where it is translated in the English version as:

> If the Tausves-Jontof's nothing,
> What is left? O vile detractor!

This time, however, the Jewish renaissance would arise not from Spain, southern France or even the Holy Land, but from Prague in Bohemia and Cracow in the Polish-Lithuanian commonwealth, the two chambers of the Yiddish civilisation's beating heart.

CRACOW

The middle of the sixteenth century saw Cracow rejoice in its golden age. Commerce prospered. Scientists, artists and humanist thinkers gathered from all over the Slav world, as well as from Italy, Germany and further afield. Polish intellectual life burst into full flower at the Cracow Academy (known since 1818 as the Jagiellonian University), which had been founded in 1364 by Casimir the Great, with faculties of law, medicine and the liberal arts, and then re-established by King Władysław Jagiełło in 1400, with an additional faculty of theology graciously sanctioned by the pope. The Academy soon became the world's foremost centre for the study of astronomy, the only European university to hold a separate chair for the subject, later adding a second. By 1495 a German chronicler was reporting that no other city could compare with Cracow's predominance in this subject.

The university's story had long been bound up with that of Cracow's Jews. When Casimir founded his Academy, classes were first held in a number of temporary premises while a purpose-built palace of scholarship was planned. The king's intention was to create a grand university complex outside the city walls, choosing as his preferred location an old village called Bawół (Buffalo), on an island in the Vistula river where the road from the salt mine at nearby Wieliczka met the ancient transcontinental slave route from Russia. Around his new centre of learning he founded a town which came to be called Kazimierz after him. However, building work was halted when he died, and the university's next patron, King Jagiełło, favoured a much more central location, preferably not too far from Poland's most magnificent Gothic church, the recently completed Basilica of St. Mary, in the city's great Market Square, the Rynek Główny.

An obvious choice was Ulica Żydowska (Jewish Street), today renamed for St. Anne, which still runs into the square's southern end. Here, as a first step, the large stone house belonging to the Jew Jossman was compulsorily purchased. As the university expanded, further property was bought, sometimes extorted with menaces, and occasionally expropriated outright, from the Jewish community.

The university students proved to be neighbours from hell. Students and apprentices were famed all over Europe for their riotous and destructive behaviour. Shopkeepers in all the great cities would rush to put up shutters, and stallholders would stow their merchandise in panic, whenever the cry of "'ware 'prentices!" went up. In 1209 pitched battles between students and townsmen in Oxford, the Town and Gown Riots, prompted a group of academics to leave the city and set up a new place of study in Cambridge. In 1408, Bohemian students at the University of Prague rioted, objecting to privileges granted to German students by the emperor, and drove their rivals out with much bloodshed. In the Apprentice Riots of London's Evil May Day 1517, 135 Flemings were hacked to death. Incidentally, these were not all necessarily testosterone-fuelled young men; someone studying for a doctorate in theology at Oxford in the sixteenth century could expect to be attending university for sixteen years or more.

In the English colleges, antagonism was directed towards northerners and Welshmen.[18] In Cracow Jews were the students' neighbours and thus their closest available and most convenient targets. And those attending the faculty of Catholic theology were anyway ideologically strongly predisposed to anti-Jewish agitation, especially when acting in concert with German burghers keen to wipe out competition, and even more particularly when egged on by visiting missionary rabble-rousers like John Capistrano, sworn enemy of all non-Catholics.

Eventually street violence forced the Jewish community to move first to the area around St. Stephen's Square near the northern end of the Rynek, and ultimately in 1495, by royal decree, out of Cracow altogether, to join the community already established in neighbouring Kazimierz, the township where Casimir had first intended to site his house of study. Specifically, they resettled themselves around Ulica Szeroka (Broad Street), where the monumental Old Synagogue, created in the sixteenth century by a Gucci ancestor called Matteo, still stands by the old town wall on the site of Bawoł village—the very spot the king had designated for his seat of learning. There, in a satisfying tit-for-tat against their Cracovian competitors, the Jewish elders sought, and in 1568 were granted, the royal

Privilegia de non tolerandis Christianis, a ban on non-Jewish residence in their part of the municipality.

As usual, though legally obliged to live in Kazimierz, the Jews retained their places of business in all the main streets of Cracow, even on the Market Square, and heavy penalties were imposed on anyone who perpetrated acts of violence against them. What is more, their faith was continuing to attract Slav converts even in this late period, for in 1539 Katharina Zelazewska, a well-known alderman's widow, was burned at the stake for embracing Judaism, as an example to other less prominent Cracow folk for whom both the self-imposed restrictions of orthodox Jewish life, as well as the antagonism of their former co-religionists, were apparently not discouraging enough.

Walking the tourist-thronged streets of Kazimierz today, past the many synagogues raised in diverse styles ranging from Renaissance to nineteenth-century oriental pastiche, by the green-roofed ritual bathhouse that looks like a country villa and now houses a kosher café, through the market place with its round central kiosk once occupied by the ritual slaughterers, alongside the substantial, if time-ravaged, houses—like the red-rendered building that local guides always point out as the birthplace of cosmetics empress and philanthropist Helena Rubinstein (though she herself claimed a different family home, whose appearance she thought classier)—it is not easy to conjure up an image of Kazimierz's overcrowded sixteenth-century past. Since that time even the street plan has changed somewhat, a fact underlined by the notice on one wall as a warning to everyone called Cohen, members of the priestly caste, for whom contact with the dead is defiling. "COHANIM BEWARE!!!" it shouts in Polish, English and Hebrew. "Only the opposite sidewalk can be used for walking on this street!!! The sidewalk on this side and a part of the roadway have been paved over graves."

Back in the sixteenth and seventeenth centuries, the Jewish part of town housed some four and a half thousand residents, more or less the same number as the non-Jewish sector, which was, however, spread over five times the Jews' area. By 1653 a survey showed that, apart from synagogues, hospitals, bath and dance houses, the community headquarters and other public buildings, there were 67 tenements and 121 wooden houses. By which one should understand neither simple log cabins nor alpine chalets, but the sort of multi-storeyed, plank-patched, sagging-roofed, broken-staired, glassless-windowed edifice shown in old illustrations like the 1869 drawing of the market place printed in the *Jewish*

Encyclopedia. Many families would have been crammed into this unprepossessing and unhygienic warren, perhaps even—as in some early twentieth-century New York City dwellings—one family per room.

Yet in the very same period, the shabby township was the focus, the centre, the very heart of the Yiddish civilisation, a place where the German-speaking West and the Slavic-speaking East were united, in a land where its principal and world-famous rabbi, Moses Isserles, said that it was preferable to live even "on dry bread" than in other places more dangerous for Jews. He jokingly derived the name of the country, Polin in Yiddish, from the Hebrew *poh lin*, "here shall you rest."

Precisely where Isserles lived in Kazimierz is now unknown and unknowable. His remains are buried in the old cemetery named after him, in a tomb around which, until the Nazi war, pilgrims from all over the world would assemble in his honour on the day of his death, the 18th of the Hebrew month of Iyyar, a minor holiday.[19] On the stone are written the words: "From Moses to Moses there was none like Moses," a slightly mysterious compliment in this context, since the saying was originally coined in reference to the Prophet Moses and the philosopher Moses Maimonides.

Where the great rabbi worshipped and taught, on the other hand, is well-known. What is more, the place still exists: a pretty little synagogue with pale cream-coloured masonry and red-tiled roof, sheltering behind a round-arched gateway off Szeroka Street. Inside you can still find the chair on which—so the guides tell you and maybe it is even true—the great man himself sat.

His full name was Moses Isserel-Lazarus, abbreviated to Isserls or Isserles, but mostly known by the Hebrew acronym Rema.[20] He was born in Cracow, some time between 1520 and 1530, into a family surnamed Luria, a famous and widespread clan, which had already provided medieval Jewry with some of its brightest luminaries and would continue to do so long after the Rema's day. Moses's grandfather was rabbi of Brest, his father was famed for both his wealth and his scholarship, and he himself, after childhood lessons from his father and his uncle, was sent to study with a well-known Talmudic scholar in Lublin, where he married his teacher's daughter. On returning to Cracow, he set up a seminary, a yeshivah, whose pupils he supported out of his own well-endowed pocket. When his wife died—sadly prematurely at the age of only twenty—he founded in her memory, and his father paid for, the synagogue off Szeroka Street still known by his name. There he taught, attended services, carried out charitable works, and concentrated on his own life's task of rabbinical scholarship.

The Rema's best-known bequest to posterity is his commentary on Sephardic Rabbi Joseph Caro's summary of Jewish practice, *The Prepared Table* (*Shulkhan Aruch*), which Isserles believed did not fairly represent eastern European, Yiddish custom. He called his notes the Tablecloth, the *Mappah*, and few editions of the *Shulkhan Aruch* printed since his day have failed to spread the Polish Rema's cloth over the original author's structure.

Thus far, Rabbi Moses Isserles seems to have been simply following the millennial Jewish tradition of devoting all his energies to the eternally unfinished business of reinterpreting the Hebrew sacred texts for a new age and holding his congregation to their religious duties. But this age was different from all previous ages. Natural philosophers were in the process of developing an entirely new understanding of the universe and its workings. And this was happening right here, in Cracow.

A young Prussian cleric from Toruń called Niklas Koppernick—better known Latinised to Copernicus—attended the Cracow Academy at the end of the fifteenth century to study astronomy. Fifty years later, in 1543, when on his deathbed in Frauenburg (now Frombork) on the Baltic coast, he finally allowed the publication of a treatise that threatened to upset the composure of sixteenth-century Christianity as roughly as Darwin's *On the Origin of Species* rocked the Church's complacency in the nineteenth. His book was called *On the Revolutions of the Celestial Spheres* (*De revolutionibus orbium coelestium*) and though still not quite describing our modern sun-centred solar system, it began the process of displacing the earth from the centre of the universe, a position taken for granted in every religious text.

Given the importance of astronomy to the Cracow Academy, located in the very part of the city where the Jews' quarter had once stood and where they still had their places of business, and almost next door to the Jewish town in Kazimierz, it would be very surprising if at least some of the college's heady intellectual ferment did not froth over into the Yiddish community. And it would surely have been impossible for any informed person, let alone a mind as capacious and perceptive as the Rema's, to ignore the tumultuous renaissance of philosophical, scientific thought, and fail to formulate some kind of response to it. Isserles was not found wanting. David Fishman, professor of history at the Jewish Theological Seminary of America, has pointed out that in taking on the new ideas with which he was surrounded, he not only picked up the rationalist tradition

begun by Maimonides, but broadened and expanded it. "While his for-
bears had delved exclusively into Maimonides' conception of God, Isserles
revived whole dimensions of Maimonidean thought that had been
neglected by them."[21] These included astronomy, the rationalist interpretation of rabbinic tales and the search for logical reasons for the commandments. The Rema himself wrote, "The aim of man is to search for the
cause and the meaning of things."[22]

Rabbi Isserles's most original contribution to religious astronomy, if
not to science, was in the course of a difficult work called the *Law of the
Burnt Offering* (*Torat ha-Olah*), in which he applied to the study of the
heavens principles derived from the mystical esoteric tradition of Judaism,
the Kabbalah.

Kabbalah has one foot in the esoteric, Gnostic (concerning hidden
knowledge) literature of the middle of the first Christian millennium,
developed under Greek and Persian influence, as in its first major text the
Book of Creation (*Sefer Yetzirah*), and the other in a fragmented collection
of traditions ascribed to the Babylonian sages of the Talmud, the *Book of
Brightness* (*Sefer ha-Bahir*). A complete theosophical system was first
developed in thirteenth-century Provence and Spain during the upwelling
of exotic beliefs that at much the same time was stimulating the Cathar
heresy among Christians. Kabbalah's most influential work, the *Book of
Light* (*Sefer ha-Zohar*), was compiled—and perhaps written—in Spain
between 1270 and 1300 by Moses ben Shem Tov de Leon.

In the sixteenth century the non-rationalist Kabbalistic way of thinking was becoming increasingly influential in eastern Europe, partly in reaction to the shattering expulsion from Spain in 1492 of Judaism's most
glamorous community, which could only be, in the eyes of many, a prelim-
inary to the end of the world. The focus of mystical creativity now shifted
to Safed in the Holy Land, where contemporaries of the Rema, Moses
Cordovero and Isaac Luria, added to it a strong messianic colouring.

To sum up the ideas of Kabbalah in brief is impossible and even to try
ridiculous. But in a suggestion of its approach, one might say that just as
the sounds of words like good, evil, joy, sorrow, beauty, or ugliness are
physical vibrations in the air, real enough in their own way but in no sense
directly connected with the phenomena they describe and instead are
merely symbols for them, so is the Torah, the Jewish religion, indeed the
entire physical universe, but a set of symbols representing matters beyond
normal human comprehension. The task of Kabbalah is to unlock the
symbolic code.

In the *Law of the Burnt Offering* Rabbi Isserles deciphers the Jerusalem Temple, interpreting it as a microcosm that models in miniature the entire universe: the rotations of the sun and moon, the variations of climate and sunlight on the earth, the paths of the stars. In the course of his dissertation, Isserles puts across a considerable amount of astronomical lore, including ideas propounded by anonymous non-Jewish "scholars of astronomy." The result is a tour de force combination of allegorical symbolism with genuine astronomical learning drawn from a wide array of sources. One might see it as the first tentative step towards building up a Yiddish astronomy, a science marked with the preoccupations, interests and intellectual traditions of eastern European Jewry.

The Rema's other written contribution to natural philosophy was educational: an explanatory commentary on *The Course of the Stars*,[23] the Hebrew translation of a popular astronomy book of the time, the *New Theory of the Planets* (*Theoricae Novae Planetarum*) by George von Peuerbach, a precursor of Copernicus, first published in 1460. In his introduction, the Rema puts forward his purpose clearly: "so that every man of intelligence who is capable of logical reasoning may study it and understand all its words." In a foreword to this commentary by the seventeenth-century rabbinic astronomer Chaim Lisker, we find the explanation for the inscription on Isserles's tombstone. " 'From Moses to Moses there was none like Moses,' " wrote his admirer. "For from Moses Maimonides until Moses Isserls these matters were concealed and hidden, until he came with his commentary to this book." To his followers, the Rema was the pioneer who picked up the baton where Maimonides had dropped it.

This caused him much grief from his more conservative contemporaries. In an exchange of letters well-known to scholars, his relative Solomon Luria, head of a yeshivah in Lublin, took him to task for citing "the uncircumcised Aristotle" and the "researchers into nature"[24] in the context of adjudicating on religious law. Isserles rejected the admonition, writing that there was no ban on "the study of the words of wise men and their investigations into the essence of reality and its natural manifestations."

Yet the Rema was still restricted by certain fundamentals of belief which nothing could be allowed to threaten. His image of the solar system was still firmly as described in the second-century Alexandrian astronomer Ptolemy's *Almagest*, with a central earth around which revolve all the heavenly bodies. How could it be otherwise when this picture of the heavens had been accepted by Talmudic authority? Any clash between the "scholars of astronomy" and the sages of the Talmud must be declared no contest. So fundamental was the Talmud to the whole Yiddish intellectual world that it was simply not possible for its sages ever to have been wrong—or even unaware of matters discovered since their time, since they "knew the secrets of astronomy as much as the gentile scholars, and even more than them."

Thus while always positive about science, calling its study "a stroll in the pleasure gardens" and encouraging his students to range widely in their pursuit of knowledge, Rabbi Moses Isserles himself was not quite able to take the next step and seek a way to combine the wisdom of the gentiles with that of the Jews. However, so good a teacher could not fail to inspire others to boldly go where no rabbi had gone before. His example made it possible to map out an identifiably Yiddish path through the pleasure gardens of scientific knowledge. But not in Cracow.

PRAGUE

The way led 250 miles westwards out of the Polish-Lithuanian common-wealth to Prague in Bohemia—the domain from 1583 to 1612 of Rudolf II, Holy Roman Emperor, King of Bohemia and Hungary. And just as Cracow's inspiration, echoing the Yiddish tradition, was the creative friction between Germanic and Slavonic culture, so too in Prague did western and eastern influences vie with each other and finally combine in a cultural whole that was greater than the sum of its parts.

In the sixteenth century the Emperor Rudolf raised patronage at the Bohemian court to new heights and with it the splendour, both material and intellectual, of his bustling German-Slav capital, Prague, whose wealth and security is still evident today. The Jewish population in the 1590s is estimated at some six thousand, a significant proportion of the city total.

If you walk from the fourteenth-century tourist-infested Charles Bridge into the Old Town, across the square with its town hall (the one bearing the famous fifteenth-century astronomical clock from which a procession of wooden apostles emerges every hour on the hour) down the boulevard called Parizska, you enter the Jewish quarter, the district now called Josefov, after the Emperor Joseph II, whose 1781 Edict of Tolerance would change the situation of the Jews throughout the Austrian Empire considerably for the better. There isn't anything left today of the rather squalid tangle of alleyways and ramshackle unsanitary housing that were swept away by redevelopment at the end of the nineteenth century—what Franz Kafka, who was born there, remembered as "dark corners, mysterious corridors, blind windows, dirty backyards, noisy pubs, and closed inns," but there remain enough historic buildings to give at least an idea of how numerous and prosperous were Prague's Jewish inhabitants in early modern times—the High synagogue, the Gothic Altneuschul with its fingered brick gable, the Maisel, Klausen and Pinkas synagogues and the Jewish town hall with its Hebrew-lettered clock face and reverse-moving hands, remodelled in the Rococo 1760s and now painted in fairy pink (leading some tourists to confuse it with the Pinkas synagogue). Several of these buildings, as well as the paving of the area's streets, were the gift of Marcus Mordechai Maisel (1528–1601), mayor of the Jewish quarter, considered by the historian Heinrich Graetz the first true Jewish capitalist, on whose tombstone are written the words, "None of his contemporaries was his equal in deeds of charity."

From the 1580s until the emperor's death some thirty years later Rudolfine Prague, as historians have called it, prospered mightily, to shine out as a beacon of European arts and sciences, attracting major European painters, architects, scientists, philosophers and thinkers. The British historian Hugh Trevor-Roper wrote that the ruling ideology of the multicultural Habsburg court was to be found in "humanism, in science, in the study of nature, in Platonic philosophy,"[25] for these were fields that ignored—or rather transcended—differences in language, nationality and religion. Indeed, the emperor's supreme self-confidence gave him a uniquely relaxed attitude to religious orthodoxy, attracting to his circle Catholics, Protestants, other Christian nonconformists and Jews. The Elizabethan travel writer Fynes Moryson observed, with some surprise, on his visit to the city in the 1590s that:

> generally, in all the kingdome, there was great confusion of Religions, so as in the same Citty some were Caluinists, some Lutherans, some Hussites, some Anabaptists, some Picards, some Papists . . . And as the Jewes haue a peculyar Citty at Prage, so they had freedome throughout all the kingdome . . . I founde Emperour Rudulphus's subjects in Bohemia more differing in opinions of Religion yet to converse in strange amity and peace together.[26]

This remarkable ecumenical atmosphere, this multi-sided tolerance and interest in others' views, whatever their religious allegiance might be, allowed Yiddish-speaking thinkers to flourish, taking up the challenge from Moses Isserles in Cracow and raising their sights yet further, to arrive ever closer to the ultimate aim of establishing the Jewish perspective as an independent and equally valid view of reality. Several of the Rema's pupils found a sympathetic home in Prague, each making his own particular contribution to the collective enterprise. But first these Yiddish proto-scientists had to come to terms with a new and revolutionary Renaissance idea, one very difficult for them to digest: that there could be such a thing as progress, that understanding might increase over time, and that all new knowledge did not have to accord precisely with the Holy Scriptures and the writings of the ancient sages.

Paradoxically this step was made possible by the deep conservatism of the most celebrated authority of the day, Moses Isserles's contemporary, the Prague Rabbi Judah Loew—best known for supposedly having moulded a Golem out of clay (the word, taken from Psalm 139:16, means a homunculus of "unshaped flesh"). He called it Yossele and brought it to life by placing a piece of paper with the name of God (the *Shem*) into its mouth—which he would withdraw every Friday evening to prevent his creature from violating the Sabbath. It is presumably unnecessary to underline that this story has no basis in fact, that it first appeared in the late eighteenth century, and that it was originally told not about Rabbi Loew but about a certain Rabbi Elijah of Chelm in Poland, a devotee of Kabbalah, who died in 1583. Similar stories of miracles and superhuman power circulated around the Rema too. (Worth noting, however, is that the concept was updated for the twentieth century when Czech playwright Karel Čapek re-imagined the Golem as a mechanical worker that he called a "robot" and gave the word to the English language.)

Rabbi Loew's full name was Judah Loew Ben Bezalel, otherwise referred to by his acronym Maharal.[27] Though of German origin—his family came from Worms and he himself was possibly born there too—he spent his working life in the Slav world, Moravia, Bohemia and Poland. He died at Prague in 1609 and devotees still come to pray by his tomb in the Old Jewish Cemetery, easily recognisable from a carved lion motif (signifying the German *Loewe*, lion) and the many scraps of paper, inscribed with petitions to his shade, inserted into cracks in the stone. Elsewhere in Prague's Jewish town, the Maharal's twenty-first-century admirers still visit the Klausen synagogue, built in 1604 on the site of three buildings (Klausen is German for retreats or cells) erected by the mayor to mark the Emperor Maximilian's progress through the Jewish quarter in

1573, in one of which some claim that the Maharal held his Talmudic tutorials. Also linked with his name is the Altneuschul, the oldest and most famous of all Prague's synagogues, the earliest part of which, now merely the entrance lobby, dates from the 1220s or 1230s, with a double nave added in the 1280s or 1290s, and further developed with its signature brick comb-edged gables in the fifteenth century, and in whose attic, so they say, the remains of Rabbi Loew's Golem are still hidden.

Revered for his piety, asceticism, and mystical inspiration, the Maharal's scholarship was not confined to Torah and Talmud, but embraced secular fields as well, including mathematics and astronomy. However, he rejected Aristotle's view, as propounded by Maimonides, that intellectual attainment through rational thought is the supreme human goal. Only through study of the Torah and observance of its laws can humanity achieve perfection and communion with God. "If a person labours and becomes wiser than all the ancients [in worldly knowledge] there is no doubt that this is to be considered nothing compared to a small intellectual attainment concerning the hosts of heaven."

Yet Rabbi Loew was as far as a man can be from an ignorant obscurantist, and was perfectly well aware of the revolutionary developments in natural philosophy taking place in his own day. Though he remained utterly faithful to the rabbinic view of the universe, which had been received from Moses at Sinai, who had received it directly from God, who alone can possibly know the truth, he was aware of the discovery of America—"they say that recently a certain place has been found, called by them a new world, previously undiscovered"—and hoped that the remnants of the lost ten tribes might turn out to be living there. He knew of Copernicus: "One came who was called the Master of the New Astronomy, who provided a different picture . . . of the path of the stars and constellations and heavenly bodies." He may even have been familiar with Copernicus's book itself, for he seemed to know of the anonymous preface that Lutheran Pastor Andreas Osiander added to the work, calling its claims into question: "Even he himself wrote that he has still not resolved everything." (Osiander's aim was to avoid the book's proscription by the Church.)

How then did this great scholar, with his firmly medieval rabbinical views, make it possible for younger others to break out of the Talmudic mould and entertain notions that seem to contradict both the Bible and the Jewish sages? In an article about the Jewish response to early modern science,[28] Professor Noah Efron of Bar-Ilan University explains that the

Maharal believed science merely dealt in superficialities and had nothing to do with ultimate truth. Scientists were, after all, constantly revising their ideas and contradicting what their predecessors claimed, so how could such an unstable process compete with the certainties of the religious canon? The notion that science should progress by successive, ever closer approximations to truth, each invalidating the previous, was unknown to him. Indeed, Efron adds, "the Maharal went so far as to call all statements of the natural philosophers 'lies,' of more or less flagrant varieties." He quotes from the Rabbi's book *The Well of Exile:*

> It is not even appropriate to call the science of astronomy a science, because science is only attainable by one who actually knows something as it is, and that condition you will never find in their [so-called] science, for no one can verify its truth, and what is the difference if one lies a great deal or lies a little?[29]

Since science had no claim, unlike Torah, to absolute truth, was in other words merely a collection of greater or lesser lies, what scientists said was of no importance in the greater scheme of things. So there need be in Judaism no equivalent of the Catholic Church's fight against the new astronomy, no threats of torture or burning at the stake, no Jewish *Index Librorum Prohibitorum* (Index of Forbidden Books) such as was instituted by the Council of Trent in 1557, no forcing of believers, like Galileo, to recant their views.

Even greater freedom to consider scientific results, in spite of their contradiction of scripture, was afforded by the Maharal's uniquely relativistic stance. Too rational simply to accept biblical miracles at face value, he proposed an explanation that Einstein might have been proud of. Taking as his text the story in chapter ten of the Book of Joshua, when Joshua "said in the sight of Israel, Sun, stand thou still upon Gibeon; and thou, Moon, in the valley of Ajalon. And the sun stood still, and the moon stayed, until the people had avenged themselves upon their enemies," the Maharal wrote,

> It is possible that the sun followed its accustomed course while [at the same time] it miraculously stood still. For it is possible for one subject to possess two opposite conditions because of two opposite perspectives—the course of nature being one and the unnatural the other ... Thus for Joshua and his people who needed an

unnatural miracle, [the sun] stood still, but for the rest of the
world who did not require the miracle, they experienced the natural course [of the sun].[30]

So science and religion belong to two different worlds that do not have to
match. Now Jewish scholars could accept the novel facts that science was
delivering daily without disloyalty to Torah and Talmud—no different
from the separation of domains that the pious of all religions maintain in
their minds today, able to allow both the stories in the biblical Book of
Genesis as well as the findings of palaeontology at the same time. Now
nothing prevented the Yiddish-speaking people from making a specifically
Jewish contribution to Europe's collective scientific enterprise.

DOVID GANS

Take a few paces from the Maharal's splendid tomb in Prague's Old Jewish
Cemetery and you will find another, rather humbler, grave with a narrow
headstone bearing a Hebrew inscription, surmounted by a carved goose
perched on a slightly miscarved Star of David, the very first time the symbol appears on a Jewish gravestone. This is the last resting place of Rabbi
Dovid Gans, disciple of Rabbi Isserles of Cracow and Rabbi Loew of
Prague. The three elements carved on the headstone, the inscription, the
goose and the Star of David, sum up the man and his contribution. The
stone's dedication reads, "Here is buried our teacher, the righteous Dovid
Gans, author of *The Shoot of David*";[31] the goose refers to his family name
(*Gans* is German for goose), and the hexagram indicates both his name
David, as well as the title of a book on astronomy, *Mogen Dovid* (*The Shield
of David* as the symbol is called in Hebrew), for which he issued a brief
prospectus shortly before he died, but which would have to wait 130 years
before publication under a different title. It is not much to have left behind
for a man who struggled so hard, yet who was completely ignored in the
writings of his contemporaries and is largely forgotten by history, but who
did more than any other to give expression to a Yiddish voice among the
councils of the great thinkers of the Prague renaissance.

In his moving and sympathetic account of Gans's life and work,[32] the
late historian and theologian André Neher wrote, "I am sorry for his sake:
all the more so in that it is through him, through his chronicle, through his
astronomical work, that we are acquainted with so many personalities,
events, items, curiosities which enable us to reconstruct a whole universe

throbbing with life." Yet, though Neher makes the case strongly that Gans's posthumously published astronomy book, renamed for unknown reasons *Delightful and Pleasant*,[33] was a scientifically significant work, the first in Hebrew to give an account of the Copernican sun-centred solar system, he admits that his subject was not in the first rank of thinkers. "For we have to admit, David Gans was not on the level of the geniuses with whom he was associated. In today's universities we would place him among the technical assistants . . . Neither in Jewish studies nor in the general sciences was David Gans more than a modest workman."

Yet if Gans's greatness did not lie in his contribution to astronomical science, it may instead be found in his overall purpose, which was brilliantly achieved in the one book that he did see off the press. For Gans was at heart an educator, content to find an honourable role in presenting the work of the intellectual élite in a form accessible to the many. And the whole point of this education was to make it possible for the Yiddish-speaking Jews to take their rightful place among the European nations. This was neither to be achieved by assimilating to gentile ways and values nor, God forbid, by converting to Christianity. Gans was a rabbi after all, steeped in Talmudic learning. His aim was to lift Jewish horizons to include with their basic grounding in Torah and Talmud both the latest ideas of the natural philosophers as well as a greater familiarity with the Jews' own mundane history and that of the wider world.

Born in 1541 in Westphalia, north Germany, after a basic rabbinical education in Germany, Gans made the great trek east to study under the wing of Rabbi Moses Isserles in his famous Cracow yeshivah. Along the way he stopped with a relative, on whose library shelves he found a Hebrew translation of Euclid's *Elements*. He did not, he later related, merely leaf through the book but studied it carefully. *Elements* opened the young student's eyes to a stunning revelation: an entirely unexpected new world of shapes and numbers not only fascinating in itself, but also providing a key to unlock the secrets of the skies. "Euclid's book is like a ladder thrown between earth and heaven," wrote Gans, "and its top reaches heaven. Take away the book and it will be impossible for you to mount heavenwards."

Perhaps an inkling of his future interests had already led Gans to select the Rema as his teacher, for far from discouraging the young man's passion for geometry, mathematics and astronomy, the Cracow yeshivah where he was to spend the next years was the one place in the Yiddish world where they were likely to be further strengthened. Moreover, Rabbi Isserles introduced him to another aspect of secular learning that would have found little encouragement anywhere else, namely history. Then, when he moved to Prague in his mid-twenties, Gans came under the influence of the great Rabbi Loew, the Maharal, who had his own interest in philosophy, mathematics and astronomy, and encouraged the young disciple yet further. Thus David Gans was educated by the very best minds that sixteenth-century Yiddish society could offer.

Unlike other rabbinical writers, he penned no commentaries on religious texts, no ethical works or homiletic pamphlets—at least none that we know of. In fact, how he spent most of his life and how he earned his living are a mystery. He seems to have married twice—he left descendants—and was probably active in business, making frequent journeys back to his home town in Germany. All one can be sure of is that through the next twenty-five years of silence, he was absorbing the unique multicultural atmosphere of Rudolfine Prague, and nurturing the ambition to become the educator of his people. He wrote many Hebrew books—the community scribe later said that he begged him daily for one or other of his works to copy and distribute, but to no avail. He wrote on mathematics, geography and astronomy. All but one of these texts are lost—maybe some were never finished (or even started?). But when he did finally launch a work into the public realm, it was worth waiting for. It ran to nine editions and was translated into Latin, which could only mean that non-Jews were reading it too, an extraordinary achievement for a sixteenth-century rabbi.

The book was called *Tsemach Dovid* (*The Shoot of David*), a phrase with a multiplicity of meanings, resonating with the famous passage in the biblical Book of Isaiah: "and there shall come forth a rod out of the stem of Jesse, and a Branch shall grow out of his roots." David is, of course, the name of the author, suggesting that the book is a shoot that has grown from the author's mind, and also—for the Hebrew word has this sense too—that it is but one shoot of many to come.

The Shoot of David is essentially a book of history, divided into two volumes, one chronicling personalities and events from the Jewish past, the other from the gentile. The content tells us little that we did not already know. But what comes through clearly is Rabbi Gans's motivation, why he believed it important for Jews to know the material which he presents to them. The book is a fascinating glimpse of precisely what constituted, to his sixteenth-century rabbinical sensibility, the general historical information with which every ordinary person should be familiar. For this was no tome for intellectuals: "I did not write this book for great scholars who are filled like pomegranates with the Torah, but for householders, and humble and young students, of my own standing."

"For the majority of readers," writes Noah Efron, "Gans aimed to promote what might be called, anachronistically, historical and scientific literacy." The author himself put it this way in the introduction:

> We are foreign residents among the gentiles, and when they tell or ask us of the first days of ancient dynasties we put our hands to our mouths and we do not know what to answer, and we seem to them like beasts who do not know their left from their right, and it is as if we were all born yesterday. But with this book, the respondent can answer and say a little about every epoch.

Gans wished to raise the Jewish tradition to a position of equal honour with the Polish, the German, the Italian and the other national traditions by which he was surrounded. His second teacher the Maharal, who forbade the reading of books by non-Jews, would probably not have approved at all, but Gans defended himself by quoting what his first teacher, the Rema, said about the pursuit of history in one of the commentary notes of his *Mappah:*

> People for whom narratives and the communication of news is a form of pleasure may indulge in it on the Sabbath as well as on weekdays . . . As for profane narratives and historical chronicles, we should point out that it is forbidden to read them only if they are written in a foreign language, but it is perfectly permissible to read them in Hebrew.

What sort of information did this pious and humble rabbi believe that his readers should have available for impressing the gentiles? A smattering of everything, in fact, even including a glancing familiarity with English dynastic politics: "1557. Mary, Queen of the Scots, rebelled against her aunt the Queen of England, and on 28 November 1577, the latter, through guile, arrested her together with her fifteen-year-old son, and ordered her to be beheaded."

He explained the Reformation:

> 1552. Martin Luther, a great scholar of their scriptures . . . set himself against the Pope and provoked a great schism among the

Christians by proposing a whole series of innovations . . . Since that fatal year until our own days more than a thousand thousands of Christians have been killed and massacred as a terrible consequence of his doctrine.

The invention of printing was important to know about:

1440. Printing was invented at Mainz by the Christian Johannes Gutenberg of Strasbourg in the first year of the reign of the Emperor Frederick the Pious. . . . Blessed be He who in His goodness has granted us such an invention, of universal benefit and unique of its kind.

He reported famous comets, royal intrigues, the St. Bartholomew's Day Massacre in Paris. He believed that his community ought to be aware of the change of the Christian calendar from the Julian to the Gregorian:

1585. Pope Gregory XIII instituted the new calendar in Rome, replacing that of the Emperor Julius Caesar . . . Instead of calling the day after the fifteenth of October the sixteenth of October, he decided that it would be the twenty-fifth of October, so that that year was shortened by ten days. We should note that the new counting of the solar year is very close to the old Jewish computation of Rav Adda bar Ahava.

Gans wanted not only to raise the standing of Jews in the eyes of Christians but also to foster a greater understanding of Christians by Jews. Throughout his chronicle, he downplays injuries to his co-religionists perpetrated by Christians and emphasises the sufferings of Christians at each other's hands as well as from outside enemies like the Turks. Noah Efron has written, "The general picture that emerged for Gans's readers was of a Christendom of admirable leaders and scholars, significant accomplishment, and some grace. Christians were often wise and benign."[34] He wanted his readers to appreciate the fine qualities of the land they lived in, and delivered himself of a long panegyric so gushing that it would make the writer of a modern tourist guide blush. "And as for Bohemia, what an abundance of population, of unfortified towns, of villages, of great and splendid cities, of palaces and of castles which outrival one another in their beauty. This land is full of the blessings of God."

Most of all, Gans wanted to demonstrate that Jews and Christians could not only improve their understanding of each other, but could even work together as equals. Proof came from his own personal experience.

In 1599, when Gans was fifty-eight years old, the Emperor Rudolf succeeded in poaching from the royal court of Denmark the celebrated nobleman and watcher of the skies Tycho Brahe, who had made his name as an astronomer some twenty-five years previously when a new star, a "nova" in the constellation of Cassiopeia, had swum into his ken. In his *Mogen Dovid* Gans described the arrival of this august figure who was to change his entire outlook:

> Our sovereign, the noble Emperor Rudolf . . . sent a mission to the land of Denmark and invited the eminent scholar Tycho Brahe . . . and installed him in a castle called Benatek, five parasangs [about eighteen miles] from the capital Prague. He lived there surrounded by his learned disciples, and received an allowance of three thousand crowns a year, together with a total provision of bread, wine, and liquor, not to speak of various gifts and donations.
>
> In this castle that I have mentioned, Tycho Brahe lived with twelve others, all learned in the astronomical sciences. Their task was to manipulate instruments which were larger and more marvellous than any which had ever been seen.
>
> The Emperor built him a series of twelve consecutive rooms. In each of these rooms was placed an instrument which enabled the position and movements of all the planets and most of the stars to be observed.

The following year, Brahe invited Johannes Kepler to join him as first assistant and pupil. This son of an innkeeper's daughter by a mercenary soldier, who had failed to complete his training as a Lutheran pastor, had written a treatise about the solar system. Though Brahe disagreed with its conclusions, the arguments Kepler brought to bear on the problem nevertheless intrigued and impressed him. The two men then proceeded to work together, laying down the observational groundwork on which the intellectual revolution that gave us modern astronomy was built. They were two of the giants on whose shoulders Isaac Newton would later claim to have stood. Gans describes their modus operandi:

Uninterruptedly, throughout the whole year, they would carry on their observations from day to day, carefully noting the movement of the sun and its position in its orbit and in longitude, its height in the sky, and its distance from the earth. Each night they would observe each of the six planets in the same way, recording their position in longitude, in latitude, their height in the sky, and the approximate variations in their distance from the earth.

One might have thought that the gap between the two Renaissance scientists gazing into the limitless vistas of the heavens, and the simple rabbi from Prague steeped in Talmudic lore, would have been unbridgeable. And yet

I should add that I, the author of this book, have had the privilege of being there three times, each time for a period of five consecutive days. Yes, I was there amongst them in the rooms used as an observatory, and I saw with my own eyes the marvellous work that was carried on there—great and marvellous undertakings, in connection not only with the planets but with most of the stars, each of which was known by its name. The procedure was as follows: three instruments, each operated by two scholars, took the astronomical determination of the star at the very moment it passed the line of midnight. These determinations were immediately transcribed into hours, minutes, and seconds at the very moment when the star stood on the line of midnight.

What is more, Gans was not only there among them, but assisting with the observations, becoming an unsung participant in the making of the history of astronomy. Tycho Brahe requested him to translate into German some astronomical tables that were only to be found in Hebrew. Could there be better proof that Jew and gentile could work together as ethnic and religious, if not intellectual and social, equals? Yes there could. For Rabbi Gans went even further, doing something that may be unique in Jewish history. He approached the Protestant scientists for help with a difficulty in Jewish ritual law.

The voyages of discovery made throughout the sixteenth century had finally established that the earth was round and that the Antipodes were both inhabitable and inhabited, not sunk into the ocean as previous generations had believed. Thus it was now clear that the day stretched around the globe for a full twenty-four hours. With remarkable perception Gans saw a serious problem coming:

> Suppose that Reuven, Shimon and Levi stand at a single point . . . Reuven sets out to the west and circles the world, Shimon circles to the east, and Levi remains in place. . . . On one and the same day it will be three days after the Sabbath for Levi who remained, two days after the Sabbath for Reuven [who circled west, with the sun], and four days after the Sabbath for Shimon [who circled east, against the sun]. The difference between Reuven and Shimon will be found to be two days.

Which, of course, would make it in principle impossible for travellers to know on which day to hold the Sabbath or any festival, a matter of considerable importance.

> You, the reader, should know that I presented these questions and perplexities before the great and extraordinary Christian scholars who reside before our Lord, Emperor Rudolf . . . clever, wise and sharp-witted people whose knowledge is inestimable. After they considered these questions for several days, and debated with me, they admitted and were not ashamed to say that they had not attained a correct and satisfactory answer.

So the emperor's court astronomers and mathematicians—presumably including Johannes Kepler himself—had thought it worth spending days discussing with a rabbi a specifically Jewish religious problem. And, as if that were not enough, contacts between the communities went even higher, to the very top, in fact. In 1592 there took place a meeting so unlikely that it immediately took on mythic proportions and ever more fantastic tales ran around the rumour circuit of Yiddish Prague.

> Out of his beneficence and out of his desire to learn the truth, our sovereign, the Emperor Rudolf . . . called to him . . . our teacher Rabbi Loew ben Bezalel, and received him most graciously, speaking to him face to face as a man speaks to his equal. As for the substance and purpose of this dialogue, it remains a secret which the two men decided not to disclose.[35]

We even know a little more about this interview than Gans did, for one of the Maharal's party made a marginal note in his copy of the Hebrew Bible which tells us that the meeting was the emperor's own initiative, and that it had been arranged by a certain Prince Bertier, using the Jewish mayor, Mordechai Maisel, as an intermediary. The emperor had first sat behind a curtain, listening to the conversation between the prince and the rabbi, and then revealed himself "in all his majesty" and exchanged words with the Maharal directly. What they spoke about, however, was not to be revealed. "The conversation having dealt with questions that affect the person of our Sovereign, discretion requires us to pass over it in silence. But if God grants us life, we shall reveal it when the moment is ripe."

The moment never came. The Emperor Rudolf died in 1612 and the court was repatriated to Vienna from Prague. Gans was lowered into his modest grave in the Old Jewish Cemetery in 1613. His dream that the following generation would make a positive Yiddish contribution to European science and culture was never fulfilled. For the pressure cooker of history, which had been slowly heating up for the previous century and a half, finally blew its gasket when, five years later, in May 1618, the imperial regents, Wilhelm Graf Slavata and Jaroslav Borzita Graf von Martinicz, together with their secretary Fabricius, were thrown out of the window of the Bohemian Chancellery in Prague Castle. (They fell on to a midden in the moat and only Slavata was slightly hurt.) This event, known to historians as the Third Defenestration of Prague, marks, by convention, the start of the Thirty Years' War, described by the great German dramatist Schiller as:

> a desolating war . . . which, from the interior of Bohemia to the mouth of the Scheldt, and from the banks of the Po to the coasts of the Baltic, devastated whole countries, destroyed harvests, and reduced towns and villages to ashes; which opened a grave for many thousand combatants, and for half a century smothered the glimmering sparks of civilization in Germany.[36]

This terrible conflict, the birth agony of our modern world, changed the Yiddish people's destiny out of all recognition and made obsolete all Rabbi Gans's hopes. Was his aim to make of the Jews another respected and accepted nationality ever realistic? Was Prague under the Emperor Rudolf a model for what might have been, a light unto the nations?

It is often said that the Bohemian capital was a unique city, the times inimitable, and the Rudolfine atmosphere impossible to emulate elsewhere, that the distance between Jews and Christians was so great that any accommodation between the two was quite impossible. Yet everything we know about Jewish life in the seventeenth and eighteenth centuries, the beginning of the modern era, suggests rather the opposite. That Yiddish-speaking Jews and their Christian neighbours could still, most of the time, live together in peace, harmony and to great mutual benefit. And not just in Bohemia, but right across the wide horizons of the *heym*.

10

Wide Horizons

By the end of the sixteenth century and the middle of the seventeenth, the Yiddish civilisation stretched right across the European continent from the Central Russian Uplands to the North Sea, from the Baltic to the Mediterranean, with the exception only of England and Russia, Scandinavia and Iberia, where none but Christians might officially reside. Yiddish-speaking communities and families were widely established in cities, towns, villages and hamlets. Historians believe that in the towns and cities of the East the Jewish populace often equalled, if not outnumbered, its Christian neighbours. Tax records are all we have to go on, and they are unlikely to tell the full story to judge by the question King Sigismund-Augustus of Poland (1520–72) asked the bishop of Cracow: "Tell me, my Lord Bishop, since you do not believe in sorcery, how is it that only 16,598 Jews pay the poll-tax, whilst 200,000 of them apparently live underground?"[1]

In *God's Playground*, Norman Davies—a scholar unlikely to inflate Jewish influence—prints a diagram showing the Jewish population of sixteenth-century Poland-Lithuania as being approximately one in twelve of the population, rising to one in ten by the eighteenth century. Whatever the real figure, it is clear that by the year 1600, in spite of furious opposition from religious and commercial rivals, in spite of anti-Jewish violence,

tragic accusations of ritual murder and other absurd and irrational allega-
tions that led to the scaffold or the pyre, the Yiddish-speaking Jews had
firmly linked their western and eastern personalities and traditions, and
established themselves as one of the core nations of Europe, outnumbering
many others, with the main population centre of their *heym* now in the
Slav East.

It may strike the citizen of a modern nation as slightly odd that a state
like Poland-Lithuania, from 1569 formally united as a single federated
commonwealth (*Rzeczpospolita*), should be regarded as a homeland to a
people whose language, culture and religion continued to link them to the
international rather than the national order. Were they not to be regarded
as a foreign intrusion?

In fact the Yiddish-speaking minority was far from alone in its extra-
territorial connections. The idea of the nation state, in which a homoge-
neous ethnic group exercise independent sovereignty over a national
territory, the ultimate legacy of the Treaty of Westphalia that ended the
Thirty Years' War, would not take full hold in eastern Europe until the
nineteenth, in some places the twentieth, century. Both the fragmented
states of the Holy Roman Empire as well as the Polish-Lithuanian commonwealth, which included today's Belarus and Ukraine and spread over
not much less than half a million square miles, containing some eleven
million inhabitants, were all perforce multi-ethnic and multicultural.
Other than the Yiddish Jews, the population consisted not only of Germans, Czechs, Poles and Lithuanians, but also of Ruthenes, White Russians, Tartars, Armenians, Scots and a sprinkling of others.

Some cities were officially German speaking, others Polish, yet others
Lithuanian. In the 1530s the Sunday services in Cracow's St. Mary's
Church were held in Polish before noon and in German after noon. German remained the official language of the courts of Cracow until the year
1600.[2] In Vilna at that time, Lithuanians, Poles, Ruthenes and Germans
took it in turn to serve as Christian guild masters. Apart from Judaism, the
people adhered to Roman Catholicism, Protestantism, eastern Orthodoxy,
numerous nonconformist Christians sects and Islam. They couldn't even
agree on the calendar until surprisingly recently. Norman Davies points
out in his book *The Heart of Europe*, "In a city like Wilno, for example,
when the Poles celebrated the Constitution of 3 May A.C.E. 1792, the
Orthodox were still on 22 April, the Jews were in the month of Iyyar after
Passover in the year 5552 a.m. and the Tartars were in the eighth month of
the year Hegira 1205."[3]

To observers from western Europe this situation seemed bizarre. A French traveller who spent five years in Poland in the 1770s noted that:

> the term Frenchman, Englishman, Spaniard includes all of the inhabitants of France, England and Spain because each individual is a constituent part of those states. It is not the same in Poland, as I have observed. The three classes that make up the inhabitants do not constitute a nation. The nation is made up exclusively of the nobility, called here the *szlachta*. The second class, that is the Jews, are foreign to the state and merely serve the material interests of the first class. The third class (the peasants) are simply the property of the first.[4]

In truth the situation was even stranger. The *szlachta*, the Polish nobility, which supposedly constituted the entire nation, was now developing its own notion—perhaps spurious, or maybe not—of foreignness. The lords took it into their heads that they themselves were by origin not Europeans at all, but Orientals, claiming to be descendants of the Sarmatians, Iranian nomads of the Eurasian steppe. It was the peasantry, by contrast, who were the authentic Slavs, and were despised for it. In support of this odd conceit, the nobility affected what they imagined was oriental behaviour, and an eastern style of dress modelled after that of the Mongol Tartars—a fashion still faithfully preserved by the pious Chassidim of modern times. Thus, in a nation ruled by a class that prided itself on its foreign and exotic origins, it was hardly possible to accuse the Yiddish speakers of being any less authentically Polish-Lithuanian than anyone else. Though the Jews were often enough attacked for their beliefs, at this stage in history none questioned their right to be considered part of the Commonwealth.

Further west, in the political patchwork that was called the Holy Roman Empire, by the end of the sixteenth century the age of greatest persecution was largely over. The communities that had survived the Crusades, the Black Death, the blood libels, the accusations of desecrating the host, the random attacks and the general devastation of war, now found themselves swimming in calmer waters. True, there would still be expulsions, but unprovoked massacres were now rare. The Reformation and the consequent Thirty Years' War had done their work of divesting the Jews of their status as Christianity's principal enemy.

Jewish numbers began to rise once more. During the seventeenth century, troubles in the East reversed the major direction of Jewish migration, which had for centuries been from west to east, and Yiddish speakers were now moving from east to west, from Poland-Lithuania into Bohemia, from Bohemia into Germany, from Germany into France.

The new states were hardly more peaceful than the old. The century after 1650 would experience the Thirteen Years' War (1654), the Great Northern War (1700), the War of the Spanish Succession (1701), the War of the Austrian Succession (1740), the Seven Years' War (1756), several Anglo-Dutch wars, numerous Turkish wars and even the War of Jenkins's Ear (1739). But the utter ghastliness of the Thirty Years' War and the new political dispensation achieved by the Peace of Westphalia had changed the nature of international conflict. From 1648 until the twentieth century, "total war," one that involved destruction of entire populations, was largely replaced by war as professional practice, fought between armies in the field and avoiding, by and large, the massive civilian casualties of earlier times.

It was these wars that offered the greatest opportunities to those who could best take advantage of them: Yiddish merchants and dealers in bulk commodities, who supplied the armies in the field with regular deliveries of weapons, ammunition, clothing, food and fodder, and honed new organisational, entrepreneurial and financial skills to a high level in the process. Hence the rise of the so-called "court Jews," the *Hofjuden*, who, in return for certain privileges—official recognition, freedom of travel and settlement, exemption from the rabbinical courts, sometimes even a salary—joined the equally ubiquitous Jewish royal physicians to render financial, commercial and diplomatic services to the crowned heads of the continent. Every self-respecting princely seat needed its court Jew in the seventeenth century: Nini Levi and Abraham Isaac in Münster, Simon Model at Ansbach, Bonaventura Sachs in Saxony, Leffmann Behrends in Hanover, Behrend Lehmann at Halberstadt, Aaron Beer at Frankfurt, the famous Samuel Oppenheimer and Samson Wertheimer at the imperial court in Vienna. Israel Aaron was for long on the payroll of the Prussian rulers; five generations of the Gompertz family served at the court of the Hohenzollerns. There were dozens of others.

Apart from supplying the army, they provided the prince and his establishment with credit and luxury merchandise, sourced precious metals for the mint, undertook commercial and diplomatic missions and carried out on the ruler's behalf the promotion and development of new trades and industries. Behrend Lehmann (1661–1730)—who travelled about in a carriage drawn by six horses and kept a household retinue of thirty, including a rabbi and a kosher slaughterer[5]—helped Frederick Augustus of Saxony mount the Polish throne. Joshua Abensur (died 1670) was sent on diplomatic missions by the Polish court; his younger brother Daniel (died 1711) was minister resident of the king of Poland in Hamburg. Vienna's vainglorious Schönbrunn Palace (begun 1696) and the unblushingly overblown Baroque Karlskirche (begun 1716) were financed by Yiddish-speaking court bankers.

Each of the great families supported dozens, if not hundreds, of others who serviced their religious and social needs, spreading the benefit of the monarch's favour throughout the communities. Everyone profited. The Yiddish-speaking people were firmly established across Europe as a nation of some importance, both politically and economically, and no little honour, as we discover from the autobiography of the merchant Glückel von Hameln, the very first full account of what it actually felt like to live within the wide horizons of the seventeenth-century *heym*.

The scene is the muddy bank of the Moselle, near where the river runs through the once German, now French, garrison city of Metz, on its way to joining the Rhine. It is the Hebrew month of Nissan in the Jewish year 5479, at about ten o'clock in the evening. A woman is kneeling by the water's edge cleaning dishes in the dark. Suddenly the landscape becomes as light as day. The woman looks up at the cloudless night sky and sees the heavens open. A great shower of sparks cascades down. Then, just as abruptly, the heavens close as if someone has jerked a curtain across and all returns to darkness.

A report of this strange and dramatic manifestation is the final entry in the *Zichroynes*, the "Memories," of Samuel Pepys's contemporary Glikl bas Judah Leib (*bas* is Hebrew for daughter-of)—dubbed Glückel von Hameln by the Austrian editor of the first published edition of her classic Yiddish autobiography.[6]

Today we might deduce that the celestial fireworks were a meteor breaking up as it entered earth's atmosphere, perhaps part of the Lyrid meteor shower which appears every April (Nissan—the first month of the Hebrew year 5479—ran from 21 March to 19 April 1719). Or just perhaps the event was related to the great fireball that Astronomer Royal Edmund Halley reported to have been seen across southern England in the March of that year.

To Halley, one of the new breed of scientists who were remaking our view of the world in the seventeenth century, the meteor phenomenon demanded a physical explanation. By comparing reports of sightings from different places, he calculated that the shooting star was 150 miles high and travelling at five and a half miles per second. To the elderly Jewish woman of Metz, whose universe was still shaped by the beliefs of the ancient sages of Babylonia as interpreted by the rabbis of the Middle Ages, sparks in the sky had a mystical significance. She found their meaning personally troubling. "May God, blessed be He, grant that it be for our good," were the last written words of the first Jewish woman in European history whose full true personality one can get to know, whose inner life, thoughts and feelings one can recognise and understand.

Other familiar names, more ancient, more prestigious, arguably more holy and certainly more scholarly, remain merely names. We may even know something of their life stories and much of what they achieved. But as human characters they remain mysterious, impenetrable. With Glikl it is quite different. In a huge break with the medieval past, she saw herself as an individual, whose experiences, opinions and inner feelings had a right to be heard—and are certainly worth the hearing. Her story has it all: comedy and tragedy, laughter and tears. She writes of love and death, business and pleasure, glorious success and abject failure. She relates personal anecdotes, family history, moral fables, religious homilies and even a short but well-crafted and artful prototype crime thriller, surely the very first example of the genre in European literature, a dark tale of serial disappearances and a criminal finally unmasked by the perseverance of a stubborn Jewish woman who refuses to give up her compulsion to solve the mystery, in the teeth of stout opposition from her husband and the Jewish authorities—foreshadowing the plot of innumerable TV dramas today.

Yet however close to us Glikl seems, as one reads the account of her life one soon recognises that she was at the same time a last, late representative of the medieval Jewish mercantile class, a woman who still lived by the centuries-old ideals, attitudes and beliefs that had always shaped the outlook of the Jewish merchants of central and eastern Europe. Her words help us sense the underlying mindset, catch a sight of the inner life, of the traders, the financiers and the people of business, those Jews who had brought the Yiddish, as well as the German and Slav, worlds into being in the course of the preceding five hundred years, the generations of medieval Jews about whose insecurities, achievements and failures, about whose struggle for existence and success, we would otherwise know next to nothing.

Conversely, the very fact that she wrote her memoirs at all, and in Yiddish, also indicates her modernity. For centuries Jewish men had written "ethical wills" in Hebrew, homilies designed to read like teachings culled from the experience of a long life, left by a dying father to the children gathered round his bedside. Though many such works began with the words "My Son," this was often mere convention; the ethical will was usually a literary form written for wide dissemination, not an actual message from one generation to the next. Or maybe such documents were more commonly written than we know but only those designed for publication survived. Certainly by Glikl's lifetime, it was not unusual for a woman to compose an ethical will. Glikl tells us of the document left by her sister's mother-in-law Pessele. "It is a wonder to read the testament that she made, may she rest in peace. I cannot write of it but anyone who wishes to read it can still find it with her children . . ." and then, in one of those touches that instantly wipes away three hundred years and makes the reader suddenly feel like an intimate, she questions with, I imagine, a quizzical frown, ". . . they would surely not have thrown it away?"

Glikl's own memoirs, however, were not intended as ethical instruction. "This, dear children, will be no book of morals. Such I could not write, and our sages have already written many." It was to be a genuine account of her life. "So far as my memory and the subject permit, I shall try to tell everything that has happened to me from my youth upward."

Glikl was revealing her familiarity with the wider world, for by the late seventeenth century women's autobiography had become an established genre in many languages. That a woman should write the story of her quotidian life was now no longer thought ridiculously presumptuous. Moreover she shows a precociously modern concern for recording family roots: "I write so that if today or tomorrow your beloved children or grandchildren come and do not know about their family, I have recorded here briefly who their people are."

WEALTH AND HONOUR

The bare outlines of her life can be briefly told. She was born, she tells us, in "the year of Creation 5407 [1646–7]" in Hamburg, a free city within the Holy Roman Empire, the second largest in Germany after Cologne, which came into prominence as a port when the medieval protectionist Hanseatic League broke up. By the middle of the seventeenth century, Hamburg had a major bank, a stock exchange and a system of shipping insurance; its vessels were the first to be escorted at sea by men-of-war.

Glikl was the daughter of Judah Joseph, aka Leib, a dealer in precious stones and a considerable local worthy. When she was three years old, the German-speaking *Hochdeutsche*—though, as so often, not the Sephardic *Portugiesisch* (Portuguese)—Jews were expelled from Hamburg and resettled themselves in Altona. Though the move disrupted their lives it didn't take them far. By Glikl's own account Altona, a possession not of the empire but of the king of Denmark, who "enjoyed the aid of the Almighty, for he was a righteous God-fearing king who had always dealt kindly with us Jews, "lay less than fifteen minutes' walk away. Today Altona is just a wealthy inner suburb lying at the end of the famous Reeperbahn. The family's life was further unsettled when in 1657 war between Denmark and Sweden triggered a Swedish attack on Altona and its Jewish inhabitants fled back to Hamburg, where they helped defend the city.

> It was early in the morning and everyone was still asleep. We jumped out of our beds, *nebbich* [an untranslatable Yiddish expression of condescension and pity, here signifying "alas, poor us"], and ran half-naked all the way to Hamburg, where we took up defensive positions, some with the Sephardim, and others alongside the Christians.

Not long after—perhaps in recognition of their loyalty, though more probably because the city just couldn't do without them—the German-speaking Jews were encouraged to resettle back in Hamburg, her father being one of the first to return. He was a progressive man, concerned to equip his children for their future. Unusually for a pious Jew of the period, "my father gave his children, girls and boys, a secular as well as a religious education." Or perhaps it was not so unusual, but rarely admitted.

This did not, however, prevent him from following age-old tradition and marrying off his daughters at the earliest age possible. At twelve Glikl was betrothed, and at fourteen married, to seventeen-year-old Chaim, the son of a successful trader from Hamelin—in Glikl's opinion a shabby, dull, deeply provincial place. Her mother couldn't get over the fact that instead of sending a carriage for the bride, Chaim's family despatched a peasant cart! As was the custom, for the first year of their marriage the teenage couple lived, in spite of Glikl's great homesickness, with Chaim's family. Then they transferred back to her own childhood home and set up in business, dealing in precious stones, the family speciality. Chaim travelled to the fairs at Leipzig and Frankfurt, imported from and exported to Amsterdam, Moscow and even London. Glikl was no stay-at-home housewife, but took her full share of the enterprise. Chaim "asked no advice from anyone else, as we always discussed everything together." They were, she wrote, "young and inexperienced and knew little or nothing of the business ways of Hamburg," but were quick to respond to changes in fashion. They noted that "non-Jewish burghers and bridegrooms were no longer wearing many gems, but fine gold chains instead," so they turned to the trade in precious metals, a business that went so well that, by the time Glikl reached the age of twenty-five, they were in a position to rent a house of their own in Hamburg's New City and engage two servants, no mean achievement.

This was particularly important to Glikl, for whom wealth and honour (*oysher un koved*), a phrase more liberally repeated than any other throughout her entire book, seemed to loom as more important than anything else in life. Like a character in a Jane Austen novel. Glikl reckoned *oysher un koved* largely in money terms: "My sister Hendele—may she rest in peace—received 1,800 Reichsthaler as her dowry, a very large sum indeed in those days . . . the whole world wondered at the large dowry." Though to her, unlike to the English gentry, it didn't matter a jot that the *oysher* had been hard earned rather than inherited. She reckoned the community leader Chaim Fürst to be worth 10,000 Reichsthaler, and assessed her father Judah Leib at 8,000. To her great pride, her son-in-law Moses became "the wealthiest man" in the community. The word rich is the adjective she most often applies to characters who receive her approval—and even some who don't. Elias Gompertz of Cleves, father-in-law to one of her daughters, whose house was "really like the dwelling of a king," was "very rich, worth 100,000 Reichsthaler or even more." But valued even more highly than money was the *koved* of aristocratic approval. A wedding she attended in Amsterdam was celebrated with great pomp and splendour; delicate titbits were served in a room "furnished like the mansion of a ruler"; jesters entertained the gathering of notables, among whom were included Count Maurice of Nassau and the young Crown Prince Frederick of Brandenburg, later to become king of Prussia, whose heart was stolen away by her little son Mordechai. "No Jew has been granted such high honour for a hundred years," she boasts.

Money loomed so large in Glikl's life that financial misfortune affected her physically, though she tried to hide it from others. One year she lost a large sum and "fell very ill because of my worry, but to the world at large I put my condition down to my pregnancy." Normal parental difficulties with her children were assessed in financial terms: "All kinds of unpleasant things and troubles befell me through my children, and it always cost me much money. But it is not necessary to write of it. They are all my dear children and I forgive them, both those who cost me much and those who cost me nothing . . ." Yet before we become irritated by her materialism, she quickly disarms us with some humorous Yiddishism that rings with unexpected familiarity to the modern ear. Of her uncle who died young she writes, "If God had spared his life, he would have become a rich man, for God had granted him good luck. If he so much as picked up—you should pardon the expression—a piece of dung, it turned to gold in his hands."

Indeed, one of Glikl's charms is the way she is able to muster a piercing self-awareness, an objectivity that excuses much of her frequent bad temper and denigration of others. She writes that her grandmother and mother had "at times not more than a crust of bread all day. Still they accepted it and trusted that God—may He be praised—would not forsake them . . . I wish I had such a nature. But God does not bestow the same character on everybody." She voices the eternal complaint of the older generation that, in contrast to when she was first married, the young now "take everything from their parents without asking whether they are in a position to give that much." But then admits that "if children had the same trouble with their parents as their parents do with them, they would soon tire of it."

Over the years, Glikl gave birth to fourteen children—"like olive shoots around my table," in the words of the psalm—of whom twelve, six boys and six girls, survived to marriageable age, and eleven became parents in their turn. This too was something of a victory, since in the seventeenth century on average more than a third of all children died before reaching puberty. She was only too conscious of the dangers of their way of life. Travelling was essential for trade, yet to embark on any journey along the roads of the period was to take a serious risk—of assault, murder or kidnap for ransom—particularly for Jews. Their own agent and family friend was robbed and killed on the journey from Hanover to Hildesheim, a road usually as safe as that between Hamburg and Altona, which she walked without fear even in the dark.

Yet when in 1689, disaster did strike Glikl personally, it was from a completely unexpected direction. One evening, hurrying into town on business, Chaim tripped and took a heavy fall. Within a few days he was dead. Asked if he had any final instructions he replied, "I can think of nothing. My wife knows everything. Let her carry on as she is used to." To her mother he said, "Only comfort my little Gliklichen." Then he died. Glikl, still in her early forties, was suddenly left a widow.

> What shall I write, dear children, of all our bitter grief? I had always stood so high in his eyes, and now I was abandoned with eight of my twelve forlorn children—and one of them, my daughter Esther, betrothed! May God have mercy on us and be the Father of my children, for He is the Father of the fatherless! I truly believe I shall never cease from mourning my dear friend. On Sunday, the 24th of Tevet 5449 [16 January 1689], he was buried with all honour. The entire community was struck with horror and grief at the sudden blow of it.[7]

Glikl could not, however, afford to indulge herself in her sorrow. She had a family to support, children to marry off, and Chaim's death had sent her snaking back to square one on life's unpredictable board game. "When his soul took wing, there flew with it all my glory, *oysher un koved*." What is more, she received little help from anyone else. "Visits of consolation kept on for two or three weeks; and then everyone forgot all about me and the very people we had helped most began to repay us with evil, as is the way of the world." Her complaint smacks of self-pity, but with the wry self-knowledge that makes her such an appealing witness, she quickly pulls herself together again. "At least I fancied so, for a widow—God forgive me—who has suddenly lost everything is quick to see and take offence, and often unjustly."

She launched herself into feverish business activity, holding Chaim's predatory creditors at bay, auctioning off his remaining goods at a profit, and successfully dedicating herself to paying off all their debts within a year. She invested in a factory making "Hamburg stockings" and sold its products far and wide. She made herself an expert in pearls, bought, cleaned, graded and resold them to appropriate clients. She was to be found in her shop at all hours, unless travelling to the important fairs at Leipzig, Brunswick and elsewhere, chaperoned—as propriety demanded—by one of her sons. At the same time, like many Jewish and Christian women, she lent small sums of money against items on pawn.

And in between all these efforts, she started composing the story of her life. "I began writing it, dear children, upon the death of your good father, in the hope of distracting my soul from the burdens laid upon it, and the bitter thought that we have lost our faithful shepherd. In this way I have managed to live through many wakeful nights, and springing from my bed shortened the sleepless hours."

Significantly she begins her saga with a story, a parable that expresses her idea of the proper relationship between parents and children:

A bird once set out to cross a windy sea with its three fledglings. The sea was so wide and the wind so strong that the father bird was forced to carry his young, one by one, in his strong claws. When he was halfway across with the first fledgling the wind turned to a gale, and he said, "My child, look how I am struggling and risking my life in your behalf. When you are grown up, will you do as much for me and provide for my old age?" The fledgling replied, "Only bring me to safety, and when you are old I shall do everything you ask of me." Whereat the father bird dropped his child into the sea, and it drowned, and he said, "So shall it be done to such a liar as you." Then the father bird returned to shore, set forth with his second fledgling, asked the same question, and receiving the same answer, drowned the second child with the cry, "You, too, are a liar!" Finally he set out with the third fledgling, and when he asked the same question, the third and last fledgling replied, "My dear father, it is true you are struggling mightily and risking your life in my behalf, and I shall be wrong not to repay you when you are old, but I cannot bind myself. This though I can promise: when I am grown up and have children of my own, I shall do as much for them as you have done for me." Whereupon the father bird said, "Well spoken, my child, and wisely; your life I will spare and I will carry you to shore in safety."

It was fitting that Glikl's confessions start with this tale, since it sums up the covenant between generations that has helped to ensure Jewish survival down the ages. The phenomenon so well known in gentile society, of elderly spinsters prevented from marrying by the expectation that they sacrifice themselves in order to look after ageing parents, was never a Jewish tradition.

Fulfilling her obligations, over the following ten years Glikl did indeed "struggle mightily" on her fledglings' behalf, managing to amass respectable dowries for her daughters, and marrying off all but one of her children to suitable families right across western Europe: to Amsterdam,

Bamberg, Berlin, Copenhagen, Metz and even London. As a still relatively young widow of substance, not to speak of her enviable business acumen, she was herself regarded as a worthy catch for some older man, "matches with the most distinguished men in the whole of Germany had been broached to me," and found herself needing to fend off frequent proposals of marriage. Finally, in her fifties, and after fulfilling nearly all her family duties, hoping for a quiet and comfortable old age she allowed herself to be persuaded to wed Hirsch (Deer, or as he was known in French Cerf) ben Isaac Levy, "a widower, an outstanding Jew, a scholar, very rich, and maintaining a fine household," a highly respected banker and leader of the community in Metz, just over the French border. After selling off her stock and repaying all remaining debts—in secret, so as to avoid alerting the authorities, and thus escape the large exit tax levied on departing Jews—Glikl and her last unmarried daughter left Hamburg for ever.

She was received with great honour, shown much respect and given a magnificent wedding, but the move was not a happy one. Glikl found her new home very different from what she was used to. She knew no French—at least no more than the few words with which a cultured person anywhere in Europe was familiar—and hated having to use an interpreter. She couldn't even exchange pleasantries with the neighbours. Everything was so fancy here, in contrast to her "straightforward German ways." There were so many servants. Men wore Paris-style wigs, *perruques*. Jewish business people discussed their affairs with non-Jews! She felt particularly uneasy about having no hand in her new husband's dealings, or even any knowledge of them. Her anxiety proved well-founded.

Less than two years later the wealthy, scholarly and highly esteemed Hirsch ben Isaac was suddenly pronounced bankrupt and everything was lost. Everything—even the furniture. Hirsch went into hiding. Bailiffs came to the house and sealed it while they made an inventory. Glikl and her maid almost starved. The Jewish community thought that there may have been "some irregularity" in his affairs but mainly blamed Hirsch's fall on the rapacity of Christians who had lent him money at exorbitant rates of interest. For a woman who had devoted her entire life to the pursuit of respectability and honour, the pain of the shame was even greater than that of the poverty. "I . . . had to live the very shame against which I had hoped to protect myself." Hirsch barely escaped a spell in a debtors' jail. Though she began dealing in precious stones once again and became known locally as "extremely skilful in their commerce," Glikl was now too old to start all over as she had done once before. The couple had no choice but to accept support from their children, which offended every one of Glikl's principles. Had she not begun her memoirs years before with a long parable to show that parents should not expect help from their offspring?

After ten years, Hirsch died, and Glikl was forced to leave the house in which she was living, move to a little room up a flight of twenty-two stairs with no stove, and cook for herself in a shared kitchen with the help of a single servant. She even had to suffer the deep shame of accepting support from the community. So she reluctantly allowed herself to be coaxed into moving in with her daughter's household in Metz, where she was much honoured and looked after with great consideration and love. Some family joys—the success of her children and the birth of grandchildren—lightened her last decade. She herself died in 1724 at the considerable age of seventy-eight.

THE GREAT DIVIDE

What struck me most forcibly when I first read Glikl's book was that, though born more than 350 years ago, she nevertheless sounds exactly like several of my relatives of the last generation, and even a few acquaintances of the present. Of course she doesn't match any individual perfectly, but if you combined their traits, you would achieve the very same combination of sympathy and snobbery, staunch courage and self-pity, patient suffering and short temper, disdain for plebeian gentiles and fawning adulation for non-Jewish nobility. I had always assumed that these characteristics were the result of the Jews' tormented recent history, but Glikl's memoirs suggest that they have a far longer background. She expresses herself, too, in a way that strikes the ear as utterly contemporary. Reading Glikl's work is a clear demonstration that the familiar Yiddish manner of speaking—and Glikl's great strength as a writer is that she sets words down on the page just as she would have said them aloud—has a much longer history than I had previously imagined. The contemporary Yiddish tone turns out, after all, not to be derived just from Polish and Russian influence, but is also inspired by the word music of Bible and prayer book.

Glikl's entire life was built upon two pillars: business and family, themselves erected over a foundation of unquestioning traditional religious belief. In her own eyes, however, all three came to much the same thing. "Go diligently about your business," she writes. "Providing a decent livelihood for your wife and children is a *mitzvah*—a command of God and the duty of man." Indeed, for Glikl business and life seem to be indistinguishable. "The first question put to a man in the next world," she advises her children, quoting the fourth-century Babylonian Rabbi Rabbah bar Huna, "is, whether he was faithful in his business dealings." Actually the quote in the Talmud reads: "Hast thou been honest in *all* thy dealings?"[8] In this conflation of work with life, I don't believe that she was influenced, as some have suggested,[9] by the new capitalist mood of the day that the sociologist Max Weber linked to Protestant Christianity. I take her to have been following the very same impulse as the long line of—first German- then Yiddish-speaking—merchants, traders, financiers and people of business who had, over the preceding half-millennium, made Jews the indispensable lubricant of the central and eastern Europe economy and to whom Germany, Bohemia, Poland and Lithuania owed much, perhaps even most, of their commercial development.

But there was also another tradition, from which Glikl implicitly and explicitly separates herself. The eastern half of the Yiddish world had quite different norms. Across the River Oder business success, though not quite despised, was far less honoured than it was to the west. The religious seminaries of the Polish-Lithuanian commonwealth were filled with lifelong students of Talmud who demanded to be, and were, maintained at their community's expense. Here a very different model of ideal family life held sway, in which the husband was expected to spend his day in the house of study, while the wife laboured and struggled with worldly affairs to support him there. True, even in Germany and France, limited public support of students was regarded as a pious duty. Talmud students and rabbis were fed by Glikl's stepdaughter and others were maintained by charitable contributions from her in-laws. When her husband Chaim's father died, ten rabbis were hired for a year, to pray and study Talmud in the old man's memory. But Chaim himself successfully managed to combine commerce with piety. However busily speeding around town trading gold, Glikl tells us, he never missed Torah study for a single day, though after his father's death he gave up travelling away from town for a year "in order not to miss a single *kaddish* [prayer for the dead]."

In an article in *A Historical Atlas of the Jewish People*,[10] Professor Eli Barnavi underlines this wide mental gap between the Jews of Germany and those of Poland in her time. Though to Glikl, Poland was respected as a land of religious learning, "with the Jews of Poland," he tells us, "one concluded neither marriages nor business." The East was a land both of Talmud and of *tsores* (troubles).

When Glikl wrote, "my son Loeb loaned some thousands to Polish

Jews, and the money, alas, was never seen again," she doesn't add "of course" but the thought is implied. When her little daughter was believed, wrongly, to be infected with plague, the two Polish Jews whose help she sought would not stir "unless paid thirty Thalers on the spot"—and on the Sabbath, of all days; rabbinical dispensation had to be sought to allow the payment. Two of Glikl's brothers-in-law were ruined by the Cossack uprising in Poland; sick Polish Jewish refugees from a Muscovite attack on Vilna were taken in by Glikl's father and tended by her grandmother, who herself succumbed to disease as a result. The Polish rabbi to whom Glikl had sent her most scholarly son to learn Talmud tried to extort money from her, "fifty or sixty Reichsthaler," with a forged letter, supposedly from her son, that played to Glikl's worst fears. "I beg you, in God's name, hasten! For if you delay I shall fall into the power, God forbid, of the Poles, and should that happen and it come to a question of ransom it will cost us tenfold." The fraud was only exposed when her son chanced to arrive home, safe and sound, knowing nothing of the affair. Though nowhere does she use it in the course of her memoirs, she, like the last generation of German Jews, would have often referred to *polnische Wirtschaft*, Polish business, an insult still used by today's Germans to refer to anything shoddy, incompetent or ill-made.

Of course, Glikl's prejudices, like most, were based less on fact than on loose stereotyping. And if she and her circle shared the German conception of Polish Jewry as ultra-conservative, anti-modern, living out a medieval fantasy, compared with their forward-looking co-religionists living in the West, they were ignoring the fact that the greatest advances in Yiddish thought of the previous century had come not from among Germany's Jews but from those of Cracow and Prague.

I had imagined that the great divide, the original division between the western and eastern, German- and Slavic-speaking parental streams that had merged to form the Yiddish nation must have long dissolved by the beginning of the eighteenth century. I had assumed that the friction between central and eastern European Jewry that I remember from my youth—and the insults hurled between the two—was a new split, dating from the emancipation of German and Austrian Jews and the resulting eastern, orthodox, reaction to the western Jewish enlightenment with its secular thrust. I was wrong.

Glikl's memoirs demonstrate that the schism was already, or rather was still, wide in the seventeenth century. We learn that, however much each had contributed to the common culture and however amicably they may at times have seemed to get along, the two had never truly amalgamated. Though they shared language, customs, religion and ancient history, and though in Glikl's lifetime each was as God-fearing as the other, the German and Slav traditions had never been able fully to dismantle the barriers that separated them.

Now it was too late. Two years after Glikl was born there began a series of massive historic blows that would continue to strike eastern Europe from all sides for a century and a half, smashing the pattern of the past and rearranging the fragments to a new and greatly impoverished design. The Yiddish *heym* would be broken into pieces. Its German and Slav halves would be for ever separated. And the Polish-Lithuanian commonwealth, the very heartland of the Yiddish civilisation, would be wiped off the map.

II

The Deluge

Not much more than a decade ago the tall chimneys of Communist Katowice's satanic mills darkened the skies of Poland for miles around, catching at the throat with their sulphurous smoke, while the clangorous din of Soviet industrial enterprise pounded on the ears. Today, most of the works, the mine heads, the forges, foundries and factories, stand silent and deserted, their windows smashed, their blackened crumbling brickwork invaded by self-seeded buddleia and red valerian, amaranth and willowherb. In twenty years it will be hard to remember that this part of Silesia was once one of Moscow's principal powerhouses. Today it is difficult to recall that less than a hundred years ago this was not Poland—no country by that name existed—but part of the German Empire, and that close by, near the old mining town of Mysłowice, the Russian and Austrian Empires began.

The three great nineteenth-century powers of Europe met at the *Dreikaisereck* (Three Emperors' Corner), where the Y-shaped confluence of the Black Przemsze and the White Przeme rivers divides the flat, treeless terrain into three triangular pie slices. The spot was marked after 1907 by an ugly, chunky, seventy-foot tower commemorating Bismarck, dismantled in 1933. These days the town is known mainly for the band called Myslovitz, one of Poland's most popular rock groups.

The grubby, muddy river junction should be better known, for it is a memorial not only to the eclipse in 1795 of the independent Polish State, when it was partitioned for the third time and vanished from the map (until 1918), but it also recalls the fateful splitting of the *heym*, the Yiddish homeland, separating for ever the two sources of the Yiddish civilisation, German and Slav, between the twin fates of assimilation and penury.

To the north-east the Russian Empire now stretched for six thousand miles to the shores of the Pacific; to the north-west Prussia waited for the opportunity to unify an imperial Germany that would reach all the way to the French border; to the south sprawled imperial and royal Austria, *Kaiserlich und Königlich*, incorporating Bohemia and Moravia, Polish Galicia, Slovenia, Croatia, Bosnia and Montenegro, and of course Hungary and Transylvania, which had become part of the Yiddish world after the Ottoman Turks were turned from the gates of Vienna by Bonnie Prince Charlie's grandfather King Jan Sobieski in 1683 and didn't stop running till they reached the safety of the southern Balkans, whereupon Yiddish-speaking Jews were encouraged to resettle the ravaged and depopulated lands.

The *Dreikaisereck* represents a sword cut through the very heart of the Yiddish civilisation, the tragic end result of two hundred years of steady Polish decline.

The long, long inflation that had begun the 1400s was brought to a crisis by a force that seemed to observers to be the hand of God in action: a sudden dramatic transformation of the weather. The summer of 1591 was wet and cold. Peasants watched helplessly as their crops were flattened by torrential rainstorms and the hay for their animals' winter feed rotted in the fields. If 1594 was as bad, 1595 was worse, 1596 disastrous and 1597 catastrophic. People called the inevitable famine, in which hundreds of thousands perished, the Great Dearth. This was more than a temporary spell, it marked a real change in the climate, the beginning of what has been called the Little Ice Age, when even deep lakes and swift-flowing rivers froze over, when the icy tentacles of mountain glaciers encroached on inhabited valleys, strangling entire villages, and when, according to one report, the Arctic ice expanded so far south that Inuit in kayaks made landfall in Scotland.[1]

The cold hand of depression squeezed the economy ever harder: the *Kipperzeit*, "time of coin-clipping." In England arguments about taxation led to civil war and King Charles losing his head outside the banqueting hall at Westminster. In France disputes over money between the Parlement de Paris and the crown sparked a series of rebellions called the Frondes. Major revolutions exploded in Catalonia and Portugal, Naples, Sicily, Denmark. Even peaceful Switzerland would descend into civil war when peasants from the valley of Entlebuch rose in protest, to the signal of an alphorn, at a devaluation of the coinage. When the inflationary wave finally crested and broke, after years of famine and disease and destitution, the Thirty Years' War, a destructive storm of a ferocity hitherto unknown, unleashed by the largest European armies since Roman times, was sweeping back and forth across almost the whole of northern and central Europe, erasing virtually everything in its path like a rubber wiping over a chalked blackboard.

The trial of strength that began at Prague in 1618, with the ejection through the castle window of the Imperial Regents Slavata and von Martinicz together with their secretary, soon got out of hand. The Protestants of Bohemia, Hungary and Transylvania rose in rebellion and thirty thousand imperial troops under Count von Tilly marched across the border. This was no rerun of the Hussite stand-off. The Protestant army was convincingly crushed at the Battle of the White Mountain near Prague; the rebel leaders were executed, twenty-seven of their heads exposed as a warning on the Charles Bridge in the centre of the capital. Nearly five hundred noble estates were confiscated. Bohemia was devastated by the imperial mercenaries and forcibly returned to the Catholic fold. All Protestant ministers were expelled and every lay person was forced to choose between Catholicism and exile. Tens of thousands became refugees, losing everything. Whole communities converted to Judaism rather than bow to Rome. By 1650 the Christian population of Bohemia had fallen to half its pre-war number. The dreams of David Gans and his circle in Prague were utterly dashed.

But the appetite for battle and the religious hatred it fed on were unsated. A limited Bohemian conflict burst its territorial bounds to become a Thirty Years' War, a continent-wide struggle between Catholics and Protestants, between imperialists and nationalists, and ultimately between all the great European powers, destroying cities and laying the countryside to waste. The details are described with stomach-churning precision in the grim eyewitness novel by Hans von Grimmelshausen that was the basis for Bertolt Brecht's coruscating play *Mother Courage*, and in the powerful visual indictment brought by French engraver Jacques Callot's heart-rending series of prints called *The Great Miseries of War*, with its depictions of horrors such as trees festooned with hanging corpses or peasants hacking wounded soldiers to death as they pleaded for mercy.

The power of the Holy Roman Emperor was broken; Germany was splintered into more than four hundred statelets. In her classic text *The Thirty Years' War*, historian Dame C. V. Wedgwood calculated that the German population fell from twenty-one to thirteen million. Another scholar[2] finds that Swedish troops alone destroyed 2,000 castles, 18,000 villages and 1,500 towns across Germany. In 1618 the Duchy of Württemberg had 350,000 registered inhabitants; in 1648 less than 120,000. In 1618 Magdeburg had 25,000 citizens; after the war 400 houses were left standing and its population had dropped to no more than 2,500.

Though Jews were mere bystanders to the action, the Yiddish-speaking inhabitants of central Europe suffered along with and in proportion to their gentile confrères, their livelihoods and lives ruined. Yet unlike the earth-rooted peasants, their history had taught them well. Once again the roads were packed with slowly shuffling columns of refugees, men, women and children dragging carts or carrying whatever they could salvage from their households on their backs, direction: eastward.

Permanent security was not, however, to be found in that quarter either. Poland-Lithuania, though constantly engaged in smaller conflicts, might count herself lucky to have escaped the frightful savagery that devastated Germany and her surroundings. But at the very same time as the Peace of Westphalia that ended the Thirty Years' War was being concluded in Münster, shaping the pattern of central Europe for the next 250 years and inaugurating the era of nation states that would in the end find no room for a Yiddish nation and civilisation, another hate match was being ignited on the far side of the continent, the first in a chain of catastrophes that the Polish people remember as the Deluge. And this time the Yiddish-speaking people of the commonwealth would not be able to stand aside.

THE COSSACKS

"It was a remarkable year, the year 1647, in which various portents in the heavens and on the earth foretold calamities and unusual occurrences." So begins *With Fire and Sword*,[3] the first of a trilogy of historical novels written towards the end of the nineteenth century by Henryk Sienkiewicz (1846–1916), the Polish Nobel Laureate (who also gave us *Quo Vadis*, filmed in 1951 by Sam Zimbalist and Mervyn LeRoy), in which the author traces the events that began the downfall of his nation from her place of honour among the European powers to her disappearance from the map 150 years later.

The story begins in the most undeveloped part of the Polish-Lithuanian commonwealth: the wild lands of the south-east, through which flow the great Dnieper and Dniester rivers, and beyond which stretch the endless steppelands and the Crimean peninsula where Tartar khans ruled.

> The last vestiges of civilised life disappeared as one went towards the south. Not far from Chigrin in the direction of the Dnieper, and from Uman in the direction of the Dniester, and then a great distance as far as the coast lakes and the sea—steppe followed steppe between the two rivers, as if framed by them. At the bend of the Dnieper, in the Nij [lowlands] beyond the rapids, Cossack life swarmed, but upon the steppes themselves, no one lived, and only on their borders were here and there patches which looked like islands in the midst of the sea. The country belonged in name to the Commonwealth, but it was a waste, and the Commonwealth permitted the Tartars to use it as a pasture-land. As the Cossacks, however, frequently defended it, the pasture ground was often turned into a battle-field.[4]

Sienkiewicz's novels shaped Poland's real history into a powerful myth. As American novelist James Michener wrote in his introduction to a recent edition, "The Sienkiewicz Trilogy stands with that handful of novels which not only depict but also help to determine the soul and character of the nation they describe."[5] Poles, faithful Catholic Poles, fighting for survival against a malevolent world swarming with bitter enemies. It is significant for twentieth-century history that one group of people is mostly absent from Sienkiewicz's narrative: the Yiddish-speaking Jews.

The south-eastern borderlands of Lithuania had long been where civilised Europe petered out and the Wild East really began. A small Jewish population, Slavic-speaking in the main, had for centuries lived here in peace and relative security, since this was the eastern route by which Jews had arrived in Europe even before the first Christian missionaries—as Martin Luther himself conceded. After the Union of 1569 which turned Poland and Lithuania into a single commonwealth, and the annexation by Poland of these lands "by the border"—old Slavic *ou kraina*, Ukraine—the undeveloped territories were opened up to ruthless Polish colonisation, settled by Polish magnates suffering from the inflationary economic wave, and eager for new land and new serfs to make up their losses. Crucial to the enterprise was the assistance, as advisers and factors, of a new generation of Yiddish-speaking pioneers who, like the minor nobility, were finding their old homes too crowded and competitive, their lives too restricted—in part by close rabbinical supervision—and who relished the wide horizons and new opportunities on offer. Recent arrivals and old residents now mingled and multiplied to become one of the most thriving of Yiddish communities, moving the centre of gravity of Poland's Jewish population bodily eastwards.

Jews were the key ingredient in the Ukraine's development. Management of much of the agricultural economy, administration of the nobles' lands, organisation of export and import, mining and quarrying, flour milling, alcohol production and sale, were either entirely or mainly in the hands of the Yiddish-speaking community, who ensured their control by subcontracting only to their relatives and co-religionists. The Polish word *arenda*, meaning the leasing for a flat fee of entire landed estates, together with their villages, their produce, services and their serfs, quickly entered the Yiddish and Hebrew languages. The Polish king decreed, "We should always aim to increase the income from our towns and castles, and through the competition of the Jews the value of our leases has always increased." At the same time Prince Piotr Zabrzeski leased all his possessions in the district of Krzemieniec, future birthplace of violinist Isaac Stern,

> including the old and new city of Krzemieniec, New Zbaraż and Kolsec with all the settlements appertaining to these estates, together with the noble boyars, the burghers, and the serfs of those cities and villages . . . all their debts, obligations and privileges, with the arendas, taverns, tolls, ponds, the mills and their revenues, the manors, the various tithes paid by the boyars, burghers and serfs of those districts, together with all the other revenues, to Mr. Mikołaj Wransowicz and to Efraim the Jew of Międzybóż, for the amount of 9,000 złoties of the Polish currency, for three years.[6]

In addition, the lease owner was also judge, enforcer of the law and implementer of its penalties: the power of life and death.

This Yiddish takeover of the wild and lawless Ukraine's economy could be expected to have involved much exploitation and corrupt abuse of monopoly. Jews tried hard to keep such businesses as the collection of customs dues and taxes to themselves. Surviving customs records from the 1580s are written in a mixture of Yiddish and Hebrew. The historian Shimon Dubnow quotes a resolution passed by the Jewish Lithuanian Council, the *Vaad Medinas Litoh*, ruling body of the Jewish estate: "We have openly seen the great danger deriving from the operation of customs in Gentile hands; for the customs to be in Jewish hands is a pivot on which everything turns, since thereby Jews may exert control."[7]

It was not just nepotism, however, but also the Yiddish entrepreneurs' expertise in management and administration that led to their dominance. In places where Jewish leasing of customs was not allowed, Jews were still in demand as silent and invisible, but executive, partners to nominal Christian leaseholders, foreshadowing the dishonourable practice of the early Nazi years.

The alliance between ruthless Polish nobles and insecure Yiddish frontiersmen proved dangerous and destructive. The Jews now held a position that nothing in their background or religious law had properly prepared them for. They had been placed in authority over another people, of another social order, another culture and another religion, a people whom the magnates, the Jews' masters, regarded as racially inferior and fair game for callous exploitation. Tragically, shaking off the restraining influence of wiser counsels of the West, the repeated warnings of the rabbis of metropolitan Cracow, Posen and Lublin, the Yiddish businessmen who flocked to the colony came to regard the peasantry in a similar contemptuous light.

Guillaume Le Vasseur de Beauplan, a French military cartographer and engineer who joined the Polish king's service, was shocked by what he found when he first visited the region in the 1650s:

> The peasants are utterly destitute, obliged as they are to work three days a week with their horses and their own hands in the service of their lord, and to pay him, according to the amount of land they hold, fatted capons, hens, goslings and chickens, payable at Easter, Pentecost, and Christmas, and also to cart their lord's wood and to perform a thousand other forced labours to which they should not be subject . . . Their lords have total authority over them, not only over their possessions, but also over their lives, so great is the power of the Polish nobility (which lives as if in paradise and the poor peasants as if they were in purgatory), such that

if it happens that these unfortunate people fall into the hands of wicked lords, they find themselves in a state more deplorable than convicts working the galleys.[8]

De Beauplan's "three days a week" may have been an understatement. In 1602 a council of rabbis and community leaders urged Jewish lessees not to force their serfs to work on the Sabbath:

> If the villagers are obliged to do the work on weekdays [i.e. Monday to Saturday for Christians] . . . let them forgo the Sabbath and [Jewish] holidays altogether. Living in exile and under the Egyptian yoke, our forefathers chose the Sabbath day for resting . . . Therefore also where Gentiles are under their hand, [the Jews] are obliged to keep the Law . . . Let them not be ungrateful to the Giver of Bounty.[9]

That this exhortation was thought necessary can only mean that its ideals were not usually observed. Indeed, records show that demanding a full seven days' work per week from each male serf was not unknown,[10] leaving his wife and under-aged children—if he had them—to grow enough food on his little plot to keep them barely alive. Peasant life on the Ukrainian estates has been compared with African-Americans' experience of *ante bellum* plantation society in the southern Confederate states of North America.

It should go without saying that the wealthy leaseholders, the *arendators*, were only a tiny minority among the Yiddish speakers—less than two per cent perhaps. The great majority, simpler folk, earned their bread as operators of mills and taverns, as artisans like hatters and tailors, or as servicers of the entrepreneurs' religious wants and needs. These were far from enriching occupations, for this was settler territory, after all. Jewish innkeepers plied their trade in smoke-filled wooden shacks, their children running half naked among the peasant drinkers sitting on stamped-earth floors, with not even bundles of straw for beds. There were also large numbers of the indigent and unemployed to be maintained at the communities' expense, estimated at up to twenty-five per cent of the Yiddish-speaking population. But as so often happens, the evil reputation earned by an unscrupulous few brought retribution on to the heads of the innocent many. The distinguished historian of Poland Professor Norman Davies's judgement is severe but probably fair:

the Jewish arendator became the master of life and death over the population of entire districts, and, having nothing but a short-term and purely financial interest in the relationship, was faced with the irresistible temptation to pare his temporary subjects to the bone . . . In 1616, well over half the Crown Estates in the Ukraine were in the hands of Jewish arendators. In the same era, Prince Konstanty Ostroróg was reputed to employ over 4,000 Jewish agents. The result was axiomatic. The Jewish community as a whole attracted the opprobrium directed originally at its most enterprising members, and became the symbol of social and economic exploitation.[11]

However, when Davies goes on to write "their participation in 'the oppressive practices of the noble-Jewish alliance' provided the most important single cause of the terrible retribution which was to descend on them on several occasions in the future," he goes too far, moving from history to polemic. The most important single cause of the approaching storm that would engulf the Ukraine was that this patch of the untamed East, on the margin between the sown and the wild, was a disputed frontier.

Just as the Yiddish speakers were moving from west to east, the Orient was steadily encroaching from the opposite direction. By the year 1600 Lithuania had lost its southern shoreline to the Turks. The Ottoman Empire now ruled all the way from the Black Sea coast to the Adriatic. The Caucasus, the Balkans, Romania and Hungary were all subjects of the Sultan. Lithuania suffered constant incursions and raids on towns and villages through her thousand-mile-long, dangerously porous steppeland border, though not from Turks—whose priority was to penetrate ever further into central Europe's heart with their repeated attempts to take Vienna—but from their Tartar vassals, the descendants of Mongol conquerors still occupying the Crimea and the "Wild Plains" north of the Black Sea.

One of the best-known responsa by Rabbi Meir of Lublin (1558–1616), known as the Maharam, vividly illustrates the everyday dangers, in this case what happened to a man, "luckless, ill, tortured by pain and suffering from epilepsy," who lived with his many children as the only Jew in a gentile village.

This happened during the time when there were disturbances in Volhynia due to the Tartar invasions. At this time, by command of the general and the officers, every man there was expected to be ready with his weapon in his hand to engage in battle and to fight the marauders.

It happened then on a certain day that the man in question was trying out his gun, as musketeers usually do. He was shooting with his weapon, which in German is called a *Büchse*, through a window in his house at a target that was fixed on the wall in his yard. But just then a man coming from the street into that yard, and wishing to enter that house, ran into the area just described and was unfortunately killed, without having been seen and certainly without having been aimed at. For the man who did the shooting had never seen the unfortunate fellow, as was later made clear by evidence offered in court on his behalf by people of his city. It was further testified that the Gentile who was the officer of the Jewish musketeer and his superior—for he was in charge of ten men—had stationed himself outside to warn anyone who might wish to enter the yard. Indeed he had done so in this case, too, for he had shouted at the intruder and had warned him not to enter, as was made clear in court.

Now this musketeer has come to me, weeping and crying in the bitterness of his soul, and has willingly offered to take upon himself any penance for the calamity which, unfortunately, happened through him.[12]

Meir of Lublin had a reputation for leniency. What that meant in the year 1600 is revealed by the penance prescribed at the behest of his sick, epileptic questioner, a man already found innocent by the civil court. Where today the accidental killer would perhaps be offered counselling, Rabbi Meir ordered—in addition to various ascetic privations to be followed for a whole year: fasting three days every week, no alcohol, no festive meals, no pillows, no clean clothes—the following routine:

First he is to go to the holy community of Ostrog and to lie down at the threshold of the synagogue as everyone goes out, and then he is to be whipped and to make confession for his sins. Afterwards he is to go to the holy community of Vinnitsya, after that to Zaslavl, then to Ostropol, then to Sinyava, and finally to the holy community of Konstantinov, and shall also do that which is prescribed above.

The Polish authorities could not, of course, depend only on amateur civilian marksmen to protect their territory. They had to make proper provision for defence. But they had neither the manpower nor the expertise for steppe skirmishing. So, in a classic error that even a brief study of Roman relations with the Germanic tribes might have warned them against, they turned for assistance to those they believed to be the natural enemies of the Tartars, the other group of outsiders who lived just within and outside the Lithuanian borderland.

The Cossacks, semi-nomadic self-governing military communes, originally composed of runaway serfs, freebooters and traders, who had settled around the Dnieper river *za porozhe*, above the rapids, had long contested control of the grasslands with the Tartar tribesmen. From the early sixteenth century Polish kings had organised these Zaporozhian Cossacks into "registered" military colonies to protect the kingdom's borders. In the seventeenth century, Cossack regiments fought in the continental wars under Polish colours. But the Cossacks were Orthodox Christian and the Poles were Catholic. The Poles thought they were the masters, the Cossacks thought they were free. Tension between the two was inevitable.

In the 1620s a minor local nobleman, educated by Polish Jesuits, with an estate in the hill country near the Dnieper river, joined the registered Cossacks and in ten years rose to the position of military chancellor, working for an understanding between his Orthodox comrades-in-arms and the Catholic Polish crown. In 1638, however, the king revoked the autonomy of the Zaporozhian host, the post of military chancellor was abolished and its holder reduced to the rank of captain. This might seem reason enough for disaffection, but the former chancellor continued to serve for some years, and with some honour, in this lowlier capacity.

However, a feud with a group of local landowners led to an armed raid on his estate and the seizure of his property. His small son was brutally beaten and died, his wife was carried off and a warrant was issued for his arrest and execution. After fruitless appeals to the law and to the royal court, he was imprisoned, but escaped—one chronicler claimed that he was helped by a Jew called Jacob Zabilenki[13]—joined the Cossack host and was voted hetman of the Zaporozhians, whom he proceeded to lead in rebellion against their Polish overlord, allying himself with his former Tartar enemies. This was Bohdan (or Bogdan) Chmelnicki (or Chmielnitsky), known to the Jews as Chmiel the Wicked and to the Ukrainians as father of their freedom. (An avenue in Odessa is named after him; it crosses Sholom Aleichem Street.)

In itself the Cossack revolt was nothing new. This was far from the first uprising of the Ukrainian hosts. But the revolt coincided with the peak of the economic disaster that had finally spread to these furthermost reaches of the Polish commonwealth. The Baltic grain trade, on which the Polish nobility's profits depended, had collapsed; customs duties had dwindled away; the wool and textiles business had shrunk to nearly nothing. As their incomes diminished, the Polish magnates put ever more financial pressure on the Jews and the Jews in turn attempted to squeeze ever more from the Ukrainian serfs. This was the final straw to lay on the peasants' backs. They rose in unrestrained fury against their oppressors, joining forces with the Cossacks, and turned a minor political rebellion into an explosion of savagery that nobody, not even the Polish army, could withstand. In 1648 and 1649 rebel bands spread carnage throughout Poland, as far west from the Ukraine as Posen and as far north as Vilna and Minsk. The *Ukrainian Eyewitness Chronicle*[14] relates:

> Wherever they found the *szlachta* [Polish nobles], royal officials or Jews, they killed them all, sparing neither women nor children. They pillaged the estates of the Jews and nobles, burned [Catholic] churches and killed their priests, leaving nothing whole. It was a rare individual in those days who had not soaked his hands in blood and participated in the pillage.

The Khmielnitsky massacres were seen by the Jews as specifically directed against them: "a great multitude of the empty-headed have gathered with weapons and dressed in coats of mail. A large number of the Tartars have joined them and are encamped around them, saying: come let us destroy Israel."[15] The slaughter is inscribed in Jewish history as the worst crime perpetrated against the Jewish people between the Roman destruction of Jerusalem and the twentieth century. Contemporaries numbered the dead at more than 100,000 and described unbearable inhumanities.

As always, scholars argue over the accuracy of contemporary Jewish accounts. The main Jewish chronicler of the massacres, Nathan Hannover, was not witness to the events he describes but based his reports on the accounts of others and on hearsay. Yet there is no question at all that the sufferings of the Yiddish Jews of the Ukraine at the hands of the Cossacks and the peasants were extreme, although it is not at all clear that Khmiel-nitsky himself was responsible for the excesses, or that he had much control over the insurgents.

It is not to diminish the Yiddish people's afflictions to note, as reported in these same grisly accounts, that the worst cruelties were practised on Polish noblemen and Catholic priests: "The Jews were led to the cemetery . . . They entered the cemetery chapel and were killed there. Afterwards the building was set on fire . . . The Catholic priests . . . were skinned alive while the dukes who had been buried for a long time were dug up from their graves and tossed aside";[16] that it was Polish nobles and priests who provided the greater number of victims: "In the city of Mogila they slaughtered 800 nobles together with their wives and children as well as 700 Jews, also with wives and children";[17] and that some of the events described are quite unrealistic and seem to belong to the class of atrocity myths that are always traded during bitter conflicts. "That, in a town taken by assault, they skinned 15,000 people alive? I declare this deed impossible, not for want of ferocity, but for lack of patience of even the most stupid of the savages," wrote French author Prosper Mérimée of the Polish clerical victims, in his account of the uprising, *The Cossacks of the Past.*[18]

Whatever the real truth, whether the martyrs numbered 50,000, 100,000, or 500,000, Professor Shmuel Ettinger of the Hebrew University of Jerusalem points out that "Jews began to return to their localities in Volhynia at the end of 1648, and a short while later were again living throughout the territory up to the Dnieper. Despite the memory of the holocaust of 1648–49, this region was one of the most densely populated by Jews during the 18th and 19th centuries."[19] The Jews suffered monstrously, but they returned. On their return, however, they lived in very reduced circumstances compared with their previous generations. The Ukrainian massacres signalled the end of Yiddish prosperity in the East. After Chmiel the Wicked, the Polish-Lithuanian commonwealth was no longer the *goldene medine,* the golden land, that it once had seemed.

POVERTY AND DISGRACE

The Cossack rebellion was just the first of an array of disasters that struck Poland-Lithuania in the mid-seventeenth century. There followed in quick succession a bewildering series of major and minor conflicts that included a devastating Swedish invasion, further battles against Tartars and Turks—including Poland's last starring performance on the world stage: the rescue of Vienna from the Ottoman army by Jan Sobieski—and finally the calamitous Great Northern War that attended the birth of the eighteenth century, in which Poland was again utterly despoiled. Famine and plague followed in the train of the ravaging armies. In 1676 the Council of Four Lands expressed the mood prevailing among the Jews of Poland:

> We have sinned grievously against the Almighty; the disturbances increase from day to day. It is becoming more and more difficult for us to live. Our people are considered as naught among other nations; and it is wonderful, in view of all our misfortunes, that we still exist. The only thing left for us to do is to form ourselves into a close union, following strictly the commands of the Lord and the precepts of our venerable teachers and guides.

By the early 1700s the once proud and mighty Polish-Lithuanian commonwealth was left ruined, her crown effectively bankrupt and her population reduced by a third or more. Even worse, Austria, Prussia and Russia, the surrounding states, were by contrast growing in strength, and looking with green and greedy eyes on the huge area of land that the wounded nation was no longer able properly to support or to defend. Attempts were made to reform the monarchy and the parliament, the *Sejm*, and even to regularise relations with the Jews and integrate them into the state, but they were too little and too late. Civil war threatened; Polish rulers became little more than puppets worked by Moscow's strings; the Polish economy was further undermined when Prussia began flooding the country with counterfeit coinage.[20] Piece by piece Russia, Austria and Prussia took bites out of the commonwealth's territory. In 1772 the *Rzeczpospolita* would lose half its population and a third of its area. In 1791 most of the rest would be taken. Finally, in 1795, Poland-Lithuania would disappear altogether and the three predatory powers that would dominate the rest of the modern era in eastern Europe would meet at the muddy river junction by Mysłowice.

In the course of that disastrous history trade faltered and almost ceased. Town and country were impoverished. Jews and Christians alike were forced to pull in their belts. Most affected were the community organisations, the Kahals, whose expenses continued growing with the size of the population, rather than diminishing with the downturn in commerce. Already, over more than a century of economic decline, the Yiddish speakers' own capital had been insufficient to finance their activities.

Increasingly they were forced to turn to the nobles and even to the Catholic Church for loans. In spite of Papal opposition, like Pope Benedict XIV's reaffirmation in his bull *Vix Pervenit* that usury was forbidden, the Polish Church seemed to regard loans to the Jews as safe and profitable investments, while the Jews may have seen in their indebtedness to the Church a guarantee against arbitrary expulsion. Large sums were involved. But now, it seems, the communities were being forced to break the first rule of responsible finance: borrow to invest, never to consume. For the first time, the Kahals were having to take out loans to fund their running expenses. The communities of Cracow, Grodno, Opatów, Pińsk and Posen all sank into debt, amounting to many hundreds of thousands of Polish złoty, perhaps several million all told, at a time when 4 złoty a month was a respectable working wage. The Yiddish speakers had turned from net creditors to net debtors. And like so many of their former clients, when the time came to repay they found that they couldn't.

In the year 1710 or shortly thereafter, a pair of travel-stained emissaries from the Community of Lublin arrived at the door of Rabbi Zvi Hirsch ben Jacob Ashkenazi, then serving as rabbi to the Yiddish-speaking Jews of the prosperous Dutch city of Amsterdam. They came bearing a begging letter endorsed by a number of other Yiddish scholars whom they had petitioned in the course of their long journey west. Please help, they implored, we cannot pay our debts, "for the money was finished, it had run out, it left our pouches, and when the creditors saw . . . that the money was finished, that money was completely gone from Israel, they purged all of their evil on us to destroy our remnant, God forbid." The community was bankrupt and its elders were apparently languishing in debtors' jail: "This the word of . . . the leaders of the holy community of Lublin who sign with their weakened hands, in prison."[21]

Rabbi Ashkenazi did what he could, raising a donation from the Yiddish-speaking Jews of Amsterdam and even, with some trepidation, approaching the local Sephardic community. His son recalled that "they responded to him and gave a certain sum, their gift, into his holy hand to give the monies to those emissaries from Lublin." The gift may have solved the problem temporarily, but Lublin, like other communities, continued to borrow, albeit on a smaller scale, never finding an alternative way to fund its essential activities and never managing to clear its debt.

The community was still fighting off its creditors when in 1764 the Polish parliament, in an attempt at reform—perhaps even well meant, as they claimed to be trying to integrate the Yiddish-speaking communities more fully into the Polish State—modernised the system of Jewish taxation, set up a committee to carry out the liquidation of the Kahals' debts, forbade them to borrow any more money, and for good measure ordered the Council of the Four Lands to be immediately wound up. "Whereas the comprehensive Jewish poll tax . . . is abrogated . . . henceforward there shall be no assemblies, apportionments or other kinds of injunctions, levies or compulsions relating to the Jews as customary hitherto . . . we abolish them in perpetuity."[22] The penalty for breaking this edict was 6,000 *Grivnas* (bars of silver), a huge sum—not to be confused with today's low-value unit of Ukrainian currency.

The community was stunned. They were shamed. They felt humiliated that "the captains, the heads of the Lands, have been dispossessed of their mite of greatness, and even this small honour has been taken from Israel."[23] To poverty had been added disgrace. No longer would there be a "Supreme Court for the Jews." No longer would the Yiddish speakers have their own administration, their claim to separate nationhood. Moreover, in spite of the *Sejm*'s intention, there was never a realistic prospect of the Yiddish-speaking people's full integration as equals into Polish society. The effect of the edict was to disempower and marginalise the Polish-Lithuanian Jews. It was the beginning of the end of the Yiddish civilisation.

As always we have only the testimony of how the good and the great felt and wrote. Perhaps ordinary working people took the loss of Jewish autonomy less hard. Many may well have felt relief to be rid of a class of oligarchs who "had authority to dispense justice to all Israel in the kingdom of Poland, to safeguard the law, to frame ordinances, and to inflict punishment as they saw fit."[24] Many may have found their new freedom from centralised control a blessed release.

For the Yiddish response to Poland's steep economic decline had been a great upwelling of popular religion, sometimes irrational, often heretical, and certainly unsanctioned by the rabbinic authorities, who fought hard but without success to retain control. Messianic fantasy, pietist enthusiasm, enlightenment rationalism had been quietly germinating through the long dark days and now, with the abolition of central control, were free to throw up strong shoots into the daylight of recorded history.

Where in former days, the Council of the Lands had successfully suppressed nonconformist movements and held the Yiddish civilisation together by force of its authority, now after its abolition, as Poland's rapacious neighbours began their project to dismantle the commonwealth, and certainly when that aim had been achieved and the three empires finally met at the *Dreikaisereck*, squeezing Poland out of existence altogether, Yiddish unity was irredeemably destroyed. "Woe to the generation that experiences this in its time," wrote a contemporary,

> the borders are redrawn . . . and the gates to the nations are closed.
> . . . The councils of the regions and the lands are no more. Since
> the elders no longer gather together, there is rarely vision. . . .
> Everyone builds a "high Place" for himself convening a council of
> rebels and a quorum for prayer in his own house, while the synagogues and study houses stand abandoned. This is the beginning
> of the decline and fall of Israel.[25]

The eighteenth-century synagogue at Przysucha with its *kuna* or pillory (below), where those deemed guilty of some misdemeanour by the town's rabbis would be chained by the neck during the Sabbath service, so that those entering or leaving could strike, spit at or revile the miscreant

Above: Isaac Leib Peretz (1852–1915), advocate of enlightenment and socialism, and one of the founders of the Yiddish Renaissance. He recognized that, since millions of European Jews knew no other language, a literature must be created for them in Yiddish if they were to be brought out of their poverty, ignorance and intolerance. *Below:* The synagogue of Zamosc, eastern Poland, built for Sephardic Jews invited to settle by the town's founder. They were later joined by thousands of Yiddish speakers fleeing the Cossack uprising. The Jewish Enlightenment in Poland first took root here.

Shalom Yankev Broido (1835–1917), father of the Yiddish Renaissance. Best known under the name of his comic character Mendele Moykher Sforim (Mendel the Book Pedlar), Broido published in Hebrew under the name Abramowitch. When he wrote in Yiddish, he feared it would ruin his reputation.

Shalom Rabinovitz (1859–1916), superstar of modern Yiddish literarture. Writing under the pseudonym Sholom Aleichem, he achieved great fame as a novelist, satirist and humorist. When he died in New York, all the sweatshops stopped work and huge crowds attended the funeral.

"To New York every Wednesday and Sunday." An 1880 poster showing one of the earlier sail-and-steam ships of the Hamburg-America Packet Shipping Company, known as HAPAG. Wags said it stood for *Haben alle Passagiere auch Geld:* Have all the passengers got money?

Left: Albert Ballin (1857–1918), shipping magnate and friend of Kaiser Wilhelm II, who made possible the survival of a branch of the Yiddish civilisation far from the old hatreds of Europe. The descendants of hundreds of thousands of Yiddish-speaking immigrants in the United States and elsewhere owe him a debt of gratitude. *Below:* The Pavilion Theatre in Whitechapel, known as "The Drury Lane of the East End," from 1906 the home of Yiddish theatre in London. Ibsen, Strindberg and Gorky were performed here in Yiddish, alternating with more populist fare, as well as with concerts, boxing matches and political meetings.

trunk? Is your luggage

טראנק איז יאהר אין לאנגדזש

ready? Everything is pre-

רעדי עווערימהינג איז פרי-

pared. — Do not forget

פעהרד דו נאט פארגעט

to write to us.

טו רייט טו אָס

I will do it with pleasure,

איי אואיללאיט דזז איטאימאה פלעזשער

Farewell, a pleasant journey

דזשעראנזצע עה פלעזענט פעהרוועל

and góod health.

ענד גוד העלטה

קאָפּפּער? איזט אייער געפּעק

פֿערטיג. (בערייט) אלעס איזט

פֿאָרגעברייטעט. פֿערגעסט ניכט

צו אונס צו שרייבען.

איך ווערדע עס טהון מיט פֿער-
גניגען.

בלייבט געזונד! אין גליקליכע
רייזע

אונד גוטע געזונדהייט.

§ 2.

Cóachman, to the railway.

קאָהטשמען טו דהי רעלאוועה

Make haste. Be quick.

קוואיק בי העהסט מעהק

The train starts in an hour.

דהי מרעהן סטאהרטם אין ען אויער

We are at the státion, Sir,

אגאי אהר עט דהי סטעשען סער

Where is the bóoking-office?

אָפֿפֿים-בוקינג דהי איז אוועהר

A ticket for Manchester,

עה טיקעט פֿאָר מענטשעסטער

if you please. What class?

איף יגה פליהם אואָט קלאהם

קוטשער, צו די אייזענבאַהן!

מאַכט שנעלל, געשווינד,

דער צוג געהט אב אין איינע
שטונדע.

וויר זינד, מיין הערר, אויף דעם
באַהנהאָף.

וואָ איזט דיא קאַסס ? ?
(בּיללעט אויסגאַבע)

איין בּיללעט נאַך מאַנטשעסטער

בּיטטע. וועלכע קלאַסס ?

The language divide, 1901. A page from a Yiddish–English phrasebook for immigrants, published by the Russo-Jewish Committee at seven pence per copy, with sections on travel, common trades and occupations and sample social and business letters. But the language is not so much Yiddish as German written with Hebrew characters.

Above: Petticoat Lane in the early 1900s, the principal Jewish market street of late-Victorian London, named for the old clothes once sold there. "The noise is often deafening, and in the babel of sounds half a dozen different languages may be distinguished—French, German, Russian, Polish, Hebrew, with the Yiddish compounds of them all, and occasionally English." *Below:* New York's Lower East Side, capital of Jewish America at the turn of the last century, its roadways blocked by merchandise spilling out of shop fronts onto the sidewalks and by pickle barrels, hot-potato stalls and unstable mountains of battered cabin trunks and cardboard suitcases—abandoned relics of immigrant journeys

The Jazz Singer. On 6 October 1927, Yom Kippur (the Day of Atonement), Warner Brothers released the very first full-length feature film with synchronised dialogue. A précis of the American odyssey of Eastern Europe's Jews, this was the story of the incorporation of the Yiddish civilisation's remains into the American Way of Life.

12

Decline . . .

Az der Rebbe Elimeylech	When Rabbi Elimelech
Iz gevoren azoy freylech,	Became so very joyful,
Iz gevoren azoy freylech, Elimeylech,	Became so very joyful, Elimelech,
Hot er oysgeton di zokn	He took off his socks
Un hot eyngedreyt di lokn	And twisted up his sidelocks
Un geshikt noch di fidler di tsvey.	And sent for the fiddlers, the two of them.

(Then, joined by pipers, cymbalom players, drummers and no doubt yet others, he jumped on to the table and began to dance.)

That, at least, is the way it was sung in my family. I didn't find the verse when I looked up the song in *Mir Trogn a Gezang,* one of the collections of Yiddish songs assembled by Eleanor Gordon Mlotek[1] in the 1970s. I did learn, however, that "Der Rebbe Elimeylech," inspired by the children's song "Old King Cole," was the work of a Communist satirist, the Galician-born American Isaac Reis, who went by the pen-name Moshe Nadir, Moses the Rare. I also discovered that in 1923, four years before the composer was ready to publish it himself, the piece had already appeared in an anonymous "folklorised" version, having almost immediately escaped its creator's control.

The jingle's provenance explains its meaning. It is a satire, but so warm-hearted and generous that anyone other than its author would be hard put to distinguish it from a loving evocation of a vanished way of life, celebration rather than mockery of the old Rebbe. Nevertheless, "Der Rebbe Elimeylech" is a faint after-echo of the genuine passions aroused by a real conflict that savagely tore the Yiddish nation apart during the eighteenth and nineteenth centuries—a struggle over nothing less than the Yiddish future and the Yiddish soul. Yet the naming of an actual rabbi, Elimelech, in the song was unusual, demonstrating how even among those most strongly critical of the way of life promoted by the charismatic wonder-working preachers of the eighteenth and nineteenth centuries, the renown of this Rebbe,[2] leader of a Chassidic community, also called a *Tsaddik* (Righteous One) or an *Admor* (an abbreviation of the Hebrew for Our Lord, Teacher and Rabbi),[3] made him impossible to forget even 150 years later.

Elimelech ben Eliezer Lipmann Weissblum (1717–87) is still well remembered in Leżajsk, now a quiet riverside market town in southern Poland lying on the main road from Lvov (Yiddish: Lemberg)[4] via Sandomir to Gdansk, which the Rebbe adopted as his home after half a lifetime of wandering from village to village, preaching and praying with his equally famous brother Zusya. (His former residence now houses the local office of the Ministry of Education.) His tomb—his *Ohel* or Tabernacle—still stands in a plot on a grassy hillock, enclosed in a gilded metal cage next to a long table for ritual dining, inside a white-painted wooden cabin surrounded by tall trees, all protected by a spiked iron fence—like a precious jewel hidden away inside a series of elaborate containers. This was once the town's Jewish cemetery before Hitler's *Wehrmacht* destroyed it and took the gravestones to pave the town square. Krystyna, the middle-aged Christian woman who lives nearby, keeps the key, tends the tomb and shows pilgrims into the building, explains that she inherited the duty from her father who had shared a Gestapo cell with Leżajsk's rabbi. The two agreed that whichever survived would do what he could for the other's family, but since none of the rabbi's kinsfolk, and only one other local Jew, outlived the war, the old man devoted himself instead to the maintenance of Rebbe Elimelech's grave and name.

Catholic Krystyna seems to have become a fervent disciple. When I visited the shrine, she immediately pulled out a navy cloth-bound tome, one of the many copies of *No'am Elimelech* (roughly: the sayings of Elimelech), the Rebbe's book of wisdom, crammed into a bookcase near the door, and tried to press it on me, explaining how much I would be improved by reading it. "If you can't read it in Hebrew," she urged, "then I will lend it to you to have translated. Every Jew should know the wonderful words of the *Tsaddik*." The traditional respect, not to say superstitious awe, in which Catholic Poles once held the spiritual leaders of the Chassidic Jews had still not quite evaporated.

No'am Elimelech contains the Rebbe's definitive formulation of the role of the Chassidic holy man. It describes the *Tsaddik* as a man with his feet on the earth but his head in paradise, who "lives below but in reality dwells in higher worlds," whose righteousness is such that heaven itself obeys his wishes when "the *Tsaddik* decrees and God fulfils," and who must first be prepared to fall into sin so as to be able to rise again even higher than before, in the process transforming evil into good and the mundane into the holy for all his community. To carry out this redemptive function he and his entourage must be released from all earthly cares by the financial support of their followers who, in return for the *Tsaddik*'s blessings and advice, pay him "ransoms,"[5] in practice, for the sake of delicacy, left discreetly on a table by the door under the eagle eyes of the *Tsaddik*'s helpers. "Whosoever lets scholars and *Tsaddikim* derive benefit from his property," wrote Elimelech, "that benefit will have the result that he will not rush to sin, to become an absolute villain and deny the Torah—Heaven forbid."

As may easily be imagined, this principle was rather prone to corruption, particularly as being a *Tsaddik* soon became a hereditary occupation—and, indeed, something of a racket—in the course of the nineteenth century. The *Tsaddik* reigned over a "court" that included his family, his associates, his assistants, numerous hangers-on and varying numbers of visiting Chassidic acolytes, leading to huge expenses that could not be covered by "ransoms" alone. So, like an American presidential candidate today, the Rebbe had often to go on long fund-raising tours, while also levying annual fees on all his followers. A careful analysis of Chassidic economics tells us that:

> the Zaddik's court maintained an existence economically apart from that of the [Jewish] host community and was generally quite indifferent to the needs of the latter's institutions. It was self-supporting, achieving its goals through such typical economic tools as fund-raising, tax collection, loans, savings, and profitable investments.[6]

Most *Tsaddikim* were no doubt quite sincere; indeed, some seemed almost embarrassed by their followers' largesse. Judah Zevi of Rozdol, brother of a more famous *Admor*, found it "difficult to understand why the masses journey to me too and give me money, for I surely know that I cannot be considered in the category of *Tsaddik* as *Axis Mundi*." However, it is difficult to know what to make of the claim that all the money given to Mordechai, the *Maggid* (Preacher) of Chernobyl, who lived in a great house in opulent luxury, was actually dedicated to the upkeep of the unknown "36 Righteous Men"[7] whose merit in each generation, the Talmud teaches, is all that keeps the world in existence. To question this was heresy and risked expulsion from the community.

Several "royal" Chassidic courts cultivated a lifestyle of considerable grandeur, paid for by the donations of their mostly penniless followers. Baruch, *Tsaddik* of Medziboz (1757–1810), grandson of the founder of Chassidism, regarded himself as rightful leader by descent of the entire movement, and announced that Shimon ben Yochai, the supposed second-century author of the Kabbalist *Book of Splendour*, the *Zohar*, had appeared to him in a dream to tell him "my beloved Baruch, you are a perfect man." Baruch lived like a Polish aristocrat, and even kept a famous wit, Hershele Ostropover, on his payroll as "court jester" to combat his depressions. I am reminded of certain Holy Hindu Gurus with their fleets of Rolls-Royces. Moreover, Chassidim came to be divided by lineage into sacred "Men of Form" and mere "Men of Matter," a caste division that was rigidly enforced and made unchallengeable by its supposed divine provenance.

Here was the unexpected outcome of a movement that had originally begun with a popular rejection of the scholarly oligarchy that had always ruled the communities, a determination among the common people to find a more accessible pathway to God in reaction to the previous century of disasters that had robbed the Yiddish-speaking Jews of their property, their homes, even their lives, and certainly their hope and their religious certainty.

WHO PERMITS THE FORBIDDEN

The crises of seventeenth-century Poland had seemed unending: the financial crash, the Cossack uprising, the Swedish invasion, the plagues and famines, the enfeebling of the throne, the depredations of Turks, Tartars and paramilitary bands called *Haidamacks* (from the Turkish command: *Haida!*, Move On!) who even apparently included renegade Jews among their number. Between 1600 and 1660 Elimelech's home town had itself suffered devastating epidemics, numerous fires that destroyed all its buildings, a private war between the Lord of Leżajsk and the owner of nearby Łancut, assaults by Tartars, with residents taken captive and shipped into slavery, and a brutal conquest by the Swedes that drove the entire citizenry to flee while King Karl Gustav himself strutted around in triumph. In the light of these inexplicable events the Yiddish Jews were quite ready to believe that the world was coming to an end.

Soon a rumour spread that a Messiah had appeared in the Middle East and was preparing to lead the Children of Israel back to their Holy Land and to raise them up above the nations. It was said that his name was Sabbatai Zvi or Shabbetei Zevi or Shabtai Tsebi, the son of a kosher poultry dealer from Smyrna in Turkey.

Today we would most likely diagnose Zvi as a man afflicted by mental illness, with symptoms that would probably be ascribed to acute manic-depressive psychosis as it used to be called, or bipolar disorder. At times given to severe ascetic practices, fasting, self-flagellation and complete withdrawal, at other times propelled by mania to frenzied activity, to declaring divine revelations and breaking the normal rules of Judaism, including—most shockingly—repeatedly and publicly pronouncing out loud the Tetragrammaton, the Ineffable Name of God, something only allowed to the High Priest in the Temple's Holy of Holies on the Day of Atonement, this highly learned but disturbed individual brought about what Gershom Sholem, the great analyst of Jewish mysticism, called "the largest and most momentous messianic movement in Jewish history subsequent to the destruction of the Temple."[8] It came close to destroying the Yiddish-speaking people.

In 1665, prompted by his discoverer, manager and principal publicist, the Kabbalah scholar Nathan of Gaza,[9] Zvi announced that he was the long-awaited Messiah and appointed twelve followers to represent the tribes of Israel. The Jewish world exploded into pandemonium. In Germany and Italy they told each other wide-eyed tales of how Zvi had paraded around Jerusalem on a white horse, accompanied by his acolytes, which everyone knew was only permitted by the sultan to Muslims of royal blood, and of how he would eat unkosher foods after pronouncing the blessing *"Boruch atoh Adoshem, Eloheinu Melech ho-olom, matir issurim"*— "Blessed art Thou Lord, our God, King of the Universe, Who permits the forbidden." In Poland, they told of his marriage to a Polish Jewish girl, orphaned in the Cossack rebellion and brought up in a convent, who had miraculously escaped to join the Messiah. (His enemies said that she was a woman of loose morals. But then they would, wouldn't they?) In Muslim Morocco it was whispered that he had performed miracles and was leading the Lost Ten Tribes in the conquest of Mecca. The talk even penetrated the Christian world, where there had long been speculation that the year 1666 would see the second coming of Christ.[10] In his *History of the Jews*, the founder of modern Jewish historiography Heinrich Graetz suggested that it was such talk in the house of an English factor in Smyrna, a sympathiser with the Fifth Monarchy Men of Cromwell's time—believers in the imminent second coming of Christ—for whom Zvi's father worked as an agent, that had first instilled messianic delusions into the troubled mind of his young son. In Amsterdam the millenarian Christian preacher Petrus Serrarius taught the arrival of the Messiah. Samuel Pepys in London heard talk of Zvi's appearance on the world stage:

> Here I am told for certain, what I have heard once or twice already, of a Jew in town, that in the name of the rest do offer to give any man £10 to be paid £100, if a certain person now at Smyrna be within these two years owned by all the Princes of the East, and particularly the grand Signor, as the King of the world, in the same manner we do the King of England here, and that this man is the true Messiah. One named a friend of his that had received ten pieces in gold upon this score, and says that the Jew hath disposed of £1,100 in this manner, which is very strange; and certainly this year of 1666 will be a year of great action; but what the consequences of it will be, God knows![11]

The news raced around the Jewish world like a forest fire. Men and women burned with messianic enthusiasm, undertook fasts, often a week at a time, constant ritual baths to keep them ever in a state of purity, and severe mortifications of the flesh, scourging themselves with thorns or lying naked in the snow. Long processions, parading placards bearing Zvi's image, wound through the Jewish streets of cities across Europe chanting Psalm 21: "The King shall joy in thy strength, O Lord; and in thy salvation how greatly shall he rejoice!" Jews rioted for Yiddish pride in Pinsk, Vilna and Lublin. Work and trade almost stopped altogether. Against the advice of the very few rabbis able to resist the hysteria, people sold their houses for the journey fare, or gave their property away outright and waited to be transported to the Holy Land on the clouds. More practical believers from the Netherlands, Germany, Poland and Italy set out by road to join the Messiah, while other communities despatched delegations bearing letters from their leaders paying homage to the new King of Israel. Across the Middle East itself, to quote the eyewitness Rabbi Leib ben Ozer:

> prophets arose in hundreds and thousands, women and men, boys and girls, and even little children; all of them prophesied in the holy tongue and in the language of the Zohar as well, and none of them knew a letter of Hebrew and all the less so of the language of the Zohar. And this is how it would be: they would fall to the ground like someone struck with epilepsy, foam would come from their mouths, and they would have convulsions and speak secrets of the Kabbalah in the holy tongue concerning many matters, and what they said, each in his own way was this: "The reign of Shabtai Zvi, our lord, our king, our messiah, has been revealed in Heaven and Earth and he has received the crown of kingship from Heaven" . . . And wherever you went you heard nothing but that Mr. So-and-So had become a prophet and that Miss So-and-So had become a prophetess; and here there was a company of prophets, some prophesying in one way and others in another, but the sum of the matter was always that Shabtai Zvi was the messiah and our righteous redeemer.[12]

In February 1666 Zvi was arrested and imprisoned by the Ottoman authorities, but this did little to dampen the flames of religious enthusiasm. The fortress at Gallipoli in which he was held "in honourable confinement" as a political prisoner was now referred to by the biblical phrase *Migdal Oz*, the Strong Tower,[13] and the fact that the Sultan had not beheaded their saviour—the casual, usual and expected punishment for troublemakers in the Ottoman Empire—was adduced as evidence of his sanctity and untouchability.

But the dramatic saga, so full of eastern promise, ended badly. All too soon Zvi's Polish followers heard that the unbelievable had happened, that in September 1666 their Messiah had been denounced to the Turks as an impostor by one Nehemiah ha-Kohen, a Polish Kabbalist from Lemberg, and brought before the Ottoman grand vizier, Ahmed Köprülü. With the sultan himself observing from behind a lattice, Zvi was faced with the choice between immediate death and conversion to Islam. He chose the turban over the headsman's sword. The new convert was honoured under the name Aziz Mehmed Effendi, awarded the title *Kapici Bashi*, Head Gatekeeper—a position which in the Ottoman court included the duties of public executioner—and granted a generous pension.

Nehemiah ha-Kohen the whistle-blower, on the other hand, found himself an outcast when he returned to Poland. Despised as the betrayer of the Messiah, he was excommunicated and expelled from the country. He had to change his name to find anonymity.

Nathan of Gaza, the Messiah's promoter, remained unrepentant, explaining that Zvi's conversion had been "in order to penetrate to the depths of the realm of evil to free the sparks [i.e. of holiness] imprisoned there," and continued to pour out an entire library of letters, tracts, pamphlets and books justifying Zvi's actions on mystical grounds, powerfully influencing the direction steered by Yiddish Judaism for the rest of its days. From then onwards the messianic lodestar ever twinkled faintly ahead.

German and Austrian rabbis, out of embarrassment for their former fervour, cleared their throats and spoke no word more about the subject, pretending that nothing had really happened. In Italy the relevant pages of the community records were torn out and burned. Further east, however, the messianic zeal of the Yiddish communities was not so easily dampened. Large numbers of the Yiddish-speaking people of Bohemia, Moravia, Poland and Lithuania refused to allow real events to stand in the way of wishful thinking. Some of Zvi's apologists explained that the Messiah's apostasy was merely a tactical device through which he hoped to persuade Muslims into the Jewish fold—though more Jews probably followed Zvi into Islam than the reverse, creating a community of secretly Jewish Muslims in Salonika who called themselves *Doenmeh*, Turners (the word in today's Turkish means transsexual), who survived into the twentieth century. Others interpreted Zvi's apostasy as a mystical event with an other-worldly meaning, a victory of Kabbalah over common sense. As the Kabbalist Jacob ben Moses Temerles wrote at the time,

> Truly all, great and small, are well instructed in the mysteries of our Lord. It consoles me in my sorrow to see the great yearning of our people to uncover hidden knowledge. All, great and lowly, strive to be admitted to the mystery of God and to live according to his precepts. Surely this means that our salvation is near at hand.[14]

Deep-mining the Torah, the Talmud, the *Zohar* and other literature of Kabbalah for precedents and predictions, self-appointed prophets came up with heavy loads of citations that by audacious and often heretical inter-pretation justified the paradox of a legitimate apostate Messiah.

Eventually, the Yiddish world learned that Zvi had been discovered by his Turkish minders sitting in a tent, singing Hebrew psalms with a con-gregation of Jews, suggesting that his adherence to Islam was somewhat less than wholehearted. The Ottoman authorities lost patience and exiled the former Messiah to a small town in the Balkans, where he died in 1676 just after his fiftieth birthday—appropriately enough on the Day of Atonement.

THE HOLY CREED OF EDOM

One might have expected that after the Messiah's demise and the failure of his promise to lead the Children of Israel back to their ancestral home, the wave of messianic belief would have broken. Yet it did not, particularly in Podolia (meaning Along the Valley), the south-eastern corner of Poland-Lithuania, lying between the Rivers Dniester and Bug, which had been occupied by the Turks between 1672 and 1699—an area that would play a leading role in the final centuries of eastern European Jewry.

Here, where the Yiddish, Russian and Turkish worlds met, Judaism, Islam and eastern Orthodox Christianity all contributed to the kind of religious environment that twentieth-century historian Arnold Toynbee memorably described as a "culture compost," a fertile seedbed that encouraged new social and spiritual conceptions to germinate and take root. The Jews brought with them their messianic hopes and their Kab-balah, the Christians their *agape* love feast and their veneration of saints, the Muslims their particular style of mysticism and oriental forms of reli-gious organisation. Each was in the process of throwing off traditional religious authority and each derived something new from the collabora-tion. Among the Christians there arose the sect of the *Doukobours*, other-wise known as Spirit Wrestlers: pacifist, anti-priest and anti-state, their ceremonial reduced to the *sobranie*, a meeting for prayer and the sharing of bread and salt. Among the Muslims, the old Bektashi Sufi order, dom-inant in Ottoman Turkey at that time, particularly among the Janissary troops posted to the imperial borderlands, was revitalised, adopting a kind of trinity comprising God, the Prophet and 'Ali his son-in-law, as well as equality for women, the ritual sharing of food and the confession of sins.

Unwittingly the Jews had already experienced aspects of Islamic Sufism through the life and mission of Sabbatai Zvi. His pronouncing out loud of God's name is recognisable as a Jewish parallel to the *Dhikr*, a ritual during which devotees repeatedly recite the names of God. He cultivated the important Sufi poet Niyazi Misri and his followers chanted Sufi verses during their devotions. According to the author Harvey Sarner,[15] his tomb in Albania became a shrine for Bektashis and was—at least until 1965—regularly visited by Sufi pilgrims.

Believers will no doubt dispute that the religious world of the Yiddish speakers of Podolia could have been infiltrated by Sufi influence, though the fact that profound change had come about, whether from within or without, would become ever clearer over the following century. There can be little argument that being in close geographical contact with their ancestral roots—the Holy Land was part of the Ottoman Empire over the border—helped Podolia's Jews throw off the dominance that German, western, influence had long held over them, bringing to the surface and widening the suppressed and hidden, but ever present, division between the Germanic and Slavic Yiddish worlds: the one side represented by the rabbis and the community hierarchy, by high respect for learning and sober demeanour; the other by ordinary simple folk, and by emotion, enthusiasm and the superiority of the heart over the head.

After Zvi's death, Sabbataian messianism slowly changed from an overwhelming mass movement to a cult—albeit very well patronised. Theory held that before the final Messiah, the Messiah ben Dovid, i.e. descended from David, there would be a forerunner, the suffering Messiah ben Joseph, i.e. a successor of Joseph. This offered an open audition to every deluded dreamer, every struggling religious showman and frustrated spiritual mountebank. A veritable flush of Sabbataian preachers, candidates for Messiahship, burst from Slav soil, from Bohemia, Moravia, Poland and Lithuania, promoting themselves as the Messiah ben Joseph and foretelling the imminent second coming of Zvi, as if he were a version of the Christian Saviour. Mordechai of Eisenstadt (1650–1729) travelled throughout Bohemia, Hungary and northern Italy, exhorting the people not to lose faith in their awaited redemption and explaining that Zvi's death was mere illusion. "In three years," he insisted, "*Moshiach* [the Messiah] will return." A former brandy distiller by the name of Zadok appeared in Grodno with a similar message. In Vilna, a goldsmith, Heshel

Zoref (1633–1700), "a simple man without wisdom" who "always performed abnegations and would cry before the ark to gain wisdom and knowledge,"[16] became Poland's most enthusiastic Sabbataian prophet, and spent some thirty years composing the *Sefer ha-Zoref* (*Zoref's Book*), the Torah of the future Messiah, whose five thousand or so pages expounded indigestible mystical and numerological explanations of the *Shema Yisroel*, Judaism's declaration of faith. In Moravia a certain Judah ben Jacob was "reborn" as Loebele Prossnitz, prophet of Zvi, and in the first years of the eighteenth century travelled across Moravia and Silesia raising numerous followers with his repertoire of magic tricks and bemusing incantations. The Polish Sabbataian Samuel Jacob Chayyim Falk narrowly escaped being burned as a wizard in Cologne and fled penniless to England, where he set himself up in a house near the Tower of London with a synagogue and an alchemical laboratory. Known to the Jews as the Ba'al Shem (Master of the Name) of London and to the English as Dr. Falk, he died in 1782 an astonishingly wealthy man.

However, in terms of material profit, the most successful adventurer of the whole genre was unquestionably Jacob Leib (1726–91) from Korolevka, a small town in Podolia, whom Heinrich Graetz described as:

> . . . one of the worst, most subtle, and most deceitful rascals of the eighteenth century. He could cheat the most sagacious, and veil his frauds so cleverly that after his death many still believed him an admirable man . . . He became a Mahometan, as afterwards a Catholic, for so long as it served his purpose, and changed his religion as one changes one's clothes.[17]

Perhaps this judgement reads too harshly. It is possible—perhaps even probable—that Leib was originally sincere, if also self-deluding. Having spent some twenty-five years in the Ottoman Empire, where he apparently joined the Jewish-Muslim *Doenmeh* sect and was initiated into Bektashi Sufism, on his return to Poland in the 1750s he adopted the ways of the formerly Spanish, Sephardic, Jews, spoke in *Ladino*, Judaeo-Spanish, and passed himself off as a *Frenk*, as the Sephardim were often called among the Yiddish speakers. He subsequently took Frank as his surname. Hailed as a prophet and as a reincarnation of Zvi, he was immediately accepted as leader of the Sabbataian cult and successfully promoted its beliefs throughout Moravia, Podolia, Galicia and Hungary, building up such a large following that the rabbis became alarmed and cast about for ways to stop his activities. They nearly succeeded in 1756, when Frank was discovered leading a Sabbataian ritual behind locked doors which, according to the prophet's opponents, amounted to nothing more than a sexual orgy. With the exception of Frank himself, who was thought to be a Turkish citizen, the entire congregation was arrested and brought before a rabbinical court, where its members were made to confess to immoral practices—the women apparently admitted to having broken their marriage vows—and punished by a severe penitential regime. Their leader escaped to Turkey, where he took the opportunity to become a full Muslim convert and renew his Sufi connections—to the great delight of the Ottoman authorities, who gleefully publicised their prestigious catch.

However, Frank was soon back in Poland again, stirring up his dangerously large heretical flock. The rabbis decided that the movement must be stamped out for good. A rabbinical council in Brody, its decision ratified by the Council of the Four Lands, excommunicated Frank and his followers, and encouraged all good Jews to persecute what they called the Sect of Sabbatai Zvi out of existence. This pushed the sectarians into the arms of the Church, who took up their cause with unsurprising relish. Frank himself encouraged his flock to convert to Catholicism, though only outwardly, explaining that all religions were mere steps on the path from illusion to reality, and that the true God was hidden and not accessible to mere human beings, but was represented in this world by the King of Kings, otherwise known as Big Brother (who was always watching you), and whose messenger was none other than Frank himself. Christianity, in this teaching, was no more than a screen behind which was to be found the ultimate true faith, what Frank called the Creed of Edom. There would be no order in this world, he proclaimed, nor would the true Messiah arrive, "until the Law of Moses is fulfilled, until they have entered the Holy Creed of Edom . . . as it is written concerning Moses: 'And Moses dispatched messengers to Edom.' Anyone who is of the seed of Abraham, Isaac and Jacob must follow this Holy Creed of Edom."

The Frankist cult was patronised principally by the well-educated and the wealthy. Ordinary Jews refused to understand the Holy Creed of Edom or recognise its legitimacy. Passionate as they were for the Messiah to appear, ready as they were to follow any charismatic leader who offered to show them the way to redemption, they were too staunchly loyal to their Jewish heritage to be able to accept the principle that only "in the abandonment of Torah is found its true fulfilment." Jacob Frank's activities were a shocking step too far, simply unacceptable to the majority.

THE FAMOUS BA'AL SHEM TOV,
MAY HIS LIGHT LONG SHINE

The fuss that attended the whole Frankist phenomenon served to obscure what would prove to be far more momentous developments. While the *heym*'s attention was focused on the self-publicists and messianic pretenders, a quiet revolution had been taking place among less educated Jews, particularly once again in Podolia, that part of the south-east on the Ottoman border where Judaism, Christianity and Islamic mysticism throve cheek-by-jowl. Zvi's brief messianic reign had undermined the rabbis' authority and Frank's success in attracting a scholarly following had shown up rabbinical pretensions in a poor light too. Resistance to the authoritarian rule of the Talmudists was growing; the common people were beginning to look to others for guidance.

The reasons are not hard to discover. Visit the little town of Przysucha in central Poland with its great barn-like synagogue, the stucco peeling away from solidly built masonry under a green mansard roof, and you will find, set into the massive stone wall next to the entrance, an arched niche, the kind that outside a church would be expected to house a devotional statue. Here, however, the purpose is quite different. Cemented into the wall at the back of the niche is a chain, and hanging on the end of the chain is a hinged iron collar so arranged that it can be closed with a padlock. This is the *kuna* or pillory, the place where those deemed guilty of some misdemeanour by Przysucha's rabbis would be chained by the neck during the Sabbath service, so that those entering or leaving could strike, spit at, or at least revile, the miscreant.

Przysucha's synagogue dates from 1750, the chain was obviously cemented in long after the wall's construction, and—to judge by the state of the rust on the contraption—the metal cannot have been subjected to the vagaries of the Polish weather for much more than 150 years or so. Here is a solid iron symbol of what granting temporal power to a self-perpetuating oligarchy of Torah and Talmud scholars had led to. As representatives of one Lithuanian community complained: "We, the Jewish citizens of Schaulen [now Siauliai], state with tears in our eyes that we need neither a rabbi nor elders . . . They practise extortion and plot evil amongst themselves, to bring us low. They are all related to each other, and they rob us of our last coins, merely to enrich themselves."[18]

In previous centuries the rabbis' authority, bestowed on them by the ruling powers, could not so easily be shrugged off. Now after the Council of the Lands had been abolished in the middle of the eighteenth century, and as Poland-Lithuania disintegrated, it was no longer possible to enforce the rule of the learned, the orthodox, the well-connected—and the rich.

In Podolia, eastern Galicia and other territories of the south-east, groups of artisans and craftspeople began to withdraw from the rabbi-dominated congregations and set up their own prayer circles and synagogues. In central Poland, the record book of the Jewish Company of Tailors of Płock—comprising several dozen members headed by three *gabbai'im*, three trustees and five accountants—tells of how it made itself independent of the *Kehile* and proudly associated itself to the local Christian guild, even though its members enjoyed no benefits and yet had to pay their dues.[19] Mystically inclined associations, *chavures*, came together, paralleling the Sufi brotherhoods across the border in Turkey, engaging like them in meditation, prayer, and physical acts of worship like dancing and acrobatics that drew derision from the orthodox but endeared them to the common people.

Popular preachers sprang up, drawn from the same social stratum as their simple audiences: wandering holy men, living saints. They taught, not Torah and Talmud, nor the mind-bendingly difficult Kabbalah of Speculation,[20] the province of the intellectual élite, but instead applied the Practical Kabbalah,[21] which emphasised magic and the occult as a way of controlling the world. Gershom Sholem described it as "an agglomeration of all the magical practices that developed in Judaism from the Talmudic period down through the Middle Ages."[22] Travelling around the countryside, sometimes claiming to have been magically transported, writing out charms and crafting talismans, dispensing magic potions, exorcising demons and evil spirits, treating sickness and madness with remedies that included the appropriate application of the Divine Name, such a practitioner came to be called a *Ba'al Shem*, Master of the Name, or *Ba'al Shem Tov*, Master of the Good (i.e. Divine) Name.

Most of these poor-people's Kabbalists have been forgotten. Only one really stands out, and not from his own time, but from the era of his followers, who collected and published tales about him, once he had been retrospectively recognised as the first leader of a religious revolution that was permanently changing eastern Europe's Jewish way of life, turning half of the Yiddish civilisation on to a new course. His name was Israel ben Eliezer and he was more than just *a Ba'al Shem Tov*. He became known as *the Ba'al Shem Tov*, abbreviated in the usual Hebrew way to the acronym *B-Sh-T* or *Besht*.

It is almost impossible to separate fact from fancy in our only near-contemporary source on Israel ben Eliezer, *Praises of the Besht*,[23] a collection of tales and legends about his life, works and miracles collected by his one-time secretary's son-in-law and owing much in their style to hagiographies of Russian Orthodox saints. The book was published fifty-five years after its subject's death and within a short time, according to an early nineteenth-century account,[24] had sold more than ten thousand copies. Even the date and place of his birth are uncertain: around the year 1700, in a small Podolian town traditionally named as Okop, yet of which there is no record on any map. All that we can be reasonably sure of is that his later followers chose to think of him as a man of simple origins, uneducated in Talmud, in his youth eking out a living as a helper in a children's religious school and as a synagogue watchman, and after marriage engaging first in lowly occupations like clay digging and, later, tavern keeping. Some time in his mid-thirties he received the call as a seer, healer and teacher. Thereafter he travelled widely throughout his region, providing the usual services of a *Ba'al Shem*: preaching, writing amulets, exorcising ghosts, and gaining much fame, to judge by contemporary references to him as "the famous *Ba'al Shem Tov*, may his light long shine."[25]

He must have possessed an extraordinarily charismatic personality, for by the end of his life he had succeeded in drawing together under his direction the many disparate anti-rabbinical groups and preachers into a single pietist movement, Chassidism, that Dr. Avraham Rubinstein of Bar-Ilan University has called "the first religious trend in Judaism since the days of the Second Temple which had a self-defined way of life and recognisable rite of worship, but yet was acknowledged (albeit somewhat grudgingly by those who differed from it) as a legitimate Jewish phenomenon."[26] Israel ben Eliezer's new Chassidism would shape the style of life of the Yiddish speakers of south-eastern Europe for the rest of their existence.

Precisely what the *Besht* taught is as hard to know as the details of his life. He wrote no books himself, and objected to anyone else writing down his sermons and homilies. Legends tell of acolytes who broke the rules and transcribed his words, but when they came later to look at what they had written found nothing but blank paper. Only after he died did several of his disciples publish collections of what they claimed to have heard from his lips. One, Jacob Joseph, expressed his ambivalence when he wrote, "These are statements that I heard from my master. I only made fragmentary notes because I feared both writing everything down but also forgetting it."[27]

What has been passed down to us from the *Besht* betrays little that is systematic and consistent, and hardly anything that is particularly new. Much of his teaching reflects the wave of pietism that was also washing over the Protestant Christian world in this very period, particularly the *Besht*'s contemporaries the brothers John and Charles Wesley, founders of Methodism. There is a strong emphasis on personal spiritual development: "Before one prays for general redemption," ben Eliezer is reported to have insisted, "one must pray for the personal salvation of one's own soul." He took from Kabbalah the concept of "cleaving to God," *devekut*, which he applied not just to times of prayer but to a person's entire life, his business and social contacts included, for "when man is occupied with material needs and his thought cleaves to God, he will be blessed." He stressed the importance of worshipping God with joy and disapproved of mortifying the flesh, warning one of his disciples against the danger of indulging in "too much fasting, which contributes to melancholy and sadness."

Reading between the lines, it is possible to detect the Sabbataian and Frankist background of the times. The *Besht* followed the Kabbalistic teaching that everything in the world contains "holy sparks," fragments of the Divine, that can be liberated by devotion to God. Jacob Frank too had concerned himself in his own unique way with liberating sparks: "A Jew once saw me eating pork. 'What are you doing?' he cried. I answered, 'Here, too, are Holy Sparks, yearning to return from whence they came. If I do not lift them up, will you?'" Israel ben Eliezer would never have eaten forbidden foods but has usually been pictured smoking, a pipe in his mouth. The *Encyclopaedia Judaica* explains that the Chassidim used tobacco to redeem "holy sparks." Smoking a pipe, it suggests, apparently not in jest, served to release subtle sparks not otherwise accessible.

There are even hints that Israel ben Eliezer may have thought of himself, like other preachers of his disturbed century, as a kind of Messiah ben Joseph, the precursor who prepares the way for the final Messiah ben Dovid. He was certainly familiar with, and persuaded by, the mystical writings of the Sabbataian prophet Heshel Zoref, for he instructed one of his disciples[28] to copy them out and distribute them. In a letter to his brother-in-law he describes how he ascended to heaven on the occasion of the Jewish New Year—an event strikingly reminiscent of the *Mi'raj*, the ascent and visit to heaven of the Prophet Muhammad, to which Sufis attach great significance.[29] While up there, "I asked the Messiah, 'When will you come, O Master,' and he answered me, 'When your learning will be made known and revealed to the world and its source will spread.' . . . I was astonished and deeply grieved by this, and wondered when it would come to pass."

Indeed, a hidden undercurrent of messianism, a residue of the Frankist times through which Israel ben Eliezer lived, handed down through the pietist groups that followed his example, occasionally surfaces to this day. The *Besht*'s grandson, the *Tsaddik* Nachman of Bratslav, was for a time convinced that he had been chosen as the Messiah. In 1994 shortly before the late Rebbe of the Lubavitch Chassidim, Menachem Mendl Shneerson, the seventh and last leader of the movement, died in New York at the age of ninety-two, some of his followers announced that he was the Messiah ben Joseph, and that after death he would be resurrected and reappear as the Messiah ben Dovid.

It took some three generations of leaders to turn the Chassidic movement into the way of life of the majority of eastern European Jewry. After Israel ben Eliezer died in 1760 there was a brief power struggle until the baton of leadership fell to Dov Baer, known as the Great *Moggid* (Preacher) of the town of Mezhirech, while the other senior contender, the *Besht*'s disciple Jacob Joseph of Polonnoye, rather embittered by his failure to win the top prize, had to content himself with becoming Chassidism's first theorist. While the Great *Moggid* sent out missionaries among the Jews of the south-east, attracting many rabbis and scholars to the movement, Jacob Joseph's work recorded "words which I heard from my teacher,"[30] and made the first attempt to systematise the teachings of Chassidism— though he also attacked the traditional leaders of the Jews and their values with such bitter criticism as could not help but sharpen the antagonism of the rabbinical hierarchy and store up trouble for the future.

Yet the traditional power of the rabbis was not fully challenged until, in the third generation, the leadership was divided between Dov Baer's students. Among them were names revered by Chassidim to this day, like Elimelech of Leżajsk, his brother Zusya of Hanipol, Menahem Mendel of Vitebsk, Nahum of Chernobyl, Shneur Zalman of Lyady, Israel of Kozienice, Levi Isaac of Berdichev, and yet others.

Inevitably, as the number of pietist centres grew, each with its own *Tsaddik*, tensions built between them, occasionally flaring up into open and bitter conflicts, as when Jacob Isaac, the Seer of Lublin,[31] broke away from his teacher Rebbe Elimelech of Leżajsk to start his own court. Nonetheless, by the beginning of the nineteenth century or shortly thereafter, Chassidism had trounced the rabbinical class. In small towns and cities from central Poland to the extreme south-east, holy *Tsaddikim* resided in their courts like monarchs surrounded by their entourages, among them the Czortkow Rebbe, the Belzer Rebbe, the Tomashover Rebbe, the Radzyner Rebbe, the Gurer Rebbe, the Slonimer Rebbe, the Lubavitcher Rebbe, the Satmarer Rebbe and many more.

The tight brotherhoods of devotees, each clustered around its own teacher and Living Saint, worshipped, ate and lived together in an atmosphere of intense other-worldliness, believing, like Menachem Mendel of the Schneerson dynasty in Lubavitch, that:

> there is no reality in created things. That is to say that in reality creation does not belong to the category of "things" as we see them with our eyes. That is only from our [human] perspective since we cannot perceive the Divine force . . . From which it follows that there is no existence whatsoever apart from His existence, blessed be He.

Such pantheistic beliefs, like the organisation of the Chassidic communities around their *Tsaddikim*, may have owed more than a little to the Sufi brotherhoods gathered around their sheikhs flourishing next door in the Ottoman realm. Yet, if so, the Jews quite outdid their mentors. Sufism was only for the few. Chassidism successfully reversed the failure of Sabbataian messianism, exploiting the Yiddish people's deep dissatisfaction to create, not merely a mass movement, but a complete social structure and way of life for most Ukrainian, Galician and Polish Jews. A way of life, it should be added, that was largely maintained in those lands until the Nazi slaughter. As the Yiddish author I. L. Peretz explained in a conference speech in 1908:

> The poor Jewish masses, the poor ignorant Jews begin to liberate themselves. They lose confidence in both the Jewish Talmudic scholar, and in the rich man. The rich man's "charity" does not fill his stomach; the Talmudic scholar's Toyre [Torah] doesn't give him any joy. The masses long, feel, want to live their own poor lives in their own way. And Chassidism emerges. Toyre for everybody.[32]

The withdrawal of such a high proportion of Yiddish speakers into otherworldly spirituality had serious consequences for the Yiddish civilisation. In the very period during which other European nationalities were embracing the modern age with all its disorientating promise, its flawed

beneficence, more than half of the Yiddish-speaking people were turning
their backs on the world and retreating into what their critics denounced
as a delusional, if comfortable, fantasy. As one mid-nineteenth-century
satirist caricatured the Chassidic response to modernity:

> Come here, you philosopher, with your brain the size of a cat's.
> Come to the Rebbe's table and learn a bit of sense.
> You've invented a steamship and think you're so superior;
> The Rebbe has only to spread out his handkerchief to cross the sea.
> You've designed a railway and think you're so smart
> The Rebbe sneers, the Rebbe laughs. To him it's totally useless.
> Do you know what the Rebbe does when he sits alone in private?
> Within a minute he has flown up to heaven
> To celebrate the third Sabbath meal.[33]

During a devastating cholera epidemic in 1831, Rebbe Hersh of Zydaczow guaranteed his followers immunity from disease if they would "recite
all the Psalms every week, give to charity after completing each of the five
books of the Psalms . . . and make sure that all the *mezuzahs* [parchment
scrolls fixed to the doorposts of Jewish homes] are kosher."[34]

At the same time, however, Chassidim promoted an attitude to
women that was far more in keeping with modernity than was acceptable
to the traditional rabbis. Odel, the daughter of the *Besht*, known as "the
most righteous" because of "the supreme qualities of her soul," had her
own following, which included men. The *Tsaddika* Frieda wrote commentaries on Torah and Chassidism. Other women were famous for their para-
bles and aphorisms. Such female prominence had been unknown in
Judaism since the daughter of Rashi, the eleventh-century sage from
Troyes in France, wrote responsa on behalf of her father in his old age.

The historian Shimon Dubnow, writing long before the current new-
age fashion for Kabbalistic and pietist revival, summed up the influence of
the movement ambivalently: "Under the influence of the Chassidim, the
Russo-Polish Jew became brighter at heart but darker in intellect."[35]

OPPOSE THEM STRONGLY

Modern Vilnius, the city that the Poles once called Wilno and the Jews
Yerusholayim de Litoh (the Jerusalem of Lithuania). Walking the streets,
it is hard to believe that Vilnius was until recently a Communist city.

"Is there anything you can see," I ask my Russian companion, as we stroll near the city centre, "which tells you that just over ten years ago, this was part of the Soviet Union?" She looks around at the well-dressed, fashionable passers-by, the new western-style shop signs, the refurbished buildings, the late-model European motor cars—not a Gaz, Moskvitch or Trabant in sight. The elegant eighteenth- and nineteenth-century buildings housing modern shops and offices appear so smugly and naturally capitalist that one can't easily imagine them any other way. Then she glances at the ground and her eyes light up. "There," she says, delighted at her discovery, and points to an iron access cover set into the pavement on which the raised lettering still gives away the former name of the state—the Lithuanian Soviet Socialist Republic.

It is just as hard to find vestiges of Jewish Vilnius—almost impossible to believe that the Jewish presence here was once so strong that the 1897 census listed just over forty-one per cent, or almost half, of the citizens, as Jews. High up on a whitewashed wall above a waist-level bricked-up archway that betrays a two-metre rise in street level since the building was first constructed, opposite a former Dominican monastery that occupies one whole side of the street, now partly an extension of the American embassy, I find the remains of a former Yiddish shopfront sign. All that is left are three Hebrew characters—ע ayin (E), מ mem (M) and ט tes (T)—as well as part of another, now indecipherable. It is impossible to guess what word these letters once spelled. Otherwise there remain no more than a few street names: Jewish Street, as if there had been only the one, and—significantly—Gaon Street.

I ask my hotelier: why Gaon Street?

"It was named after a great Jewish scientist who lived in a house along there."

Which is no more inaccurate than the paean of praise sung by the Lithuanian state to this unlikely new national hero on marking the bicentenary of his death in 1797, when the Vilna Gaon was lauded for "his intellectual openness; his humanistic values; his tolerance, which was even harnessed to buttress a plan for advancing Jewish-Christian relations; and his almost Erasmus-like humanism, which led him to perform scientific research in parallel with his religious studies."[36]

The best that can be said is that these are not qualities very often associated with Elijah ben Solomon Zalman (1720–97), known variously as the "Gaon Eliyahu," the "Vilna Gaon" or "Ha-Gra,"[37] where "Gaon" is a word drawn from the biblical Book of Psalms that can be translated as Pride,

Excellency or Genius. This ascetic founder of modern Jewish orthodoxy, indeed the Godfather of all modern mainstream Judaism, was the sage who stiffened the resistance of the rabbis against the Chassidim, and who did more than anyone to redefine on national lines the eternal Yiddish divide between eastern and western, Slavic and Germanic, heart-ruled and intellect-driven. Even after the Holocaust, descendants of Europe's Yiddish speakers, living far from the *heym*, would still class themselves either as "Litvaks," Lithuanians, who respected the legacy of the Gaon, or "Polaks," Poles, who favoured the revelations of the Chassidic *Tsaddikim*.

Where previously the two inspirations had amalgamated themselves in an extraordinarily rich, more-or-less unitary, single Yiddish civilisation, the enormous upheavals of the seventeenth and early eighteenth centuries had, by Elijah ben Solomon's day, served to separate out the Yiddish civilisation's constituent parts, like colours in a chromatograph, into a spectrum running from the very Germanised west and north to the even more Slavicised east and south. If one were forced to draw a notional boundary between them, it would hover somewhere over the Pripet Marshes, where today a border runs between Belarus and the Ukraine. North of this imaginary line, where the *heym* bordered on Prussia and Saxony, was the area where Germanic values were most familiar and most favoured. The Vilna Gaon was their most powerful representative.

Alas for the Yiddish future, however, Chassidism's greatest adversary was no more forward-looking than his opponents, and fought the *Tsaddikim* in a spirit of deepest conservatism. When not yet thirteen years old, he had himself begun to construct a Golem, a man-made homunculus to be vitalised by application of the Divine name, and had only given up, not because of the implausibility of the task, but when "an image appeared above me, and I ceased from making it, for I said, doubtless God is preventing me."[38]

True, like David Gans of Prague before him, he regarded the Talmudic scholars' lack of secular education as an insult to Israel's reputation among the nations who, he once wrote, "like the roaring of many waters, will raise their voice against us, asking: where is your wisdom?" But since he read only Hebrew and Yiddish, his secular knowledge was derived almost exclusively from medieval or even earlier Jewish sources, and his writings on mathematics, geography, astronomy, music and medicine, though prolific, would have been thought old-fashioned two hundred years earlier. His devotion to Kabbalah and his belief in the efficacy of magic spells, charms and amulets bearing the Divine name, led him to oppose "accursed" philosophy, for the study of which he berated even the great Maimonides.

Self-taught, married at eighteen, Elijah ben Solomon travelled throughout Germany and Poland before settling down in Vilna in 1748 to a life of extraordinarily ascetic scholarship, teaching a small circle of students, financially supported first by the legacy of a notable ancestor,[39] and then as the fame of his learning spread, by an allowance and rent-free lodgings provided by the community—even though he held no communal office. It was said that to avoid distraction, he would study behind closed curtains by the light of candles even during daytime, with his feet in a bucket of ice-cold water to keep him awake. Elijah's sons reported that he slept no more than two hours a night, and for only half an hour at a time. Modest almost to a fault, when drawn at the age of thirty-five into a bitter controversy between two great and famous rabbis of his day[40] on a matter that was dividing the German from the Polish communities, he responded, "Who am I, a man from a distant land, a man young in years, of retiring disposition, that they should listen to me?"

It was the appearance of the Chassidim on the scene, particularly when they had the effrontery to begin making converts in Vilna itself, a city whose Jews prided themselves in resisting all religious innovation, that drew him out of his shell and propelled him into the public arena. The rabbis of the *Kehile*, the community organisation, aghast at the pietists infiltrating their town, approached the Gaon and asked what they should do. "Oppose them strongly," was his reply, whereafter those who joined him in his anti-Chassidic stand came to be known as Opposers, *Mitnaggedim*.

The opposition was fierce and at times brutal, beginning in 1772, when the Vilna *Kehile* closed down the local Chassidic prayer rooms, arrested the Chassidic leaders, publicly burned their books and pronounced their followers excommunicated. A letter was sent out, over the Gaon's name, to other communities exhorting them to campaign against the "godless sect." When the first works of Chassidic literature began to appear, particularly the so-called *Testament of the Ba'al Shem Tov*,[41] Elijah ben Solomon chaired a rabbinical council of war, which issued circulars ordering the communities to expel all the pietists, to burn their works, to regard them as being "of another faith" and therefore not to intermarry with them, not to eat their food, nor to bury their dead: "It is the duty of every believing Jew to repudiate and pursue them with all manner of afflictions and subdue them, because they have sin in their hearts and are like a sore on the body of Israel."

Alarmed by such a level of antagonism, two of the most influential and saintly Chassidic leaders, Menachem Mendel of Vitebsk and Shneur Zalman of Lyady, asked to meet the Gaon. Their approach was rudely rebuffed. "He slammed the door upon us twice," wrote Menachem. However, the Gaon was evidently not prepared to countenance actual physical violence. Verses by the German romantic poet Adalbert von Chamisso, a good friend of the Yiddish Jews, record a dangerous fracas outside the Vilna synagogue when an orthodox crowd attacked an itinerant preacher, Abba the *Glusker Moggid*, grabbed the manuscripts of the thirteen books he was taking to be published, ripped them up, burned the shreds in the synagogue courtyard and then set about beating the preacher himself severely. He was saved from the holy mob by the appearance on the scene, in the nick of time, of the Gaon himself.[42] (The *Glusker Moggid* may, on the other hand, have been quite used to such treatment. A nineteenth-century anthology[43] quotes a parody which was said to have been improvised by him after being thrown down a flight of stairs by another enraged orthodox rabbi,[44] in Altona.)

The Gaon soon recognised that attacking the Chassidim was no answer to what he saw as a serious threat to the continuity of Yiddish Judaism. A positive effort had to be made to offer an alternative, to make the orthodox rabbinical faith as attractive to the masses as the pietistic effusions that he condemned as ignorance, pantheism and idolatry. His own intellectual stature being so high, he was personally uninclined, indeed unable, to stoop low enough to catch the ear of the small people, the uneducated, the ignorant. Instead, he encouraged his foremost disciple, Chayyim of Volozhin, to open a seminary, a yeshivah, whose students would be instructed according to the principles that he had established and would take his vision out into the Yiddish world.

As a self-taught scholar, he had rejected, or rather never acquired the taste for, *pilpul*, the elaborate casuistry of traditional rabbinical study, the piling of prosopopoeia[45] on top of metalepsis[46] on top of anthimeria[47] as practised in the Polish seminaries. "It is man's nature to desire these things," he wrote caustically, "just as he prefers games and silliness. It would be better that he should engage in a trade that requires skill, like carpentry, than study in this manner and claim that his purpose is to analyse scripture."[48] His approach to the canonical texts was sober and scientific. Words were to be understood, not for their arcane symbolism nor for the mystical numerical values represented by the letters that spelled them out, but for their meanings, as elucidated by the best philological methods then known.

The yeshivah never opened during the Gaon's own long lifetime. But after his death in 1797 the stew of resentment between Chassidim and *Mitnaggedim* boiled over. Never unbiased, the historian Heinrich Graetz claimed that "the Chassidim took vengeance upon him by dancing upon his grave, and celebrating the day of his decease as a holiday, with shouting and drunkenness." The former Rabbi of Pinsk,[49] who had a personal axe to grind after a group of pietists had engineered his dismissal, denounced the Chassidic leaders to the Russian authorities as dangerous agitators, teachers of heresy and as guilty of personal acts of treason against the state. Twenty-two *Tsaddikim*, including Shneur Zalman of Lyady, representing many thousands of individual pietists, were arrested and locked up in the St. Petersburg fortress. Released after the intervention of the czar, Zalman was again accused and imprisoned three years later, only regaining his liberty when the czar died in 1801 and an amnesty was declared.

This was no longer a mere squabble between different sections of the élite, but a real battle that threatened to tear whole towns and villages apart, pitching parent against child, sibling against sibling, congregant against congregant, across the entire Yiddish world. As the belligerents ratcheted up their aggressive rhetoric, as the two sides increasingly sought the support of the Russian authorities, as the attacks on each other increased in savagery, both parties, Chassidim and *Mitnaggedim*, were risking disaster. Strife so destructive to the Yiddish communities could not be allowed to continue. Chayyim the Gaon's disciple remembered his master's voice, recalled Elijah ben Solomon's insistence that positive must be set in place of negative, and finally in 1803 got down to the task of founding the popular public yeshivah that his teacher had always yearned for. He chose his own birthplace Volozhin, deep in the forest country between Vilna and Minsk, for the institution in which the Gaon's prescription for proper Jewish education would be applied with rigour—and love. The result for the Yiddish people was the best that Rabbi Chayyim, or even the Gaon himself, could have hoped for.

It is strange to walk around Volozhin today, a small typically shabby Belarusian town of twenty thousand or so inhabitants, to turn a corner and confront a nondescript crumbling structure, two storeys under a pitched roof, the red of its bricks bleeding through the stained and flaking rendering, with a broken 1950s-style sign on the side that reads *kulinaria* (delicatessen in Russian). And then to realise that this is it: the building that housed the most powerful institution of Lithuanian Jewry, the centre of an intellectual empire that not only controlled the lives of the Yiddish people of Lithuania, but whose writ runs to this day in orthodox synagogues across the entire world, from Sydney to San Francisco. This was Chayyim of Volozhin's yeshivah, soon dubbed *Eyts Chayyim*, The Tree of Life.[50]

A network of similar seminaries all over the region soon sprang from the Volozhin yeshivah and helped to hold the line successfully against the encroachment of Chassidism into the Gaon's domain. These were the institutions that shaped Jewish Lithuania until the Holocaust. To quote Professor Haim Hillel Ben-Sasson:

> The young men who came to the yeshivah from village, town or city, rich or poor, met at the yeshivah on equal terms and imbibed yeshivah manners, ideals and modes of thought, which they transmitted wherever they later settled. Rabbi, preacher, merchant, or shopkeeper, the yeshivah graduate remained at heart a proud and orthodox intellectual, influencing by word and deed the lower strata and imbuing them with yeshivah values. These values became all-pervading.[51]

The poet Chayyim Nachman Bialik, who studied there briefly towards the end of the nineteenth century, wrote that the yeshivah at Volozhin, and the others that grew from it, were "the moulders of the soul of the people."

The *Eyts Chayyiim* itself, however, did not survive. In 1892, as part of the attempt to force Russia's Jews to assimilate, the Minister of Education, Count Delianov, proposed a series of changes to the yeshivah's constitution: that the study day be limited to no more than twelve hours; that a minimum of three hours a day should be devoted to teaching Russian language and literature and other secular subjects; that the teachers must be approved by the government; and that the chief rabbi should be responsible for the conduct of the pupils. The yeshivah's governing body refused to countenance any of these conditions. The *Eyts Chayyim* was ordered to close.

The Yiddish civilisation in Poland, Lithuania, Galicia, Russia, Hungary and the Ukraine was thus divided between two schools of thought, between the emotionalism of the Chassidim and the intellectuality of its opposers. Yet both were essentially backward-looking, both refusing to recognise, let alone accept, the profound changes that Europe was experiencing as it entered modern times. Ultra-conservative, opposing all innovation, rejecting any form of learning that did not derive from Torah, Talmud or Kabbalah, neither the yeshivah alumni nor the devotees of the *Tsaddikim* were equipped to lead the Yiddish civilisation on into the future. That task was to be attempted further west, in Austria and Germany, where the values of rational and scientific modernism were penetrating Yiddish society and precipitating something entirely new, a Jewish Enlightenment, in Hebrew *Haskalah*, in Yiddish *Haskoleh*, represented by a man acknowledged by all, gentiles as well as Jews, to be one of the greatest minds of the eighteenth century.

13

. . . and Fall

He was born in 1729, the son of a poor Torah scribe, supposedly a descendant of Moses Isserles, the Rema of Cracow. He was hunchbacked and sickly. He stammered. He was never recognised with an official public position. Yet Moses ben Menachem Mendel (1729–86), known to Jews as Moses of Dessau and to Christians as Moses Mendelssohn, against all odds and in spite of his own better judgement, would be the one Jew who best demonstrated what the Yiddish civilisation could offer to European culture. Drawing inspiration from his own people's beliefs, he made himself a central figure in European philosophy, an essential link in the chain between classical and modern thought, between the philosophers Leibniz and Kant. Deeply religious yet at the same time a keen observer of science and industry, he welcomed the new while recognising its risks. "The discovery by Montgolfier [of hot-air balloon fame] will probably lead to great revolutions," he wrote. "Whether they will be for the good of human society nobody will as yet dare to decide. But who will on this account hesitate to promote progress?" An able pianist, he took lessons from a student of Bach[1] and helped keep the German master's musical legacy alive, passing it on to Mozart and to his grandson the composer Felix Mendelssohn-Bartholdy. He appeared in disguise as the protagonist of the German dramatist Lessing's verse play *Nathan the Wise*, and even more highly camouflaged as the Pasha Selim in Mozart's *Singspiel* or musical, *Die Ent-führung aus dem Serail* (*The Abduction from the Seraglio*). He was an international celebrity, lauded by Jews as the Third Moses (after the biblical Prophet and Maimonides) and by the world as the German Socrates or the German Plato—note: German not Jewish. He represented to the eighteenth century what Marx, Freud and Einstein, from a later lineage of the Yiddish civilisation, would be for the twentieth. Unlike them, however, he was privately religiously observant, publicly and passionately Jewish, campaigning for the value of the Jewish religion to be recognised and accepted, and offering generous encouragement, support and active assistance, like a *shtadlan* of old, to every oppressed Yiddish community that sought his help.

Moses ben Menachem Mendel received the usual Jewish education, learning Torah and Talmud first with his father and then from the rabbi of Dessau, whom he followed to Berlin when his teacher was appointed chief rabbi to the cosmopolitan Prussian capital. On arrival at the age of fourteen he could neither speak, read nor write a word of German. But he was a quick student. Apart from acquiring a German written style which would later earn praise as among the clearest and most elegant of his generation, he also learned mathematics from a Polish rabbi, French and English from a young Jewish medical student, while with a Jewish physician from Prague he studied enough Latin to make it worth his while to scrape together sufficient pennies to buy and painstakingly work his way through a Latin translation of the English philosopher John Locke's *Essay Concerning Human Understanding*. This was the first step on his lifelong philosophical journey. At twenty-one he was engaged as a teacher in the household of a wealthy silk manufacturer, rose to the position of bookkeeper and finally became a full partner in the enterprise, working in the silk business all his life, and only studying, writing and philosophising in his spare time. Married at thirty-three, he fathered six children, founding a family that would play an important part in the shaping of modern European culture.[2]

It reveals something of his driven character that he spent his honeymoon working on an essay, pitching for a prize offered by the Berlin Academy of Sciences, on "Whether metaphysical truths . . . are susceptible of the same evidence as mathematical truths." What his new wife thought of this is unrecorded, but she could only have been pleased when her bridegroom's effort beat Immanuel Kant's to first place, and won the generous purse of fifty ducats. As a further bonus, he was awarded the status of

"Protected Jew" by the king, Frederick the Great, and exempted from paying all Jewish taxes by his own community—though when the Academy elected him as a member the king refused to ratify the decision. (The Academy president regretted that Mendelssohn possessed all the qualifications for membership except a foreskin.)

Mendelssohn easily brushed off the insult and got his own back in his own way. Never one to be intimidated by authority, and in love, as he was, with the German language and its culture, he found the current fashion for all things French unacceptable, complaining that the French were "too fickle to read through a systematic treatise with due effort," and had the extraordinary temerity to publish a critique of Frederick the Great himself, for having written some verses in French rather than in his own language. Legend has it that this hunchbacked Jew, who had only learned German as a teenager, when summoned to appear before the king at Sans Souci Palace to defend himself, explained that "whoever makes verses plays at ninepins; and whoever plays at ninepins, be he king or peasant, must have the setter-up tell him how he bowls."

Moses now set himself a higher task. He wanted to read the Greek philosophers—in the original Greek, of course—and asked his Christian acquaintance Nicolai, a book dealer, whether this would be possible. Nicolai later remembered how he advised his friend "not to spend too long on the grammar, but to do as I had done, take an easy author and read him with a dictionary in your hand." Nicolai recalled Mendelssohn's impatience: "Yes, yes, I did that myself with Latin and English. If only I could have someone in front of me, while I am reading, who would act as a living dictionary." Nicolai suggested a certain Rector Damm, and so for the next two years, a time which Nicolai thereafter always remembered with great nostalgia, "the learned and worthy old man" came to his lodgings twice a week, Wednesdays and Saturdays, where for several hours the three of them read Homer and other Greek authors together.[3]

The intense study bore its fruit after Mendelssohn had finally read Plato's works—in the original—and set himself to composing a book, *Phädon*, that would update the *Phaedo*, the Greek philosopher's justification of his belief in the immortality of the soul. The project began as a translation but soon, as the author wrote in his preface,

> I saw that I needed to leave Plato behind. His evidence for the immateriality of the soul seems, to us at least, so shallow and fanciful that it hardly deserves serious disproof. Whether that is

because of our better understanding of philosophy or our poor understanding of the philosophical language of the ancients, I cannot determine.

When published in 1767, *Phädon* immediately became a best-seller. More: it was the book of the age, running to fifteen reprints and translated into many other European languages. Everyone who was anyone, from Goethe to Mozart, had to have his or her own copy. The work of an observant Yiddish-born Jew had penetrated to the very heart of German culture and thought.

There had to be a reaction. And there was. Johann Kaspar Lavater was a passionate and highly eccentric Swiss cleric who later became internationally famous, or perhaps notorious, for his treatise[4] on how to read character, personality and disposition of the soul from a person's face. (He actually presents Mendelssohn's profile in his book as an example of "understanding and exquisite penetration . . . good sense; prompt, accurate perception of truth, delicacy; but, I suspect, less acuteness.") In 1769, egged on by various noble conspirators, he challenged Mendelssohn either to refute Christianity or to convert. This caused the Jewish philosopher much angst, since he had no more intention of abandoning the religion of his fathers than of starting an argument about it, having often stated that to criticise the beliefs of others was a mere exercise in self-gratification: "One who cares more about the welfare of men than about his own glory will hesitate over such matters." Moreover, he was well aware that to attack Christianity would be absurdly impolitic, given his situation as "a member of an oppressed people." Others, too, were outraged on his behalf. The celebrated Göttingen physicist and aphorist Georg Lichtenberg[5] protested that "nothing antagonises me more than to see a young, importunate, injudicious babbler like Lavater upset the peace of mind of a thinker like Mendelssohn in order to gain heaven. It is better to serve the world with one's hands and head, as Mendelssohn does, than to assault it with volumes of enthusiasm."

The dispute sapped Mendelssohn's health and he suffered what today might be described as a nervous breakdown, rendered unable to work for several months. On his return to an even keel, he was a changed man. The assault by Lavater seems to have disabused him of the illusion that his major contribution to European philosophy had made people forget his Jewishness. From now on he would turn his attention to the fate of his own people and to the betterment of their condition.

The Jews of Dresden were threatened with expulsion. He appealed successfully to one of his admirers, a prominent official of Saxony. New anti-Jewish decrees were threatened against the Jews of Switzerland. He turned for help to Lavater who, to grant him his due, gave the Jews his support. The Koenigsberg community had been commanded to have a government-appointed supervisor present in the synagogue during services, since several prayers, particularly the one that begins with the words "it is our duty to praise the Lord of all,"[6] were thought to be anti-Christian. He explained that the prayer had been composed long before Jesus's day and that the objectionable lines "For they bow to nonsense and emptiness / and pray to a god who cannot save," referred to ancient idolaters and not to modern Christians. In the light of his assurance, the order was rescinded. (The offending lines of this ancient poem have nonetheless been censored from most modern prayer books.)

Mendelssohn provided the Prussian government with an authoritative account of Jewish matrimonial law, which was at this time being transferred from the rabbinical to the civil courts, and helped rewrite, in German rather than Yiddish, the traditional *Jusiurandum More Judaico*, the Jewish Oath taken by those who would not swear on the New Testament when appearing in a court of law. He was active in the movement to grant civil rights to the Jews that culminated with the Austrian Edict of Tolerance of 1782, the *Toleranzpatent*, arguing successfully against the prejudice that because the Jews were waiting for the advent of their Messiah and a return to Zion, they could neither identify with their host country nor fight for it. He explained that messianic hopes were a spiritual rather than temporal aspiration and had no influence on the believers' civic conduct. He was, however, concerned that many of the *Toleranzpatent*'s provisions might weaken the Jews' commitment to their religion and lead to assimilation. Most significantly of all, he established a permanent place for himself in Judaic religious literature by writing—in response to further public challenges—an account of his faith, *Jerusalem, or On Religious Power and Judaism*, that proved to be the most significant analysis of the Jewish religion since Maimonides's *Guide to the Perplexed* six hundred years earlier. To be sure, there were critics: both those who found the ideas in the book too novel, as well as those who found them too traditional. Mendelssohn took the criticism lightly, describing himself as being "in the position of a husband whose wife accuses him of impotence while his maid charges him with having made her pregnant."

Moses Mendelssohn was not the only Jewish thinker to bring

Enlightenment values to the Yiddish-speaking people. But both the quality of his contribution and the esteem in which he was held by gentiles and Jews alike, raises him head and shoulders above his contemporaries. He was even awarded a Hebrew acronym, Rambeman,[7] a sure sign of admiration and respect.

Yet this towering genius, who could have helped to establish the Yiddish civilisation among the founders of the modern European world, was so subject to the prejudices and antagonisms between the German- and Slav-influenced halves of the Yiddish realm that he colluded in denigrating the major part of his own nation. Indeed, one could say that he unwittingly began the process by which the Yiddish civilisation would eventually be written out of history.

To him the very Yiddish language was a stumbling block to any kind of progress. "Pure language" was the basis of all culture, and German as well as Hebrew, his other great love, were infinitely superior to Yiddish, which was a mere jargon that "has contributed not a little to the immorality of the common man." Centuries of "ludicrous Talmudic disputation" had deprived his people of a proper appreciation of the original Hebrew poetry of the Bible, so, initially for the benefit of his children, he spent eight years translating the Torah into German (printed in Hebrew characters), together with a commentary. This was the first direct translation from the Hebrew into a European vernacular: "a better translation and explanation of the holy scriptures than they had before. This is the first step toward culture, from which, alas, my nation is kept at such a distance that one might almost despair at the possibility of an improvement." He promised himself "great results from the increasing use of the pure German idiom among my brethren."

The Germanising of the Jews would, he believed, speed their emancipation and make them full citizens. So long as the Jews still spoke Yiddish and so long as Slavic-Yiddish culture continued to hold sway over the eastern European Jewish masses, he had little hope for their betterment. He supported the founding of a Jewish Free School in Berlin, with a modern curriculum, but did not think that much would come of it. A "person of high rank," a Saxon nobleman and diplomat,[8] approached him in 1770 with a scheme to establish a Jewish state in the Holy Land but he dismissed the idea, believing pessimistically that after their long oppression the Jewish people had lost the capacity to be "moved by the spirit of freedom, or even of joining forces for the execution of such a great act." However, with astonishing prescience, he did foresee that an independent state for the

Children of Israel could only come about "through a generalised European war, otherwise it would certainly be held up by one of the powers."

He did not anticipate where promotion of the "pure" German language would lead. He believed that a German-speaking but self-consciously Jewish people was a possibility. No friend of assimilation, while looking down on Yiddish speakers as "culturally backward," he had no time for those who wished to style themselves Germans of Jewish faith and who wanted, as later assimilators did, to be "Jews inside their homes and human beings outside." He failed to recognise the power of language to change a nation's self-perception: that in adopting the German language, former Yiddish speakers would make themselves Germans first and Jews only second—if at all. How horrified would this pious scholar have been to know that most of his descendants, together with a large number of German Jews from all levels of society, would misuse his name and reputation to justify converting to Christianity.

How pained to have found that many others would invoke his memory to push aside the hard-to-keep laws of orthodoxy and substitute a Reformed Judaism more in keeping with respectable German bourgeois values. How devastated to have learned that his rationalist arguments for the truth of religion would be totally overturned by the development of knowledge and lead many others towards outright atheism. "If our souls were mortal, reason would be a dream," he had written in *Phädon*. "We would be like animals destined only to seek food and to perish." After Darwin, when people came to believe that human beings were indeed like animals, Mendelssohn's claim was stood on its head: if we are like animals then there is no more reason to believe in the immortality of the soul.

But then neither did Moses ben Menachem Mendel predict the final and total partition of Poland in 1795, nine years after his death, which swept the European Jewish masses into the unwelcoming arms of the absolutist states of the Habsburgs, the Hohenzollerns and the Romanovs. Nor the granting of civil rights to the Austrian and German Yiddish speakers, but only on condition that they abandon their language, their customs and their Jewish national identity, leaving what remained of the Yiddish civilisation to backward Habsburg Galicia and to the East, under Moscow's ruthless rule. Nor did he foresee the rise of Romantic Nationalism with its promotion of Blood and Soil ideology, the delusion of a mystic link between a people and their land (that would eventually lead to One State, One People, One Leader—*ein Reich, ein Volk, ein Führer*), leaving no room for Jews at all.

And yet perhaps Mendelssohn would have smiled to know that the *Haskalah*—the Jewish Enlightenment of which he was at the same time instigator, product and leading representative—would be welcomed among the unredeemed Yiddish speakers of the East, and that the Hebrew language he so loved would be reborn there, eventually to become once again the everyday language of the Children of Israel. And he would surely have laughed had he learned that those who followed him in their contempt for Yiddish speech and folk ways would themselves one day be responsible for the renaissance of that "impure jargon" and for raising it, albeit briefly, to a literary language of world class. So that one day, a generation of Jews speaking the national languages of Europe, educated far beyond anything Mendelssohn could have imagined, would conjure up for themselves a romantic nostalgia for that "culturally backward" way of life.

THE "JEWISH PROBLEM"

On swallowing up the Polish-Lithuanian territories, Moscow, the Third Rome, bastion of eastern Christianity, inherited a huge population of Jews, people who regarded themselves as a separate nation, with their own language, yet without a homeland, with their own autonomous administrations, yet without a central governing body.

This "Jewish Problem," that offended every one of Moscow's autocratic and absolutist ideals, could only be solved by forcibly assimilating and absorbing these inside-outsiders into the general population. Every effort of the czars over the following century, using both stick and carrot, was to be directed towards persuading the Yiddish speakers that they were really Russians, and just too intransigent and misguided to accept their true identity.

The first step was to forbid their entry from the Polish territories into Russia proper, where no Jewish life had been sanctioned for hundreds of years. There thus came into existence a Pale of Settlement, from now on the only part of the Russian Empire, except for the underpopulated extreme south-east of the Ukraine and the Black Sea coast, where Jews were allowed to live. The Yiddish-speaking world was henceforth to be a large open prison.

Next came an order in 1804, motivated by the unfounded prejudice that Jewish enterprise was pauperising the peasantry, ordering all Jews to move away from the countryside, from all villages and hamlets, and gather in the towns and cities.

Unexpectedly, the great population movement intended by the czar was delayed by the interruption of Napoleon's attack on Russia, which saw Jews lined up on both sides of the front. Bonaparte was a pro-Semite and appointed Jewish officers, like Colonels Józef Aronowicz and Berek Jose-lewicz, as well as Berek's son Joseph who led a Jewish light cavalry regiment against the Russian armies. The czar's forces were on their side supported with prayers and even money by such important Chassidic leaders as Levi Isaac of Berdichev. The *Tsaddik* Shneur Zalman of Lyady arranged for his followers to undertake spying missions on behalf of the Russian forces, fearing the corrupting power of liberty. He explained that "if Bonaparte wins, the wealthy among Israel would increase and the greatness of Israel would be raised, but they would leave and take the heart of Israel far from Father in Heaven,"[9] a sentiment close to that of his older Christian pietist contemporary John Wesley: "wherever riches have increased, the essence of religion has decreased in the same proportion."[10] Ungratefully ignoring this Jewish support, after Napoleon's retreat from Moscow in 1812 the czar insisted that the deportations from the country-side resume.

The urban Jewish population was already growing steadily and now migration from the countryside would add to the pressure, helping to swell city numbers so greatly that, as in Vilna, previous restrictions to designated Jewish quarters of the towns had to be lifted. In Łódź, for example, where Jews had contributed some five per cent to the townspeople in 1793, by 1897 their number had swelled to over thirty per cent. In Warsaw, where in 1781 a little more than one in every twenty-five of the citizens had been Jews, in 1882 there were more than one in three. Artur Eisenbach of the post–Second World War Jewish Historical Institute in Poland calculated that not long after the mid-century, fully ninety-one and a half per cent of Polish Jewry lived in the cities.

Such large numbers, all crammed into a few places, meant that inevitably many were without gainful employment and became a charge on their communities. Some found work in the growing industrial sector, but hawking and peddling were the only recourse for the many. Perhaps one in three lived entirely on charity. For the first time there emerged a true Jewish proletariat, that class which serves society only by producing offspring, the political consequences of which can hardly be overestimated, given the important role that would be played by formerly Yiddish-speaking urban Jews in the Socialist and Communist movements.

Moscow rule tried every device it could conceive of to force the Yiddish speakers into conformity with Russian norms. Jewish children were ordered to attend Russian-language schools, though these were stubbornly avoided and evaded by the mass of Jewry. In the hope of reducing Jewish numbers, early marriage was forbidden.

Even worse was to come under the vicious Czar Nicolas I, who arrived on the throne in 1825 and was said to have "frozen Russia for thirty years." It was not enough for his government to issue decrees forbidding Jews their traditional costume and banning sidelocks, for to him even the last vestiges of Jewish self-government, the Kahals, were an affront. In 1844 he issued an *ukaz* stating in its preamble that:

> By stubbornly avoiding fusion with the society amid which they live, they still support themselves, as formerly, by the labour of their neighbours, thus justify the incessant complaints of the population . . . His Majesty the Emperor, with respect to the social state of the Jews, . . . has therefore deemed it requisite to withdraw the Jews from their dependence on the several Kahals, and to place them under the ordinary public authorities.[11]

With these words, the *Kehile*, the institution that had over so many centuries given the Yiddish speakers control over their own lives, that had served them so long and so effectively for both good and ill, was in effect abolished, its authority strictly limited to religious affairs. It was the final end of Jewish autonomy in Europe. More: it represented the last act in the annulment of Yiddish national identity. For the next hundred years, until the establishment of the State of Israel in 1948, nowhere in the world would Jews, let alone Yiddish speakers, be recognised as a separate people. In that sense the czar's decree of 1844 brought the story of the Yiddish civilisation to a close.

But not the torments of Russia's Jews. The czar, whose response to a plea for Jewish emancipation was "such a thing is inconceivable, and as long as I live, such a thing shall not take place,"[12] now demanded that they be divided into the categories Useful and Useless, a classification terrifyingly prophetic of Nazi concentration camp "selections." The Useless were to be conscripted into the military for training in crafts and agriculture, then forced to work on the land. By the infamous Cantonist system, Jewish youths were pressed into the Russian armed forces for twenty-five years' service, an attempt at mass re-education and conversion to Christianity.

They were taken as far from their birthplace as possible. Those mobilised at Kiev were sent to Perm, over 1,000 miles away; those at Brest to Nizhniy-Novgorod, not much less a distance. During the disastrous Crimean War, thirty boys were taken for every 1,000 adult males. Large numbers did not survive.

The Russian socialist libertarian Alexander Herzen described meeting a group of Cantonists on the road:

> The officer who escorted them said, "They have collected a crowd of cursed little Jew boys of eight or nine years old. Whether they are taking them for the navy or what, I can't say. At first the orders were to drive them to Perm; then there was a change and we are driving them to Kazan. I took them over a hundred versts farther back." The officer who handed them over said, "It's dreadful, and that's all about it; a third were left on the way" (and the officer pointed to the earth). "Not half will reach their destination," he said.
>
> "Have there been epidemics, or what?" I asked, deeply moved.
>
> "No, not epidemics, but they just die off like flies. A Jew boy, you know, is such a frail, weakly creature, like a skinned cat; he is not used to tramping in the mud for ten hours a day and eating biscuit—then again, being among strangers, no father nor mother nor petting; well, they cough and cough until they cough themselves into their graves. And I ask you, what use is it to them? What can they do with little boys?"[13]

The death of Czar Nicolas in 1855 brought some respite to the sufferings of both Jews and Russians. The next czar, Alexander II, a reformer known as "The Liberator" for abolishing serfdom, cancelled the forced abduction of Jewish children and gave Useful Jews the right to live throughout Russia. He did not, however, abandon the aim of persuading Yiddish speakers to accept the Russian language and culture. In 1874, needing troops for his expansion into Central Asia, the czar introduced general conscription for the first time, making young men of all religions and classes liable to military service, though this time for a "mere" six or seven years. (The young Polish-speaking Joseph Conrad fled his native Ukraine at this time to avoid the draft.) Those with a Russian secondary education were treated more favourably,[14] so under threat of being called up to arms—a fearful prospect for a young Russian even today—ever larger numbers of Jewish parents now pushed their children to speak Russian and sought for them a Russian education, producing a large new class of Russified Useful Jews.

Alexander was as good as his word and encouraged them to participate ever more in the nation's industrial, intellectual and cultural life: in railways, mining and the textile industry, in law, medicine, journalism, literature, in painting, sculpture, music and the arts in general. Jews soon became prominent in the ranks of the professional classes and a widespread belief began to spread that at last Jewish emancipation was a real possibility—though only by abandoning their past, their language and their more than 800-year-old Yiddish heritage. The stage was now set for the entry of the *Haskoleh*, the Jewish Enlightenment, into the czar's dominions.

WORDS THAT FALL ON US LIKE LASHES

"The Jewish Enlightenment came to Poland," wrote Isaac Leib Peretz, one of the great stars of the Yiddish literary revival, "and outside of Warsaw, Zamość was the most natural place for it to take root."

Today's Zamość, inscribed in UNESCO's list of world heritage sites, looks an unlikely setting for a rebirth of Yiddish literature, for it appears irrefutably, if beautifully, gentile. Built as a model town in the 1580s for the local magnate Jan Zamojski by the Italian architect Bernardo Morando, and rightly nicknamed "The Polish Padua," its gracious, expansive Market Square surrounds a magnificent pink-and-white, Italian and Polish, Renaissance and Gothic town hall, supporting a fifty-two-metre clock tower, its double flight of stone steps first climbing to a kind of saluting platform, as if the multicoloured colonnaded Armenian merchants' houses standing at attention all around are on parade. The Jewish quarter and even the synagogue, with its red, green and gold interior decor, follow the same design style. One might even say that so did the original Jewish community, for this place of worship was built for Sephardic Jews invited in to settle by Zamojski—they were, as ever, considered high-class and would not bring down Zamość's Renaissance tone. They were, however, later joined by thousands of Yiddish speakers fleeing from the Cossack uprising—though many died of famine in 1648 during a protracted siege of the town. Peretz's surname, Pérez in Spanish, points to his origin in the Sephardic community.

Perhaps the airy and elegant environment in Zamość encourages enlightenment. No Chassidic *Tsaddik* was ever welcome here. According to Peretz, "if Zamość got word that a Rebbe was on his way, the police were asked to set a guard at every gate, and the community provided a Jew to stand by him on watch. When the wagon appeared, it was challenged: *'Kudie?'* Where to? *'Nazad!'* Go back to where you came from!"[15]

Rabbi Israel of Zamość, who taught Moses Mendelssohn mathematics, had come from here. As had Shloyme Ettinger, a local physician who wrote volumes of ballads, epigrams, poems and dramas (not one of which was published in his lifetime). Jacob Gelber adopted the name Eichenbaum to get a permit to reside here while he translated Euclid into Hebrew. Alexander Zederbaum left this town for Odessa, a city famous for its freethinking apostasy, where he founded *Ha-Melitz* (*The Advocate*), the first Hebrew weekly in Russia—and two years later its pioneering Yiddish supplement *Kol Mevasser* (*The Voice That Announces*). In Peretz's day the richest man in town was Abraham Luxemburg, whose large house fronted a walled garden in which his young daughter Rosa, a very clever girl but so unprepossessing to look at that she was "afraid to show herself on the street," sat and read all day. And not uplifting works of spiritual guidance either. At the age of forty-eight she would be murdered by army officers after being arrested as a revolutionary in Berlin, having founded the German Communist Party.

One can easily imagine the successful lawyer Jacob Peretz, some time in the 1870s, striding along U Perec, the street now named after him, in a short German-style jacket known locally as a Berliner (after Moses Mendelssohn) rather than the long coat worn by orthodox Jews. "In compliance with *Haskoleh* directives," Peretz wrote, "people began to shorten their coats to modern style." After busy working hours advising clients and pleading their cases he would retire to his home, eat his meal, then devote what was left of the day to his real task in life: pouring out a rich stream of Hebrew and Polish poems, songs protesting against anti-Semitism, and articles attacking with bitter ridicule Zamość's Jewish communal institutions.

As a *maskil*, a follower of *Haskoleh*, Peretz had little respect for the Yiddish language. He believed, like other *maskilim*, that Hebrew was the only proper language for Jewish literature, and that the local language of the state—in his case Polish—was the appropriate medium for all other forms of communication. But this demanded a different kind of education from that normally available to the Yiddish speakers of Poland. So in whatever time the law and literature left to him, he set up a school for poor children and night classes for working men, where he no doubt also prop-agated his egalitarian views, for the local Jewish community was soon complaining to the authorities about his "socialistic tendencies." After some years the school was shut down and in 1889 even his licence to prac-tise law was withdrawn. When he appealed, the minister merely shrugged: "So, there will be one less talented Jewish lawyer in Russia." Yet what was Zamość's litigants' loss was literature's gain. Peretz moved to Warsaw and worked on a statistical survey, for which he had to travel around many provincial villages and *shtetlach* (small Jewish towns), a journey which would provide much raw material for the rest of his writing life.

Now word reached him that someone in Kiev called Shalom was look-ing for contributions to a collection of Yiddish writings called The Popu-lar Jewish Library (*Di Yidishe Folks-Biblyotek*). Out of touch and out of sympathy with the Yiddish-speaking intellectual world, yet desperately needing both money and a readership—"here am I, observing the ways of our people and attempting to write for them stories . . . in the holy tongue, yet most of them do not even know this tongue. Their language is Yiddish. And what life is there for a writer . . . if he is of no use to his people?"[16]— he sent a letter under the mistaken impression that he was addressing a well-known author of the previous generation, Shalom Jacob Abramow-itsh, who hid his real identity behind the fictional character Mendele Moykher Sforim (Mendel the Book Pedlar), and is considered to be the founder of the modern Yiddish literary movement. In actual fact the wealthy young publisher was a different Shalom, Shalom Rabinovitz, who would become even more famous under his pseudonym Sholom Alei-chem.

These three, Abramowitsh (1836–1917), Peretz (1852–1915) and Sholom Aleichem (1859–1916), the leading personalities of the nineteenth-century revival of Yiddish literature, had much in common. All received a tradi-tional Jewish education, Torah and Talmud. All came under the spell of the Jewish Enlightenment and tasked themselves to promote its values among what they perceived as the ignorant, poverty-stricken Yiddish-speaking masses in superstitious thrall to yeshivah or *Tsaddik*'s court. But how to communicate with them? Too few could make sense of the pol-ished Hebrew prose and verse that the enlighteners yearned to make once again the common literary language of the Jews. Too few could read or even understand the Polish or Russian of their gentile neighbours.

The only recourse available to a Jewish writer in eastern Europe who wished to address the majority of his people was to use their everyday language: Yiddish. And herein lay a difficulty. Like other Enlightenment thinkers, these writers had little sense of history and were unaware of the riches of the Yiddish past. What little they did know of they utterly despised. As self-conscious artists, they wished to supplant what they thought of as vulgar folk writing with proper literature, replacing the *Bove Buch* with the novel, the Chassidic parable with the short story, the "nonsensical and degrading" medieval epic with educative satire.

Yet not only was the despised jargon held responsible for the very failings that the *maskilim* were trying to correct, but it was too limited a language to be able to express fully the manifold experiences of life that these writers longed to explore. When as a young man Peretz had begun to throw off the religious convictions of his orthodox religious upbringing, he had desperately wanted to discuss his feelings. Yet:

> to whom could I talk to about all this? To whom could I pour out my lament for the ruins in my mind and the corpses in my heart? To the people around me? I lacked the very language to speak to them. I couldn't express these things in Yiddish, because I had no words for these ideas in Yiddish. I couldn't even talk about them to myself when I tried.[17]

Throughout the centuries the literary standard had been set by the western Yiddish dialect that looked to High German for its models. Now that the western Yiddish world had been severed from the Slavic by the partition of Poland—with the exception of Galicia, which never accepted that it was no longer Polish—and the Jews of the western *heym* were following Moses Mendelssohn and abandoning their traditional tongue in favour of German, a new standard had to be created, based on eastern Yiddish. What is more, this dialect itself came in several different varieties, of which perhaps the most important were the northern Lithuanian, the central Polish and the south-eastern Ukrainian.

In order to communicate with the masses, a common eastern literary Yiddish had first to be created, one that would be understood wherever it was read. (It would later come to be called *Klal Sprach*, popular language.) Thus, before he could achieve anything with his work, a Yiddish writer must first forge the very tools of his trade, the words, idioms, images and figures of speech.

In "Monish," Peretz's first Yiddish poem to be published, by Sholom Aleichem's Popular Jewish Library, the poet bewails the hardship of the task. How much better his verse would ring, he wrote, if composed in the language of the country,

> Not in Yiddish, in "Jargon,"
> That has no proper sound or tone,
> It has no words for sex appeal,
> And for such things as lovers feel.
>
> Yiddish has but quips and flashes,
> Words that fall on us like lashes,
> Words that stab like poisoned spears,
> And laughter that is full of fears,
> And there is a touch of gall,
> Of bitterness about it all.
>   . . .
> In Yiddish I have never heard
> A single warm and glowing word.[18]

Adding to the writers' problems was anxiety about the reaction of their friends, colleagues and relatives. It is no accident that two out of the three great writers hid behind pseudonyms. Shalom Rabinovitz admitted that he chose the pen-name Sholom Aleichem so that his family would not know he was writing in the contemptible jargon. Shalom Yankev Broido changed his family name to Abramowitsh—perhaps to escape the Russian military draft—and happily published in Hebrew under that name. "How perplexed I was then," he wrote, "when I thought of writing in Yiddish, for I feared it would be the ruin of my reputation."[19] So when he sent off his first story to the new Yiddish periodical that was just budding off from the Hebrew journal *Ha-Melitz*, he chose for the character who narrates the tale the sobriquet Senderl Moykher Sforim (Little Sender the Book Pedlar), after a real tradesman fondly remembered from his childhood. But Sender is Yiddish for Alexander, and the publication's editor, Alexander Zederbaum, thought he was being mocked. Without asking he changed the byline to Mendele Moykher Sforim instead. And it was that name that achieved literary immortality for Shalom Abramowitsh.

The principal social aim of these "enlightened" writers was to encourage their Yiddish-speaking compatriots to give up their traditionalism, their adherence to a medieval way of life, and enter the modern world. Their principal weapons were ridicule and satire. One only has to leaf through *No Star Too Beautiful*,[20] Joachim Neugroschel's fine collection of Yiddish stories translated into English, to find on nearly every page attacks on Yiddish Jews, Yiddish customs or Yiddish manners. Mendele's story "The Little Man," for example, is an extended catalogue of the corruption and injustice apparently endemic in the Polish-Jewish environment. The tone is apparent from the very first line of the story, which tells us that the protagonist, Yitsik Avrom, the Little Man himself, was born in a town called Hypocritia. Even in a story about a railway journey, like "Shem and Japheth on a Train," the writer can't resist comparing Jews unfavourably with gentiles:

> We Jews bustle and jostle like crazy to scramble aboard, terrified that we may miss the departure—Heaven help us! Yet all the while we kowtow to the conductors, virtually praying to them: "Please take pity and let us travel!" The gentile passengers, in contrast, keep strolling nonchalantly to and fro on the platform, with their hands clasped in back of them, and it's only when the bell rings a third time that they leisurely climb in to the train. Why the difference?

In Aizik Méyer Dik's 1868 piece "The Town of Hérres', which deals with the panic that ensued after Moscow's *ukaz* that attempted to shrink the Jewish population by banning early marriage among Jews, we read how the Yiddish wives protested: "You see, each woman recalled that she had been divorced by the age of sixteen, or at least that her marriage had been on the rocks. And now her daughter wouldn't even be married by that age!"

Where characters evoke the writer's sympathy, they are often presented as victims of an absurd, pathological, culture. Peretz's short tale "Kabbalists," for example, first written in Hebrew in 1891 and later translated into Yiddish by the author, depicting a destitute Rebbe and his sole remaining acolyte, amounts to a moving meditation on the old joke about the rabbi who is so poor and short of food that if he didn't fast on Mondays and Thursdays he would starve to death. At the end of Peretz's tale the student expires. "After fasting just a few more days," sighed the Rebbe, "he would have died an easy death—with the kiss of God!"

Mendele, Peretz and Sholom Aleichem, the three great stars of the nineteenth-century rise of Yiddish fiction, were far from alone. A host of others joined in the assault, though their acid tone is no longer perceived by enthusiastic readers and their cutting condemnations are misread as fond nostalgia. Was the criticism warranted? Isaac Linetzki's account of his childhood, in the semi-autobiographical novel *The Polish Lad*, first published in instalments in 1867, suggests that conditions in many places were as bad as can possibly be imagined. Here, for example, is the way he introduces us to his Hebrew infants' school, his *cheder*.

> Filth was everywhere; near the entrance were a round cistern and a mouldy slop pail . . . Three infants, their skirts pinned up under their arms, crawled about in the mire. A long, narrow, rickety table was held by twine and baling wire; its plank top was gouged, charred, and covered with ink stains. More planks, rough-hewn and studded with knotholes, were set on sawhorses to serve as benches for pupils of various ages, who sat huddled together with their backs against the dripping walls. The single tattered prayer book that did service as the text for ten pupils was swollen by the damp to three times its original thickness . . . Through an open door in one corner there was a glimpse into an adjoining room, where the teacher's wife, her face clammy with sweat, and wearing a greasy cap, was shoving a poker into the oven. Near the oven, our tutor held the place of honour: having shed the gabardine, he wore only his *tallit katan*, the four-cornered undergarment, whose ritual fringes were yellow with age; the dirty threadbare *yarmulka* that covered his bald head looked more like a potholder or a mustard plaster than a skullcap. In one hand he clutched a cat-o'-nine-tails, while with the other he scratched his hairy chest, which the unbuttoned and grimy shirt had left exposed.[21]

Whatever the original aims of the new Yiddish writers, their new Yiddish readers quickly developed a genuine thirst for modern fiction written in their own everyday language and reflecting the reality of their everyday lives—even when that was presented in a less than flattering light. However cruel its attack, *The Polish Lad* was a fantastic publishing success, even among those it savaged. Mordkhe Spektor, a Chassidic youth who grew up to become a popular Yiddish writer himself, remembered in his memoirs that:

> Chassidim young and old read the book through. They roundly cursed the author, but read it they did. Linetzki's *Poylish Yingl*

[*Polish Lad*] was "looked into" even in the *Tsaddikim*'s very "courts," and—who knows—perhaps even by the *Tsaddik* himself. Here too the author was met with dire curses, called by the most humiliating names; still his book did not go out of circulation . . . Whoever got the book passed it on. Accompanied by curses it went from hand to hand, till in a few weeks it looked like grand-mother's tattered, disintegrating prayer book.[22]

SHAKESPEAREAN TRAGEDY

The creators of the Yiddish literary revival hoped to raise the common people's cultural standing so that Jews would be able stand shoulder-to-shoulder with Christians in a liberalised Russian Empire. The terrible times under Czar Nicolas I were, they believed, an aberration; the better days under Alexander II would from now on be the norm.

Only a few years later such hopes lay in ruin. On Sunday, 13 March 1881, Czar Alexander went to take the salute at a military parade. The famous anarchist Prince Peter Kropotkin described what happened to him on the way back:

A bomb was thrown under his iron-clad carriage to stop it. Several Circassians of the escort were wounded . . . Then, although the coachman of the Czar earnestly advised him not to get out, saying that he could still drive him in the slightly damaged carriage, he insisted upon alighting. He felt that his military dignity required him to see the wounded Circassians . . . and as he passed close by another young man . . . the latter threw a bomb between himself and Alexander II, so that both of them should be killed. They both lived but a few hours.

There Alexander II lay upon the snow, profusely bleeding, abandoned by every one of his followers. All had disappeared. It was cadets, returning from the parade, who lifted the suffering Czar from the snow and put him in a sledge, covering his shivering body with a cadet mantle and his bare head with a cadet cap. And it was one of the terrorists . . . with a bomb wrapped in paper under his arm, who, at the risk of being arrested on the spot and hanged, rushed with the cadets to the help of the wounded man . . .

Thus ended the tragedy of Alexander II's life. People could

not understand how it was possible that a Czar who had done so much for Russia should have met his death at the hands of revolutionists. To me . . . it seemed that the tragedy developed with the unavoidable fatality of one of Shakespeare's dramas.[23]

The tragedy was not the czar's alone.

As long as the sad and poverty-stricken descendants of the once powerful and influential Yiddish-speaking nation had kept their place in the Russian social hierarchy, i.e. outside it or at least near the bottom rung, their presence could be tolerated. But the Jews' penetration into the mainstream, their new prominence in Russian industry, culture and academic life was, it seems, not to be endured. The greater the Jews' success, the more did anti-Jewish resentment spread and fester among many of their gentile compatriots, particularly imperial bureaucrats, minor landowners and the lower middle class.

What is more, in the mood of general rebelliousness, disappointed hopes and frustrated ambitions that pervaded the Russian Empire during much of Alexander's reformist rule, and in the atmosphere of patriotic Polish agitation, with Jews supporting the 1863 national uprising against the czar under the slogan "for your and our freedom," many Yiddish speakers had been attracted to extremist politics. Now a Jewish woman, Gesia Gelfman, was found among those held responsible for the czar's assassination. (She was condemned to death, but being pregnant her sentence was commuted—she died of peritonitis soon after giving birth to a daughter.)

The naming of a single Jew was enough to break the dam holding back the enmity of so many of the Russians. A tidal wave of pogroms crashed across the Pale of Settlement. Perhaps the government saw anti-Jewish violence as a useful diversion, for where it did not actively promote the outrages, it did nothing to stop them. Jews were assaulted and killed, and their property destroyed, in cities and towns over all the provinces of the empire: Elizavetgrad, Kiev, Konotop, Nizhniy-Novgorod, Nyezhin, Pereyaslav, Odessa, Smyela and Warsaw in 1881, Balta in 1882, Ekaterinoslav and Rostov-on-Don in 1883, Nizhniy-Novgorod again in 1884.[24]

To bring the disturbances under control, the czar established a commission to investigate the cause. This body reported that the disorders had been the result of "Jewish exploitation" and, "now that the government has firmly suppressed the riots and lawlessness in order to protect the Jews, justice demands that it immediately impose severe regulations which will alter the unfair relations between the general inhabitants and the Jews and protect the former from the harmful activity of the latter."

The government responded by enacting the harshly repressive May Laws, restricting Jews' rights of residence yet further, severely limiting their ability to become shareholders, take out leases or sign contracts, and banning them outright from holding office in joint stock companies. The aim of these measures was succinctly put in a statement attributed to the then head of the Russian Orthodox Church:[25] "One-third of the Jews will die, one-third will flee the country, and the last third will be completely assimilated within the Russian people." Russians were making it clear that they were no longer prepared to allow any room at all for the nation with whom the Slavs had shared their land for more than a thousand years.

The threat to the Yiddish presence in the Russian Empire called for three possible responses. The first was to ignore it, to bury one's head in a prayer shawl, pray for the coming of the Messiah and continue to live by the old rules, in small country towns where all life revolved around the synagogue and to go to the theatre was tantamount to not believing in God. There were many who took this course.

The second was to accede to anti-Semitism and accept that Jews had no place in Slav society, either by emigrating to freer and more developed lands, or perhaps to join the growing Zionist movement and dream of the day when the Yiddish language would disappear as a mother tongue and the Yiddish culture would vanish as a way of life, to be replaced in the Holy Land by a population of brawny, brainy, self-sufficient Jewish farmer-settlers speaking a revived Hebrew, no longer just a written liturgical museum language but once more a living, spoken tongue.

The only other possibility was to stay put, resist the pressure and demand recognition for the Yiddish-speaking Jews as one of Europe's peoples, with as much right to exist as Poles and Lithuanians, Hungarians, Romanians, Ruthenes and Russians. The pogroms that followed the czar's assassination seem to have been the wake-up call for which the Yiddish-speaking people had long been waiting. Across the Yiddish-speaking world a bewildering variety of political organisations now sprang into lively being.

Social democracy had always attracted Europe's Jews, since its principle of equality, of treating all members of society as if they belong to one family, chimes well with traditional Jewish values and with the group solidarity of a persecuted minority. Marxism, founded by a (baptised) Jew who looked and wrote like an Old Testament prophet, and based on the core Jewish belief that history has meaning, purpose and pattern, attracted many more.

In the following decades, many Yiddish speakers would be active in the radical politics of the Left. Though only a small minority among the Jews, they would contribute an all too visible proportion of the new revolutionary class: perhaps most famously Trotsky (Lev Davidovich Bronstein); the leaders of the Menshevik faction in Russia, Pavel Akselrod and L. Martov (*nom de guerre* of Yuly Osipovich Tsederbaum, favourite grandson of the founder of *Ha-Melitz*); three of the six Politburo members who formed the Russian Bolshevik government in 1920; revolutionaries Rosa Luxemburg in Berlin, Kurt Eisner in Munich, Béla Kun in Hungary; and many more, including the greatest survivor of them all, Lazar Moiseyevich Kaganovich, born 1893 in Kabana near Kiev, trained as a bootmaker, Party member from 1911, close protégé of Stalin, creator of the Moscow Metro, commissar for transport and communications, and for heavy industry, First Deputy Premier of the USSR, mentor to Khrushchev and Brezhnev, and accused by some of responsibility for the purges of the 1930s and the murder of more Russian Jews than even Cossack leader Bohdan Khmielnitsky. He would die unrepentant in 1991 at the age of ninety-eight, having lived through the entire Bolshevik experiment from bloody start to pathetic finish.

Most of these Socialists and Communists, being secularists and internationalists, hoped and believed that with the coming of the Utopia for which they were working, all Jewish disabilities would come to an end—and with them all notion of Jews as a separate people. Yet the rising antagonism and anti-Semitism of the peasantry and the workers, what the German Socialist August Bebel (1840–1913) memorably called "The Socialism of Fools," cast doubt on the possibility of forging class solidarity across the religious divide. The consequence was the emergence of a new, specifically Jewish Socialist politics, strongly promoted by, among others, the writers and thinkers who had previously tried to reform the way of life of the Yiddish-speaking masses with their satirical attacks. "Jewish intellectuals," exhorted I. L. Peretz in 1891, "don't assume that you are doing your duty by working for a greater entity, for so-called humanity-at-large . . . Humanity-at-large does not yet exist. Cultural groups, distinct peoples, differing civilizations are now the actors on the stage of the world . . . Come back to your own people."[26]

In October 1897 a group of workers, artisans and intellectuals met in Vilna, ever since the Gaon's time the centre of Yiddish intellectual life, to establish the General Jewish Workers' Union in Lithuania, Poland and Russia (*Algemeyner Yidisher Arbeter Bund in Lite, Poyln un Rusland*). The new body grew rapidly, organising strikes and boycotts, and successfully helping to improve the conditions of the Jewish working class. In contrast to Zionism, which they felt to be a petit-bourgois movement, guilty of abandoning a thousand years of heritage, members of the *Bund* emphasised the importance of stubborn *doykeyt* (being here) and saw itself as part of the great international labour movement.

Indeed, in 1898 the *Bund* supplied three of the nine delegates who convened to found the Social Democratic Labour Party of Russia, the parent body of both Bolsheviks and Mensheviks. Yet even the most doctrinaire class warriors could not help but be aware of the rising tide of nationalism among all the different peoples of the Russian Empire, of Germany and the Balkans. Poles, Ukrainians and Finns were in revolt against their Russian masters, and the language question was threatening to break Austria-Hungary into pieces. Now, at the eleventh hour and against all their best anti-sectarian instincts, activists finally came to feel that it was time to recognise the Yiddish-speaking Jews as a distinct European nationality, with its separate traditions, its unique culture and its own language. A *Bund* publication of 1904 pointed out that:

> It is said that the Jews are not a nation because they do not possess a language of their own . . . The statistics of 1897 show that 80 to 90 per cent of the Jewish population uses the Jargon as its mother tongue. Then is it not their folk language? It is true that the language is still underdeveloped but it has made great progress. It has a sizeable literature and writers like Peretz and Abramowitsh would also be a credit to the great European literatures.[27]

The last-ditch struggle for the recognition of eastern European Jews as a nation, with Yiddish as their language, now became a war on two fronts: against the imperial authorities of Austria and Russia on the one side, and on the other against the promoters of Zionism, emigration to the Holy Land and the revival of Hebrew—a movement whose polemics refused to accept the validity of a Yiddish-speaking identity. "Those miserable stunted jargons, those ghetto languages which we now employ, are the stealthy tongues of prisoners,"[28] wrote Zionist leader Theodor Herzl dismissively in 1896. "He who knows no Hebrew may be an ignoramus," riposted supporters of the *Bund*, "but he who knows no Yiddish is a gentile."

The failure of the Russian 1905 rebellion and the cruel political repression that followed tore the heart out of Yiddish Socialism in Russia. Though the *Bund* survived for another twenty years, and even longer in Poland, it lost political influence. Its leading role among the Jewish intelligentsia was now taken by a passionate campaign for recognition of the Yiddish language. Political activism being too dangerous, it was replaced by a strong drive towards linguistic nationalism. If a change in the political make-up of the czar's empire was impossible, let the Yiddish speakers at least be recognised as a separate language community. One triumph was registered overseas when in 1906 the British South African colonies accepted Yiddish as "a European language, a cultural language, and the language of the Jewish people,"[29] thereby making it possible for Yiddish speakers to fulfil the literacy conditions required for entry.

The high point in the language movement came in 1908 when a conference was held in Czernowitz, within the Austrian Empire, to which all the leading lights of the Yiddish political and literary worlds were invited. It shows how divided Yiddish intellectuals were over the language issue, even at this late stage, that of the three great founding fathers of modern Yiddish literature only Peretz deigned to turn up. Sholom Aleichem pleaded (diplomatic) illness and Abramowitsh didn't even bother to send an excuse. The brilliant young Sholem Asch did attend but the important novelist and playwright David Pinsky said that he was busy writing a book. In the end seventy delegates presented themselves, fourteen from Russia, one from Romania and fifty-five locals, who included students, merchants, bookkeepers, craftsmen and one wedding entertainer (a *badkhn*). Those who attended had only one thing in common, wrote an observer, "They could afford the fare."[30] The organisation was chaotic, the discussions stormy, the conclusions vague: little more than to declare that Yiddish was *a*, rather than *the*, Jewish national language.

The conference had been welcomed by one Socialist Cracow newssheet, the *Sotsyal-Demokrat*, with the words: "The significance of the conference is augmented by the fact that it takes place in Austria, where Yiddish is closest to official recognition."[31] For some time university students, who had to enter their nationality on application papers but were forbidden to write "Jew," had tried to avoid boosting the statistical proportion of the German-speaking majority by entering such languages as

"Hottentot" or "Malay" as their mother tongue.[32] Now, for the census of 1910, a great effort was made finally to persuade the Austrian authorities to add Yiddish, as the national language of the Jews of Galicia, to the nine national languages already recognised by Vienna. Thousands marched through the streets and presented a petition to the provincial government on behalf of the entire Jewish population. Thousands disobeyed official instructions and steadfastly entered Yiddish as their language of everyday communication on the census form. The Austrian government regarded this as a criminal act and the thousands were fined or jailed.

Though the language movement failed to move the imperial bureaucrats, it did add impetus and authority to an astonishing flowering of new Yiddish writing. Now that the Yiddish language had gained the respect of at least some of the Jewish intelligentsia, political pamphlets, philosophical essays, religious homilies, science textbooks and many other non-fiction genres achieved a wide readership among a people thirsty for self-improvement. Not to mention the host of novelists and short-story writers who were appearing on the scene to add their contribution to the burgeoning literary renaissance. Joining Peretz, Abramowitsh and Sholom Aleichem came S. Ansky, Sholem Asch, Dovid Bergelson, H. Leivick, Der Nister (Pinhes Kahanovitch), David Pinsky, Mordkhe Spektor and a whole host of others.

It seems strange that so few of these managed to break through the language barrier and appear in translation to join the canon of world literature. Perhaps only Sholom Aleichem and, much later, Isaac Bashevis Singer managed that difficult transition, to become genuinely well-known among non-Jewish readers. Two Yiddish-speaking authors, Isaac Babel and Ilya Ilf (Ilya Arnoldovich Fainzilberg),[33] did achieve international fame, but only by writing their short stories and satires in Russian. Many of the rest limited their appeal by submitting to an all-conquering vogue for what critic Dan Miron has called the "lachrymose and sentimental style,"[34] confining themselves to maudlin accounts of small town, *shtetl*, life, to describing a world already in the past.

An article in *Poetics Today* by two leading scholars offers a possible reason. At the very same time as Yiddish "gradually crystallized as a modern literary language," they explain,

> sizeable sectors of the Jewish intelligentsia started using other languages, such as Russian and Polish . . . In the families of many of the Yiddish writers themselves (among whom one finds the pillars

of Yiddish literature, Mendele, Peretz, and Sholom Aleichem), either the wife or children spoke Russian or Polish. No longer used for a large range of subjects current in the daily life of a central social stratum of the Jewish people, Yiddish thus was actually prevented from developing ways to relate to these subjects.[35]

Their contention is confirmed by the greatest name of all in modern Yiddish literature, Nobel Laureate Isaac Bashevis Singer.

> In the Yiddish prose written in Poland you will hardly find a Jewish doctor or lawyer, teacher and party leader, secondary school student (*gimnazist*) and university student. You will not encounter the strange metamorphoses of the Jewish communist, the Zionist Pioneer (*Chaluts*), the Revisionist, the assimilationist . . . the Galician doctors, the ladies of the health resorts, the elegant young Jewish ladies who filled up the Polish theatres, cafés and cabarets . . .

The reason, says Bashevis Singer, is that the Yiddish language simply does not have the vocabulary to describe such people, no words with which to write about "farmers, hunters, fishermen, miners, sportsmen, train workers, mechanics, policemen, soldiers, boats, horse-races, universities, society salons and a thousand and one other objects and people . . . He [the writer] could not even label in Yiddish all those flowers . . . which he saw on his way out of town."[36] Thus in spite of the richness, variety and occasional excellence of the new Yiddish writing, there was often something lacking. To reserve a place in world literature, an author must take as his or her subject what it is to be a human being. Too many Yiddish writers restricted themselves to exploring what it is to be a Jew.

Perhaps the Yiddish national movement could never have succeeded. Perhaps it was already a century too late. In any case greater forces would soon intervene and make the promotion of political and cultural autonomy for the Jews of eastern Europe an impossible dream. All Europe was accelerating towards the bloodiest war in its history, and imperial Austria and Russia in particular were hastening towards their own final demise.

The assassination of the Austrian crown prince and his wife in June 1914 smashed the old European order irretrievably. The resulting First World War, and the civil war in Russia that followed, changed everything. Russian and German forces, armies of Poles, of Ukrainians, of Communist Reds, of reactionary Whites, criss-crossed the Yiddish *heym*, leaving death and devastation in their wake. The Yiddish speakers learned to fear the Ukrainians and the Whites most, for the Reds were generally not ill-disposed towards the Jews while many Whites, as well as Ukrainian nationalist General Petlyura's ragbag forces, burned with anti-Jewish hatred. Some 400 towns were attacked, almost 1,000 pogroms instigated, more than 50,000 killed. In Russia the *Bund* backed the more moderate, Menshevik, side during the Bolshevik *coup d'état* of 1917 and lost.

The peace treaties that ended hostilities dismembered the multinational empires, thereby rendering all dreams of a united European Yiddish nation, whether religious or secular, capitalist or Socialist, irrelevant. Once great Austria-Hungary was left a tiny rump. Reborn Poland, with its millions of impoverished Yiddish speakers, rejoiced in its Polishness, ignored the stipulations of the Treaty of Versailles—that the rights of minorities be respected and that non-Poles be allowed to foster their national traditions—and shunned its Jews, referring to its Yiddish-speaking town and city quarters as "the dark continent."

The Soviets played at granting Jews national status, with Yiddish as their language, Marxism-Leninism as their religion, and from 1928 onwards 14,000 square miles of swampy wilderness in far-off eastern Siberia as their national homeland. Unsurprisingly, few went to live there, a fact which Khrushchev later blamed on "Jewish individualism." In any case autonomy was never more than a pretence; in Stalin's ever more paranoid USSR no group was allowed to be anything other than a division of the international proletariat.

The dispossession of the Yiddish-speaking Jews had been slow but inexorable. The abolition of the Council of the Lands in 1765 by the Polish National Assembly had been the beginning of the end of the Yiddish civilisation. After the third partition of Poland in 1795, Moscow's anti-Semitism would constrain its final days. The czar's petulant dissolution of the Kahals in 1844, removing the last vestige of Jewish self-rule, had been the second stage in the eradication of an autonomous Jewish existence in eastern Europe. Finally the pogroms that followed Alexander's assassination in 1881 showed those with eyes to see and ears to hear that an independent Yiddish world in eastern Europe was no longer achievable. Jews might be recognised as a religious minority, might gain emancipation, acceptance and even de jure (if never de facto) equality with gentiles, might develop history-changing Yiddish politics and a world-class Yiddish literature, but would never, ever again, be recognised as a separate European people. The destruction of the old multi-ethnic empires by the First World War and its aftermath confirmed that diagnosis. After 1881 the Yiddish day as a European civilisation was done. Fifty-eight years later, less than a lifetime, Hitler's murderous onslaught would bring the story crashing to a final stop that is still shuddering half a century later.

EXODUS

People do not tear up their roots and move home lightly, even in the face of repression. Attacks and massacres in previous centuries had seen survivors return to their former homes and hope for better times to come. But now better times could no longer be expected; life among the debris of the Yiddish civilisation had too little to offer. A great exodus began, in which at least one part of the vile prediction of the head of the Russian Orthodox Church was fulfilled: as many as a third of the entire Jewish population of the Russian Empire abandoned their homeland and their past, fully recognising that in doing so they would also have to relinquish their Yiddish national identity.

For most the gain was worth the loss. As Professor John Klier of University College London points out in a recent book review,[37] contrary to the common myth it was not just anti-Semitism that emigrants wanted to leave behind—they had no guarantee that tolerance would be greater elsewhere—but more the claustrophobia of *shtetl* existence, its class and clan divisions, its ruthless dominance by reactionary *Tsaddikim* or ultra-conservative rabbinical oligarchies, its self-imposed limitations on living a full, rich and successful life.

Some went to western Europe, to Germany, the Netherlands, France, Italy and Britain. Spain was largely avoided, as the Hebrew *cherem*, or ban, put on that country after the expulsion of 1492 was still strong in the memory—Jews were not tolerated in Spain until the constitutional reform of 1868. (Forty years ago my mother would still raise her eyebrows at the willingness of Jewish holidaymakers to throng the tourist Costas, given that the 1492 Decree of Expulsion was not actually repealed until the 1960s.)

Most Yiddish emigrants, however, chose to leave Europe behind altogether and set sail for new and more promising worlds, for South Africa, Australia, the Caribbean and—the vast majority—for the United States of America (where there was no income tax until 1913). Not all arrived at their intended destination; many were deposited by unscrupulous ship's officers at Rotterdam in Holland instead of Buenos Aires in Argentina, or dumped in Cardiff in Wales instead of New York, USA—and, knowing no language other than Yiddish, it sometimes took the unfortunates several days to discover that they had been gulled.

The consequences of this huge population movement can hardly be overestimated, for it established a new focus of Yiddish Jewish life in the United States. And for that we have to thank, at least in part, one particular German Jew who, more than anyone else, made it possible for poor Yiddish-speaking emigrants from Russia to achieve their dream of travelling to a new golden land, the *goldene medine* of America.

Albert Ballin's background was not promising. His father Joel was a second-hand clothes dealer in Hamburg who, though never learning to write German, had prospered enough to set up a small clothing factory, but was ruined by the Great Fire of 1842. Some ten years later, having tried and failed at several other businesses, and now truly desperate to find a way of making a living, Ballin Senior eventually became part owner of what seemed at the time a highly risky venture for a man with no experience or knowledge of the transport industry, one, moreover, with much the same shady reputation borne by today's "people traffickers": a bureau that arranged boat passages for emigrants to the USA.[38]

This time, however, he had made a good choice. The middle of the nineteenth century was witnessing a huge growth in transatlantic travel by migrants anxious to escape the economic and political consequences of the failed 1848 revolutions and drawn to the United States by travellers' tales of American prosperity and the "Forty-Niner" California Gold Rush. Germans, Austrians, Czechs, Poles, Lithuanians, Hungarians, Russians and others, Christians for the most part, streamed towards Bremen and Hamburg, looking for cheap berths on overloaded passenger vessels. Between 1841 and 1846, Bremen had shipped 115,000 passengers to America, but Hamburg only 11,000. The shipowners of Hamburg could not stomach being overshadowed by old rival Bremen, and sought every means to replace her as the main port of embarkation from Germany. Ballin's enterprise did well.

In 1874, the elder Ballin died and his eighteen-year-old son Albert took over his father's share of the business. Six years later the assassination of the czar that signalled the coming end of Jewish Europe sent hundreds of thousands, eventually millions, of Yiddish speakers flocking towards north Germany in the search for a way out of unemployment, poverty and the threat of violence. Albert Ballin was well placed to help them and astute enough to know how.

He teamed up with Edward Carr, nephew of the owner of a shipping line that sailed trampships out of Hamburg, and persuaded him to convert a number of cargo vessels for passenger use. The first left Hamburg on 7 June 1881 with 800 passengers aboard. Over the next two years he was able to arrange relatively low-cost passage for 16,500 emigrants, the ships returning from the USA profitably loaded with guano, cotton and industrial goods. Charging a fare of some £300–500 at today's values (about US$500–800), the project was successful enough to challenge the largest, best-established and most influential passenger line in Hamburg, the Hamburg-America Packet Company, Hapag[39] for short (wags said it stood for *Haben alle Passagiere auch Geld?*—Have all the passengers got money?). In 1886, Hapag bought an interest in Ballin's business and persuaded its owner to take the post of director of their passenger department; in 1888 they offered him a seat on the board; in 1899 he was appointed general director of the entire company. Within a decade Ballin had made Hapag the largest and most successful shipping company in the world.

Under Ballin's direction, Hapag built a huge "emigrant city" in the Veddel area of Hamburg's port, which could house up to 5,000 travellers at a time while they waited to board ship, with dormitories for families and for single men and women, kosher canteens, recreation grounds and a synagogue. It was officially opened in 1901. Migrants had to undergo fourteen days' quarantine before being able to embark on the twelve- to fourteen-day crossing direct to Ellis Island, New York City, and Ballin's Yiddish new town made the wait bearable. It was a winning formula. Those taking other lines had to find their own accommodation in Hamburg. Many had first to sail to Hull on the north-east coast of England, take a cross-country train to Liverpool on the west coast, and only then begin the Atlantic crossing.

Ballin became very rich and built himself a palatial villa in the city— nicknamed "Little Potsdam" and now occupied by a UNESCO institute. Had he been prepared to give up his Jewish faith he would have been treated as an equal in the very highest circles of imperial Germany. Loyal to his religion as he was, he nevertheless maintained a personal relationship with Emperor Wilhelm, who wrote to him as "My friend"—though the empress and courtiers strongly disapproved—and had a specially wide drive laid to the front of his villa so that Wilhelm could ride up in his carriage.

Though he married a Christian, Ballin never forgot his Jewish roots, never gave up his Yiddish allegiance, never stopped trying to help his co-religionists fulfil their dreams of freedom, and never stopped attempting to prevent a war in Europe, which he knew would be catastrophic both for his business and his people. He spent the first half of the year 1914 shuttling between Berlin and London seeking, and of course failing, to bring the two sides closer together. In 1918 he attempted, equally unsuccessfully, to persuade Kaiser Wilhelm to take up American President Wilson's Fourteen Point peace plan. Germany collapsed; Wilhelm abdicated. On the day before the emperor left for his long afterlife in Dutch exile, Albert Ballin swallowed an overdose of sleeping tablets and died the following morning.

In 1947, to wipe away some of the shame of the Nazi era, which had ruthlessly erased all references to Hapag's greatest director and the man who did more than most to put Hamburg's name on the modern map, the city council recognised Ballin's contribution by giving the name Ballindamm to the *grand allée* where Hapag's main office, now the Hapag-Lloyd Haus, still stands. There are moves to restore one of the large emigration halls at Veddel as a memento of German-Jewish history.

Tens of thousands of the descendants of Yiddish-speaking emigrants, in the USA and elsewhere, owe the Hamburg shipping magnate a debt of gratitude. They should raise a glass to him every 15 August, his birthday. For Albert Ballin made possible the survival of a branch of the Yiddish civilisation far from the old hatreds of Europe and safe from the destruction wrought by evil millenarian fantasists who promised that their empire would last a thousand years but brought both it and Europe down in flames within twelve. It was in good measure thanks to Albert Ballin that after the old European *heym* was annihilated by Hitler's maniacal programme, the lineage of the Yiddish-speaking Jews still survived.

14

A Winter Flowering

"It is a pouring wet day," wrote the London-based journalist and pioneering social reformer George Sims in 1901, describing the very first Jewish migration to be fully documented by outside observers.

> The rain is coming down in torrents, and one has to wade through small lakes and rivulets of mud to reach the narrow pathway leading to Irongate Stairs, where the immigrant passengers of the vessel lying at anchor in the Thames are to land . . . The wretched immigrants are taken off in small boats and rowed to the steps. Look at them, the men thin and hungry-eyed, the women with their heads bare and only a thin shawl over their shoulders, the children terrified by the swaying of the boat that lies off waiting to land when the other boats have discharged their load . . . When at last they land it is in a dark archway crowded with loafers and touts all busily trying to confuse them, to seize their luggage, almost fighting to get possession of it.
>
> Fortunately Mr. Somper, the Superintendent of the Poor Jews' Temporary Shelter is here also. As the scared and shivering foreigners step ashore he speaks to them either in Yiddish or Lettish, and finds out if they have an address to go to. Most of them have

something written on a piece of paper which they produce creased and soiled from a pocket. It is the address of a friend or relative, or of a boarding-house . . . For most of them have friends somewhere. It may be a brother, it may be only a fellow townsman or fellow villager, who came to London years ago. In the shelter they are taken care of with their money and their baggage until their friends can be communicated with or employment obtained.[1]

In later years, many immigrants themselves wrote memoirs of their arrival in London or New York. Yet how hard it is not to cover up the reality of what must have been a disorientating and frightening experience under a warm blanket of nostalgia for lost youth and forgotten innocence. Solomon Ginsburg, a Polish rabbi's son, arrived in Hamburg at the age of fifteen with three 10-pfennig coins in his pocket.

No vessel to New York would take me over and I found a sailing boat, carrying horses to London, that was willing to take me. I was to do some kind of work, but we had a very rough sea and I suffered great agonies until we reached the Thames. I will never forget the arrival in London on that early September morning of 1882. I at once seemed to smell the warm odors of a bakershop and, entering, placed my three German nickels on the counter and pointed to a loaf of bread. How rapidly this bread disappeared can more easily be imagined than described, as I had not had any food for three days.

In London I found an uncle of mine, my mother's brother, who owned a large dry goods store in the East End who gladly took me in and gave me work in his office as assistant bookkeeper. He was a splendid man, a typical orthodox Jew, adhering strictly to all that Moses and the Holy Fathers required. I had my own room in the attic and was taking special lessons in mercantile bookkeeping as well as in the English language.[2]

Though many of the immigrants were just passing through London on their way to Liverpool and thence to the Americas—Ginsburg converted to Christianity and emigrated to Brazil as a missionary—about 100,000 settled in Whitechapel, Stepney, Hackney and Bethnal Green, collectively known as the East End, a rough, tough district, Jack-the-Ripper territory, where whores outnumbered housewives, and policemen only patrolled in fours, a neighbourhood which had previously sheltered French Huguenot Protestant exiles and would much later become home to immigrants from Bangladesh. One double-fronted building on Brick Lane[3] was originally built as a Huguenot church, was next converted to a Methodist chapel, then became a synagogue and from 1976 has been in use as a mosque.

In these five square miles or so there sprang up the colourful and chaotic community so nostalgically glorified in the memories of the older generations of my youth, and that the writer Israel Zangwill, a fully anglicised English gentleman and scion of an earlier immigration, described with such patronising sentimentality in *Children of the Ghetto*:

> Hawkers and pedlars, tailors and cigar-makers, cobblers and furriers, glaziers and cap-makers—this was in sum their life: to pray much and to work long; to beg a little and to cheat a little; to eat not over much and to "drink" scarce at all; to beget annual children by chaste wives (disallowed them half the year), and to rear them not over-well; to study the Law and the Prophets, and to reverence the Rabbinical tradition and the chaos of commentaries surrounding it; to know no work on Sabbath and no rest on weekday.[4]

Most newcomers to this Jewish quarter, "greeners" as they were known, would soon find that their dreams of streets paved with gold were quickly dashed by the reality of arriving penniless in a foreign land. Many would find employment in the burgeoning sweatshops of the rag and leather trades, crafting dresses, coats, jackets and trousers, belts, gloves, hats, boots and shoes, in cramped, damp, airless and unsanitary workshops set up in private dwellings, often in properties that had once belonged to Huguenots and even on occasion taking over their defunct businesses, for French Protestants, like Jews, had been much engaged in the textile trade. Factory Act regulations, drawn up to protect workers from exploitation, did not apply to domestic premises and inspectors had no right of access. The human consequence shocked English observers like Sims:

> The Russian "greener" lives on next to nothing. A cup of tea and a herring are frequently all the food he will have in the twenty-four hours. How can he afford more on the starvation wages he receives from the sweater? Not long ago a Russian who appeared before the Sweating Committee said he had that week worked

from 6.30 a.m. to 2.30 a.m. on the following day with only one hour for dinner. He worked harder in London than in Warsaw and made less. But the emigration agent had painted London as a land of gold and tempted him to invest all he had in the world in a ticket.

The struggle is sometimes too terrible even for a Russian Jew. Recently a young "greener" hanged himself. He had brought his newly-wedded wife from Russia to London thinking he would get a living. He learnt boot finishing and earned 12s. to 15s. a week. To earn £1 a week he would have to work twenty-two hours out of the twenty-four. At the inquest it was proved that he had tried to do this and his brain had given way. In a fit of madness and despair he hanged himself in the room he occupied with his young wife.[5]

As Sims was quick to point out, the sweatshop system was not always, or even usually, a case of workers ruthlessly exploited by greedy employers. The boss was "no wealthy spider sucking the life-blood from the flies he has caught in his web," but most often "a worker also, a man sweating because he himself sweated."

To sustain the struggling population of impoverished orthodox Yiddish-speaking Londoners there grew up a thriving secondary economy of bakers, butchers, fishmongers and grocers, jewellers, second-hand clothes merchants and pawnbrokers, sellers of religious wares, scribes, certified kosher slaughterers and circumcisers, and all the other specialists that Yiddish communal life demanded. Jewish shops and stalls lined the thoroughfares. Jewish traders packed the market places, where "the noise is often deafening, and in the babel of sounds half a dozen different languages may be distinguished—French, German, Russian, Polish, Hebrew, with the Yiddish compounds of them all, and occasionally English."[6]

Some of the shopkeepers became very rich indeed, at least by the standards of the day. In a single generation a family of fishmongers in the 400-year-old market called Petticoat Lane,[7] rose to ownership of an entire estate outside London near Epping Forest, with a pool for breeding carp, an apple orchard with a summer house and a private synagogue.[8]

Mental sustenance was not lacking either. According to the journalist David Mazower, great-grandson of the Yiddish author Sholem Asch, several small printing houses were already publishing pamphlets and books in Yiddish by the 1880s, and in the 1890s "the East End could boast three Yiddish dailies as well as a range of Zionist, Socialist and Marxist period-

icals. And there was an increasingly enthusiastic audience for Yiddish theatre—the main form of entertainment for the immigrant working class."[9]

There were popular music halls like the Cambridge, where Charlie
Chaplin first appeared before the public and whose faux-Moorish façade
betrayed its origins as a synagogue, or "that Whitechapel resort fancifully
named 'Wonderland,' " as H. Chance Newton wrote in his account of
"Music-Hall London."

> In this big hall are provided entertainments of the most extraordi-
> nary description. They include little plays, songs, and sketches,
> given first in Yiddish dialect and afterwards translated into more
> or less choice English by, as a rule, a Hebraic interpreter. This
> interpreter often improves the occasion by calling the attention of
> kind—and mostly alien—friends in front to certain side shows
> consisting of all sorts of armless, legless, skeleton, or spotted
> "freaks" scattered around the recesses of this great galleryless hall.
> When once the "freaks" have been examined, or the "greeners" and
> other foreign and East-End "sweated" Jew toilers have utilised the
> interval to indulge in a little light refreshment according to their
> respective tastes, the Yiddish sketches and songs—comic and oth-
> erwise—are resumed until closing time.[10]

There was little show-business glamour to London's Yiddish theatre
world. The performers worked under conditions almost as harsh as did
their audience of sweatshop toilers, putting on four or five shows a night in
different theatres and music halls, or on tiny stages in cramped assembly
rooms, urgently battling their way through dense traffic from one engage-
ment to the next by horse-drawn brougham. "If the sweating system was
terrible in the tailoring shops, it was still more terrible in the Yiddish theatre," wrote the radical journalist Morris Winchewsky.[11] The rewards were
no less miserly either.

Perhaps in consequence of the miserable working conditions, possibly
because of the relative tolerance of the British authorities, maybe because
of the polyglot population drawn from all quarters of the Continent, or
most likely because of the leading role played by the Yiddish-speaking
Jews in the European Socialist movement, after 1881 the East End of London became a major world centre of left-wing politics. The 1907 Congress
of the Russian Social Democratic Labour Party, precursor of the Bolshevik
Party, was held in a building just off the Whitechapel Road. Before 1917

Lenin was a frequent visitor and Stalin came to stay in a flat near the famous bell foundry (where the American Liberty Bell had been cast in 1752). In 1911 a group of Latvian anarchists, holed up in Mrs. Betsy Gershon's flat in Sidney Street, exchanged rifle shots with the police and a detachment of Scots Guards from the nearby Tower of London, until the building caught fire and a young Home Secretary called Winston Churchill, who was directing operations on the spot, refused to allow the Fire Brigade to extinguish the flames.

The political ferment could not help but make a strong impression on the suffering sweatshop workers, particularly after Rudolf Rocker, the German, Yiddish-speaking though Christian, editor of the Yiddish anarchist newspaper *Der Arbeter Fraynd* (*The Workers' Friend*), whose portrait still hung in the Whitechapel Library until not long ago, began organising resistance among them. Soon many were joining trade unions. There was a Jewish Furniture Workers Union, with a marching banner inscribed in Hebrew lettering, which conducted its business in Yiddish. According to Solly Kaye, a former Communist councillor, it later amalgamated with the National Furniture Trades Association and became known as the No. 15 branch, "renowned for its militancy during the whole of the 1930s and after."[12] There was a Jewish Bakers' Union and Kaye remembers "loaves from Kossoff's bakery which carried a little label 'Baked by Union Labour.'" As is the way of the world, fiery radicalism declined as material prospects improved.

The Yiddish-speaking East End was inevitably fated to be merely a temporary ornament on British society and contributed little directly to English culture or language. The number of Yiddish speakers was far too small, the strength of the host culture far too great and its antagonism far too sharp, not just to the Yiddish way of life but to the language itself, and not only from gentiles but even more importantly from the well-established Anglo-Jewish community. Largely Sephardic by origin and aristocratic by aspiration, they had learned to see themselves as Jewish Britons rather than British Jews, and were indescribably appalled by the vulgar Yiddish-speaking rabble from Russia now storming up the Thames river stairs and threatening their comfortable retreat. Damn it all, hadn't the Anglo-Jews supplied their country with a prime minister, Benjamin Disraeli, baptised though he may have been? Even when giving a favourable review to a Yiddish theatre performance, the *Jewish Chronicle*—founded in 1841—couldn't restrain itself: "The plays performed were in the

Jüdisch-Deutsch dialect, a language which we should be the last to encourage any efforts to preserve."[13]

The *Jewish Chronicle* got its way in the end. Not many years after the First World War, in the 1920s, the community began its long, slow dispersal from Stepney and Whitechapel towards the suburbs, many of the better-off moving upwind, away from the East End's smoky, polluted and crime-ridden streets towards more salubrious districts in London's northwest, many of the less successful travelling downwind, eastwards along the Mile End Road, the historic route out into the less sought-after suburbs of Essex, while the most God-fearing relocated directly north to Stoke Newington and Stamford Hill. Yiddish language and culture did not easily survive the transition to busy suburban high-street terraces or leafy lanes bordered by semi-detached villas, where the neighbours only knew English and the men had to gather in the local barber's shop to hear Yiddish spoken and bet pennies on a hand or two of Hungarian Kalabriasz.[14]

The second generation were still able to understand the language but not to speak it with much fluency, still knew the traditions but chose not to observe them with any dedication. By the third generation even most of the knowledge was gone. These accountants, dentists, doctors, lawyers, writers and painters tried to distance themselves from their origins as far as and as fast as they could. David Bomberg, brought up in Whitechapel and founder member of the "London Group" of artists, went further than most when he fled to Palestine to record the work of the Zionist pioneers—but he fell out with them after refusing to paint what he regarded as propaganda.

On the other side of the Atlantic, however, Yiddish numbers were vastly greater and every US citizen was either an immigrant or the descendant of an immigrant. Here a true Yiddish-speaking society was briefly reincarnated, represented by a building that stands at the southern end of Manhattan, below the area known as the East Village, not far from where the knee of New York's Lower East Side juts into the East River to confront the Williamsburg district of Brooklyn. Here you will find the Lower East Side Tenement Museum.

In 1863 an immigrant German tailor scraped together enough cash to erect a six-storey, twenty-two-apartment red-brick tenement at 97 Orchard Street, a road that before the American Revolution had led to the apple plantation on British Lieutenant-Governor James Delancey's 300-acre farm. The building still stands, 140 years and 7,000 tenants later, grimier and more dishevelled but still sound, although most everything else has changed about the neighbourhood around it.

A hundred years ago these streets teemed with life, as noisy and aromatic as an oriental souk. Old photographs show huge crowds of bearded elders in fur hats, matriarchs and matrons in boots and headscarves, white aprons protecting their ground-trailing skirts with little girls in plaits towed at arm's length unwillingly behind, skull-capped boys cavorting with their shirt-tails hanging out and their sidelocks swinging, fighting their way among horse-drawn carts and push-barrows, past merchandise spilling out of shopfronts on to the sidewalks, past pickle barrels, hot-potato stalls, unstable mountains of battered cabin trunks and cardboard suitcases, abandoned relics of immigrant journeys. All around are signs in Yiddish and German enticing buyers to purchase kosher chickens, fancy dresses, luggage, second-hand clothes, sacred books, clocks and watches, cloth remnants and fents, superior haircuts. Irrepressible *shleppers* in bowler hats and bow ties are trying to drag reluctant customers into shop doorways, while above them the iron fire escapes are festooned with drying washing as if with flags on a national holiday.

Today the area is much quieter, the streets almost empty; only the stores promoting cut-price clothing and bargain jewellery hint at its vanished former industries. The languages are different too. Instead of Yiddish and German, you are now much more likely to hear Mandarin, Cantonese or Spanish. But 97 Orchard Street still stands proudly as a reminder of the past.

The building is a physical record of the passage of the final phase of the Yiddish civilisation across the seas from the old world to the new. In these cramped and gloomy three-roomed apartments, only one room of which boasts natural light and which originally had neither running water nor interior sanitation, many Yiddish-speaking families lived their early American years.

A tour of the museum introduces the visitor to three such families: one from what was then Germany, one from Poland and one from Lithuania, representing the irresistible wave of emigration that washed west to east across Europe during the second half of the nineteenth century, sweeping up a colossal mass movement that prompted a third of the Jews to abandon their homes in the once but no longer golden land of the Yiddish *heym*, for the promise of a better life in the new *goldene medine* of the USA.

The Gumpertz couple arrived separately in the 1850s, Nathalia from a small town some twenty miles from Breslau in Silesia. As subjects of Prussia they were probably bilingual in Yiddish and German, since some years after husband Julius disappeared mysteriously during the fearful depression of 1874, leaving for work on the morning of 7 October, never to be seen or heard of again, wife Nathalia moved to the Upper East Side, which was then a German-speaking neighbourhood. At this time New York had the largest German-speaking population in the world after Berlin and Vienna.

The Yiddish-speaking Levines, Harris and Jennie, emigrated from a town some way north of Warsaw in 1890, apparently while on their honeymoon, and stayed on the Lower East Side for five years before moving on to Brooklyn.

The Rogarshevskys came with their six children in 1901, having made the ten-day Atlantic crossing on the Steamship *Graf Waldersee*, a converted freighter of 12,830 tons, an old-fashioned vessel with four tall masts and a fat funnel amidships, one of the boats pressed into service by Albert Ballin's Hamburg-America line. They had travelled by stages from the yeshivah city of Telz, now Telsiai, in Lithuania, and by all accounts remained strictly observant of Jewish law in their new home. Abraham, the husband, was president of the local synagogue. He worked as a presser in a tailoring sweatshop until he died of tuberculosis in 1918. The thousand-year German-Slav divide seems even then to have been important in the Rogarshevskys' self-image. They soon began to call themselves Rosenthal, as if hoping to associate themselves with their higher-class, longer-resident and by now better-established German co-religionists.

It should, of course, be no surprise that many immigrants failed to make a success of their move. Around a quarter of those who left the *heym* for America were unable to establish themselves in their new land and returned to eastern Europe. Perhaps another quarter would have eagerly done so had they been able to raise the money for the fare. Not a few committed suicide in their despair, like the father of New York painter Philip Guston (Goldstein), who took his own life from a sense of demeaning failure—he could only find work as a refuse collector.

Yet in spite of the difficulties they faced, most of those who remained in America prospered. The first few generations of New York Jewish immigrants from Europe remained strongly attached to their language, religion and social mores, and to serve this rapidly growing community— soon to constitute the largest number of Yiddish speakers gathered together in any city—a great, late, winter flowering of Yiddish culture burst into life.

Yiddish writers and poets set themselves up in New York to serve the

Jewish masses. In the absence of a developed book publishing industry, they provided material for the large number of Yiddish publications that were soon hitting the streets, space limitations forcing authors to perfect the characteristic Yiddish form: the short story, sketch or *skitse*. The American Yiddish daily press, having been born in 1870 with the first appearance of *Di Yidishe Tsaytung* (*The Jewish Newspaper*), was joined over the following decades by publications of almost every political stance and interest: for the religious, for Socialists, for anarchists, for Communists, for those looking for a laugh. There were specialist journals for women, for theatregoers, for sports enthusiasts, even for vegetarians. Some of the greatest names in Yiddish literature flourished on these pages: Sholom Aleichem, Sholem Asch, H. Leivick and the Singer brothers, Israel Joshua and Isaac Bashevis, who were published in the daily *Forverts* (*Forward*), founded in 1897, which at its peak had a circulation of more than a quarter of a million and printed eleven local and regional editions reaching as far west as Chicago. *Forverts* is still published as a weekly today.

Creative talents of every kind were attracted away from the *heym* and from other cities of settlement like London and Buenos Aires to have a share in New York's phenomenal Yiddish success story: Yiddish composers, songwriters and musicians, Yiddish theatre directors and film makers. Some two dozen Yiddish theatres played to a total audience of more than two million in the year 1900. When cinema became a business, hundreds of Yiddish films were produced—and even distributed back in the old country. Thousands upon thousands of klezmer, Jewish entertainment music, recordings were pressed. All Yiddish life was there. As the first line of the 1918 theatre song "Lebn Zol Kolombus" (Long Live Columbus) put it: "A *shtetl* is Amerike!"[15]

But *shtetl* America had brought with it a sadly narrowed view of the Yiddish civilisation that it had left behind in Europe, distorted through the perspective of the Yiddish satires and the fantasy history of the lachrymose and sentimental stories which, apart from bitter memories, were its main inheritance from the *heym*.

Real Yiddish history was lost, the centuries of true Yiddish civilisation forgotten. It was as if the Jews of eastern Europe had somehow and at some unknown time been spirited magically to the *heym* from the Holy Land, converted in the blink of an eye from noble ancient Israelites to impoverished and oppressed Yiddish *shtetlites*: "It is as if we were all born yesterday," as David Gans wrote all those centuries ago. The great figures of the past, the men and women who had contributed not just to Jewish life but to the history of Europe and the world, were consigned to oblivion. No longer would anyone remember the pious Kalonymos family who came north from Italy, wealthy Samuel Belassar who kept sumptuous house in Regensburg, learned Litte of Ratisbon who composed the *Shmuel Buch*, grand Josel of Rosheim who confronted the leaders of the Protestant Reformation, the scholarly Rema and Maharal who jousted over philosophy and science, worthy David Gans who tried to be the educator of the Yiddish-speaking Jews, hard-working Glikl of Hamelin who wrote the first great Yiddish autobiography, or even the brilliant Moses Mendelssohn, the most important Yiddish-speaking link in the chain of the European musical and philosophical traditions.

In any case, *shtetl* America itself could not, of course, last. The Yiddish world was dying in the *heym*. The American *shtetl* was no more than an errant brightly glowing spark that sprang from the thousand-year-old Yiddish fire just as it was being stamped out by its enemies. A spark that flared up all too briefly before it too finally went cold. Or, to change the metaphor, like a cutting taken from a dying plant that quickly puts out leaves but fails to root and then shrivels. Even the daily *Forverts*, American Yiddish speakers' main source of information, education and entertainment, under its legendary editor Abraham Cahan, pursued a Socialist, modernist line, denigrating the Yiddish past and urging its readers to adopt the English language and assimilate to American culture, thus working towards the extinction of its own readership.

Yiddish-speaking Americans were fated to become, wanted to become, Americans *tout court*. Julius Gumpertz took American citizenship seven years after his arrival and Harris Levine after fourteen. They had not travelled across 4,000 miles of wild ocean simply to re-create all they had fled. Though it took two or three generations for the immigrants to become indistinguishably American, the gradual change can be encapsulated into a single moment, a single representative event that was significant not only to the Yiddish-speaking Jews of America but to the cultural future of the United States, and indeed to all the world.

On 6 October 1927, the Day of Atonement, Yom Kippur, and the day after Sam Warner, co-founder of Warner Brothers, died, his studio released *The Jazz Singer*, the very first full-length feature film with synchronised dialogue. When it opened in New York's Warner Theater—after sunset so that Jews could attend—the modern movie era began and with it, in some sense, the modern world.

And what is the film's plot? A précis of the Yiddish Jews' American odyssey, the story of the incorporation of the Yiddish civilisation's remains into the American Way of Life. In the opening scene we hear Cantor Rabinowitz of the Orchard Street Synagogue—where Abraham Rogarshevsky was president—singing "Kol Nidrey," the Jewish prayer for the evening before the Day of Atonement. The closing scene shows his son Jakie, played of course by Al Jolson (Asa Joelson), having sung the prayer out of grudging respect for his father, now putting his background for ever behind him and turning his cantorial skills to belting out the kitsch "Mammy," in blackface, to his mother in front of a packed audience in the Winter Garden Theater.

The Jazz Singer struck a deep chord in the heart of America's Jews. They took it as their own universal story as they made their way from minority to mainstream. It must have spoken for other new Americans too, for it was a phenomenal triumph, making three and a half million dollars at the box office, a colossal sum for those days.

It was no accident that success, and full acceptance as an American, should have come for Jakie Rabinowitz—as for his impersonator Al Jolson—through show business. On his first visit to New York as late as 1959, the important Italian writer Italo Calvino was amazed to find that American banks "are completely closed to Jews, as are the universities. The few Jewish doctors are regarded as the best because such difficulties are put in the way of Jews trying to get into university and to pass exams that those who do succeed in graduating in medicine have to be of extraordinary brilliance." Unable to participate easily in medicine or politics or banking or heavy industry, it fell to the immigrant Yiddish speakers to create their own space in their new home, by taking up popular culture. Calvino observed that "Seventy-five per cent of the publishing world here is Jewish. Ninety per cent of the theatre is Jewish. The ready-to-wear clothes industry, New York's major industry, is almost exclusively Jewish."[16]

Neal Gabler's well-known book, *An Empire of Their Own: How the Jews Invented Hollywood*,[17] documents how, by going into the movie business, eastern European immigrants like the Warner Brothers, Samuel Goldwyn, Universal Studios founder Carl Laemmle, Louis B. Mayer of MGM, William Fox of 20th Century Fox, and Paramount's Adolf Zukor, sold their own Yiddish vision of an ideal world to the public and made it America's own. It was the son of a cantor and kosher slaughterer, Israel Baline, Irving Berlin of the Lower East Side, who wrote many of the USA's most popular anthems: "God Bless America," "This Is a Great Country," "This Is the Army, Mr. Jones." The great songwriter Jerome

Kern, Jewish but no Yiddish speaker, said of Berlin, "He doesn't have a place in American music; he *is* American music." "White Christmas," the most famous popular musical evocation ever of a Christian religious festival and the most performed holiday song in history, with over 500 versions recorded in twenty-five languages, was inspired by Jewish childhood memories of winter in his birthplace Mogilev, where still today "the tree-tops glisten and children listen to hear sleigh bells in the snow." Rabbi Emanuel Goldsmith, Professor of Jewish Studies at Queens College of the City of New York, has written, with perhaps a little forgivable exaggeration, "You can't understand American culture without knowing Yiddish."[18]

So although the Yiddish world was ruthlessly extirpated from Europe, and its American offshoot consigned to assimilation, amnesia and the myth-making of younger generations, some part of the Yiddish civilisation was not lost, but was incorporated into the foundations of the American dream. Though precisely which aspects were Yiddish-inspired is an issue that will no doubt fuel debate for a long time to come.

The example I most hope is true was told me by a friend who is an authority on kitchen history.[19] Albert Ballin, the shipping magnate who made his name and his fortune by conveying poor Jews across the Atlantic from Hamburg to New York, saw his responsibility as ending with the provision of transport. Emigrants travelling steerage had to provide their own food for the ten- to fourteen-day crossing. It needed to be simple to prepare and uncomplicated to serve, strictly kosher and above all low cost. Kosher meat, being salted, keeps well. When minced it goes further than steak. Rolled into balls, flattened into patties, it can be rapidly cooked on a hot-plate and served on bread. The dish soon became so well known as the staple of Hamburg-America's steerage class that it was nicknamed Hamburger steak, the first explicit recipe appearing in *Aunt Babette's Cook Book* of 1889:[20] "Hamburger steak is made of round steak chopped extremely fine and seasoned with salt and pepper. You may grate in part of an onion or fry with onions."

Every spring, Jews celebrate the Passover, the matzo festival, during which they eat unleavened bread in memory of the Exodus of the Children of Israel from Egypt, "because they were thrust out of Egypt and could not tarry."[21] At the service round the dinner table, the whole company raises the plate of matzos and recites: "This is the bread of affliction that our forefathers ate in the Land of Egypt. All who are hungry, let them come and eat."

There is no annual hamburger festival. Hamburg-America's steerage fare is on the menu all year round and all over the globe, from Adelaide to Anchorage to Ashkhabad, from Beijing to Bombay to Buenos Aires. The diners may not know it but they are celebrating the Exodus of the Yiddish people from Europe. This is the food that sustained the survivors from the shipwreck of the Yiddish civilisation. All who are hungry, let them come and eat.

Notes

INTRODUCTION

1. Dovid ben Solomon Gans (1541–1613).
2. Roman Vishniac, *A Vanished World*, Farrar, Straus & Giroux, New York, 1983.

1

Bist a Yid?

1. Howard Jacobson, *Roots Schmoots: Journeys Among Jews*, Penguin, 1993.
2. Henry Sapoznik, *The Compleat Klezmer*, Tara Publications, 1987.
3. Steven J. Zipperstein, *Stanford News*, 22 May 1996, and in *Imagining Russian Jewry: Memory, History, Identity*, University of Washington Press, 1999.
4. David Grupper and David G. Klein, *The Paper Shtetl, a Complete Model of an East European Jewish Town*, Schocken Books, 1984.
5. Bernard S. Bachrach, *Jews in Barbarian Europe*, Coronado Press, 1977.

2

The Jews of Rome

1. "And thou shalt make a candlestick of pure gold: of beaten work . . . And six branches shall come out of the sides of it; three branches of the candlestick out of the one side, and three branches of the candlestick out of the other side," Authorised Version: Exodus, 25:31–32.
2. "Make thee two trumpets of silver; . . . that thou mayest use them for the calling of the assembly . . . ," Numbers, 10:2.
3. "Thou shalt also make a table of shittim [Acacia] wood . . . And thou shalt

overlay it with pure gold, and make thereto a crown of gold round about . . . And thou shalt set upon the table shewbread before me always," Exodus, 25:23–30.

4. Flavius Josephus, *The Wars of the Jews or History of the Destruction of Jerusalem*.
5. Persius, *Satire* 5.
6. Juvenal, *Satire* 6.
7. Cecil Roth, *A Short History of the Jewish People*, Macmillan, 1936.
8. More boringly, others derive the name from Latin *piper* (pepper).
9. Flavius Josephus, *Jewish Antiquities* 2.80.
10. Glenn R. Storey, "The Population of Ancient Rome," *Antiquity* 71 (1997).
11. Tacitus, *Histories* 5:5.
12. "*Corpora hominum salubria et ferentia laborum*," *Historia*, v. 6.
13. Juvenal, *Satire* 14.
14. Ibid., 3.
15. Tractate Shabbat, 33b.

3

From the Mediterranean to the Baltic

1. *PHOBOUMENOI TON THEON HUPSISTON.*
2. *Jewish Encyclopedia.*
3. Salo Wittmayer Baron, *A Social and Religious History of the Jews,* Columbia University Press, 1976.
4. Acts of the Apostles, 6.1.
5. The Tatars were originally a Turkic-speaking people from north-eastern Siberia. After they joined the Mongol leader Genghis Khan's horde and inter-mixed with the Mongols, Europeans labelled all the invaders Tatars (or Tartars, as they considered them to have come from hell, *Tartarus* in Latin).
6. S. M. Dubnow, *The History of the Jews in Russia and Poland,* Jewish Publication Society of America, 1916.
7. Writing in the *Encyclopaedia Judaica*.
8. Colossians, 3:11.
9. Modern western Jews classify themselves either as Ashkenazim, who originally lived in Ashkenaz, Germany, and Sephardim, who—before they were expelled in 1492—inhabited Sepharad, Spain. We know from inscriptions that Sepharad, as used in the biblical book of Obadiah, originally meant the region around Sardis, capital of Lydia in Asia Minor. In the first centuries of the Christian era the name was applied to other settlements, like the Greek colonies north of the Black Sea, founded by Lydian emigrants, and was only transferred to Iberia after the Muslim conquest.
   The name Ashkenaz, on the other hand, refers in the Bible to an ancient

people that the book of Genesis traces back to a son of Gomer, who was in turn a grandson of Noah. "Now these are the generations of the sons of Noah, Shem, Ham, and Japheth . . . The sons of Japheth were Gomer, Magog, Madai, Javan, Tubal, Meshech and Tiras. And the sons of Gomer were Ashkenaz, Riphath and Togarmah." God incites the Ashkenaz, among others, to arms against Babylon, commanding in the Book of Jeremiah: "call together against her the kingdoms of Ararat, Minni, and Ashkenaz."

The application of the name Ashkenaz to Germany and its Jews, dating from the eleventh century onwards, has in the past defied a believable explanation. Recent linguistic and historical analysis, however, has established that the biblical Gomer represented the Cimmerians, a nomadic Iranian people who once controlled the western end of the Eurasian steppe and were dispersed around 500 BCE—possibly leaving their name to the peninsula still called Crimea. They were expelled and absorbed by their kinsmen and successors—hence "sons of Gomer"—the Scythians, also an Iranian people, originally called in Semitic *a-Shkuz* (the Skyths), but misread or miscopied by a later scribe as *a-Shkenaz* as the letters "u" ו and "n" נ look much alike in Hebrew. Thus אשכנז instead of אשכוז. Assyrian and other ancient texts describing the geopolitics of the time show that Jeremiah's kingdoms of Ararat, Minni and Ashkenaz originally referred to Urartu (now in Kurdistan), Armenia and Scythia, but the true meanings of the names were lost with the passage of time. Where and when, during the first post-Christian millennium, eastern European Jewry came to be labelled with the Hebrew name of their Scythian neighbours on the Black Sea steppe is unknown, but ever since then it has been Ashkenazi, Scythian, Jews who were associated with that part of eastern Europe which ancient and medieval geographers called Scythia, as if recognising the importance of the steppe nomads to the dispersal of Jews across the eastern half of the European subcontinent.

10. *The Itinerary of Benjamin of Tudela,* Critical Text, translation and commentary by Marcus Adler, OUP, 1907.

11. Quoted in Paul Wexler, *The Ashkenazic Jews: A Slavo-Turkic People in Search of a Jewish Identity,* Slavica Publishers Inc., 1993.

12. Quoted in Kevin Allen Brook, *The Jews of Khazaria,* Jason Aronson Inc., 1999.

13. Arthur Koestler, *The Thirteenth Tribe,* Hutchinson & Co., 1976.

14. Ibid.

15. Dunash Ibn Labrat (*c.*920–*c.*90).

16. Quoted in Brook, *The Jews of Khazaria.*

17. Quoted in Aleksander Gieysztor, "Beginnings of Jewish settlement in Poland," in *The Jews in Poland,* eds. Abramsky, Jachimczyk and Polonsky, Blackwell, 1986.

18. The *Salzburger Formellsammlung.*

19. Koestler, *The Thirteenth Tribe.*

20. Small leather boxes containing passages of scripture, bound by straps on to the

left arm and forehead during all morning services other than on the Sabbath and holidays.

21. *Encyclopaedia Judaica.*
22. Brook, *The Jews of Khazaria.*
23. Norman Davies, *God's Playground, a History of Poland,* vol. 1, OUP, 1981.
24. W. Reddaway (ed.), *The Cambridge History of Poland,* CUP, 1941–50 (quoted in Davies).
25. *Al-Masalik wa-al-Mamalik* by the Arab geographer al-Bakri (died 1074).
26. Even Adolf Hitler, in spite of his psychotically racist anti-Semitism, wrote in his political testament shortly before his welcome end, "We speak of the Jewish race only as a linguistic convenience, for in the true sense of the word, and from a genetic standpoint, there is no Jewish race . . . The Jewish race is above all a community of the spirit." *Adolf Hitler, Politisches Testament: Die Bormann-Diktate,* February and April 1945 (published Hamburg, 1981).

4

The Remaking of Western Europe

1. Massimo Livi-Bacci, *A Concise History of World Population,* Blackwell, 1997.
2. A. Fitzgerald, *The Letters of Synesius of Cyrene,* London, 1926.
3. In David Hackett Fischer, *The Great Wave, Price Revolutions and the Rhythm of History,* OUP, 1996.
4. James William Brodman, *Ransoming Captives in Crusader Spain,* University of Pennsylvania Press, 1986.
5. A. Mitchell Innes, "What is Money?," *Banking Law Journal,* May 1913.
6. Doris Stenton, *English Society in the Early Middle Ages,* Penguin Books, 1951.
7. Bishop Agila quoted in Gregory of Tours, *Historia Francorum.*
8. Cassiodorus, *Variae,* book 2.
9. Adolf Helfferich, *Westgothischer Arianismus und die Spanische Ketzergeschichte,* Springer, Berlin, 1860.
10. *Encyclopaedia Judaica.*
11. *Gesta Caroli Magni ad Carcassonam et Naribonam,* Philomena, in the Codex Laurentianus of Florence, dating from the ninth century.
12. Dr. Bernhard Blumenkrantz of the Centre Nationale de la Recherche Scientifique in Paris, quoting Gustave Saige, *Histoire des Juifs du Languedoc antérieur au XIVe siècle,* Paris, 1881.
13. Quoted in the *Jewish Encyclopedia.*
14. John Peckham in Gilbert Dahan, *Les intellectuels chrétiens et les juifs au moyen âge,* Cerf, Paris, 1990.
15. John Geipel, *Mame Loshn, The Making of Yiddish,* Journeyman Press, 1982.
16. "Matzref le-Hokhmah" (the Crucible of Wisdom), translation adapted from *Encyclopaedia Judaica.*

17. Bishop of Speyer: Grant of Lands and Privileges to the Jews, 1084.
18. The other is Levi ben Gershom, known as Gersonides.
19. Stephen E. Sachs, *The "Countinghouse Theory" and the Medieval Revival of Arithmetic,* http://www.stevesachs.com/papers/paper_90a.html
20. *The History of Accounting—An International Encyclopedia,* New York and London, 1996.
21. "Whan that Aprille with his shoures soote, The droghte of March hath perced to the roote . . . Thanne longen folk to goon on pilgrimages."
22. According to a witness, Fulcher of Chartres, in his *History of the Expedition to Jerusalem.*
23. Mainz Anonymous.
24. Ibid.
25. Bachrach, *Jews in Barbarian Europe.*
26. Writing in the *Encyclopaedia Judaica.*
27. G. G. Coulton, *The Medieval Village,* CUP, 1925.
28. Ibid.
29. Ibid.
30. Ibid.
31. *Shir Yedidoth,* Song of Friendship, Cracow, 1644.
32. *Sefer Chassidim.*
33. Fischer, *The Great Wave.*
34. Responsum by Rabbi Israel ben Chayyim of Bruna (*c.*1400–80).
35. Letter dated *c.*1200, by Rabbi Eliezer ben Yitzchak of Bohemia, quoted in Brook, *The Jews of Khazaria.*
36. Quoted in Wexler, *The Ashkenazic Jews.*

5

At the Crossroads

1. Israel Abrahams, *Jewish Life in the Middle Ages,* Jewish Publication Society of America, 1896, quoting Joseph Wertheimer's *Jahrbuch für Israeliten* (*Yearbook for Jews*), published in 1856.
2. Abrahams, *Jewish Life in the Middle Ages.*
3. Baron, *A Social and Religious History of the Jews.*
4. http://www.metmuseum.org/works_of_art/viewone.asp?dep=9&item=26.72.68
5. Abrahams, *Jewish Life in the Middle Ages.*
6. Davies, *God's Playground.*
7. Ibid.
8. *Encyclopaedia Britannica.*
9. *Encyclopaedia Judaica.*
10. Robert D. King, "Migration and Linguistics as Illustrated by Yiddish," in

Reconstructing Languages and Cultures, eds. Edgar C. Polemé and Werner Winter, Mouton de Gruyter, 1992.

11. C. Roth and I. H. Levine (eds.), *The Dark Ages, Jews and Christian Europe 711–1096,* New Brunswick, NJ, 1966.

12. Baron, *A Social and Religious History of the Jews.*

13. *Sefer Chassidim.*

14. "A woman must not put on men's clothing and a man shall not wear women's clothing," Deuteronomy, 22:5.

15. Tractate Bava Batra, 10a.

16. By a synod convened in Germany around 1220, says the *Encyclopaedia Judaica.*

17. In Bachrach, *Jews in Barbarian Europe.*

18. http://www.panorama-miast.com.pl/33/html/wloclawek.htm

19. Quoted in James Buchan, *Frozen Desire, an Inquiry into the Meaning of Money,* Picador, 1997.

20. Fischer, *The Great Wave.*

21. Isidore Loeb, "Réflections sur les Juifs," in the *Revue des Études Juives,* 1891.

6

The New Yiddish World

1. The late Dr. Basil Greenhill, Director of the Greenwich Maritime Museum, *Dreams, Realities, Montages,* BBC Radio 3, 21 November 1983.

2. *Sefer Chassidim.*

3. Rabbi Israel ben Hayyim Bruna, "Teshuvot Mahari Brunna 71," from Avraham Yaakov Finkel, *The Responsa Anthology,* Jason Aronson Inc., 1990.

4. "*Le cour est une mer, dont sourt / Vagues d'orgueil, d'envie orages . . . / Ire esmeut debats et outrages, / Qui les nefs jettent souvent bas: / Traison y fait son personage. / Nage aultre part pour tes ebats.*" Quoted in Huizinga, *The Waning of the Middle Ages.*

5. Roger of Hoveden, *The Annals, comprising The History of England and of Other Countries of Europe from AD 732 to AD 1201,* translated by Henry Riley, H. G. Bohn, London, 1853.

6. "*O Fortuna*
   velut luna statu variabilis
   semper crescis aut decrescis;
   vita detestabilis nunc obdurat
   et tunc curat ludo mentis aciem,
   egestatem, potestatem
   dissolvit ut glaciem."

7. "Thou shalt not seethe a kid in his mother's milk," Exodus, 23:19, 34:26, Deuteronomy, 14:21.

8. "Neither shall a garment mingled of linen and woollen come upon thee," Leviticus, 19:19. The material is called linsey-woolsey in English, and was probably the original meaning (French: *tiretaine*: "a kind of cloth, half wool, half linen," *OED*) of the word tartan.

9. Stated in Wexler, *The Ashkenazic Jews*.

10. Source: http://www.heraldica.org/topics/jewish.htm

11. Davies, *God's Playground*.

12. http://www.backtowhen.com/pages/tudor_and_historical_goods/jewellery/pilgrim_badges/

13. *Encyclopaedia Judaica*.

14. "*A shprakh iz a diyalekt mit an armey un a flot*," stated in the 1945 article "Der yivo un di problemen fun undzer tsayt" (*Yivo* and the problems of our time) in the periodical *Yivo-bleter* (Yivo pages) 25.1.13. YIVO stands for "Yiddisher Vissenshaftlicher Institut": Yiddish Scientific Institute.

15. In Wexler, *The Ashkenazic Jews*.

16. Peter Wapnewski, "Über die Miniatur des Süezkint im Codex Manesse," *ZEITmagazin*, Hamburg, 1988.

17. "*Ich var ûf der tôren vart*
    mit mîner künste zwâre,
    daz mir die herren nicht went geben.
    des ich ir hof wil fliehen
    und wil mir einen langen bart
    lân wachsen grîser hâre:
    ich wil in alter juden leben
    mich hinnân fürwert ziehen.
    mîn mantel der sol wesen lanc,
    tief under einem huote,
    dêmüeteclich sol sîn mîn ganc
    und selten mê ich singe in hovelîchen sanc,
    sîd mich die herren scheiden von ir guote."

18. Dietrich Gerhardt, *Süsskind von Trimberg*, Peter Lang, 1997.

19. The *Melochim Buch*.

20. The *Shmuel Buch*.

21. Song of Songs. 3:11.

22. *Shloyshe She'orim* (*The Three Gates*), by Sore bas Tovim (Sarah daughter of the Good Ones), probably the pseudonym of a man.

23. *Encyclopaedia Judaica*.

24. Martin Przybilski, *Spuren des Kulturtransfers zwischen Juden und Christen in der deutschen Literatur des Hoch- und Spätmittelalters (Habilitationsprojekt)*, University of Würzburg, 2001.

25. Taken from the English "Sir Bewes of Hamptoun" and ultimately derived from the Anglo-Norman "Boeve de Haumtone."

26. *"Drum libe hern ir solt schouen*
    Was umglik kumt fun den besen weibn,
    Seht was Schlome HaMelech buchr schrejbn,
    Wie er sucht ein frou ein rejne,
    Un al sejn tag fand er ni kejne."

27. Genesis, 49.9.

28. A theme repeated by Rabbi Yomtov Lipmann Muelhausen, appointed *Judex Judaeorum* of Prague in 1407: "Deceive none, either Jew or non-Jew."

29. *Sefer Chasidim,* translated by Avraham Yaakov Finkel, Jason Aronson Inc., 1997.

30. *Encyclopaedia Judaica.*

31. *"Brengt der shadkhn mir a khosn*
    An Oysnam fun ale.
    Heyst er Vladek, nor a tsore—
    Vladeks mame heyst oykh Sore,
    Punkt vi ikh, zayn kale—
    Oy, vil zi nisht di kale."
    From Eleanor Gordon Mlotek, *Mir Trogn a Gezang, Favourite Yiddish Songs of Our Generation,* 5th edition 1989, published by the Workmen's Circle Education Department.

32. Slavery was abolished in Poland in the fifteenth century and in Lithuania in 1588. In Russia agricultural slaves were converted into serfs in 1679, but household slaves not until 1723.

33. Synod of Breslau: *"quum adhuc Terra Polonica sit in corpore christianitatis nova plantatio, ne forte eo facilius populus christianus a cohabitantium Iudeorum superstitionibus et pravis moribus inficiatur."*

34. *Encyclopaedia Judaica.*

35. Report by V. A. Dymshits at http://judaica.spb.ru/artcl/a2/Azer_e.shtml

36. Solomon ben Jehiel Luria (*c.*1510–74), the *Maharshal.*

37. Abrahams, *Jewish Life in the Middle Ages.*

38. Noted by Abraham ben Meir de Balmes (*c.*1440–1523), physician, philosopher, translator and grammarian in his book *Mikneh Avram,* Latin: *Peculium Abrae* (*Abraham's Property*).

39. Tractate Megillah, 32b.

40. Known in Yiddish as *gemore nign* (Gemara tune).

41. Professor Chaim Ben-Sasson of the Hebrew University of Jerusalem in the *Encyclopaedia Judaica.*

42. Talmud, Baba Metzia, 33a.

43. *Mizbeach haZahav* (*The Golden Altar*), Rabbi Shlomo ben Mordechai of Merezich (sixteenth-century student of the *Maharshal*).

44. Rabbi Yosef Haan of Frankfurt quoted in Rabbi Mordechai Breuer, *The Study*

of *Tanach in the Yeshiva Curriculum,* Studies Presented to Moshe Arend, Jerusalem, 1996.

45. *Orchot Zaddikim.*

7

Political Consolidation

1. Barbara Tuchman, *A Distant Mirror: The Calamitous Fourteenth Century,* Random House, 1978.
2. Flemish chronicler Johannes de Beka.
3. Fischer, *The Great Wave.*
4. *Jewish Encyclopedia.*
5. Tuchman, *A Distant Mirror.*
6. Claudia Roden, *The Book of Jewish Food: An Odyssey from Samarkand to New York,* Knopf, 1996.
7. Hebrew: *Bes Chatanes.*
8. Proverbs, 11:21.
9. Abrahams, *Jewish Life in the Middle Ages.*
10. Morenu ha-Rav Shelomo Luria (Our teacher the Rabbi Solomon Luria).
11. Myer S. Lew, *The Jews of Poland: Their Political, Economic, Social and Communal Life in the Sixteenth Century as Reflected in the Works of Rabbi Moses Isserles,* E. Goldston, London, 1944.
12. *Encyclopaedia Judaica.*
13. References in Brook, *The Jews of Khazaria.*
14. Andres Bernaldez, *Historia de los Reyes Católicos.*
15. "Anthropological Structure of the Jewish People in the Light of Polish Analyses," *Jewish Journal of Sociology,* 1960.
16. In his "Letter to the English," quoted in *Encyclopaedia Judaica.*
17. Coulton, *The Medieval Village.*
18. Davies, *God's Playground,* vol. 1.
19. Myer S. Lew, *The Jews of Poland.*
20. *Encyclopaedia Judaica.*
21. Nathan Hannover, "Yeven Matsulah" (The Deep Mire), quoted in Abrahams, *Jewish Life in the Middle Ages.*
22. Ibid.
23. *Jewish Encyclopedia.*
24. *Encyclopaedia Judaica.*
25. Rashi: responsa no. 159.
26. *Encyclopaedia Judaica.*
27. English State Papers.

28. Quoted in Natalie Zemon Davis, *Women on the Margins, Three Seventeenth Century Lives*, Harvard University Press, 1995.
29. *Wer ein Jude ist, das bestimme ich.*
30. Published with a French translation in *Revue des Études Juives,* 1888.

8

The Reformation

1. *Darkhei ha-Nikkud ve-ha-Neginot* (*The Ways of Punctuation and Accentuation*).
2. Hebrew: *Berechiah Natronai ha-Nakdan,* French: *Benedictus le Puncteur.*
3. The *Quaestiones Naturales.*
4. In Hebrew *Mishlei Shu'alim.*
5. The *Anglo-Saxon Chronicle.*
6. The last full blood-libel trial was the Beilis affair, initiated by the czarist authorities of Kiev in 1911, while the 1946 Kielce pogrom in Poland, when a mob dragged forty-two Holocaust survivors out of their hostel and beat them to death in the street, was the result of a seven-year-old called Henryk, afraid of getting into trouble for having run away from home, claiming that he had escaped from the clutches of a Jew who had abducted him and intended to draw off his blood. (Some ten years ago, an American rabbi, a relative of one of those who died, visited Henryk at his home. He was received courteously and the two spent an hour talking about those fifty-year-old events. At the end of their conversation, the rabbi asked Henryk, "Do you realise that everything which happened was the result of the lie you told?" "So it seems," Henryk said, and shrugged.
7. John Wycliffe, *Speculum Secularium Dominorum, Opera Minora,* ed. John Loserth, Wycliffe Society, London, 1913, p. 74; cited in the introduction to the *Wycliffe New Testament.*
8. "For it is made that all people should know it," from the preface to Wycliffe's English Bible.
9. Vojtech Rankuv of Jesova, otherwise known as the Magister Adalbertus Rankonis de Ericinio.
10. *Encyclopaedia Judaica.*
11. By a writer unnamed in both Baron and the *Encyclopaedia Judaica.*
12. From the contemporary *Articuli et errores Taboritorum,* an anti-Taborite tract, quoted in Norman Cohn, *The Pursuit of the Millennium,* Secker & Warburg, 1957.
13. David Gans in *Tsemach Dovid.*
14. *Věstník židovských náboženských obcí v československu* (*Guide to Jewish religious communities in Czechoslovakia*) no. 11, 1949.
15. Baron, *A Social and Religious History of the Jews.*

16. H. H. Ben-Sasson, "The Reformation in Contemporary Jewish Eyes," Proceedings of the Israeli Academy of Sciences and Humanities, 4, 1970.

17. Sebastian Franck, *Chronik, Geschichte und Zeitbuch aller Sachen und Handlungen*, 1531.

18. I. Kracauer, "Rabbi Joselmann De Rosheym," in *Revue des Études Juives* 16, Paris, 1888.

19. *Wider die räuberischen und mörderischen Rotten der Bauern.*

20. *Der gantz Jüdisch glaub.*

21. *Von den Juden und ihre Lügen.*

22. *Vom Schem Hamphoras und vom Geschlecht Christi.*

23. *Eine Vermahnung wider die Juden.*

24. Arraigned before the International War Crimes Tribunal in Nuremberg, Julius Streicher said, "In his book *On the Jews and Their Lies* Dr. Martin Luther wrote that the Jews are a nest of snakes. Their synagogues should be burned down and they should be destroyed. That is exactly what we did."

25. When in 1936 German Lutheran pastors protested to Hitler about the mistreatment of the Jews, they were given short shrift: "What are you complaining about? I am only following what you have been teaching for centuries."

26. Repeated in an often quoted exhortation by Spanish Rabbi Moses ben Nachman, known as Nachmanides or Ramban (1194–1270): *Tisnaheig tomid ledabeir kol devorecho benachas lechol odom uvechol eis, uvezeh tinotzeil min haka'as* (Always speak calmly to everyone and you will be saved from anger).

27. *Ad quaestiones et obiecta Judaei cuiusdam Responsio.*

28. Richard Stauffer, *The Humanness of John Calvin*, translated by George Shriver, Abingdon Press, 1971.

29. Speech to the House of Lords, 19 May 1772.

30. S. A. Bershadski, "Saul Wahl, Yevrei Korol Polski," in *Voskhod*, 1889.

31. Saul Judisch was the son of Rabbi Katzenellenbogen of Padua.

9

The Yiddish Renaissance

1. Fischer, *The Great Wave.*

2. Quoted in Ben-Sasson (ed.), *A History of the Jewish People.*

3. *Jewish Encyclopedia.*

4. Ibid.

5. Rabbi Samuel Adels in Lew, *The Jews of Poland.*

6. Quotes from Elchanan Reiner, "The Attitude of Ashkenazi Society to the New Science in the Sixteenth Century," *Science in Context*, vol. 10:4, 1997.

7. Ibid.

8. *Yesh Nochalin.*

9. *Khochmah yavanit* in the Talmud.
10. *Tsemach Dovid* (*The Shoot of David*).
11. Cecil Roth, *The Jews in the Renaissance*, Harper & Row, 1959.
12. *Tractatus de duabus Sarmatiis*, 1517.
13. In his poem "Devorekho be-Mor Over Rekuhim."
14. All quoted in Reiner, "The Attitude of Ashkenazi Society to the New Science in the Sixteenth Century."
15. "History of the Talmud," in *The Babylonian Talmud*, translated by Michael L. Rodkinson, 1918.
16. Rabbi Jedaiah ben Abraham Bedersi, *Iggereth Hinatzelut*.
17. *Me'il Tsedakah* (*The Robe of Righteousness*).
18. Glenys Patterson, *The University: From Ancient Greece to the 20th Century*, Dunmore Press, 1997.
19. The thirty-third day—in Hebrew numerals ל״ג, "lg," hence *lag*—of the Omer, the period of seven weeks between Passover and Pentecost (Leviticus, 16:9). This is the only day on which—like *Mi-carême* during Catholic Lent—traditional mourning customs are suspended. It is a favourite day for weddings.
20. Rabbi Moses Isserles, the "I" being the Hebrew Aleph, א, a mute consonant which can carry any vowel.
21. Paper presented at a conference on "Tradition and crisis revisited," Harvard University, October 1988.
22. *Torat ha-Olah.*
23. Hebrew: *Mahalloch ha-cochavim.*
24. Hebrew: *hokrim be-tiviot.*
25. Hugh Trevor-Roper, *Princes and Artists, Patronage and Ideology at Four Hapsburg Courts, 1517–1633*, Thames & Hudson, 1991.
26. *An itinerary vvritten by Fynes Moryson Gent. first in the Latine tongue, and then translated by him into English: containing his ten yeeres travell throvgh the tvvelve domjnions of Germany, Bohmerland, Sweitzerland, Netherland, Denmarke, Poland, Jtaly, Turky, France, England, Scotland, and Ireland*, London, John Beale, 1617 (modern edition: Glasgow: James MacLehose & Sons, 1907–8).
27. Morenu (our teacher) Ha-Rav (the Rabbi) Liwa (Loew).
28. "Jewish Thought and Scientific Discovery in Early Modern Europe," *Journal of the History of Ideas*, 1997.
29. *Be'er ha-Golah.*
30. Ibid.
31. *He-Chassid Morenu Dovid Gans ba'al Tsemach Dovid.*
32. André Neher, *David Gans, disciple du Maharal de Prague, assistant de Tycho Brahe et de Jean Kepler*, Klincksieck, 1974, translated by David Maisel as *Jewish Thought and the Scientific Revolution of the Sixteenth Century*, OUP, 1986.
33. *Nechmad ve-Na'im.*

34. "Irenism and Natural Philosophy in Rudolfine Prague," *Science in Context,* 1997.
35. Gans, *Tsemach Dovid.*
36. Johann Cristoph Friedrich von Schiller, *The History of the Thirty Years' War,* translated by A. J. W. Morrison.

10

Wide Horizons

1. Davies, *God's Playground.*
2. Ibid.
3. Norman Davies, *The Heart of Europe,* OUP, 1986.
4. Maria Cholewo-Flandrin (ed.), *La Pologne de XVIIIe siècle vue par un precepteur Français, Huber Vautrin,* Paris, 1966.
5. *Encyclopaedia Judaica.*
6. *The Memoirs of Glückel of Hameln,* translated with notes by Marvin Lowenthal, Schocken Books, 1977.
7. Ibid.
8. "Rabbah said, 'When one stands at the judgement-seat of God, these questions are asked: Hast thou been honest in all thy dealings? Hast thou set aside a portion of thy time for the study of Torah? Hast thou observed the First Commandment [Thou shalt have no other gods before me]? Hast thou, in trouble, still hoped and believed in God? Hast thou spoken wisely?'" Talmud, Tractate Shabbat, 31a.
9. Eli Barnavi (ed.), *A Historical Atlas of the Jewish People,* Schocken Books, 1995.
10. "An examination of the idea of Jewish space in the life (1646–1724) of a female German Jewish merchant," in *A Historical Atlas of the Jewish People.*

11

The Deluge

1. Noted in Fischer, *The Great Wave.*
2. Herbert Langer, *The Thirty Years' War,* translated by C. S. V. Salt, Blandford Press, 1980.
3. *Ogniem i mieczem.*
4. Henryk Sienkiewicz, *With Fire and Sword: A Tale of the Past,* vol. 1, Fredonia Books, 2002.
5. Hippocrene Books, 1991.
6. Dubnow, *History of the Jews in Russia and Poland.*

7. Ibid.
8. Guillaume Le Vasseur de Beauplan, *La description d'Ukranie,* Rouen, 1650.
9. *Encyclopaedia Judaica.*
10. Paul Magocsi, *A History of the Ukraine,* University of Washington Press, 1996.
11. Davies, *God's Playground.*
12. Jacob R. Marcus, *The Jew in the Medieval World,* Harper & Row, 1965.
13. Nathan Hannover.
14. *Litopys Samovydtsia.*
15. Shabbetai ben Meir ha-Kohen, *Megillah Afah.*
16. Ibid.
17. Ibid.
18. *Les Cosaques d'Autrefois.*
19. *Encyclopaedia Judaica.*
20. Fischer, *The Great Wave.*
21. Moshe Rosman, "The Indebtedness of the Lublin Kahal in the 18th Century," A. Teller (ed.), *Studies in the History of the Jews in Old Poland in Honor of Jacob Goldberg, Scripta Hierosolymitana,* vol. 38, Magnus Press, Hebrew University of Jerusalem, 1998.
22. *Encyclopaedia Judaica.*
23. Ibid.
24. Nathan Hannover.
25. Hillel ben Ze'ev Wolf, *Hellel ben Shachar* (Venus, the morning star).

12

Decline . . .

1. Mlotek, *Mir Trogen a Gezang.*
2. Though cognate with "Rabbi," the title "Rebbe" in Yiddish is usually reserved for a Chassidic leader, while non-Chassidim are called "Rov."
3. Adonai, Morenu ve-Rabbi.
4. A city of many names: Latin Lemburga, Greek Leopolis, Polish Lwów, Russian and Czech Lvov, Italian Leopoli, even occasionally Levensburg.
5. *Pidyoynes.*
6. "'Money for Household Expenses': Economic Aspects of the Chassidic Courts," by Dr. David Assaf of Tel Aviv University, *Scripta Hierosolymitana,* vol. 38; Teller (ed.), *Studies in the History of the Jews in Old Poland.*
7. ל"ו (*Lamed Vov*) Tsaddikim.
8. *Encyclopaedia Judaica.*
9. Abraham Nathan ben Elisha Hayyim Ashkenazi.
10. Presumably because the three sixes in the date related to the number 666, with its eschatological meaning derived from the biblical Book of Revelation, 13:18:

"Let him that hath understanding count the number of the beast: for it is the number of a man; and his number is six hundred threescore and six."

11. Entry for 19 February 1666.

12. Harris Lenowitz, *The Jewish Messiahs: From the Galilee to Crown Heights*, OUP, 1998.

13. Proverbs, 18:10: "The name of the Lord is a Strong Tower: the righteous runneth into it, and is safe."

14. Lenowitz, *The Jewish Messiahs*.

15. Harvey Sarner, *Rescue in Albania: One Hundred Percent of Jews in Albania Rescued from Holocaust*, Brunswick Press, 1997.

16. *Encyclopaedia Judaica*.

17. Heinrich Graetz, *Popular History of the Jews*, 1889.

18. Translated from Haim Hillel Ben-Sasson, *Geschichte des Jüdischen Volkes*, Munich, 1980.

19. *Pinkas Hakehilot, Encyclopedia of Jewish Communities, Poland*, vol. 4, *Warsaw and District*, Yad Vashem, Jerusalem, 1989.

20. *Kabbalah Iyyunit*.

21. *Kabbalah Ma'asit*.

22. Gershom Sholem, *Kabbalah*, Hippocrene Books, 1988.

23. *Shivchei ha-Besht*.

24. Josef Perl (ed.), *Über das Wesen der Sekte Chassidim*, A. Rubinstein, Jerusalem, 1977.

25. In Joseph ben Meir Teomim, *Nofet Tsufim Ray Peninim* (*The Honeycombs' Flow, Many Pearls*), 1772.

26. *Encyclopaedia Judaica*.

27. *Todedot Ya'akov Josef* (*The Annals of Jacob Joseph*).

28. Shabbetai of Raschkow.

29. Referred to in the seventeenth Sura of the Qur'an, which is about God's punishment of the Children of Israel for disobedience.

30. *Toledot Ya'akov Yosef*.

31. Known as *Hozeh MiLublin*.

32. Peretz's address to the 1908 Czernowitz Language Conference.

33. "*Kum aher, du filosof, mit dayn ketsishn meykhl.*
    Oy kum aher tsum rebns tish und lern a bisl seykhel.
    A dampfshif hostu oysgetrakht und nemst dermit zikh iber;
    Der rebbe shpreyt zayn tikhl oys und shpant dem yam ariber.
    An ayzenban hostu oysgeklert und meynst du bist a khorets;
    Der rebbe spet, der rebbe lakht, er darf dos oyf kapores.
    Tsi veystu den, vos der rebbe tut beys er zitst b'yekhides?
    In eyn minut in himl flit und pravet dort shaleshides."
    Benyiman-Wolf Eherenkranz, 1826–83, writing under the name of Velvl Zbarzher.

34. Ralph Mahler, *Hasidism and the Jewish Enlightenment,* Jewish Publication Society of America, 1985.
35. *Jewish Encyclopedia.*
36. Lawrence Schiffman, "The Selling of the Gaon: Lithuanians Retell History to Approach Jews," *Jewish Sentinel,* October 1997.
37. Ha-Gaon Rabbi Eliyahu.
38. Hayyim of Volozhin, *Sifra de Zeni'uta* (with a commentary by the Vilna Gaon).
39. Rabbi Moses Rivkes, who died in 1672.
40. Jacob Emden and Jonathan Eybeschuetz. In 1751 Eybeschuetz, Chief Rabbi of Hamburg, was accused of writing amulets containing the words, "In the name of Y——H, the God of Israel, who dwelleth in the beauty of His strength, the God of His anointed one Shabbethai Zebi, who with the breath of His lips shall slay the wicked, I decree and command that no evil spirit plague, or accident harm, the bearer of this amulet." The *Encyclopaedia Judaica* says, "While most of the German rabbis opposed Eybeschuetz, his support came from the rabbis of Poland and Moravia."
41. *Tsavva'at ha-Ribash.*
42. Adalbert von Chamisso (1781–1838), *Abba Glusk Leczeka.*
43. By Max (Meir Halevy) Letteris, Austrian scholar and poet.
44. Jacob Emden.
45. Representation of imaginary speakers or actors; attributing life, speech or vitality to an inanimate object.
46. Multiple substitutions of cause for effect.
47. Noun used as a verb or vice versa.
48. Rabbi Elijah ben Solomon, *Derech Chayyim* (*The Road of Life*), Cracow, 1589.
49. Avigdor ben Joseph Hayyim.
50. The title of a famous work of Kabbalah and punning on Chayyim's name.
51. *Encyclopaedia Judaica.*

13

. . . and Fall

1. Johann Philipp Kirnberger (1721–83).
2. Apart from his most famous grandchildren, the composers Felix and Fanny, Moses Mendelssohn's son Joseph was a patron of the great naturalist Alexander von Humboldt, his daughter Dorothea wrote *Florentin,* one of the founding novels of literary romanticism, his daughter Henriette hosted a salon that was attended by the luminaries of the age, his grandsons Johannes and Philipp Veit were important painters of their day, and his grandson Arnold was a

patron of socialist and political philosopher Ferdinand Lasalle. His great-grandsons Franz and Ernst were ennobled.

3. F. Nicolai, "Etwas über den verstorbenen Rektor Damm und Moses Mendelssohn," *Berlinische Monatschrift,* 1783–1811, year 1800, vol. 1, digitised at http://www.ub.uni-bielefeld.de/diglib/aufkl/browse/berlmon/11800.html

4. Johann Kaspar Lavater, *Physiognomische Fragmente zur Beförderung der Menschenkenntniss und Menschenliebe,* Leipzig and Winterthur, 1775, digitised at http://www.newcastle.edu.au/discipline/fine-art/pubs/lavater/

5. Lived 1742–99.

6. *Oleinu leshabeiach la-Adon ha-kol.*

7. Rabbi Moshe ben Menachem Mendel.

8. Graf Rochus Friedrich zu Lynar (who also introduced ice-skating to Prussia).

9. *Encyclopaedia Judaica.*

10. Quoted in Jerry Z. Muller, *The Mind and the Market, Capitalism in Modern European Thought,* Knopf, 2002.

11. As reported in *The Occident and American Jewish Advocate,* 1846.

12. *Encyclopaedia Judaica.*

13. Ibid.

14. Soldiers served six years and were then placed on reserve, sailors seven years. Those with elementary school education served three years, grammar school graduates one year and six months, high school graduates six months. In her memoirs, Golda Meir, fourth prime minister of the State of Israel, recalled that her grandfather had served thirteen years and only just survived.

15. *The I. L. Peretz Reader* (Library of Yiddish Classics), ed. Ruth R. Wisse, Schocken Books, 1996.

16. P. Mendes-Flohr and J. Reinharz (eds.), *The Jew in the Modern World,* Oxford, 1980.

17. *The I. L. Peretz Reader.*

18. *Nor nisht far yidn, nisht zhargon.*
   Keyn rekhtn klang, keyn rekhtn ton,
   Keyn eyntsik vort nit un keyn stil
   Hob ikh far "libe," far 'gefil . . . .
   Undzer yidish hot not vitsn,
   Hot nor dunern un blitsn;
   Zi hot nor verter vi di shpizen.
   In 'im lakhn veynen rizn.
   Zi dresht dos layb vi mit riter;
   Zi iz vi gal, vi pyolun biter . . . .
   Un khotch do lopne oyfn ort,—
   Es hot keyn leblekh, varm vort.
   English translation by J. Leftwich, *The Golden Peacock, A Worldwide Treasury of Yiddish Poetry,* Thomas Yoseloff, 1961.

19. *The Jew in the Modern World.*
20. Joachim Neugroschel (ed. and trans.), *No Star Too Beautiful, an Anthology of Yiddish Stories from 1382 to the Present,* W. W. Norton, 2002.
21. Isaac J. Linetzki, *The Polish Lad,* translated by M. Spiegel, Jewish Publication Society of America, 1975.
22. M. Spektor, *Mayn Lebn (My Life),* Warsaw, 1927.
23. James Harvey Robinson and Charles Beard (eds.), from *Readings in Modern European History,* Boston, Ginn & Co., 1908.
24. Martin Gilbert, *The Jews of Russia,* National Council for Soviet Jewry of the United Kingdom and Ireland, 1976.
25. Konstantin Petrovich Pobedonostsev (1827–1907).
26. "Education," introductory article in *Di Yidishe Bibliotek,* 1891.
27. *Di Geshikhte fun Bund,* New York, 1960.
28. Theodor Herzl, *Der Judenstaat,* 1896.
29. Emanuel S. Goldsmith, *Modern Yiddish Culture, the Story of the Yiddish Language Movement,* Fordham University Press, 1997.
30. Ibid.
31. Joshua A. Fishman (ed.), *Never Say Die! A Thousand Years of Yiddish in Jewish Life and Letters,* Mouton de Gruyter, 1981.
32. Ibid.
33. Co-authors of *The Golden Calf* and *The Twelve Chairs,* filmed in 1970 by Mel Brooks:
    "TIKON   One night, about ten years ago, was a fearful noise. There was bombs and cannons and soldiers shooting, it was terrible, terrible.
    BENDER   Ah, I think that was called the revolution."
34. Dan Miron, *A Traveler Disguised, the Rise of Modern Yiddish Fiction in the Nineteenth Century,* Schocken Books, 1973.
35. Itamar Even-Zohar and Khone Shmeruk, "Authentic Language and Authentic Reported Speech: Hebrew vs Yiddish," *Poetics Today,* 1990.
36. Ibid.
37. "No Prize for History, John Klier reviews Aleksander Solzhenitsyn's recent venture into the history of his native country," *History Today,* November 2002.
38. Auswanderer-Agentur Morris und Co.
39. Hamburg Amerikanische Paketfahrt Aktiengesellschaft.

14

A Winter Flowering

1. George R. Sims, "Sweated London," in *Living London,* George R. Sims (ed.), Cassell, 1901.
2. Solomon L. Ginsburg, *A Wandering Jew in Brazil: An Autobiography,*

Nashville Tennessee Sunday School Board, Southern Baptist Convention, 1922.

3. On the corner with Fournier Street.

4. Israel Zangwill, *Children of the Ghetto: A Study of a Peculiar People*, William Heinemann, 1892.

5. Sims, *Living London*.

6. *The Queen's London: A Pictorial and Descriptive Record of the Streets, Buildings, Parks and Scenery of the Great Metropolis*, 1896.

7. Now Middlesex Street and Wentworth Street.

8. Ruth E., *Memories of the Ruda family*, at http://www.olamgadol.pwp .blueyonder.co.uk/eastendtalk.html

9. David Mazower, *Yiddish Theatre in London*, Museum of the Jewish East End, 1987.

10. H. Chance Newton, "Music-Hall London," in *Living London*.

11. Mazower, *Yiddish Theatre in London*.

12. In his review of *London Jews and British Communism 1935–45* by Henry Felix Srebrnik at http://lesl.man.ac.uk/chnn/CHNN03LJB.html

13. *Jewish Chronicle*, 26 March 1880.

14. A card game also known as Klobiosh, Klabberjass, Bela and Belote.

15. Louis Gilrod, Arnold Perlmutter and Herman Wohl, "Leb'n zol Columbus," © 1918, Joneil Music Co., Carlstadt, NJ, given in *Mir Trogn a Gesang*.

16. Italo Calvino, *The Hermit in Paris*, Pantheon Books, 2004.

17. Anchor Books, 1989.

18. "Yiddish Lit, Close To Home," *The Jewish Week*, New York, 4 July 2003.

19. Josephine Bacon, writer, translator and historian of Jewish food. Among many other books she is the translator and publisher of Edouard de Pomiane, *The Jews of Poland, Recollections and Recipes*, Pholiota, 1985.

20. *Aunt Babette's Cook Book: Foreign and Domestic Receipts for the Household: A Valuable Collection of Receipts and Hints for the Housewife, Many of Which Are Not to be Found Elsewhere*, Bloch Pub. and Print Co., Cincinnati, 1889. The expensive Hamburg Steak that appeared on a printed Delmonico's restaurant menu in 1834 seems to have been a different dish: steak tartare.

21. Exodus 12:39.

Bibliography

Encyclopaedias

Jewish history is well served by encyclopaedias. My major sources were the *Encyclopaedia Judaica*, CD ROM Edition, Judaica Multimedia (Israel) Ltd., 1997, and the *Jewish Encyclopedia*, published between 1901 and 1906, and generously made available on the World Wide Web at http:// www.jewishencyclopedia.com by the Kopelman Foundation. Also consulted were the *Vallentine's Jewish Encyclopaedia*, published by Shapiro, Vallentine & Co., 1950, and the *Encyclopedia of Jewish History*, English edition published by Facts on File Inc., 1986.

Works of History

The canonical works of general Jewish history proved disappointing in their lack of attention to eastern Europe during the earlier medieval period.

Heinrich Graetz (1817–91), rabbi and Ph.D., the founder of the genre, was the first scholar to embark on a new kind of non-theological study of Jewish history. His German-language *Popular History of the Jews* (*Volkstümliche Geschichte der Juden*), abridged from a massive eleven-volume masterwork, was first published in 1889 and became a huge success, remaining in print and in translation until the 1930s—six volumes, translated by Rabbi A. B. Rhine, edited by Alexander Harkavy, published by the Hebrew Publishing Company, New York. Graetz's great theme was the unique messianic destiny of the Jews, "whose soul is the Torah and whose body is the Holy Land," their struggle for survival, the tragedy of their exile, and the suffering of their martyrs at the hands of their cruel enemies and persecutors. Under his pen history becomes a very depressing affair. One wonders how a people subject to such oppression managed to flourish so mightily in the eastern European lands. Unfortunately, though born hardly sixty miles from

Posen, seat of Poland's most venerable Jewish community, he had no interest in the Jews of the Slav world, and though he opposed liberal reform of the Synagogue liturgy, expressed nothing but contempt for what he called "the fossilized Polish Talmudists," with their ridiculous gibberish of a Yiddish language.

The next important milestone in Jewish history writing was the work of the Belorusian-born Jewish nationalist Shimon Dubnow (1860–1941). Non-religious, self-taught ("at the home university"), a journalist and a teacher, Dubnow took the opposite tack to Graetz and saw Jews as a people formed by their exile. In his *History of the Jews in Russia and Poland,* published by the Jewish Publication Society of America in 1916, he argued that the history of the Jews was a story of successive centres of culture, each in turn taking over from the last. So, after the original Palestinian homeland was destroyed, Babylon became the focus of Jewish life in the early Middle Ages, to be followed by Spain and then the Rhineland. From the late Middle Ages and the beginning of modern times it was Poland and Lithuania that received top billing, while in the next period of Jewish history, the starring role would be taken by the Russian-Polish centre. The Jews of the following centuries, he believed, would be Yiddish-speaking and definitely non-religious—a model for all the other nations to be incorporated into the multi-ethnic states of the future. Yet he still devotes fewer than thirty pages, in a work totalling well over a thousand, to the first three or four centuries of Polish-Lithuanian-Jewish history.

Tragically, Dubnow's dreams were demolished by the Nazis. He was killed in his eighty-second year during the Nazi deportation of the Jews of Riga in Latvia, where he had sought refuge from Berlin—by a Gestapo officer said to have been one of his former students.

Salo Wittmayer Baron (1895–1989), a Viennese-American ordained rabbi as well as a highly respected historian, was the first member of an American university faculty to teach Jewish studies. Baron carried his ideology much more lightly than his predecessors, stressing the importance to the future of both the newly re-created Land of Israel as well as the diaspora. Yet his monumental and exhaustive seventeen-volume *Social and Religious History of the Jews,* published by Columbia University Press between 1952 and 1980, devotes no more than thirty pages to the total early history of the whole of eastern Europe. Admittedly, he followed it soon after with an entire volume on Poland and Lithuania—but only between the years 1500 to 1650.

Max Margolis (1886–1932) and Alexander Marx (1878–1953) produced their one-volume *History of the Jewish People* in 1927 (Jewish Publication Society of America, Philadelphia), with new printings for twenty more years. Though concise and clear, the work's 737 pages are too limited in their scope to afford much of a picture of the life of the Jews in the Yiddish *heym.*

Cecil Bezalel Roth (1899–1970), doyen of British Jewish historians, belonged to a more English Whig school of history writing, in the tradition of Macaulay, treating Jewish history as if it were a long run-up to the founding of the State of Israel, where he spent much of the last part of his life—for the rest he lived in New York. He wrote brilliantly of the Jews of England, of Italy and of Spain, and even of the Dead Sea Scrolls, but Poland and Lithuania didn't interest him much, even though his family name suggests that, not too many generations earlier, his own antecedents must have come from Germany or further east.

Of the latest generation, the most prolific has been Sir Martin Gilbert (born 1936). In between writing his gigantic biography of Winston Churchill—some ten million words in eight volumes, of the last of which one reviewer said "four inches thick, 1,348 pages long, a book you would be ill-advised to drop on your foot" (Richard M. Langworth, Proceedings of the International Churchill Societies 1990–1)—he has somehow found time to author a steady and apparently unending stream of works on Jewish history. But even Sir Martin's voluminous output has had little to say about the first six centuries of Jewish life in eastern Europe.

Other Works Consulted

Abrahams, Israel, *Jewish Life in the Middle Ages,* Jewish Publication Society, 1993.

Adler, Elkan Nathan (ed.), *Jewish Travellers in the Middle Ages,* Dover, 1987.

Ascherson, Neal, *Black Sea,* Jonathan Cape, 1995.

Bermant, Chaim, *The Jews,* Weidenfeld & Nicolson, 1977.

Brook, Kevin Allen, *The Jews of Khazaria,* Jason Aronson, 1999.

Browne, Lewis (ed.), *The Wisdom of Israel,* Michael Joseph, 1955.

Cantor, Norman, *The Sacred Chain, A History of the Jews,* HarperCollins, 1995.

Cohen, Abraham, *Everyman's Talmud,* Schocken, 1975.

Cohn, Norman, *The Pursuit of the Millennium,* Oxford University Press, 1970.

Cooper, John, *Eat and Be Satisfied, A Social History of Jewish Food,* Jason Aronson, 1993.

Coulton, G. G., *The Medieval Village,* Cambridge University Press, 1925.

Davies, Norman, *Europe, A History,* Pimlico, 1996.

Feinsilver, Lillian Mermin, *The Taste of Yiddish,* Thomas Yoseloff, 1970.

Fishman, Joshua A. (ed.), *Never Say Die! A Thousand Years of Yiddish in Jewish Life and Letters,* Mouton de Gruyter, 1981.

Frank, Ben G., *A Travel Guide to Jewish Russia and Ukraine,* Pelican, Gretna, 2000.

Galvin, Herman, and Tamarkin, Stan, *The Yiddish Dictionary Sourcebook,* Ktav, 1986.

Geipel, John, *Mame Loshn, The Making of Yiddish,* Journeyman, 1982.

Goldin, H. E., *The Yiddish Teacher,* Hebrew Publishing Company, 1999.

Goldsmith, Emanuel S., *Modern Yiddish Culture, the Story of the Yiddish Language Movement,* Fordham University Press, 1997.

Green, Ruth M., *A Brief History of Jewish Dress,* Safira Publications, 2001.

Bibliography

Greenbaum, Masha, *The Jews of Lithuania,* Gefen, 1995.

Gruber, Ruth Ellen, *Jewish Heritage Travel,* Jason Aronson, 1999.

Haumann, Heiko, *A History of East European Jews,* Central European University Press, 2002.

Hertz, Aleksander, *The Jews in Polish Culture,* Northwestern University Press, 1988.

Hoffman, Eva, *Shtetl,* Secker & Warburg, 1997.

The Jerusalem Bible, Koren Publishers, 1997.

Klier, John Doyle, *Russia Gathers Her Jews,* Northern Illinois University Press, 1986.

Levin, Dov, *The Litvaks, A Short History of the Jews of Lithuania,* Yad Vashem, 2000.

Marcus, Jacob R., *The Jew in the Medieval World,* Harper Torchbook, 1965.

McEvedy, Colin, *The New Penguin Atlas of Medieval History,* Penguin, 1992.

————, *The Penguin Atlas of Ancient History,* Penguin, 1967.

Miron, Dan, *A Traveller Disguised, the Rise of Modern Yiddish Fiction in the Nineteenth Century,* Schocken Books, 1973.

de Pomiane, Edouard, *The Jews of Poland, Recollections and Recipes,* Pholiota, 1985.

Schauss, Hayyim, *The Jewish Festivals,* Schocken, 1962.

Tannahill, Reay, *Food in History,* Penguin, 1988.

Teller, Adam (ed.), *Studies in the History of the Jews in Old Poland,* Magnes Press, 1998.

Wexler, Paul, *The Non-Jewish Origins of the Sephardic Jews* (Suny Series in Anthropology and Judaic Studies), State University of New York, Albany, 1996.

Zimmels, H. Jacob, *Magicians, Theologians, and Doctors,* Jason Aronson, 1997.

Dictionaries Used

English–Polish Polish–English Dictionary, J. Stanisławski.

Kapesni Anglicko-Český Česko-Anglický Slovník, KP Publishing House.

Meridian Hebrew/English English/Hebrew Dictionary, Dov Ben-Abba.

Modern English-Yiddish Yiddish-English Dictionary, Uriel Weinreich.

Index

ALSO BY PAUL KRIWACZEK

"*Fascinating. . . . One vacillates between wonder at the story told and admiration at the genial intellectual virtuosity of the storyteller. . . . A delight.*"
—Fort Lauderdale Sun-Sentinel

IN SEARCH OF ZARATHUSTRA

Across Iran and Central Asia to Find the World's First Prophet

Long before the first Hebrew temple, before the birth of Christ or the mission of Muhammad, there lived in Persia a prophet to whom we owe the ideas of a single god, the cosmic struggle between good and evil, and the Apocalypse. His name was Zarathustra, and his teachings eventually held sway from the Indus to the Nile and spread as far as Britain. Following Zarathustra's elusive trail back through time and across the Islamic, Christian, and Jewish worlds, Paul Kriwaczek uncovers his legacy at a wedding ceremony in present-day Central Asia, in the Cathar heresy of medieval France, and among the mystery cults of the Roman empire. He explores pre-Muslim Iran and Central Asia, ultimately bringing us face to face with the prophet himself, a teacher whose radical humility shocked and challenged his age, and whose teachings have had an enduring effect on Western thought.

History/Travel/1-4000-3142-7